gilbert
LAW SUMMARIES

EVIDENCE

Seventeenth Edition

Jon R. Waltz
Professor of Law
Northwestern University

Roger C. Park
Professor of Law
University of California, Hastings

THE barbri GROUP

HARCOURT BRACE LEGAL AND PROFESSIONAL PUBLICATIONS, INC.
EDITORIAL OFFICES: 111 W. Jackson Blvd., 7th Floor, Chicago, IL 60604

gilbert
LAW SUMMARIES

REGIONAL OFFICES: Chicago, Dallas, Los Angeles, New York, Washington, D.C
Distributed by: **Harcourt Brace & Company** 6277 Sea Harbor Drive, Orlando, FL 32887 (800)787-8717

PROJECT EDITOR
Deborah A. Grimm, B.A., J.D.
Attorney At Law

QUALITY CONTROL EDITOR
Blythe C. Smith, B.A.

SUMMARY OF CONTENTS

TEXT CORRELATION CHART

Gilbert Law Summary Evidence	Green, Nesson Problems, Cases, and Materials on Evidence 1994 (2nd ed.)	Lempert, Saltzburg A Modern Approach to Evidence 1982 (2nd ed.)	Mueller, Kirkpatrick Evidence Under the Rules 1996 (3rd ed.)	Strong, Broun, Mosteller Evidence—Cases and Materials 1995 (5th ed.)	Sutton, Wellborn Cases and Materials on Evidence 1996 (8th ed.)	Waltz, Park Cases and Materials on Evidence 1995 (8th ed.)
I. INTRODUCTION TO EVIDENCE						
A. Background—Development of Evidence Codes		1189-1196	2-5			
B. Evidence and the Litigation Process	1-23	1-102	1-2, 5-31	2-53, 190-209		1-63, 65-67
II. THE TYPES AND FORMS OF EVIDENCE						
A. The Two Basic Types of Evidence	44-46, 69-95	150-151	60-61	101-118		29-30
B. The Three Basic Forms of Evidence	73-74	988-991	22-35, 986-991			11-12, 29
III. PROCEDURE FOR ADMITTING OR EXCLUDING EVIDENCE						
A. Admissibility	94-106	155-156, 1056	22-35	39	377-392, 393-403	32, 38-44
B. Rulings on Admissibility of Evidence at the Trial Level	52-60, 133-134, 982	1056-1109	35-48	25-28, 36-43, 51-53		
C. Appellate Review of Trial Court Rulings on Admissibility	60-68, 171, 864	529, 852-858	49-57	25-43	377-392	39-60
D. Preliminary Determinations Concerning Admissibility	52-60, 95-123, 207-210, 277-279, 368-369, 441-447, 455-456, 459, 461-462, 794-795, 829, 919, 924, 940	1056-1068	91-94	2-25, 484	54-61, 213-232, 392-393	135-139, 166-170, 182-188, 400-405
IV. RELEVANCY AND ITS COUNTERWEIGHTS						
A. Relevancy, Materiality, and Probativeness Defined	25-52	148-150, 187, 219	59-78	212-213	1-14	64-81
B. Limits on Admissibility of Relevant Evidence	52-59, 186-200	68-69, 152-153, 186, 224	86-90	43-50	393-395	
C. Discretionary Exclusion of Evidence	52-68	152-153, 156-157, 189, 230-231	78-86, 90	83, 213-214, 222	15-24	72-73, 77-80
D. Examples of Relevancy Problems	69-95	208-215		237-255	24-40	351-365
E. Character Evidence	175-357	215-254, 634-644, 1099-1102	463-505	258-308, 590-621	41-108	366-414, 439-447

TEXT CORRELATION CHART (Continued)

Gilbert Law Summary Evidence	Green, Nesson Problems, Cases, and Materials on Evidence 1994 (2nd ed.)	Lempert, Saltzburg A Modern Approach to Evidence 1982 (2nd ed.)	Mueller, Kirkpatrick Evidence Under the Rules 1996 (3rd ed.)	Strong, Broun, Mosteller Evidence—Cases and Materials 1995 (5th ed.)	Sutton, Wellborn Cases and Materials on Evidence 1996 (8th ed.)	Waltz, Park Cases and Materials on Evidence 1995 (8th ed.)
F. Evidence Affected by Extrinsic Policies	133-174	186-215	505-523	214-236, 343-357	108-137	414-439
V. THE HEARSAY RULE AND ITS EXCEPTIONS						82-350
A. Introduction	404-405	347-355	115-116			82-89
B. General Nature of Hearsay	405-472, 561-565	355-381, 407-415	115-177	642-666, 906	138-174	82-131
C. Statements Exempted from Hearsay Rule by the Federal Rules of Evidence	425-472	383-407, 507-519	179-226	655-656, 660-732	155-186, 195-227	99-103, 115-116, 164-170, 172-176, 180-188, 236-241
D. Admissible Hearsay—the So-Called Exceptions to the Hearsay Rule		407-497		757-905		131-301
1. Introduction	425, 434-435, 446-447, 554-561	407-415	115-119, 263			
2. Former Testimony	472-475	473-482	357-368	856-871	186-195	188-199
3. Admissions	425-465	425-465	211-263	700-732	195-227	162-188
4. Confessions	425-426, 466, 476-478, 567-569, 573-578, 588-595, 600-622	761, 1063, 1102-1104	216-217	50, 71-73, 878-889	230-252	
5. Declarations Against Interest	475-478	486-495	372-393	875-889	227-252	199-208, 339-350
6. Dying Declarations	478-482	482-486	368-372	871-875	253-257	131-139
7. Excited Utterances	482-492	417-419	264, 269-276	760-767	258-266	139-147, 154-156
8. Declarations of Present Sense Impressions	482-484, 490-492	415-417	263-268	757-760	266-269	147-162
9. Declarations of Physical Condition ("State of Body" Cases)	483, 484	419-422	297-306	789-796	269-280	233-236
10. Declarations of Mental Condition ("State of Mind" Cases)	483, 485-492	422-436	276-297	768-789	280-309	209-233
11. Past Recollection Recorded	492-494	436-439	263, 306-313	797-807	309-314	24-26, 241-252
12. Business Records	494-500	439-446	313-326	807-832	315-330	26-28, 253-276, 281-289
13. Official Records	500-509, 945-978	446-461, 463	326-344	832-846	330-348	276-290
14. Judgments		467-468	327, 396-397	905	352-356	192, 291-292

TEXT CORRELATION CHART (Continued)

Gilbert Law Summary Evidence	Green, Nesson Problems, Cases, and Materials on Evidence 1994 (2nd ed.)	Lempert, Saltzburg A Modern Approach to Evidence 1982 (2nd ed.)	Mueller, Kirkpatrick Evidence Under the Rules 1996 (3rd ed.)	Strong, Broun, Mosteller Evidence—Cases and Materials 1995 (5th ed.)	Sutton, Wellborn Cases and Materials on Evidence 1996 (8th ed.)	Waltz, Park Cases and Materials on Evidence 1995 (8th ed.)
15. Declarations Concerning Family History ("Pedigree")		466, 495-496	393-395, 398, 399			294-295
16. Records to Prove "Pedigree"		464	327, 398-399			B-99
17. Reputation Evidence		466-467	398-399	621-625		295, B102-103
18. Ancient Documents Affecting Property	951-952	465	395-396	893, 905		295-296
19. Learned Treatises	872, 939	465-466	263, 344-345	905	349-352	292-294, 740-742
20. Other Exceptions	510-549	461-469	180-211, 342, 345, 374, 396, 399-418	889-904	374-376	309-312
E. Hearsay and the Right to Confrontation	567-688	550-609	418-462	733-756	230-252, 356-374	312-339
VI. PRIVILEGE						
A. Introduction	686-696	645-791		908-910	691-832	521-611
B. General Principles Applicable to All Privileges	709-710	645-652 646-651	865-867	993-994		522-524
C. Specific Privileges						
1. Attorney-Client Privilege	705-797	652-708	868-920	925-969	700-746	521-546
2. Physician-Patient Privilege	695, 705	708-713	926	986-987, 989-991	749-750	546-552
3. Psychotherapist-Patient Privilege	689	713-718	920-926	977-989, 991-992	746-750	553-562
4. Sexual Assault Victim-Counselor Privilege			926	993	748-749	
5. Privilege (and Competency) Based on the Marital Relationship	797-815	718-729	926-943	910-925	691-700	562-568
6. Clergy-Penitent Privilege	689-695, 705	729-731		992	788	569-570
7. Official Information Privilege	690-691	731-743		1004-1057	750-760	583-598
8. Identity of Police Informer Privilege		743-752		995-1004	760-769	598-608
9. News Reporter's Privilege	696-704	766-788		969-977	769-787	572-582
10. Other Privileges	689-696, 808-815	752-754, 788-791	961-963	993	787-788	570-572
11. Privilege Against Self-Incrimination	273-274	754-766	943-960		788-832	

TEXT CORRELATION CHART (Continued)

Gilbert Law Summary Evidence	Green, Nesson Problems, Cases, and Materials on Evidence 1994 (2nd ed.)	Lempert, Saltzburg A Modern Approach to Evidence 1982 (2nd ed.)	Mueller, Kirkpatrick Evidence Under the Rules 1996 (3rd ed.)	Strong, Broun, Mosteller Evidence—Cases and Materials 1995 (5th ed.)	Sutton, Wellborn Cases and Materials on Evidence 1996 (8th ed.)	Waltz, Park Cases and Materials on Evidence 1995 (8th ed.)
VII. COMPETENCY TO TESTIFY						
A. General Rules of Competency	366-367	4, 12	525-530	468		627-661 / 629-633
B. Specific Rules Affecting Competency	176, 367-373		530-557	468-490	404-445	627-661
VIII. OPINION EVIDENCE AND EXPERT WITNESSES						
A. Introduction	817-819	43-44	687-688	514-517		725-777
B. Opinion Testimony by Nonexpert Witnesses	818-823	43-44, 165-166, 1198	688-695	517-529	571-580	725-727
C. Opinion Testimony by Expert Witnesses	824-937	42-44, 166-167, 859-987, 1198	695-716	529-567, 584-590	581-604, 635-647	725-731 / 731-777
IX. EXAMINATION, CROSS-EXAMINATION, AND IMPEACHMENT					445-570	
A. Form of Examination	373-404, 492-494	11-12, 17-19, 52-53, 255-284, 508-513, 520-522, 620-621, 624-625	559-581	2-12, 59, 194-206, 490-514, 568-571, 578-582	498-570	12-29, 241-252, 448-461, 474-480, 507
B. Impeachment and Rehabilitation	266-267, 270-357, 465-472	281-346	583-685	567-640	159-174, 445-500	462-520
X. REAL, DEMONSTRATIVE, AND SCIENTIFIC EVIDENCE						
A. Real Evidence	939-1015	150-152, 988-1001, 1007-1015, 1019-1055	31-32, 965-986, 993-1017	385-467	648-672, 674-690	29-33, 612-626
B. Demonstrative Evidence	73-74	988-999, 1002-1004, 1019-1025	33-34, 986-991	385-414	672-673	33-37, 836-843
C. Scientific Evidence	828-929	60, 327-328, 861-862, 944-978, 1019	716-759	308-343	404-416, 604-635	635-655, 777-836
XI. JUDICIAL NOTICE						
A. Nature of Judicial Notice	924	839-851	837-839	360-384, 369-374, 379-384	886-906	662-675, 684-687
B. Scope of Matters Noticed		839	839-863	360-384	896-898	37-38, 662-686
C. Procedure				364-369	886-906	37-38, 675
D. Effect of Judicial Notice		838-851		369-375	886-890, 894, 900-903	671, 684-687

gilbert
capsule summary
evidence

Text
Section

I. INTRODUCTION TO EVIDENCE

  A. BACKGROUND—DEVELOPMENT OF EVIDENCE CODES

    1. **Early Codifications:** Nearly all evidentiary rules were derived from common law until the Uniform Rules of Evidence were published in 1954. Although influential, few jurisdictions adopted the Rules .... [1]

    2. **Present Codes:** The U.S. Supreme Court has developed rules of evidence (adopted by Congress) for use in the federal courts (Federal Rules of Evidence). Using the federal code as a model, many states have now adopted evidence codes .... [2]

    3. **Comment:** Evidentiary rules are basically attempts to codify common law. For this reason and because jurisdictions without codes are still governed by case law, a knowledge of evidence case law is essential to an understanding of evidentiary principles .... [3]

  B. EVIDENCE AND THE LITIGATION PROCESS

    1. **Fact Questions and Law Propositions:** The outcome of trials is determined by questions of fact and propositions of law. *Examples:* .... [4]

      a. **Fact question:** Did D deliberately and with premeditation stab V in the chest with a knife in an effort to kill him?

      b. **Law proposition:** Stabbing a person to death intentionally and with premeditation constitutes the crime of first degree murder.

    2. **Role of Evidence in Resolving Fact Questions:** Fact questions are often more influential than propositions of law on the outcome of litigation. Evidence is the material *offered* to persuade the trier of fact about fact questions, and rules of evidence govern which of this material the trier of fact may consider .... [5]

      a. **Evidence defined:** "Evidence" is the material from which inferences may be drawn as the basis for proof of the truth or falsity of a disputed fact .... [6]

      b. **Rules governing admissibility and use of evidence:** Not all evidence is admissible. Analysis focuses on: .... [9]

        (1) What material should be *admitted* at trial?

        (2) What *use* may then be made of the admitted material?

II. TYPES AND FORMS OF EVIDENCE

  A. TWO BASIC TYPES OF EVIDENCE

    1. **Direct Evidence:** Evidence that proves a proposition without relying on any inference is direct evidence .... [16]

    2. **Indirect or Circumstantial Evidence:** This is evidence of a *subsidiary* fact from which the existence of an ultimate fact may be inferred .... [17]

    3. **Rules of Admissibility:** Direct evidence is almost always admissible. Circumstantial evidence is more often subject to the exclusionary rules of evidence and rules on relevancy .... [18]

  B. THREE BASIC FORMS OF EVIDENCE

    1. **Testimonial Evidence:** This is *oral testimony* given under oath by a witness in court or in a pretrial deposition .... [20]

III. PROCEDURE FOR ADMITTING OR EXCLUDING EVIDENCE

A. ADMISSIBILITY

B. RULINGS ON ADMISSIBILITY OF EVIDENCE AT TRIAL LEVEL

C. APPELLATE REVIEW OF TRIAL COURT RULINGS ON ADMISSIBILITY

D. PRELIMINARY DETERMINATIONS CONCERNING ADMISSIBILITY

dence is admissible as to a witness's credibility or lack thereof. Any witness may be impeached by showing her **poor reputation for truth** and veracity, or a **prior felony conviction**. A witness who has been impeached may be rehabilitated by showing her good reputation for veracity . . . . [179]

    d.   **Sex crimes:** Federal Rules 413 through 415 create a special exception to the rule against character evidence for the crimes of sexual assault and child molestation. Contrary to other exceptions, these Rules do not provide for reputation or opinion evidence; rather they specifically allow testimony of prior acts of D. Further, the other-crimes evidence need not be that of a prior conviction . . . . [182]

5.   **Character of Animals:** Evidence of an animal's character (or habit) to show action in conformity therewith is admissible (*e.g.*, evidence that dog has bitten before is relevant to its propensity to bite) . . . . [185]

6.   **Compare—Habit or Custom**

    a.   **Distinguished from "character":** "Character" evidence refers to a person's **traits** (*e.g.*, honest, careful). "Habit" evidence refers to a person's **specific, routine, and continuous behavior** in particular situations . . . . [186]

    b.   **Types of evidence admissible:** Habit or custom may be proved by opinion evidence or specific past acts . . . . [189]

    c.   **Purposes for which admissible:** Habit evidence is admissible to prove the doing of a particular act in accordance with the habit, to show the standard of care in negligence cases, and to illuminate the terms of a contract . . . . . . [190]

F.   **EVIDENCE AFFECTED BY EXTRINSIC POLICIES**

1.   **Introduction:** Some relevant evidence is excluded to encourage certain conduct . . . . [197]

2.   **Subsequent Remedial Measures**

    a.   **General rule—inadmissible to show negligence:** Evidence of repairs made or precautions taken by D after injury to P is **not** admissible to prove D's negligence . . . . [198]

    b.   **Admissible for other purposes:** However, evidence of subsequent repairs is admissible for the following purposes: . . . . [199]

        (1)   **To impeach** D's witnesses as to the safety of the condition;

        (2)   **To show ownership or control** of the injury-producing instrumentality;

        (3)   **To show D's attempts to conceal or destroy** evidence; and

        (4)   **To show that precautionary measures were feasible**.

    c.   **Strict liability cases:** Under the Federal Rules, subsequent remedial measures are **inadmissible** to prove a defect in a product or its design, or a need for a warning or instruction . . . . [200]

3.   **Matters Claimed as Admissions of Negligence or Liability**

    a.   **Offers to compromise:** D's offer to settle a **disputed claim** is not admissible to show liability. Also, most jurisdictions exclude any conduct or statement made during negotiations. However, offers and statements made thereof are admissible if sufficiently probative on some issue **other than liability** . . . . [201]

    b.   **Payment of medical expenses:** D's offer to pay P's medical expenses is not admissible. However, under the Federal Rules, any **admission of fact** accompanying D's offer to pay medical expenses is **admissible** . . . . [206]

    c.   **Settlement with third person:** D's settlement with a third person on a claim arising out of the same incident is also excluded . . . . [207]

    d.   **Failure to meet professional or company standards**

        (1)   **Violation of company rules:** In an action against an employer based on respondeat superior, evidence that the employee violated a company rule **is** generally admissible . . . . [209]

rule are: published market reports, prior consistent or inconsistent statements by a witness as substantive evidence, affidavits, depositions and discovery proceedings, and forfeiture by wrongdoing . . . . [534]

    a. **"Catch-all" exception:** The Federal Rules created a "catch-all" exception to allow otherwise unaccounted-for kinds of hearsay into evidence, as long as the evidence meets the standards of ***necessity*** and ***trustworthiness*** . [540]

E. HEARSAY AND THE RIGHT TO CONFRONTATION

In all ***criminal*** cases, the accused has the right "to be confronted with the witnesses against him. . . ." Hearsay used against D can arguably make the declarant a "witness," thus depriving D of confrontation. However, the Confrontation Clause has been interpreted as excluding only hearsay considered especially dubious, dangerous, or unnecessary . . . . [546]

  1. **Two-Pronged Test of *Ohio v. Roberts*:** In order to admit hearsay without violating the Confrontation Clause, the declarant must be ***unavailable*** and the hearsay must be ***reliable*** such that it possesses sufficient indicia of trustworthiness . . . . [547]

    a. **Note:** The *Roberts* Court indicated that the two requirements above might not be applied in all cases. The unavailability prong would not apply in unusual cases where the utility of confrontation is remote. Furthermore, there is no need for a particularized showing of trustworthiness for hearsay admitted under a "***firmly rooted***" exception.

  2. **Application of Confrontation Clause:** The following types of hearsay have been addressed by the Supreme Court: . . . . [548]

    a. **Former testimony:** The Court's view of the scope of the *Roberts* test has wavered so that recent decisions raise the possibility that the *Roberts* analysis may apply only to former testimony cases such as *Roberts* . . . . [549]

    b. **Co-conspirator's statements:** In effect, the Confrontation Clause does not pose any barrier to the admission of co-conspirator's statements as long as they are offered under an exception similar to the federal exception. A showing of unavailability and trustworthiness is not required . . . . . . [550]

    c. **"Catch-all" exceptions:** Catch-all exceptions are not "firmly rooted." Thus, a child's statement concerning sexual abuse offered under the catch-all hearsay exception is admissible if there is a ***particularized showing of trustworthiness*** arising only from the circumstances surrounding the making of the statement . . . . [551]

    d. **Excited utterances; statements for medical treatment:** Such statements fall within firmly rooted hearsay exceptions and are admissible without a particularized showing of trustworthiness . . . . [552]

    e. **Confessions by accomplices:** A confession by an accomplice (incriminating D) may not be used against D. However, if that part of the confession that incriminates D falls under a firmly rooted hearsay exception, it is admissible under that exception . . . . [553]

VI. PRIVILEGE

A. INTRODUCTION

  1. **"Privilege" Defined:** A privilege is a rule of law that, to protect a particular relationship or interest, either permits a witness to refrain from giving testimony he otherwise could be compelled to give, or permits someone (usually one of the parties) to prevent the witness from revealing certain information . . . . [554]

    a. **Enforcement of confidentiality:** A privilege may be seen as a method of enforcing the broad legal guarantee of confidentiality or privacy that encourages certain relationships . . . . [555]

VIII. OPINION EVIDENCE AND EXPERT WITNESSES

A. INTRODUCTION

X. REAL, DEMONSTRATIVE, AND SCIENTIFIC EVIDENCE

XI. JUDICIAL NOTICE

approach to exams

Although evidence questions can cover many different issues, most questions generally come down to whether the evidence is admissible. Some exam questions ask you just that—is this evidence admissible? Others bring out specific issues of admissibility, asking (although not in so many words) is this relevant, is this hearsay, has a proper foundation been laid, etc.? In constructing your answer to evidence questions, use some or all of the following framework (depending on your question). And be sure to review the detailed chapter approach sections at the beginning of each chapter.

1. **Is There a Timely and Specific OBJECTION?** Unless there is, the trial court can admit almost any kind of evidence. (§33)

2. **Is There a Proper FOUNDATION?** Is there a showing that the evidence comes from a *source* that is legally competent?

   a. **Oral testimony:** Is the witness *competent* to testify? (§§811 *et seq.*) Remember that the witness almost always is competent.

   b. **Real evidence:** Is the item properly identified and its *authenticity* established? (§§1128-1139)

   c. **Documentary evidence:** Is the document *authenticated* (proper foundation laid)? (§§1159-1189)

   d. **Scientific evidence:** Is the experiment or test *reliable*? (§§1224-1266)

   e. **Procedure:** Has the judge made a determination as to proper foundation (or other preliminary fact) prior to admitting the evidence? (§§61 *et seq.*)

3. **Is the Evidence Presented in Proper FORM?**

   a. **Form of questions:** Is the question misleading, argumentative, conclusionary, etc.? (§§939 *et seq.*) Consider the limits on use of *leading questions* with "one's own" witness.

   b. **Form of answers:** Does the answer state an *opinion or conclusion* of the witness? (§945)

      (1) Are the requirements for admissibility of *lay opinion* evidence met? Consider whether the evidence is based on personal observation and helpful to the jury. (§§873-890)

      (2) Are the requirements for admissibility of *expert opinion* evidence met? Consider the expert's qualifications, basis of opinion, and helpfulness to the jury. (§§891-938)

   c. **Contents of documents:** Where the *contents* of a document are in issue, will the "*best evidence rule*" require that the "original writing" be produced? Consider whether the document is admissible under an exception to the rule, or whether non-production of the original is justified. (§§1190-1213)

   d. **Qualification:** Keep in mind that evidence in *any* form may be used *to "refresh" a witness's memory,* even though the evidence itself is not admissible. (§§964-973)

4. **Is the Evidence RELEVANT?** Does it have *probative value*?

    a. **Purpose of evidence:** Determine the purpose for which the evidence is offered. (§§78-80)

        (1) **As affirmative proof:** Does it *tend to prove* any fact in issue under the pleadings, or explain or clarify such facts? (§81)

        (2) **To impeach:** Does it reflect on the *credibility* of a witness? (§§1011 *et seq.*) Consider:

            (a) *Grounds* for impeachment (conviction of crime, bias, prior inconsistent statement, etc.) (§§1015-1087);

            (b) Permissible *methods* of impeachment (cross-examination vs. extrinsic evidence) (§§1006-1012);

            (c) Evidentiary *effect* of impeachment evidence (whether also admissible as substantive proof) (§§1040, 1081-1087); and

            (d) *Limitations* on impeachment ("one's own" witness; "collateral" matters) (§§952-961, 1088-1089).

        (3) **To rehabilitate:** If a witness is impeached, does the evidence *restore* credibility? (§§1090-1116)

    b. **Doctrine of limited admissibility:** Is the evidence admissible for one purpose but not another? (§§87-90) If so, the jury must be *instructed* (upon request) to consider it only for the relevant purpose.

5. **Even if Relevant, Is the Evidence Subject to Some EXCLUSIONARY RULE?** Are there countervailing factors (some mandatory, others discretionary) that *outweigh* the probative value of the evidence, and require its exclusion?

    a. **Mandatory rules of exclusion**

        (1) **Rules of PRIVILEGE:** Does a privilege favoring protection of particular relationships (husband-wife, attorney-client, etc.) or interests (against self-incrimination) apply? (§§554 *et seq.*) Consider:

            (a) Who is the *holder* of the privilege (*i.e.*, who may assert)? (§§563-566)

            (b) What is the *scope* of the privilege (assertable in what types of proceedings, covers what kinds of evidence)?

            (c) Are there any indications of *waiver* (by consent, failure to object)? (§§571-577)

        (2) **HEARSAY rule:** Does the evidence consist of statements or conduct *outside* of court, or documentary evidence, so that the opportunity for cross-examination is precluded? (§§221 *et seq.*) If so, consider:

            (a) Is the evidence being offered to prove the *truth of the assertion* (or the declarant's belief in its truth)? (§§229-244)

(b) If the evidence is hearsay, are there recognized factors establishing its "***trustworthiness***," and sufficient "***necessity***" for its use so as to justify an ***exception*** to the hearsay rule? (§§263 *et seq.*) Consider also whether other requirements of the exception are met (availability or unavailability of declarant, personal knowledge, etc.).

(3) **Rule against CHARACTER EVIDENCE:** Is the evidence being offered to show a person's trait of ***character*** (*e.g.*, carelessness, dishonesty) for the further purpose of ***showing that the person acted in conformity*** with that trait on a particular occasion? If so, the evidence is generally inadmissible character evidence. But consider:

(a) Whether the evidence can be admitted under an ***exception*** to the rule against character evidence (*e.g.*, the accused in a criminal case may introduce evidence of good character and the prosecution may rebut that evidence; under certain circumstances the character of the victim in a criminal case may be examined; and character evidence may be used to prove a defendant's propensity to commit a sex crime). (§§145 *et seq.*)

(b) If specific act evidence, can it be used for ***another purpose***, such as to show motive, intent, knowledge, plan, preparation, etc.? If so, does the danger that it will be used prejudicially to show bad character substantially outweigh its probative value for the proper purpose? (§§125-144)

(4) **SCIENTIFIC EVIDENCE:** If scientific evidence is being offered, has a sufficient foundation been laid showing that the evidence is accepted or scientifically valid? (§§1225-1239)

(5) **PAROL EVIDENCE rule:** Does the strong policy of the law to uphold written instruments over conflicting oral testimony render otherwise relevant oral testimony ***inadmissible***? (§§1355-1356) Consider:

(a) Is there an ***integrated*** written agreement? (§§1365-1371)

(b) Is the parol testimony in ***conflict*** with that agreement—or is the testimony merely collateral thereto or explanatory thereof? (§§1373-1387)

(c) Is the parol admissible under an ***exception*** to the rule (to show fraud, condition precedent, etc.)? (§§1388-1397)

(6) **EXTRINSIC POLICIES:** Is there some other policy of the law that precludes admission of the evidence (*e.g., policy of encouraging settlements, insurance coverage, repairs, etc.*)? (§§197-219)

b. **Discretionary grounds:** Is there a risk of undue prejudice, delay, confusion of issues, or lack of trustworthiness that ***outweighs*** the probative value of the evidence? These are important means of excluding evidence. (§§91-96)

6. **What is the EFFECT of the Evidence?** Once particular evidence is held admissible, its evidentiary effect (weight) is usually up to the trier of fact, with the following qualifications:

a. **Evidence meeting burden of proof:** Is the evidence admitted legally sufficient to prove each element of the party's case, thus shifting the "***burden of going forward***" to the adversary? (§§1301-1319)

b. **Substitutes for evidence:** If evidence of some fact is lacking, are there any *substitutes* for formal proof—*presumptions* or *judicial notice*?

   (1) **If the evidence creates a presumption:** Is the presumption "conclusive" or "rebuttable"? (§§1330-1354)

      (a) If "rebuttable," is there *any* counter-evidence? If so, consider whether the presumption is entitled to any further evidentiary effect.

   (2) **Judicial notice:** Is judicial notice on the matter mandatory or permissive? (§§1267-1290)

7. **Policy Factors:** Close cases may often be resolved by considering the major purposes of the rules of evidence: *i.e.,* "to secure *fairness* in administration, *elimination of unjustifiable expense and delay*, and promotion of growth and development of the law of evidence to the end that the *truth* may be ascertained and proceedings justly determined." [Fed. R. Evid. 102]

I. INTRODUCTION TO EVIDENCE

chapter approach

This chapter introduces you to some of the most basic concepts of evidence. The ultimate issue in almost all evidence problems will be the **_admissibility_** of evidence. Although the law of evidence developed over many years, there has been a widespread movement toward codification. The most influential code today is the Federal Rules of Evidence, which is taught in most law school evidence courses.

A. BACKGROUND—DEVELOPMENT OF EVIDENCE CODES

1. **Early Codifications:** [§1]   Not all that long ago it would have been reasonably accurate to say that almost all evidentiary rules were judge-made—that they were, in other words, a product of the common law. An early effort to codify the rules of evidence, the American Law Institute's 1942 Model Code of Evidence, was not adopted anywhere. Similarly, the Uniform Rules of Evidence, drafted by the Commissioners on Uniform State Laws and published in 1954, were influential but were adopted in only a few jurisdictions.

2. **Present Codes:** [§2]   The United States Supreme Court developed rules of evidence for use in the federal courts. These Federal Rules of Evidence for United States Courts and Magistrates ("Fed. R. Evid.") were substantially revised and then adopted by Congress, effective July 1, 1975. Most states have now adopted evidence codes using the federal code as a model.

3. **Scope of Summary:** [§3]   Efforts to develop evidentiary codes are, in the main, attempts to codify existing common law evidentiary principles (although the codes do contain some innovations). Consequently, knowledge of the case law of evidence is important to an understanding of both the emerging evidentiary codes and the governing evidentiary principles in those jurisdictions that have not adopted codifications of the rules of evidence. Accordingly, this Summary makes reference to both the case law and the codes.

B. EVIDENCE AND THE LITIGATION PROCESS

1. **Fact Questions and Law Propositions:** [§4]   The outcome of trials is determined by questions of fact and propositions of law.

   a. **Example of a fact question:** Did D deliberately and with premeditation stab V in the chest with a knife in an effort to kill him?

   b. **Example of a proposition of law:** Stabbing a person to death intentionally and with premeditation constitutes the crime of first degree murder.

2. **Role of Evidence in Resolving Fact Questions:** [§5]   In most litigation, questions of fact exert greater influence than propositions of law on the litigation's outcome. "Evidence" is the material **_offered_** to persuade the trier of fact (in this Summary the

jury, but in nonjury cases, the judge) about the fact questions in a lawsuit. "Rules of evidence" govern which of these materials can be *considered* by the trier of fact in resolving such questions.

a. **Evidence defined:** [§6]   A broad definition of "evidence" is the material from which *inferences* (*infra,* §1315) may be drawn as the basis for proof (*infra,* §1302) of the truth or falsity of a fact in dispute.

   (1) **Admissibility not required:** [§7]   As noted above, evidence includes *anything offered* at the time of hearing or trial, whether or not admissible. Thus, for example, testimony given in the form of objectionable hearsay is evidence, as is a rejected exhibit.

   (2) **Other definitions:** [§8]   "Evidence" is given a somewhat more restricted definition in some codes. For example, under California Evidence Code section 140, "evidence means testimony, writings, material objects, or other things *presented to the senses* that are offered to prove the existence or nonexistence of fact." (Emphasis supplied.)

     (a) **Note:** This definition makes it reasonably clear that *presumptions* (*infra,* §1320) are technically *not* evidence since they are not "presented to the senses." However, as will be seen, they may operate as a *substitute* for evidence.

b. **Rules governing admissibility and use of evidence:** [§9]   Since not all evidence is admissible at trial, the two main problems addressed by the rules of evidence are: (i) what matters and what materials should be *admitted* (received) at trial for the fact finder to consider; and (ii) what *use* can properly be made by the fact finder of those matters and materials that are ruled admissible?

   (1) **Primary focus on admissibility:** [§10]   Most of the rules of evidence pertain to the first of these two problems—*i.e.,* the decision of what matters and materials will be admitted for the fact finder to examine (hear, see, read, touch, taste, or smell) and consider. Three principal concerns underlie the legal rule of admissibility:

     (a) **Time consumption:** [§11]   Some limitations on the matters and materials to be considered during a trial are essential to the trial's resolution; otherwise the litigation might go on forever. Hence, one effect of the rules of evidence is to establish some outer bounds on the sheer *amount* of evidence to be received.

     (b) **The jury system:** [§12]   Since the jury system relies on nonexperts to decide cases, an even more pressing concern of the admissibility decision is the protection of inexperienced jurors from improper or inappropriate influences. Hence, the crucial question becomes, "What matters and materials can lay jurors safely be permitted to see, hear, etc.?"

       1) **Example:** Many evidentiary problems result from attempts by trial lawyers to score points with a lay jury by using forensic

methods which, while perhaps dramatic, would probably not have as powerful an impact on an experienced trial judge acting as the trier of fact in a so-called bench (nonjury) trial.

    2)   **Example:** Similarly, hearsay evidence is often excluded for fear that a lay jury cannot fully appreciate all the various reasons that such evidence may be inaccurate, and hence the jury may overvalue it.

(c) **Societal values:** [§13]   Finally, certain kinds of highly probative materials are kept out of evidence in order to encourage certain confidential relationships and to protect the privacy and dignity of the individual.

    1)   **Example:** Privileged communications and unconstitutionally seized evidence fall into this category.

(2) **Use of admissible evidence:** [§14]   Beyond the problem of admissibility itself is the question of what *use* should be made of those matters and materials admitted into evidence. No effective means exist to control the way a fact finder deals with items of received evidence except for the judge's ability to issue a limiting instruction and to direct a verdict on an issue when the admissible evidence usable on that issue is insufficient to support the verdict.

(a) **Example—purpose of evidence:** In a criminal case, a trial judge can instruct the jury (fact finder) that certain evidence (*e.g.,* an unsworn prior inconsistent statement by the witness) is admissible only for the purpose of casting doubt on (impeaching) the witness's credibility and *not* as substantive evidence of any element of the alleged offense. This is a so-called limiting instruction. But, consciously or unconsciously, the jurors may nonetheless consider the evidence of the prior inconsistent statement's content as proof of guilt.

(b) **Example—weight of evidence:** Even more striking is the absence of any specific rules regarding how much weight the fact finder should give particular materials admitted into evidence. This matter is left entirely to the discretion of the fact finder.

II. THE TYPES AND FORMS OF EVIDENCE

chapter approach

Although the classifications of evidence set out in this chapter are important to the understanding of the laws of evidence, they generally do not come up in evidence questions. The codes do not use terms such as "circumstantial evidence" or "tangible evidence"; rather they analyze questions with respect to the issues discussed later in this Summary, such as relevance (*see* chapter IV), hearsay (*see* chapter V), and privilege (*see* chapter VI). Nonetheless, these definitions are helpful in understanding court opinions, where these terms are still commonly used.

A. THE TWO BASIC TYPES OF EVIDENCE [§15]

There are two fundamental *types*, as distinguished from *forms*, of evidence: (i) direct and (ii) indirect or circumstantial evidence.

1. **Direct Evidence:** [§16] Direct evidence, sometimes simplistically termed "eyewitness" evidence, proves a proposition *directly* (in one step) rather than by inference.

    a. **Example:** Testimony offered in a homicide case, "I saw the defendant pull a knife from his belt and plunge it into the neck of the man standing beside him at the bar," is direct evidence that the defendant stabbed the man in the neck.

2. **Indirect or Circumstantial Evidence:** [§17] Circumstantial (indirect) evidence depends on *inferences* for its relationship to the proposition (material issue) to be proved. It is evidence of a subsidiary fact from which, alone or in conjunction with other facts, the existence of an ultimate fact (proposition, material issue) can be inferred.

    a. **Example:** A and B are observed entering a room that has only one means of ingress and egress, a door. They lock the door behind them. A loud bang is heard coming from inside the room. When the door is broken down, A is observed standing over the fallen body of B, who has a bleeding circular wound in his neck. A is holding a pistol in her hand. There is one spent cartridge, still warm, in the chamber. All of this is *circumstantial* evidence that A shot B in the neck. It is not direct evidence that she did so since no one actually saw A shoot B.

3. **Rules of Admissibility:** [§18] Most of the rules concerning relevancy (*infra,* §§76-85), and most of the so-called exclusionary rules of evidence (*infra,* §§91-96) relate to *circumstantial* evidence since it raises the most problems of reliability and the like. *Direct* evidence, such as eyewitness accounts, is almost invariably admissible because of its obvious relevance and apparent reliability.

B. THE THREE BASIC FORMS OF EVIDENCE [§19]

The two fundamental *types* of evidence may be offered in three basic *forms*: (i) testimonial evidence, (ii) tangible evidence, and (iii) tangible-testimonial evidence.

1. **Testimonial Evidence:** [§20]   Testimonial evidence is oral testimony given by a witness, under oath or solemn affirmation, in court from the witness stand or by way of pretrial deposition.

2. **Tangible Evidence:** [§21]   Exhibits—tangible things—may also be offered for the fact finder to consider. They are of two basic sorts:

   a. **Real evidence:** [§22]   Real evidence is the *"real thing"* at issue in the case—*e.g.,* the actual murder weapon, the written contract on which the lawsuit is based, the allegedly defective product.

   b. **Demonstrative evidence:** [§23]   Demonstrative evidence is *not* the real item involved in the case. Rather, it is a *visual* or *audiovisual aid* for the fact finder. Such evidence would include an anatomical model, a chart, or a diagram. (This subject is discussed in detail in the chapter on scientific and demonstrative evidence, *see infra,* §§1216-1266.)

3. **Tangible-Testimonial Evidence:** [§24]   A hybrid of the above two forms of evidence is tangible-testimonial evidence. Although essentially testimonial in nature, it is tangible in form. The best examples of this type of evidence would be a transcribed deposition and a transcript of previous trial testimony.

4. **Compare—Judicial Notice:** [§25]   Some matters need not be proved in the customary manner (*i.e.,* with witnesses and exhibits) because they are common knowledge in the jurisdiction or are subject to certain verification through reference to a highly reliable source (such as a calendar, actuarial table, or history text). When this is the case, a court will take judicial notice of such matters and instruct the jurors to consider them established in the case without formal proof. Judicial notice thus acts as a *substitute for formal proof.* (*See infra,* §§1267 *et seq.* for further discussion of judicial notice.)

   a. **Judicial notice as evidence:** [§26]   There has been disagreement as to whether matters judicially noticed constitute "evidence" at all. Some courts have held that facts judicially noticed can be *disputed* by the parties and that the jury can *refuse* to accept them as facts. However, the prevailing view now is the other way around: A ruling by the trial court that a fact will be judicially noticed *precludes contrary evidence*. This means that matters judicially noticed, though technically they do not constitute "evidence," are in a very real sense a substitute for evidence.

III. PROCEDURE FOR ADMITTING OR EXCLUDING EVIDENCE

chapter approach

Questions involving the procedures for admission of evidence are not common on examinations since questions usually ask whether evidence has been properly admitted rather than whether a ruling has been preserved for review. Nonetheless, occasionally a question will direct your attention to this matter, and in any event, the subject is extremely important in the trial of cases.

Moreover, the distribution of functions between judge and jury is extremely important to the understanding of all the rules of evidence. It often arises in an exam where there is a question as to who determines the foundational facts necessary to make a piece of evidence admissible. Ask yourself:

1. Who has the burden of proof as to the preliminary matter?

2. What is the judge's role in the preliminary fact determination?

3. What is the jury's role as to the preliminary matter?

A. ADMISSIBILITY [§27]

Questions about admissibility arise when a party's offer of evidence draws an objection from another party. (In the absence of any objection, all but the most plainly improper evidence can be received and considered by the fact finder; *see infra*, §33.)

1. **Objection to Admissibility Sustained:** [§28]   If the objection is sustained by the trial judge, the evidence is *excluded* from the fact finder's consideration. For purposes of possible appellate review, a record of the rejected evidence is made by *identification* and *physical inclusion* in the record of exhibits and by *offer of proof* of any testimonial evidence (*see infra*, §§56-59).

2. **Objection to Admissibility Overruled:** [§29]   If the objection is overruled, the evidence is *received* and *can be considered* by the fact finder. When error in the overruling of the objection is asserted, the making of the objection preserves the objecting party's rights on appeal. (In some common law jurisdictions, an objection alone is not enough. After the trial judge overrules an objection, the party opposing the introduction of evidence has to announce that she is taking an "exception" to the ruling in order to preserve her right to appeal. Modern jurisdictions have dropped the "exception" requirement.)

B. RULINGS ON ADMISSIBILITY OF EVIDENCE AT THE TRIAL LEVEL

1. **Roles of the Court and Jury**

   a. **Court:** [§30]   The *admissibility* of evidence is determined solely and exclusively by the trial judge. The judge alone decides whether an item of evidence can be considered by the fact finder; the jury has no say in the matter.

b. **Jury:** [§31]   On the other hand, the ***weight and credibility*** of received evidence (with the possible exception of matters judicially noticed) are always up to the jury to decide.

c. **Summary:** [§32]   In short, ***admissibility*** is a question of law (evidence law) to be resolved by the ***trial court***; what ***weight*** is to be accorded evidence that the trial judge has ruled admissible is a matter to be resolved by the ***fact finder*** (jury). This is simply a practical way of stating the twin propositions that the judge is the judge of the ***law***, while the jurors are the judges of the ***facts***.

2. **Where No Objection Made:** [§33]   As indicated, unless some objection is made by opposing counsel, almost any kind of evidence can be received. Failure to object is considered a ***waiver*** of any existing ground for objection; the trial judge ordinarily is not obligated to raise grounds of objection on his own. (For an exception where receipt of the evidence constitutes "plain error," *see infra,* §§42-43.)

3. **Loss of Right to Object by Reason of Own Evidence ("Opening the Door"):** [§34]   Simple failure to object is not the only way counsel may waive the right to object to improper evidence. A party may be held to have waived the right to object as a consequence of her own tactics.

   a. **Introducing part of transaction:** [§35]   Where the plaintiff introduces evidence as to part of a conversation or event (the part favorable to the plaintiff), the defendant can cross-examine or introduce rebuttal evidence as to any other part of the same transaction necessary to make it fully understandable. Any objection the plaintiff might have invoked as to the defendant's evidence (privilege, hearsay, etc.) is deemed waived since it was the plaintiff who ***elected*** to introduce part of the transaction. [United States v. Salsedo, 607 F.2d 318 (9th Cir. 1979)]

      (1) **Compare—writings:** [§36]   Where a writing or recorded statement is offered, the adverse party need not wait for cross-examination or rebuttal; he can insist that the proponent of the evidence introduce any other part "which ought in fairness to be considered contemporaneously with it." [Fed. R. Evid. 106; United States v. Rubin, 591 F.2d 278 (5th Cir. 1979); *and see infra,* §§1214-1215]

   b. **Introducing inadmissible evidence:** [§37]   There is a second way offering counsel may "open the door." Many courts hold that where the plaintiff introduced evidence that was legally inadmissible (*e.g.,* hearsay) and the trial judge erroneously received it, plaintiff is deemed to have waived any right to object to evidence offered by the defendant to rebut it, even though defendant's evidence may be equally objectionable. In other words, the defendant is entitled to "fight fire with fire." [Bogk v. Gassert, 149 U.S. 17 (1893); Reyes v. Missouri Pacific Railway, 589 F.2d 791 (5th Cir. 1979)]

C.   APPELLATE REVIEW OF TRIAL COURT RULINGS ON ADMISSIBILITY [§38]

The trial court's rulings admitting or excluding evidence are reviewable on appeal from the final judgment in the case. However, an appellate court will not reverse the judgment unless one of the following grounds is present:

1. **Evidence Erroneously Admitted—Requirements for Reversal on Appeal:** [§39] The following are the grounds for reversal on appeal for the improper receipt of evidence:

   (i) There was a *specific objection*;

   (ii) That was *timely* made;

   (iii) The ground for the objection was *valid*; and

   (iv) The error in overruling the objection was *prejudicial*.

   a. **Specific objection:** [§40] The trial record must show that the appellant made a specific objection (unless the ground is apparent from the context). [Fed. R. Evid. 103(a)(1)]

      (1) **"Specific" defined:** [§41] "Specific" means that the objection must state the *particular legal ground or reason* that the evidence was inadmissible.

      (2) **General objections inadequate:** [§42] "We object" (without further elaboration) and "Objection—incompetent, irrelevant, and immaterial" are general objections. "Objection—no foundation" also is considered a general objection. [United States v. Barbee, 968 F.2d 1026 (10th Cir. 1992)] These objections are all too broad to inform the judge and the opposing party of the precise basis for the objection. They are not sufficient to preserve questions on appeal unless the ground for objection was apparent from the context or unless it was "plain error" to admit the evidence.

         (a) **Exceptions:** [§43] There are exceptions to the general rule:

            1) If the specific ground for objection is patently *obvious* from the context of the question, the ground need *not* be stated explicitly to preserve the issue for appeal. [Fed. R. Evid. 103(a)(1)]

            2) There is also some authority for the proposition that if a question is *objectionable from every standpoint* (improper under any theory), a general objection is sufficient. [*See* cases collected at 157 A.L.R. 598]

            3) In *criminal cases*, at least, if the error in admission (or exclusion) of evidence is so fundamental that it has *deprived the accused of a fair trial*, it constitutes a ground for reversal even though the accused failed to object with specificity at the trial level. [Fed. R. Evid. 103(d); Payton v. United States, 222 F.2d 794 (D.C. Cir. 1955)—reversing conviction based on coerced confession even though accused made no objection at trial; *and see* United States v. Castenada, 555 F.2d 605 (7th Cir. 1977)]

               a) The Federal Rules would authorize application of this "plain error" doctrine in civil cases as well. However, courts usually hesitate to employ it, fearing that it might become a crutch or "incantation" for a reviewing court that can find no other basis for reversal. [*See* Finch v. Monumental Life Insurance Co., 820 F.2d 1426 (6th Cir. 1987)]

b. **Timely objection:** [§44] The objection must have been timely, which means that ordinarily it must have been interposed **before** the evidence was received (*i.e.,* before the witness answered, or before the exhibit was shown to the fact finder). [Waltz, "Making the Record," in Waltz & Park, *Cases and Materials on Evidence* 39-41 (8th ed. 1995)] However, in some instances, evidence already received can be attacked by means of a **motion to strike**.

(1) **Motion to strike:** [§45] A motion to strike is, in effect, an objection to evidence made after it has already come in. (Thus, the motion to strike is sometimes referred to as an "after-objection.") It is effective only where there was **no opportunity** or **basis** for an earlier objection.

(a) **Examples:** A motion to strike is proper when:

1) The witness responds to an objectionable question before opposing counsel has a chance to make an objection.

2) The question itself is unobjectionable ("What color was the traffic light?"), but the answer emerges as objectionable ("My mother told me it was green").

3) Evidence admitted earlier in the case becomes objectionable later on, perhaps because its relevance was not "connected up."

(b) **Time of making:** [§46] A motion to strike, like an objection, must be made as soon as the ground for it appears. Failure to make a motion to strike **waives** the defect to the same extent as failure to object.

(c) **Instruction to disregard:** [§47] Because the rejected evidence cannot in any physical sense be "stricken from the record" and the jurors have already heard it, a sustained motion to strike is usually followed by the trial judge's instruction to jurors that they are to disregard the improper evidence.

c. **Ground for objection valid:** [§48] The evidence must, in fact, have been legally inadmissible **for the reason(s) stated in the objection**. It is immaterial that another **unstated** ground for objection existed; the unstated ground **cannot** be raised on appeal for the first time.

d. **Prejudicial error:** [§49] The overruling of the objection and receipt of the evidence must have constituted prejudicial error, which means that it probably had a **substantial influence** on the verdict or otherwise "affected a substantial right" of the party objecting to the evidence. [Fed. R. Evid. 103(a)]

(1) **Application:** There can be no fixed rule as to when an error in the admission of evidence becomes "prejudicial." However, the more closely balanced the evidence, or the more heavily circumstantial, the more

likely it is that an appellate court will find prejudice, especially in serious criminal cases.

(2) **Constitutional standards:** [§50]   Where evidence was obtained in violation of an accused's constitutional rights (*e.g.,* by an illegal search and seizure), "prejudicial" error, as distinguished from "harmless" error, is measured by due process standards. To affirm a conviction on appeal, the reviewing court must be convinced beyond a reasonable doubt that admission of the illegal evidence could not have affected the jury's verdict; the reviewing court must, in other words, be convinced that the jury would have convicted the accused anyway. [Fahy v. Connecticut, 375 U.S. 85 (1963); *and see* Constitutional Law Summary]

2. **Evidence Erroneously Excluded—Requirements for Reversal on Appeal:** [§51] A reviewing court will reverse the judgment of a trial court on the ground that evidence was erroneously *excluded* at the trial only if it is established that:

(i)   There is *no valid ground* for objection;

(ii) An *offer of proof* was made; and

(iii) The error in excluding evidence was *prejudicial*.

a. **No valid ground for objection:** [§52]   First of all, the appellant must establish that the evidence was *legally admissible* so that its exclusion was erroneous.

(1) **Incorrect specific objection:** [§53]   If the evidence was legally inadmissible on *any* ground, the trial court's judgment will be upheld. This is true even though the ground was *not* the one urged in the trial court, as long as the defect in the evidence was one that could not have been cured if it had been specifically called to the proponent's attention in the trial court (*e.g.,* cure might be possible where the only valid objection was to the *form* of the proponent's question, perhaps because it was *leading*).

(a) **Rationale:** The requirement of specific and correct objection is relaxed here. There is a strong policy favoring the affirmance of trial court judgments unless an asserted error was prejudicial.

(2) **General objection sufficient:** [§54]   Consistent with the above, the making of a *general* objection ("Your Honor, we object") or even an objection based on the *wrong ground* will not prevent appellate affirmance of a ruling excluding evidence as long as some *valid* ground for objection was available. It is assumed that the trial judge had the right reason in mind when she rejected the evidence. [Waltz, "Making the Record," in Waltz & Park, *Cases and Materials on Evidence* 45-46 (8th ed. 1995)]

(3) **Raising issue on appeal:** [§55]   This, then, is one of the rare situations in which a reviewing court will permit the parties to argue points on appeal that were not properly raised in the trial court.

b. **Offer of proof made:** [§56]   Following the sustaining of an objection, the party who sought to introduce the rejected evidence must have made an offer of proof, showing the substance of the excluded evidence and its relevance (unless the substance and purpose are apparent from the context). [Fed. R. Evid. 103(a)(2); United States v. Leisure, 844 F.2d 1347 (8th Cir. 1988)]

(1) **Function of offer:** [§57]   The function of an offer of proof is to perfect a record for appellate review; otherwise, a reviewing court would have no way of knowing the significance of the proponent's evidentiary loss. Hence, the offer must show the relevancy of the evidence (*i.e.,* what it tends to prove), and its admissibility under the rules of evidence (*e.g.,* if hearsay, how it falls within some exception to the rule against hearsay).

(2) **Procedure:** [§58]   An offer of proof is ordinarily made outside the hearing of the jury to prevent jurors from speculating about excluded matters. Sometimes the offer is made in narrative form by proponent's counsel ("Your Honor, had the witness been permitted to answer my question he would have testified to such and such"). Often it is made in question and answer form, using the witness on the stand. If the rejected evidence was an exhibit, the offer can be accomplished by including the exhibit in the record. [Waltz, The Offer of Proof, 16 Trial Lawyer's Guide 385 (1973)]

(3) **Absolute right:** [§59]   The right to make an offer of proof is virtually absolute. [State v. Shaw, 565 P.2d 1057 (N.M. 1977)]

c. **Prejudicial error:** [§60]   The overruling of the objection—*i.e.,* the exclusion of the evidence—must have constituted *prejudicial* error, *see supra,* §49.

D. PRELIMINARY DETERMINATIONS CONCERNING ADMISSIBILITY [§61]

Ordinarily, before a trial court can rule on the admissibility of offered evidence, it must determine one or more *preliminary facts*; *e.g.,* is the witness "qualified" to testify (*see infra,* §§815 *et seq.*); is the witness "privileged" not to give testimony (*see infra,* §§554 *et seq.*); was the accused's confession "voluntary" (*see infra,* §§358 *et seq.*)?

1. **Burden of Proof of Preliminary Fact:** [§62]   The proponent (offeror) of the evidence or the claimant of a privilege has the burden of proof as to the preliminary fact. [Cal. Evid. Code §405]

2. **Preliminary Facts About Which Judge Makes Ultimate Decision—Legal Admissibility:** [§63]   Where the preliminary fact relates to the *legal admissibility* of the offered evidence (*e.g.,* the qualifications of an "expert" witness or the existence of a privilege), the existence of the preliminary fact is generally determined by the trial judge alone. The proponent of the evidence must establish the preliminary fact by a *preponderance* of the evidence. [Fed. R. Evid. 104(a); Bourjaily v. United States, 483 U.S. 171 (1987)—noting that the Court has traditionally required that preliminary factual questions relating to the admissibility of evidence be determined by a "preponderance of proof standard"]

a. **Examples**

(1) **Expert's qualifications:** When an expert witness is called by a party to testify in some specialized field, that party's counsel must persuade the

trial judge that the expert possesses expert qualifications (training, experience, etc.). If the expert's qualifications are disputed, the judge must decide the issue on the basis of the preponderance of the evidence. [Fed. R. Evid. 702; *and see infra*, §§915-918]

(2) **Privilege:** Where a party invokes a privilege, he must establish by a preponderance of the evidence that the privileged relationship (attorney-client, physician-patient, etc.) in fact existed. [Robinson v. United States, 144 F.2d 392 (9th Cir. 1944); Phelps Dodge Corp. v. Guerrero, 273 F. 415 (9th Cir. 1921)]

(3) **Hearsay exception:** The proponent of hearsay evidence usually must persuade the trial court of the existence of any facts essential to bring the evidence within some exception to the rule against hearsay (*e.g.,* that an out-of-court declaration was made in contemplation of impending death). [*See, e.g.,* Bourjaily v. United States, *supra*]

(4) **Copy of writing:** Where the proponent of a writing offers a copy in lieu of the original on the ground that the original has been lost, the trial judge must determine, by a preponderance of the evidence, that the document was in fact lost. [Fed. R. Evid. 1008; *and see infra*, §1209]

(a) **But compare:** If the issue presented is whether there ever *was* an original of any such document, or whether the copy offered was a *true* (accurate) copy, the question passes *beyond* a mere "preliminary fact" determination concerning legal admissibility; instead, the question involves *credibility* or *relevance* and would ultimately have to be decided by the jury. [Fed. R. Evid. 1008]

b. **Procedure:** [§64] Questions of legal admissibility must be decided by the trial court *before* the evidence is admitted. Once the jury hears disputed evidence, the damage is done since there is a real risk that any instruction to disregard it will be ineffective. As a prominent trial lawyer once put it, "You can't unring a bell."

(1) **Compare—questions of relevancy:** [§65] When, on the other hand, the preliminary fact relates to the *relevancy* or *weight* of the evidence, it is assumed that jurors will ignore the offered evidence if they do not find the preliminary fact to exist (*e.g.,* they will give no weight to the contents of a letter where they have *not* found the preliminary fact of *genuineness*—where, in other words, they have found the exhibit to be a forgery).

3. **Role of Jury:** [§66] It would ordinarily be *error* for a trial judge to permit the jury to determine the *admissibility* of evidence, as distinguished from its *weight* or *believability*. In other words, the judge's findings as to preliminary facts on which legal admissibility depends cannot ordinarily be *reconsidered* by the jurors. For example, it would be erroneous for the trial court to instruct the jurors to determine whether a particular witness is *qualified* to give expert testimony.

a. **Exceptional cases in which jury may reconsider preliminary facts underlying admissibility:** [§67] There are, however, a few exceptional situations in which, for policy reasons, some courts allow the jury a "second crack" at the preliminary fact on which legal admissibility depends.

(1) **Examples**

    (a) **Voluntary confession:** Some courts permit the jury to make its own independent determination as to whether an accused's confession was voluntary. [*See* Stein v. New York, 346 U.S. 156 (1953)—upholding the constitutionality of this approach, often called the "New York procedure"]

        1) **Compare:** The so-called orthodox rule allows the trial court *alone* to make the determination of voluntariness. [Jackson v. Denno, 378 U.S. 368 (1964); *and see infra*, §362]

    (b) **Dying declaration:** Some courts also give the jury at least some part in determining whether a dying declaration was made in fear of impending death. [State v. Proctor, 269 S.W.2d 624 (Mo. 1954); *but see* Soles v. State, 119 So. 791 (Fla. 1929)—contra]

(2) **Criticism:** Permitting the jurors to decide preliminary fact matters lets the trial judge "pass the buck" in close cases. It may also allow inadmissible and prejudicial evidence to reach the jurors; *i.e.*, it is unrealistic to expect a jury to make a preliminary fact determination (*e.g.*, the voluntariness of a confession) without considering the details of the confession itself.

b. **Modern trend contra:** [§68] Recognizing the validity of the above criticism, the current trend is to require the trial judge to make *all* preliminary fact determinations relating to the admissibility of evidence. Under this view, the jury is not permitted to reconsider such preliminary fact matters; its functions are to determine the *weight* and *credibility* of the received evidence. [*See* Fed. R. Evid. 104(a); *and see* cases catalogued in Appendix A to Opinion of Black, J., Jackson v. Denno, *supra*]

4. Procedure in Making Preliminary Fact Determinations

a. **Presence of jury discretionary:** [§69] It is up to the trial judge to decide whether the determination of a preliminary fact issue shall be conducted in or out of the jury's presence. In practice, the jurors are usually excused whenever the evidence, if found inadmissible, might have a prejudicial impact on them. [Fed. R. Evid. 104(c)]

    (1) **Exception—admissibility of confession:** [§70] Because of the obviously prejudicial nature of *confessions* to crime, hearings on their admissibility *must* be made outside the jury's hearing. [Fed. R. Evid. 104(c); *and see infra*, §363]

    (2) **Exception—testimony by accused:** [§71] Similarly, if in a criminal case the accused elects to take the witness stand to testify on a *preliminary* fact question (*e.g.*, the circumstances surrounding an allegedly illegal search), the jury must be excused *if the accused so requests*. [Fed. R. Evid. 104(c)]

        (a) **Note—no waiver of privilege against self-incrimination:** [§72] The accused's testimony on a preliminary fact issue does *not* waive any Fifth Amendment privilege to refuse to testify *generally* in the case. [Fed. R. Evid. 104(d); *and see infra,* §804] Here, excusing the jury on the accused's request, so as to prevent it from drawing any adverse inference from the accused's failure to testify on other matters, is essential to preserve the privilege.

b. **Evidence that can be considered**

(1) **General view—only admissible evidence:** [§73]   The prevailing view in *state* courts is that the trial judge can consider only *admissible* evidence in ruling on preliminary fact questions; *i.e.,* the rules of evidence apply.

(2) **Federal Rule—any nonprivileged evidence:** [§74]   However, the Federal Rules of Evidence, and the emerging trend in state courts, permit the trial judge to consider *any nonprivileged relevant evidence*. Thus, the rules of evidence, except as to privilege, do *not* apply in preliminary fact determinations. [Fed. R. Evid. 104(a); *and see infra,* §347]

(a) **Application:** Under the federal approach, the trial judge can rely on affidavits and other forms of hearsay to determine the admissibility of *other* evidence. [*See, e.g.,* United States v. Haldeman, 559 F.2d 31 (D.C. Cir. 1976)—testimony at prior hearing, later read into the record, that recording of conversations in the Oval Office was authorized by President Nixon; *and see* Bourjaily v. United States, *supra,* §63—hearsay statement of alleged co-conspirator can be used to lay the foundation for its own admissibility]

5. **Preliminary Facts as to Which Jury Makes Ultimate Decision—Conditional Relevance:** [§75]   Where the preliminary fact goes to the *relevancy, credibility, or weight* of evidence, the trial judge initially determines only whether there has been a *minimal* showing of the preliminary fact—*i.e.,* a showing that would be sufficient to sustain a finding of fact on appeal. If there has been such a minimum showing, the trial judge will admit the evidence. However, the *ultimate* determination of the preliminary fact is for the jury. [Fed. R. Evid. 104(b)]

a. **Example:** P offers in evidence a letter that appears to have been written by D and contains damaging admissions. D *denies* having written the letter. A preliminary fact issue—the *authenticity* of the letter—therefore arises. This issue goes to the letter's *relevancy*; the letter has no probative value if D was not its author.

(1) **Role of trial judge:** The trial judge makes the initial determination as to the letter's authenticity. The trial court's determination is simply whether there is *some credible evidence* that D wrote the letter. The judge must admit the letter if the proponent can produce the minimum amount of evidence that, on appeal, would support a finding of fact by the jury that the letter was authentic. [Fed. R. Evid. 104(b), 901(a)]

(2) **Order of proof:** The trial judge will usually require that this minimal showing of authenticity be made before the letter is received into evidence. However, this is *not* mandatory. The court has discretion to admit the letter *subject to* the necessary minimal showing later in the trial—

failing which, of course, the letter will be stricken from the record. [Fed. R. Evid. 104(b)]

(3) **Role of jury:** The trial judge's initial determination of the fact question is *not* final. The jurors are free to arrive at a contrary conclusion. For example, they can find that the letter was not written by D, even though the judge found that there was sufficient evidence of authenticity to support admission of the letter initially.

   (a) **Note:** Standard practice is for the trial judge to instruct the jury that although the evidence (*e.g.,* the letter) has been ruled admissible, the jury must decide for itself whether the preliminary fact in issue exists (*e.g.,* whether D wrote the letter).

   (b) **Compare:** Or, in a case where the judge admits the evidence at first, but then later determines that no reasonable jury could find that the necessary preliminary fact exists (*e.g.,* perhaps overwhelming evidence of forgery has been introduced), she must instruct the jury at this point to disregard the evidence. [Fed. R. Evid. 104(b)]

b. **Another example:** P offers testimony by X that X told D about a dangerous condition on D's premises. Whether the statement constituted notice to D depends on whether D *heard it*. (If D did *not* hear the statement, it would be irrelevant.) Therefore, there must be *some* credible evidence that D heard the statement before it can be received. If the minimum amount of evidence is forthcoming, the trial judge will rule that X's testimony is admissible. But if D *denies* having heard X, it will be up to the jury ultimately to decide whether D in fact heard X's statement.

IV. RELEVANCY AND ITS COUNTERWEIGHTS

chapter approach

Relevancy is the first issue in almost all evidence questions since relevancy is the primary basis for admitting evidence. The two rules for you to remember are:

(i) **Only** relevant evidence is admissible; and

(ii) **All** relevant evidence is admissible **unless** there is a legal reason to the contrary (*e.g.,* rule against hearsay, etc.).

1. Thus, the first step in answering a question concerning admissibility of evidence is to determine **whether the evidence is relevant**. Ask yourself:

    —What is the evidence **trying to show**?

    —Is this **an issue** in the case? (Materiality)

    —Is the evidence **helpful** for its purpose? (Probativeness)

2. The answers to these questions will tell you whether the evidence is relevant. If so, proceed to the second step, that is, determining whether there is **some legal rule that excludes this evidence**. Consider:

    —**Discretionary exclusion** of evidence if it is unfairly prejudicial, confusing, etc. [Fed. R. Evid. 403]

    —Rules restricting the admissibility of **character evidence**. [Fed. R. Evid. 404-405, 412-415]

    —**Extrinsic policies** that justify excluding the evidence (regarding subsequent repairs, liability insurance, etc.). [Fed. R. Evid. 407-411]

    —The **hearsay rule** and all other "technical" exclusionary rules of evidence. [Fed. R. Evid. 801-802]

A. RELEVANCY, MATERIALITY, AND PROBATIVENESS DEFINED [§76]

The basic purpose of all trials is to determine the truth as to the issues presented. However, rather than admitting all the evidence that might conceivably be offered by the parties, the trial court will admit only evidence that bears such a **sufficient relationship** to the matters in dispute that it may be deemed **"relevant."** This is the first and foremost exclusionary rule in the law of evidence; *i.e.,* only relevant evidence is admissible. [Fed. R. Evid. 402]

1. **Relevancy:** [§77]   One of the many definitions of relevancy is a relation between an item of evidence and a proposition sought to be proved. If an item of evidence **tends to prove or to disprove** any proposition, it is relevant to that proposition. In

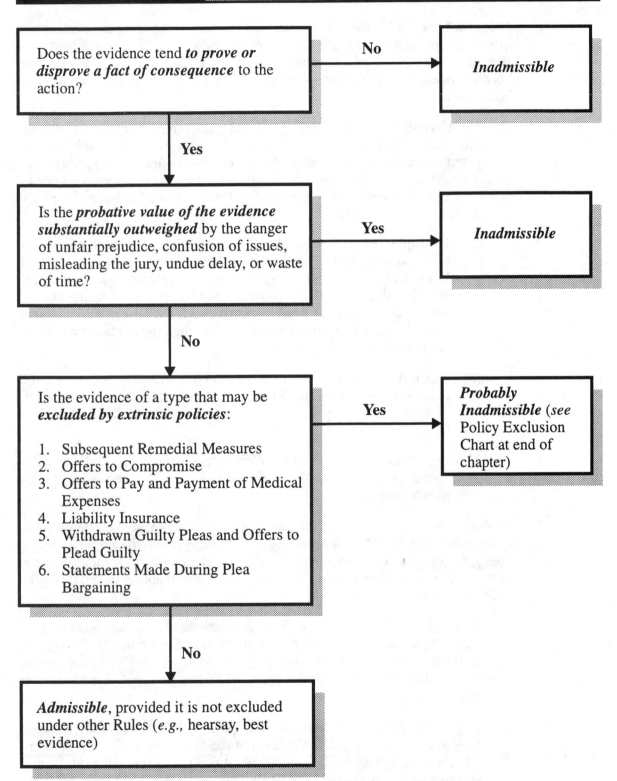

Does the evidence tend *to prove or disprove a fact of consequence* to the action?

No → *Inadmissible*

Yes ↓

Is the *probative value of the evidence substantially outweighed* by the danger of unfair prejudice, confusion of issues, misleading the jury, undue delay, or waste of time?

Yes → *Inadmissible*

No ↓

Is the evidence of a type that may be *excluded by extrinsic policies*:

1. Subsequent Remedial Measures
2. Offers to Compromise
3. Offers to Pay and Payment of Medical Expenses
4. Liability Insurance
5. Withdrawn Guilty Pleas and Offers to Plead Guilty
6. Statements Made During Plea Bargaining

Yes → *Probably Inadmissible* (*see* Policy Exclusion Chart at end of chapter)

No ↓

Admissible, provided it is not excluded under other Rules (*e.g.,* hearsay, best evidence)

Federal Rule 401, relevant evidence is defined as "evidence having any tendency to make the existence of any fact that is of consequence to the determination of the action more probable or less probable than it would be without the evidence." Whatever definition is used, the concept of relevancy can be broken down into two quite different concepts—*materiality* and *probativeness*.

a. **Materiality:** [§78]   The test of materiality relates to whether the evidence is offered upon a matter properly *in issue*—*i.e.,* whether it is directed toward a fact "within the range of allowable controversy." In other words, the question "Is this evidence relevant?" must be followed by the question "Relevant to what issue?"

   (1) **Which matters are in issue?** [§79]   Which matters in a case are in issue (and hence what evidence is "material") is determined mainly by the *pleadings*, the applicable *principles of substantive law*, and by *pretrial orders*, if any. Usually, where the issues are clear and the evidence goes to only one of those issues, the question "Relevant to what issue?" is really answered.

      (a) **Example:** Evidence that D was driving without lights at night, two to ten minutes before the accident, (if relevant at all) will go toward D's exercise of due care at the time of the accident; also, perhaps, if properly pleaded, to P's contributory negligence (in not seeing D); but not, of course, to the issue of damages. If, however, liability were conceded, and due care was not in issue, then the evidence would be immaterial and hence irrelevant.

      (b) **Example:** Similarly, where P sues D on a written contract, and the only defense pleaded by D is a denial that he executed the contract, evidence offered by him as to a release would be immaterial, and hence irrelevant.

   (2) **Matters always in issue:** [§80]   Certain matters are always deemed "in issue" even though not raised in the pleadings—*e.g.,* the credibility of each witness who testifies.

b. **Probativeness:** [§81]   In addition to materiality, the evidence offered must have probative value; *i.e.,* it must logically tend to prove the proposition for which it is offered. This concept of sufficient probativeness is sometimes erroneously referred to as materiality. However, as indicated above, materiality generally means something quite different.

   (1) **Test:** [§82]   Under this definition, probativeness is a matter of common sense, logic, and experience. For example, whether a defendant's flight is relevant to the issue of his guilt depends upon whether courts accept as true the Biblical view that "the guilty flee when no man pursueth but the innocent is bold as a lion."

   (2) **Degree of probativeness required:** [§83]   To be relevant, evidence need not be absolutely determinative of the fact to which it is directed; in other words, it need not be conclusive. It need not even make the factual proposition *substantially* more likely than not. All it need do is make the fact *somewhat* more likely than it would be without that evidence. In other words, to be relevant, the evidence must merely help a little.

(a) **Example:** Flight by no means proves guilt or makes guilt more likely than not. Evidence of flight merely makes guilt somewhat more likely, and thus it is relevant because it is somewhat helpful.

(b) **Example:** The fact that a driver has an excessive amount of liability insurance is arguably relevant to show that the driver was negligent. The insured driver might have a more reckless attitude toward driving because he has less to lose economically. However, heavily insured drivers also are likely to be prudent by nature. They may take fewer chances and, hence, buy insurance to reduce risk. These two equally plausible possibilities cancel each other out, and the evidence of insurance would be irrelevant even under the permissive test of Federal Rule 401. (To remove any doubt, Federal Rule 411 specifically prohibits evidence of insurance to prove negligence.)

(3) **Effect of finding of probativeness:** [§84]   A determination of probativeness, then, is the legal conclusion that there exists a sufficient relationship between the evidence offered and the fact sought to be proved such that reasonable persons might be helped in inferring one from the other.

2. **Materiality and Probativeness as Single Concept:** [§85]   The trend of the law today is to regard "materiality" and "probativeness" merely as parts of a broader "relevancy" test. Indeed, the definition in Federal Rule 401 (*supra,* §77) makes it clear that the concepts of materiality (*i.e.,* whether the evidence goes to a fact of consequence to the action) and probativeness (*i.e.,* whether the evidence tends to make the fact more or less probable) are but parts of a single test for "relevant evidence."

B. LIMITS ON ADMISSIBILITY OF RELEVANT EVIDENCE

1. **Introduction:** [§86]   The converse of the basic rule stated above (*i.e.,* that *only* relevant evidence is admissible) is that *all* relevant evidence is admissible unless excluded by some specific rule. Federal Rule 402 states: "All relevant evidence is admissible, except as otherwise provided. . . ." Thus, if the evidence is relevant, it must be admitted unless it violates some exclusionary rule. Indeed, the concept of relevancy, plus the reasons for excluding relevant evidence, constitute almost all of the law of evidence.

2. **Doctrine of Limited Admissibility**

a. **Purpose for which evidence offered:** [§87]   As indicated above, to determine the relevancy of any item of proof, the purpose for which it is sought to be introduced must first be known—*i.e.,* on what issue in the case is it being offered? Where the evidence is relevant on only one issue, no problems arise. Where, however, the evidence could be relevant on several issues, it may be admissible on one issue, but for some reason inadmissible on another.

(1) **Example:** In a criminal case, the prosecution offers a certified copy of D's prior felony conviction. Its admissibility depends upon the purpose for which it is being offered: if offered to show that D was likely to have committed the crime presently charged, it is probably inadmissible (*see infra,* §123); but if offered only to impeach D's testimony as a witness, it is probably admissible for that purpose (*see infra,* §§1014-1027).

(2) **Example:** Evidence may be offered against several parties and be admissible against only one of them. Thus, where Pedestrian sues two auto drivers for injuries resulting from a collision and seeks to introduce a statement by Driver No. 1 that "both cars were going too fast," this could be admissible against Driver No. 1, but may be inadmissible hearsay as to Driver No. 2.

b. **Rule of limited admissibility:** [§88]   Where evidence is admissible for one purpose (or as to one party), it is not rendered inadmissible solely because it is improper or irrelevant for some other purpose (or as to some other party). [Fed. R. Evid. 105; United States v. Garcia, 530 F.2d 650 (5th Cir. 1976)]

(1) **Instruction to jury:** [§89]   However, in such a case, the trial judge must, upon request, instruct the jury that it is to consider the evidence *only* for the purpose for which the evidence is admissible, and to disregard it for any other purpose (*e.g.,* to consider a prior felony conviction only as impeachment of D's testimony, and not as showing D guilty of the crime presently charged). [Fed. R. Evid. 105]

(a) **Note:** As a practical matter, few juries are able to abide by such instructions. Most feel that "evidence is evidence" and consider it for any and all purposes.

(2) **Severance:** [§90]   Alternatively, where evidence is admissible as to one party, but highly prejudicial as to some other party, the trial court has inherent power to order a severance as to the prejudiced party in the interests of justice. (*See* Civil Procedure Summary.)

C. DISCRETIONARY EXCLUSION OF EVIDENCE

1. **Grounds for Exclusion of Relevant Evidence:** [§91]   In addition to the specific exclusionary rules discussed later in the Summary (hearsay, privilege, etc.), in modern practice the trial judge is vested with broad discretion to exclude evidence—no matter how relevant—where "its *probative value is substantially outweighed* by the danger of unfair prejudice, confusion of the issues, or misleading the jury, or by considerations of undue delay, waste of time, or needless presentation of *cumulative* evidence." [Fed. R. Evid. 403] When engaging in this balancing process, the judge must assume that the offered evidence will be *believed* by the jury. It cannot properly be excluded simply because the judge does not consider it credible. [*See* Ballou v. Henri Studios, Inc., 656 F.2d 1147 (5th Cir. 1981)]

a. **Unfair surprise:** [§92]   Unfair surprise is recognized as an additional discretionary ground for exclusion under some state codes (*see* Uniform Rule 45); but it is not a ground for exclusion under the Federal Rules on the theory that modern discovery rules provide the parties with adequate opportunity to anticipate what will be offered, and any "unfairness" can be cured by a continuance rather than by exclusion of relevant evidence. [*See* Fed. R. Evid. 403, note]

b. **Waste of time:** [§93]   To be admissible, relevant evidence must be sufficiently probative so that time spent on the matter would not be wasted. Thus, evidence that an accused armed robber was poor may be slightly probative on the issue of guilt—*i.e.,* the likelihood of a poor person being an armed robber is probably somewhat greater than the likelihood of a rich person being an armed robber. Nonetheless, because the probative value of this kind of evidence is so low (not to mention moral compunctions about using it), the evidence would be excluded because the time wasted in pursuing it would substantially outweigh its value. [Fed. R. Evid. 403]

2. **Extent of Judge's Discretion:** [§94]   The trial judge's discretion to admit or exclude evidence on these grounds is very broad. Her rulings are reviewable on appeal only for abuse of discretion or disregard of restrictive guidelines and, as a result, are rarely reversed. [*See* Waltz, Judicial Discretion in the Admission of Evidence Under the Federal Rules of Evidence, 79 Nw. U. L. Rev. 1097 (1985)]

   a. **Rationale:** This breadth of discretion is allowed the trial judge for two reasons:

      (1) *The number of fact situations* upon which the trial judge must rule are so *varied* that the appellate courts and legislators have been unable to create hard and fast rules of exclusion for every case.

      (2) *Also, many variables may affect the judge's exercise of discretion* (*e.g.,* the judge's perception of the intelligence of the jury, the ability of counsel to eliminate confusion, the other evidence in the case) and thus appellate courts generally will not second-guess the judge's decision.

   b. **Mechanics:** At common law, judges did not have to articulate on the record their reasons for excluding evidence. An appellate court would affirm the exclusion if any reasonable basis for it existed. However, some courts now require that the trial court's reasoning be set forth in the record if the exclusion has been objected to. In fact, at least one court has reversed where the trial court failed to make an explanation on the record of its Rule 403 exclusion in the face of counsel's request for such explanation. [*See, e.g.,* United States v. Dwyer, 539 F.2d 924 (2d Cir. 1976); Contemporary Mission, Inc. v. Famous Music Corp., 557 F.2d 918 (2d Cir. 1977)]

   c. **Prejudicial evidence:** [§95]   As stated above, if prejudice substantially outweighs probative value, the evidence is inadmissible. [Fed. R. Evid. 403] For example, a videotape showing a personal injury plaintiff in sentimental scenes with her family may be more prejudicial than probative. However, despite their wide discretion, as a practical matter, judges rarely exercise their discretion to exclude admissible evidence merely because it is prejudicial, unless they are directly commanded to do so by decisions or statutes.

3. **Application of Principle of Discretionary Exclusion:** [§96]   According to the rule of discretionary exclusion, even where evidence is admissible under the doctrine of limited admissibility because it is relevant and admissible on one issue, the judge nonetheless has discretion to exclude the evidence altogether if he feels that it will have such weight on another issue (as to which it is not admissible) that the jury will disregard any instruction not to consider it on the inadmissible issue.

   a. **Example—gruesome photographs:** The issue of the judge's discretion is commonly raised in cases involving gruesome photographs. Such photos, while perhaps probative on some issue in the case (*e.g.,* cause of death), nonetheless might have such an inflammatory effect upon the jury that the judge may decide to keep them out of evidence altogether. [Waltz, *Introduction to Criminal Evidence* 422-423 (3d ed. 1991)]

D. EXAMPLES OF RELEVANCY PROBLEMS

1. **Introduction:** [§97]   Most problems involving relevancy of evidence are those in which the evidence is circumstantial (*supra*, §17)—*i.e.*, tending to prove the issue only indirectly, through inference or deduction. Usually, the judge's problem is to determine at what point the circumstantial evidence is of such little probative value as to be "irrelevant," or so full of probative dangers (undue prejudice, confusing issues, etc.) that it should be excluded on the discretionary grounds discussed above.

   a. **Limits on discretion:** [§98]   In some areas, discretionary rulings of trial judges have been codified. Where statutes (or appellate court decisions) have already established that the prejudicial value of certain kinds of evidence outweighs the probative value, the judge is required to exclude evidence that might otherwise have been within her discretion to admit. Sometimes these predetermined rules of relevance are quite specific (particularly in the character areas; *see infra*, §§119-185). In other instances, the rules are framed in general terms that still allow the judge considerable discretion. The latter type of rules include those governing admissibility of evidence of similar happenings or transactions (*see* below).

2. **Previous Tort Claims by Plaintiff:** [§99]   The mere fact that the plaintiff has been involved in previous accidents, or has previously filed claims for injuries, ordinarily is not relevant in a personal injury case. While such evidence may tend to show that the plaintiff is litigation-prone, its probative value is deemed outweighed by the risk of: (i) confusion of issues; (ii) undue prejudice; and (iii) possible impairment of the plaintiff's constitutional right to use the courts. [Zabner v. Howard Johnsons, Inc., 227 So. 2d 543 (Fla. 1969)—rejecting evidence that plaintiff had 15 other similar lawsuits on file]

   a. **Similar injuries:** [§100]   However, evidence of prior injuries, or claims of injury, becomes relevant where plaintiff claims present injury to the same portion of his body; it has probative value as to whether the plaintiff's present condition is attributable in whole or in part to the prior injury. [Brown v. Affonso, 185 Cal. App. 2d 235 (1960)]

   b. **False claims:** [§101]   There is also at least some authority holding that evidence of plaintiff's prior false claims of personal injury should be admissible to reflect on plaintiff's credibility in the present case. [*See* 69 A.L.R.2d 609]

   c. **Fraudulent schemes:** [§102]   Evidence of prior *false* claims (especially if there were several of them) for the same type of accident against similar defendants would certainly be admissible to show that the plaintiff had formed a scheme or plan to bring such false lawsuits, and hence that the instant lawsuit was a false one.

3. **Accidents and Injuries to Others in Negligence Cases**

   a. **Prior accidents:** [§103]   Suppose that evidence of other prior accidents (*e.g.*, other people's falls on a theater carpet) is offered by the plaintiff in a negligence case to show that the condition was dangerous (*i.e.*, that the carpet was loose and likely to cause falls). Courts traditionally have been reluctant to admit such evidence in the absence of a showing of: (i) substantial identity of conditions;

(ii) substantial identity of the human behavior involved; and (iii) no serious danger of confusion of issues. [Robitaille v. Netoco Community Theaters, 245 N.E.2d 749 (Mass. 1940)]

(1) **Federal approach—consider purpose:** [§104]   In jurisdictions following the Federal Rules of Evidence, the admissibility of prior-accident evidence is governed by Federal Rule 403. The trial judge must balance the probative value of the evidence against the dangers of prejudice, confusion, and waste of time. [Simon v. Town of Kennebunkport, 417 A.2d 982 (Me. 1980)—applying Maine rule based on Federal Rule 403] In exercising discretion under Rule 403, trial judges will consider the purpose for which the evidence is offered. When the evidence is offered to show *dangerousness of condition*, the proponent often is required to show a relatively high degree of similarity. When the evidence is offered to show that the prior accidents provided the defendant with *notice* of a hazard, the requirement of similarity is relaxed. The proponent of the evidence need only show that the prior accidents were similar enough to alert the defendant to the danger. [Exum v. General Electric Co., 819 F.2d 1158 (D.C. Cir. 1987)]

(2) **Inadmissible to prove negligence:** [§105]   The prior accident may *never* be used simply to show that the defendant was negligent at the prior time. The fact that defendant was negligent on some earlier occasion would be inadmissible character evidence when offered to prove negligence at the time of the current accident (*see infra*, §123).

b. **Subsequent accidents**

(1) **Inadmissible to prove causation or knowledge:** [§106]   Evidence of a subsequent accident is generally held not admissible to show either causation of the plaintiff's injury or knowledge by the defendant of the danger involved at the time of plaintiff's injury—even if there is substantial identity in human behavior, conditions, etc. [Wills v. Price, 26 Cal. App. 2d 338 (1938)]

(2) **Admissible to show dangerous condition:** [§107]   However, evidence of a subsequent accident may be admissible to show the existence of a dangerous condition at the time in issue; *i.e.*, an inference that the condition existed at a previous time may be drawn from the evidence that it continued to exist at a subsequent time, if this would be expected in common experience. [81 A.L.R. 685]

(a) **Example:** Evidence as to the defective condition of D's brakes several days after an accident is admissible as to their condition at the time of the accident.

(b) **Limitation:** However, the subsequent accident must follow shortly after the original accident, or no inference can logically be made as to the prior condition.

c. **Absence of prior accidents or complaints:** [§108]   It would seem that if evidence of prior injuries is admissible to show that plaintiff's injury was caused in a certain way, or that a certain condition was dangerous (*see* above), then evidence of the absence of such accidents during a similar period would generally be allowed to show the nonexistence of such danger or causation.

(1) **Minority view:** [§109]   A minority of courts advocate admissibility of such evidence—particularly where the condition is static and the danger is not obvious. [Rathbun v. Humphrey Co., 113 N.E.2d 877 (Ohio 1953)—roller coaster rider claimed he was injured by tree limb during ride; absence of prior injuries to others held admissible to refute his claim]

   (a) **Rationale:** Past experience—negative or affirmative—is at least some evidence of what is dangerous. [McCormick §167; 61 Harv. L. Rev. 213 (1948)]

(2) **Majority view:** [§110]   However, the general rule is that absence of other accidents or complaints is ***not*** admissible to prove the nonexistence of the dangerous condition or the unlikelihood that the condition caused plaintiff's present injuries. [Blackwell v. J. J. Newberry Co., 156 S.W.2d 14 (Mo. 1941)]

   (a) **Rationale:** Such evidence would have weak probative effect and would raise too many collateral issues. Also, not all persons who are injured report their accidents or make claims. [31 A.L.R.2d 190; *but see* Silver v. New York Central Railroad, 105 N.E.2d 923 (Mass. 1952)—absence of passenger complaints that railroad car was abnormally cold admissible to prove that it was not]

(3) **Compare—admissible on whether defendant knew of danger:** [§111] Absence of prior accidents is admissible evidence on the question of defendant's knowledge; *i.e.,* defendant may testify that he received no reports of prior accidents as tending to show that he lacked knowledge of any danger.

4.   Other Contracts

a.   **Contracts between same parties:** [§112]   Evidence of past contractual relations between a plaintiff and defendant may be held admissible for the purpose of ***interpreting the terms*** of their present contract. [Hartford Steam Boiler Inspection & Insurance Co. v. Schwartzman Packing Co., 423 F.2d 1170 (10th Cir. 1970); *and see* U.C.C. §1-205] It is, however, less likely to be admitted to prove the formation of a present contract.

b.   **Contracts with third persons:** [§113]   Evidence of a defendant's contractual dealings with third persons is generally held ***inadmissible*** to reflect either on the making or interpretation of the defendant's contract with the plaintiff. [McKee v. State, 172 Cal. App. 2d 560 (1959)]

   (1) **Compare:** Where the facts indicate a ***common plan, scheme, habit, or usage*** in all of a defendant's contracts, the defendant's dealings with third persons may be admissible. [Firlotte v. Jessee, 76 Cal. App. 2d 207 (1946); Moody v. Peirano, 4 Cal. App. 411 (1907)]

5. **Sales of Same or Similar Property as Evidence of Value**

    a. **Real property:** [§114] Where the issue is the value of land (*e.g.,* in condemnation cases), most courts will admit evidence on direct examination, not only as to the price paid for the particular parcel, but also as to reasonably recent sales prices for other property in the vicinity—as long as the other property is shown to be similar (in usability, improvements, etc.) to the property in question. [Village of Lawrence v. Greenwood, 300 N.Y. 231 (1949)]

        (1) **Rationale:** Although each parcel of land is "unique," there is really no practical way to fix land values other than by reference to sales prices of other property. Indeed, this is the type of evidence upon which expert witnesses generally rely in evaluating a particular parcel. The possibility that reference to sales of other property may raise collateral issues is outweighed by the probative value of the evidence. [County of Los Angeles v. Faus, 48 Cal. 2d 672 (1957)]

    b. **Personal property:** [§115] When the issue is the value of personal property, the almost universal rule allows admission of evidence of sales prices of similar personal property. Published price lists, market quotations, etc., are admissible for this purpose. [Fed. R. Evid. 803(17)]

    c. **Sales vs. offers:** [§116] When dealing with either real or personal property, the prices must be sales prices. Prices quoted in mere offers are not admissible; efforts to determine their genuineness would lead to collateral disputes. [Peagler v. Davis, 84 S.E. 59 (Ga. 1914)]

        (1) **Offer as admission:** [§117] However, if one of the parties to the present action has recently offered to buy or sell the property in question or similar property, and he now asserts some different estimate of its value, evidence of his offer may be used against him as an admission (*see infra,* §§294-298). [Springer v. City of Chicago, 26 N.E. 514 (Ill. 1891)]

6. **Fees Charged for Similar Services:** [§118] Evidence of fees charged for similar services previously rendered (*e.g.,* medical fees for similar care) is generally admissible to fix the value of services rendered in the present transaction. [Joseph v. Krull Wholesale Drug Co., 245 F.2d 231 (3d Cir. 1957)]

E. CHARACTER EVIDENCE

1. **Introduction:** [§119] The judge's usual discretion to balance the probative value of evidence against its prejudicial effect has been frozen into hard and fast rules mainly in the area of evidence bearing on the character of an individual.

    a. **Definition:** [§120] "Character" evidence is evidence of a general human trait, such as honesty, violence, cowardice, or carefulness. It is sometimes called "propensity" evidence.

    b. **Purpose for which offered:** [§121] The admissibility of character evidence depends upon the purpose for which it is being offered. Consider whether it is being offered:

        (i) To show a person's *action in conformity with character*?

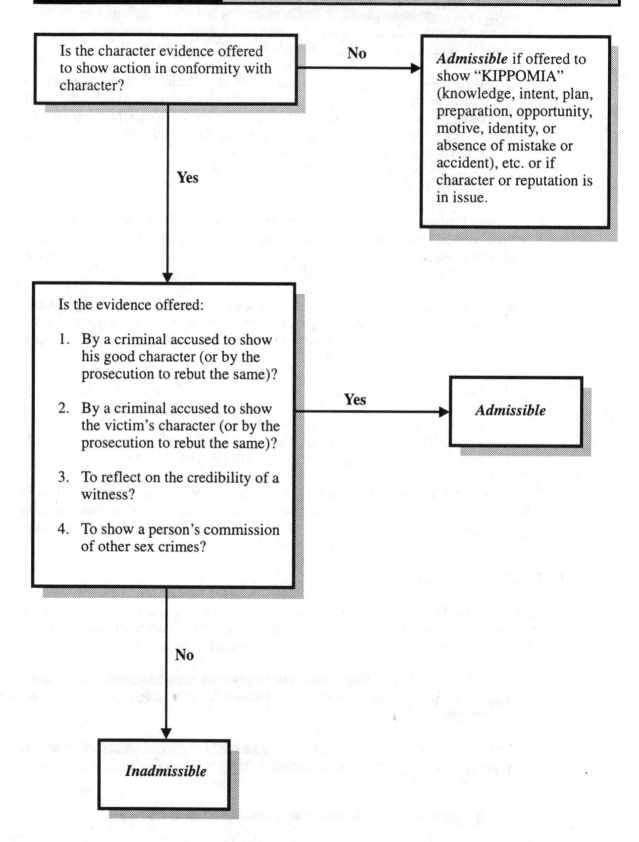

Is the character evidence offered to show action in conformity with character?

No →

Admissible if offered to show "KIPPOMIA" (knowledge, intent, plan, preparation, opportunity, motive, identity, or absence of mistake or accident), etc. or if character or reputation is in issue.

Yes ↓

Is the evidence offered:

1. By a criminal accused to show his good character (or by the prosecution to rebut the same)?

2. By a criminal accused to show the victim's character (or by the prosecution to rebut the same)?

3. To reflect on the credibility of a witness?

4. To show a person's commission of other sex crimes?

Yes → *Admissible*

No ↓

Inadmissible

    (ii)   For a ***purpose other than*** showing character?

    (iii) To prove a person's ***character***, where the question of that person's character is ***one of the issues*** in the case?

    (iv) To prove a person's ***reputation***, this being ***in issue***?

    (v)   By a ***criminal accused*** to show his ***good character*** (or by the prosecution to rebut the same)?

    (vi) By a criminal accused to show the ***victim's character*** (or by the prosecution to rebut the same)?

    (vii) Merely to ***impeach*** or ***rehabilitate*** a person as a witness? (*See* discussion of impeachment, *infra,* §§1003 *et seq.* and rehabilitation, *infra,* §§1090 *et seq.*) or

    (viii) To show that a person committed other ***sex crimes***?

  c. **Types of character evidence:** [§122] In those cases in which character evidence is admissible, three basic types of evidence may be offered to prove a particular trait of a person's character:

    (i)   ***Testimony by witnesses who know the person*** as to their opinions of his character;

    (ii) ***Testimony by witnesses who may or may not actually know the person*** as to his ***reputation*** in the community; or

    (iii) ***Testimony or proof as to specific acts*** (past conduct) by the person that reflect on the particular character trait involved.

Which type of evidence is admissible will again depend on the purpose for which it is being offered (*see* below).

2. **General Rule—Character Evidence Is Inadmissible to Show Action in Conformity with Character:** [§123] Evidence of a trait of character is generally ***not*** admissible to show action in conformity with that trait on a particular occasion. Thus, in a criminal case the prosecution generally cannot introduce evidence that the accused is a "bad" person or that he has a propensity to commit the crime with which he is presently charged. "Once a thief, always a thief" is not good law. [Fed. R. Evid. 404(b)] Similarly, evidence of a "pattern" of bad conduct is not, in and of itself, permissible; "pattern" is simply another way of saying "propensity." [United States v. Beasley, 809 F.2d 1273 (7th Cir. 1987)]

  a. **Applies to all types of character evidence:** This rule applies whether the evidence offered is opinion, reputation testimony, or evidence of other crimes or misconduct by the accused (even if established by the accused's own admission). [Fed. R. Evid. 404]

  b. **Example:** Evidence that D had previously violated liquor laws is inadmissible to prove that he violated such laws on the occasion in question. [United States v. Harris, 331 F.2d 185 (4th Cir. 1964)]

c. **Rationale:** Whatever relevancy such evidence might have is simply outweighed by the risks of undue prejudice and confusion of the issues; *i.e.*, such evidence might influence the jury to punish the "bad" person despite what the evidence in the particular case shows. [People v. Hendricks, 560 N.E.2d 611 (Ill. 1990); Jones v. Commonwealth, 198 S.W.2d 969 (Ky. 1947)]

d. **Scope of general rule:** [§124]   Under the Federal Rules of Evidence and the law of many states, some character evidence may be admissible despite the general rule. There are four recognized exceptions to the general rule (*see infra,* §§145-184), and there are some uses of character evidence that are not considered "exceptions" at all because they are offered for some purpose outside the scope of the rule, such as to show motive to commit a crime (*see infra,* §§125-144).

3. **Evidence Falling Outside General Rule**

a. **Other crimes and acts offered for a purpose other than showing character:** [§125]   Evidence of other crimes and acts is admissible when it is offered to show something other than character. For example, if a defendant is charged with stealing money from a safe, the prosecution would be permitted to show that the defendant earlier had stolen the key to the safe. That earlier crime would not be offered to show that the defendant had a general propensity to steal, but merely to show the defendant's plan, preparation, and opportunity to commit the charged crime.

(1) **"KIPPOMIA" list:** [§126]   A standard list of such noncharacter uses of other-crimes evidence is set forth in Federal Rule 404(b), and is sometimes called the "KIPPOMIA" list:

Knowledge
Intent
Plan
Preparation
Opportunity
Motive
Identity
Absence of mistake or accident.

Note that under the Federal Rules, the prosecution generally must, upon request of the accused, provide pretrial notice to the accused of the general nature of any such evidence the prosecution intends to introduce at trial. [Fed. R. Evid. 404(b); People v. Peete, 28 Cal. 2d 306 (1946)]

(a) **State of mind—knowledge, intent, motive:** [§127]   Evidence of prior crimes by the accused is admissible to show the accused's knowledge, intent, motive, scienter, etc. For example, in a prosecution for embezzlement, evidence of other embezzlements by the accused may be admitted to show his intent to appropriate. [*See* United States v. Zimeri-Safie, 585 F.2d 1318 (5th Cir. 1978)]

1) **Prior crimes to show intent:** [§128]   Where evidence of prior crimes is admissible as bearing on *intent*, the present crime charged must require a specific intent—*e.g.,* larceny.

2) **Prior crimes to show motive:** [§129]   Where evidence of prior crimes is admitted to reflect on *motive*, the defendant must be given an opportunity to deny his commission of the past crimes, or otherwise to show that he had no such motive.

3) **Prior crimes to rebut insanity:** [§130]   Some courts hold that where a defendant pleads *insanity* as a defense to a criminal charge, the prosecution is entitled to introduce evidence as to prior crimes; *i.e.*, "all relevant words and conduct" are admissible to refute the insanity claim. For example, proof that D had been convicted of larceny shortly before the present crime may be relevant to show that D had the mental ability to form a felonious intent. [Mears v. State, 422 P.2d 230 (Nev. 1967)]

(b) **Common plan or scheme:** [§131]   Evidence of prior criminal acts by the accused is admissible to prove the existence of a larger continuing plan, scheme, or conspiracy of which the present crime charged is a part. [United States v. Arroyo-Angulo, 580 F.2d 1137 (2d Cir. 1978)]

1) **Example:** D was charged with murder by insulin poisoning. Evidence was offered that D had murdered three other victims by the same means and for the same motive (money). (D had not been charged with or convicted of these murders.) This evidence was held admissible under the "common plan" exception as tending to show malice and knowledge of the means used to commit the crime charged in the present case. [People v. Archerd, 3 Cal. 3d 615 (1970)]

(c) **Preparation:** [§132]   Evidence of prior crimes by the accused is admissible to show the accused's preparation to commit the charged crime. For example, evidence that the defendant stole a car is admissible to show the defendant's preparation to facilitate the charged crime of robbing a bank.

(d) **Opportunity:** [§133]   Evidence of prior crimes by the accused is admissible to show the accused's opportunity to commit the charged crime. For example, if the defendant is charged with stealing a package from a locked mailroom of which he had no authority to enter, proof that the defendant was seen in the room is admissible to show the defendant's opportunity to steal the package.

(e) **Identity:** [§134]   Evidence of prior crimes by the accused is admissible to establish his identity. Thus, evidence that defendant committed a previous crime is admissible if the *modus operandi* in both crimes are similar and unusual enough to indicate that the same person perpetrated both. The *modus operandi* must be a veritable criminal "signature." [United States v. Benedetto, 571 F.2d 1246 (2d Cir. 1978); *and see* People v. Maston, 69 Cal. 2d 233 (1968)]

1) **Defendant may rebut evidence:** [§135]   Where the prosecution introduces evidence of other crimes alleged to have been committed by defendant on this theory, defendant is entitled to

rebut such evidence by proof that someone else committed the other crimes. [People v. Zerillo, 36 Cal. 2d 222 (1950)]

(f) **Absence of mistake or accident:** [§136] Evidence of prior crimes may also be admitted to show absence of mistake or accident in the commission of the present act—*i.e.,* to rebut the accused's assertions that it was all an innocent mistake, etc. [United States v. Young, 573 F.2d 1137 (9th Cir. 1978)]

(2) **Effect of limited admissibility:** [§137] Note that, in the above cases, the prosecution is not, at least in theory, offering the evidence of prior crimes to show the defendant's bad character. Thus, even where such evidence is successfully introduced, it can be used only to show a specific point as to identity, common plan, etc., for which it was introduced. The prosecution will not be permitted to argue to the jury that these crimes also show the defendant to be a bad person and, hence, more likely to have committed the crime presently charged.

(a) **Comment:** Of course, as a practical matter, once the evidence is received the jurors will probably consider it for whatever purpose they please.

(3) **KIPPOMIA list not exhaustive:** [§138] Many courts hold that the "pigeon hole" purposes listed above are not the only purposes for which prior crimes are admissible. Rather, they hold that evidence of past crimes or misconduct is admissible when offered for any purpose other than showing generalized criminal propensity (*i.e.,* for any purpose other than showing the accused is a "bad" person). [United States v. Woods, 484 F.2d 127 (4th Cir. 1973)—murder of baby proved by evidence that over a period of 25 years, six other infants left alone with the defendant had died of same symptoms of strangulation]

(a) **But note:** Whichever approach is taken, admissibility is still subject to the rule that the evidentiary value of the past crimes must outweigh the risk of prejudice flowing from use thereof (*supra,* §91). [*See* United States v. Beasley, 809 F.2d 1273 (7th Cir. 1987)]

(4) **Quantum of proof required:** [§139] Where evidence of other crimes or bad acts is admissible to show identity, motive, intent, plan, etc., the proponent need not show that anyone was actually *convicted* of the other crimes or acts. It is enough to prove that the other acts occurred. Some courts have held that the other acts must be proven by a *preponderance of the evidence* or even by *clear and convincing evidence*. [*See* Tucker v. State, 412 P.2d 970 (Nev. 1966)]

(a) **But note:** The United States Supreme Court, however, has *rejected* the above view. In *Huddleston v. United States*, 485 U.S. 681 (1988), it held that the prosecution was not even required to show by a preponderance of the evidence that the defendant had committed the prior crimes. This decision was based upon the view that Federal Rule 104(b) governed the reception of the other-crimes evidence, and under that rule evidence whose relevancy depends upon the fulfillment of a condition of fact is admissible when there is evidence sufficient to support a finding that the condition has been fulfilled. In the case of other-crimes evidence, the "condition" is that the defendant be the person guilty of the other crimes. The proponent is entitled to get to the jury on the issue of whether the defendant committed the other crimes once it introduces enough evidence to *permit a reasonable jury to decide in its favor* (it does not have to introduce enough evidence to convince the judge that the defendant was guilty of the other crimes).

(b) **Effect of acquittal on admissibility of evidence:** [§140]   In some jurisdictions, where sufficient evidence that the defendant committed the prior crime exists, such evidence is admissible even if the defendant was acquitted of the prior crime. [*See, e.g.,* Dowling v. United States, 439 U.S. 342 (1990); People v. Massey, 196 Cal. App. 2d 230 (1961)]

1) **Compare:** Other jurisdictions, however, have held that collateral estoppel will prevent the use of an otherwise admissible prior crime if the defendant has been acquitted of it. Note that if the acquittal was in a different jurisdiction, collateral estoppel would not apply against the prosecution in the current case.

b. **Character evidence where character itself (and not conduct) is in issue:** [§141]   Whenever a party's character is in issue under the pleadings—civil or criminal—character evidence is admissible. In such cases, character is an ultimate fact in dispute, and it must be proved by competent evidence. [Fed. R. Evid. 405(b)]

(1) **Examples**

(a) **Defamation:** Where a defamation action is based on statements as to P's character ("P is a crook") and D pleads truth as a defense, P's character is in issue, and hence character evidence may generally be offered on either side. [Davis v. Hearst, 160 Cal. 143 (1911)]

(b) **Negligent entrustment:** Where the owner of a dangerous instrumentality is being sued for negligent entrustment (*i.e.,* permitting use of the instrumentality by an incompetent person), the character of the user (for carefulness) is in issue. [120 A.L.R. 1298]

(2) **Types of evidence admissible**

(a) **Majority view—reputation and conduct only:** [§142]   When character itself is the ultimate issue, most courts admit evidence of either the party's reputation in the community or specific instances of the party's past conduct, to reflect on such character. [*See* 120 A.L.R. 1298]

1) **Note:** Opinion evidence is held *not* admissible on the rationale that it is not as reliable as the other types of character evidence. [People v. Wendt, 244 N.E.2d 384 (Ill. 1968)]

(b) **Modern trend—opinion admissible:** [§143]   However, the modern trend is to allow opinion evidence as well. Federal Rule 405(b) provides that any of the three kinds of character evidence is admissible where character itself is the ultimate fact in dispute.

c. **Reputation evidence where reputation (and not conduct or character) is in issue:** [§144]   There are a few situations where the reputation (as distinguished from character) of a person may be in issue. Where reputation alone is in issue, it may be proved only by testimony of witnesses as to the party's reputation in the community—not by opinions of the witnesses or by evidence of specific acts or conduct, except as they may be used to cross-examine the witnesses on their testimony regarding reputation.

(1) **Example:** Probably the most common cases in this area are defamation actions, where the plaintiff alleges injuries to reputation. In such a case, the plaintiff's business or personal reputation is deemed in issue, and evidence of it can be offered on either side. [Scott v. Times-Mirror, 178 Cal. 688 (1918)]

4. **Exceptions to General Rule**

a. **Criminal cases—accused's evidence of good character:** [§145]   As a matter of fairness, the accused in a criminal prosecution may always introduce evidence of his good character to show the improbability that he committed the crime of which he is charged. This is true whether or not the accused takes the witness stand on his own behalf. [Fed. R. Evid. 404(a)(1); Commonwealth v. Beal, 50 N.E.2d 14 (Mass. 1943)]

(1) **Pertinent traits required:** [§146]   Some courts permit general proof of "good" character. [*See, e.g.,* United States v. Cylkovski, 556 F.2d 799 (6th Cir. 1977)] But most insist that the character evidence be *relevant to the charges* made against the accused—*e.g.,* in a theft case, evidence that defendant is an honest person. [Fed. R. Evid. 404(a)(1); United States v. Staggs, 553 F.2d 1073 (7th Cir. 1977)]

(2) **Types of evidence admissible**

(a) **Traditional view—reputation only:** [§147]   The traditional view admits testimony only as to defendant's reputation in the community at the time of the crime charged. [People v. Van Gaasbeck, 189 N.Y. 408 (1907)]

1) **Opinions and specific acts inadmissible:** [§148]   Witnesses are usually not allowed to testify as to their personal opinions of defendant's character, or as to any specific conduct or acts that may reflect on defendant's good character (*e.g.,* acts of heroism in military service, etc.). [*See* 9 A.L.R.2d 606] (*Compare:* The prosecution can inquire into prior conduct on cross-examination of defendant's character witnesses; *see* below.)

(b) **Modern view (Federal Rules of Evidence)—opinion also admissible:** [§149]   Modern codes, however, expand this view by allowing the use of reputation or opinion evidence—testimony of witnesses who know the defendant personally and give their opinion as to defendant's character traits. [Fed. R. Evid. 405(a)] (In reality, witnesses who claim to be testifying as to defendant's "reputation" are usually only stating their personal opinions.)

(c) **Specific conduct disallowed:** [§150]   Note that evidence of specific acts may not be used by the defendant to show good character (*e.g.,* the defendant in a larceny trial may not introduce evidence that he once found some money and sought out the owner to return it). The rationale is that such evidence takes too much time, raises too many collateral issues, and is really not very probative on the issue of defendant's conduct on a later occasion.

(3) **Prosecution may rebut evidence of good character:** [§151]   While the prosecution is ordinarily forbidden to introduce evidence of the bad character of the accused (*infra,* §160), if the defendant introduces reputation evidence of good character, the prosecution is then entitled to rebut defendant's evidence by showing defendant's bad character. The defendant is said to have "opened the door" on the issue of his reputation, so that the prosecution can now go into the matter using the same type of evidence. [Michelson v. United States, 335 U.S. 469 (1948); Fed. R. Evid. 404(a)(1)]

(a) **Types of evidence prosecution can introduce:** [§152]   In states where the defendant is limited to the use of reputation evidence to show good character (*see* above), the prosecutor may normally introduce only the same type of evidence (*i.e.,* reputation) as to whatever aspect of the defendant's character is involved (*e.g.,* witnesses who testify that the defendant's reputation in the community is "violent" or "dishonest," etc.). [United States v. Corey, 566 F.2d 429 (2d Cir. 1977)]

(b) **Cross-examination of defendant's character witnesses:** [§153]   However, by far the more frequent (and effective) prosecution evidence usually comes from cross-examination of the defendant's character witnesses. To test the credibility of their statements as to defendant's good reputation, the prosecutor is permitted to attempt impeachment by examining them as to defendant's past crimes and misconduct (specific acts), which otherwise would not be permitted into evidence. [Fed. R. Evid. 405(a)]

1) **Scope of cross-examination:** [§154]   Defendant's character witnesses can be asked about anything that might logically reflect on defendant's reputation; *i.e.,* the prosecutor can bring up mere arrests or indictments, as well as actual convictions. [McNaulty v. State, 135 S.W.2d 987 (Tex. 1939)]

a) **Note:** Such cross-examination may even include questions about the specific acts for which defendant is presently on trial on the rationale that these acts reflect on defendant's reputation as much as any others. [People v. Lee, 48 Cal. App. 3d 516 (1975)]

b) **Limitation:** Any crimes or misconduct raised must have some relevancy to whatever aspect of defendant's character is in issue. Thus, where defendant's character witness testified only as to defendant's reputation for honesty, it is improper to cross-examine as to defendant's arrest on "white slavery" charges. [People v. Angelopoulos, 30 Cal. App. 2d 538 (1939)]

2) **Proper form of questioning**

a) **Majority view—"have you heard?"** [§155]   The majority view is that since the defendant's witnesses can testify only as to the defendant's *reputation* (*see* above), the prosecutor may question them on cross-examination only by asking: "Have you heard that . . . ?" (and not, "Do you know that . . . ?"). [Michelson v. United States, *supra*, §151; United States v. Bright, 588 F.2d 504 (5th Cir. 1979); 47 A.L.R.2d 1258]

b) **Modern trend—"do you know?"** [§156]   Under the modern codes, which permit defendant's witnesses to testify as to their own opinions of defendant's character (*see* above), cross-examination in either form (*i.e.,* "Do you know that . . . ?") would be proper. [Fed. R. Evid. 405, note; *and see* United States v. Tempesta, 587 F.2d 931 (8th Cir. 1978)]

1/ **And note:** Some courts allow the "do you know" form of questioning even where the character witnesses have testified only to the reputation of the defendant and not to their own opinions. [Fed. R. Evid. 405, note]

3) **Independent evidence of defendant's prior crimes:** [§157] What if the defendant's character witnesses claim no knowledge of the defendant's past misdeeds; can the prosecutor introduce records of the arrests or convictions involved? While the authorities are split, the probable majority view is that the prosecutor *cannot* introduce such independent evidence—*i.e.,* she is bound by the answers given by the defendant's witnesses. [Fed. R. Evid. 405; Cal. Evid. Code §1002; *but see* N.Y. Civ. Prac. Law §60.40—contra]

4) **Note—limitation on cross-examination of defendant:** [§158] When testimony as to the defendant's good character is given by the defendant himself, some courts do not allow inquiry into specific instances of misconduct on cross-examination.

a) **Rationale:** Asking the defendant whether he has "heard of" his own acts of misconduct serves no purpose other than to get the prejudicial question before the jury.

b) **Alternative methods of testing defendant's credibility:**
[§159]   Thus, the prosecution must either rebut the defendant's evidence of good character (*see* above), or attempt to impeach the defendant in the same manner as any other witness (*see infra,* §§1003 *et seq.*). [People v. Wagner, 13 Cal. 3d 612 (1975)]

(4) **Where accused offers no character evidence:** [§160]   If the accused never offers evidence of good character, the prosecution ordinarily cannot inquire into such matters at all.

    (a) **Note:** The accused does not "open the door" merely by taking the stand (although this does raise the possibility of using character evidence to *impeach his credibility*; *see infra,* §§179-180).

    (b) **And note:** The accused's failure to "open up" the issue of his reputation cannot be made the basis for any presumption that he has a bad reputation or character, nor can the prosecutor make any comment to the jury on this issue.

(5) **Character evidence in civil action:** [§161]   The general rule in civil cases is the same as in criminal cases: Evidence of either party's character is generally held not admissible to reflect on whether a party acted (or did not act) in a certain way on any particular occasion. [Fed. R. Evid. 404(a)] Thus, for example, P cannot prove negligence against D by evidence that D has a reputation for being a "careless" driver or "accident prone." [Towle v. Pacific Implement Co., 98 Cal. 342 (1893)] This is because the slight probative value of such evidence is outweighed by the possible confusion of issues. [Vance v. Richardson, 110 Cal. 414 (1895)]

    (a) **Exception—limited use of evidence of good character:** [§162]   A number of courts permit a defendant who is charged with *fraud* or another tort involving moral turpitude to introduce evidence of good character to rebut the charge. [Perrin v. Anderson, 784 F.2d 1040 (10th Cir. 1986)] *Rationale:* A verdict against the defendant in such a case can be as serious as a criminal conviction, and in criminal cases the defendant can introduce evidence of her good character (*see supra,* §§145-150).

b. **Criminal cases—evidence of victim's character to show action in conformity:** [§163]   In certain cases, evidence of a pertinent character trait of the victim may be admissible to show action by the victim in conformity therewith. [Fed. R. Evid. 404(a)(2)]

(1) **Examples**

    (a) **Homicide cases—self-defense:** [§164]   The character of a homicide victim is often in issue where the accused claims to have killed in self-defense. [34 A.L.R.2d 447]

1) **Evidence of victim's bad character:** [§165] The defendant may introduce evidence of the victim's violent nature or disposition in an attempt to show either: (i) the likelihood that the victim was the aggressor; or (ii) that the accused's apprehension of harm from the victim was reasonable. [State v. Padula, 138 A. 456 (Conn. 1927)]

   a) **Note:** Evidence that the victim's violent nature was *communicated* to the defendant is *not* hearsay since it is offered not for the truth of the matter asserted, but to show cause for a reasonable apprehension of harm on the part of the defendant. (*See infra*, §§220 *et seq.* for discussion of hearsay.)

2) **Rebuttal evidence:** [§166] In rebuttal, the prosecution may introduce evidence as to the "peacefulness" of the homicide victim—to offset any inference that the victim was the first aggressor. [Fed. R. Evid. 404(a)(2)]

   a) **Compare:** In most courts, the prosecution cannot introduce rebuttal evidence of the accused's reputation for violence as tending to show that the accused was the aggressor.

(b) **Rape cases—consent:** [§167] Before the "rape shield" legislation of the 1970s and 1980s, a man accused of rape who claimed that the victim consented to sexual intercourse was, in many jurisdictions, entitled to introduce evidence of the victim's reputation for promiscuity to show the likelihood of such consent. [People v. Collins, 185 N.E.2d 147 (Ill. 1962)]

   1) **Rebuttal evidence:** [§168] To rebut such evidence, the prosecutor might counter with evidence of the victim's chastity, good moral character, etc., as evidence of the improbability of her consent. [35 A.L.R.3d 1452]

   2) **Statutory changes:** [§169] "Rape shield" legislation changes this rule. To prevent putting the victim's prior sex life "on trial," "rape shield" statutes provide that evidence of the victim's sexual conduct with other men is *inadmissible* on the issue of whether she consented to sexual intercourse with the accused. [Fed. R. Evid. 412]

      a) **Rationale:** Evidence that the alleged victim had intercourse with others is considered of very little probative value on the issue of whether she consented to sexual intercourse with the defendant. [*See* State v. Cassidy, 489 A.2d 386, *cert. denied*, 492 A.2d 1239 (Conn. 1985)]

      b) **Admissibility of evidence for other purposes:** [§170] A number of statutes that forbid a defendant's introduction of character evidence to show the victim's propensity to engage in sexual acts nonetheless allow evidence of the victim's unchastity to show that a condition such as pregnancy or venereal disease, which the prosecution alleges was caused by intercourse with the defendant, was in fact caused by intercourse with someone else.

1/ **Note:** It is not yet clear in many jurisdictions whether this can be done with reputation or opinion testimony, or whether specific acts with others must be shown. The *Federal Rules* provide that for this purpose specific acts must be shown. [Fed. R. Evid. 412(b)]

2/ **Not character evidence:** [§171] If specific acts with others must be shown to account for the victim's condition, this is not *character* evidence.

3/ **Not evidence of consent:** [§172] The evidence is not being used to show consent, but rather to refute the prosecution's evidence of *identity* (whether the defendant had intercourse with the victim, with or without consent).

  a/ **Consent:** [§173] In some cases, even on the issue of consent, the character of the victim might actually be highly relevant. This is especially clear if the victim had made a practice, for example, of picking up men in bars and having intercourse with them. Such evidence would make it more likely, though of course not certain, that under similar conditions the victim consented to intercourse with the defendant.

    1] **But note:** Such evidence, however, is better called scheme or plan evidence rather than character testimony, and if so, specific act evidence, rather than reputation or opinion evidence, should be required. Note, however, that the Federal Rules exclude specific act evidence on this issue. [Fed. R. Evid. 412(b)]

c) **Compare—prior intercourse with defendant:** [§174] Evidence of the victim's prior sexual conduct with the defendant is *not* excluded by most "rape shield" statutes. *Rationale:* Such evidence is obviously far more relevant on the issue of consent than intercourse between the victim and a third party. [Fed. R. Evid. 412(b)]

d) **Constitutionality of "rape shield" statutes:** [§175] Although the Supreme Court has not yet had occasion to decide whether any of these statutes unreasonably impair an accused's Sixth Amendment confrontation rights [*see* State v. Cassidy, *supra,* §169], it has determined that, under certain circumstances, the accused has a Sixth Amendment right to cross-examine the alleged victim regarding her relationships with other men [Olden v. Kentucky, 488 U.S. 227

(1988)—defendant should be allowed to ask the victim about her cohabitation with another man because it might give her motive to lie about the nature of the incident]. The Court also has not decided whether a "rape shield" law impairs the defendant's due process right to a fair trial [*see, e.g.,* Chambers v. Mississippi, 410 U.S. 284 (1973); United States v. Nez, 661 F.2d 1203 (10th Cir. 1981)], or his rights to trial by jury (as where a judge makes determinations of witness credibility in finding a condition of fact upon which the relevancy of the proffered evidence depends).

(2) **Types of evidence admissible**

(a) **Majority view:** [§176] Where evidence of the victim's character is admissible to show action in conformity therewith (*e.g.,* in a homicide case where defendant asserts that the victim was the first aggressor), most courts limit the accused (or prosecutor in rebuttal) to testimony as to the victim's *reputation in the community* for the character trait in question. [121 A.L.R. 380]

(b) **Modern codes:** [§177] Again, however, the modern codes are more liberal and also allow *opinion* testimony by witnesses who knew the victim personally. [Fed. R. Evid. 405(a); *see supra,* §149]

(c) **Cross-examination:** [§178] And again, on cross-examination, inquiry is permitted into *specific instances* of past conduct (past crimes, etc.); *see* discussion *supra,* §153.

c. **Character evidence to reflect on credibility of witness:** [§179] Character evidence may also be admissible to reflect on a witness's credibility or lack thereof. [Fed. R. Evid. 404(a)(3)]

(1) **To impeach:** [§180] Any time a witness takes the stand, her reputation for truthfulness is deemed to be in issue. This applies to all witnesses—including the parties to a civil action and the accused in a criminal prosecution (if the accused chooses to take the stand). Hence, the rule is that *any witness* can be impeached by a showing of either:

(a) *Poor reputation for truth and veracity* (*see infra,* §§1048-1055); or

(b) *Prior felony conviction* (*see infra,* §§1015-1040), reflecting the debatable notion that felons are more likely than other persons to lie on the witness stand.

(2) **To rehabilitate:** [§181] A witness who has been impeached by the adverse party may be rehabilitated by the party who called that witness by proof of her good reputation for veracity (*see infra,* §1097).

d. **Sex crimes:** [§182] Federal Rules of Evidence 413 through 415 create a special exception to the rule against character evidence for sex crime cases. Under Rule 413, when a criminal defendant is accused of sexual assault, the prosecution may introduce evidence that the defendant committed other such crimes to show his propensity to commit sexual assault. Federal Rule 414 creates a comparable rule for cases in which a criminal defendant is charged with child molestation, and Federal Rule 415 provides for the admissibility of evidence of other offenses in civil cases involving sexual assault or child molestation.

(1) **Rule 403 applicability:** [§183]   Although Rules 413 through 415 appear to provide for blanket admissibility of other sexual assault or child molestation offenses, it seems likely that judges will use Rule 403 to exclude other-offense evidence if its probative value is substantially outweighed by unfair prejudice (*e.g.*, judge will likely use Rule 403 to exclude other sexual assault that occurred 30 years prior to alleged assault).

(2) **Types of evidence admissible:** [§184]   Most of the other exceptions to the rule against character evidence require that the character evidence be presented in the form of reputation or opinion testimony. Rules 413 through 415 are quite different in that they do not provide for reputation or opinion testimony. Instead, they specifically allow testimony about prior acts of the defendant. Also, the other-crimes evidence need not be evidence of a prior conviction; if a victim comes forward for the first time after the defendant has been accused of raping another woman, her testimony will be admissible under the Rules.

5. **Character of Animals:** [§185]   Evidence of an animal's character (or perhaps evidence of an animal's "habit"; *see infra*, §§186-188) to show action in conformity therewith is more often admissible than evidence of human character traits (*see supra*, §§119-184). For example, evidence that D's dog has bitten others is generally held relevant to establish the dog's propensity for biting and hence to make it more likely that the dog bit P on a particular occasion. [Marks v. Columbia County Lumber Co., 149 P. 1041 (Or. 1915)]

6. **Compare—Habit or Custom**

a. **Distinguished from "character":** [§186]   "Character" evidence refers to a person's *general propensity*. Character traits, such as honesty, prudence, violence, and the like, are thought to influence behavior in a variety of quite different situations. On the other hand, "habit" evidence refers to the person's *routine reactions* in particular situations. This distinction is sometimes easier to describe than to detect. [*See, e.g.,* Reyes v. Missouri Pacific Railway, *supra,* §37; Perrin v. Anderson, *supra,* §162]

(1) **Example:** P may offer evidence in an accident case showing that: (i) she is a careful driver; (ii) she never exceeds the speed limit; and (iii) she always comes to a full stop at a particular intersection.

(a) **"Character":** The evidence that P is a careful driver is really "character" evidence, and, as seen *supra*, is generally held not admissible to prove whether P was driving carefully at the time of the accident.

(b) **"Habit":** The other evidence (in (ii) and (iii), above) may be admissible as "habit" evidence, in accordance with the principles set forth below.

gilbert LAW SUMMARIES	CHARACTER EVIDENCE VS. HABIT EVIDENCE
Character Evidence	**Habit Evidence**
"Sally is always in a hurry."	"Sally always takes the stairs two at a time."
"Bart is a drunk."	"Bart stops at Charlie's tavern every night after work and has exactly four beers."
"Jeff is a careless driver."	"Jeff never slows down for the YIELD sign at the end of the street."
"Lara is very conscientious about taking care of her possessions."	"Lara checks the brakes on her car every Sunday before church."

b. **Requirements for admissibility of "habit" evidence:** [§187] The acts claimed to be a "habit" must be *specific*, *routine* (performed without deliberation), *and continuous*. Some courts add the requirement that the routine acts be "invariable" (*see* below).

   (1) **Minority view:** [§188] A few states add the requirement that habit evidence is admissible only if corroborated or if there is no eyewitness or other direct evidence as to the performance of the acts in question. [Envirex, Inc. v. Ecological Recovery Associations, Inc., 454 F. Supp. 1329 (M.D. Pa. 1978); Young v. Patrick, 153 N.E. 623 (Ill. 1926)] (Federal Rule 406 specifically rejects such requirements.)

c. **Types of evidence admissible:** [§189] Habit or custom may be proved by either opinion evidence or evidence of specific behavior.

   (1) **Opinion evidence:** In many jurisdictions, the person, or anyone who knows the person, may testify as to her opinion on the habit in question.

   (2) **Specific behavior:** More common is testimony as to specific acts of past behavior, where the instances are sufficient in number to establish the routine, semiautomatic response that is "habit." [Meyer v. United States, 464 F. Supp. 317 (D. Colo. 1979)]

   (3) **Compare—Federal Rules:** The Federal Rules are purposefully vague as to what kind of evidence is admissible to prove habit or custom. Congress indicated that the method of proof should be left to the courts to deal with on a case-by-case basis (and did not specifically authorize any general use of opinion evidence in this area).

d. **Purposes for which admissible**

(1) **To prove the doing of an act:** [§190]   Evidence of human habit, or the routine practice of an organization, is admissible to prove that on a given occasion a particular act was done in accordance with that habit or routine. [Fed. R. Evid. 406]

  (a) **Degree of proof required:** [§191]   However, where habit evidence is sought to reflect on the doing of the very act in issue (and particularly when there is no other satisfactory evidence of same) many courts tend to require a strong showing that the habit was "invariable." As a result, evidence as to driving habits, etc., is frequently difficult to establish. Note, however, that a few courts go to the other extreme and stretch the "habit" concept so that nonroutine acts, such as an individual's repeated violent reaction to encounters with police officers, are considered "habit." [*See, e.g.,* Perrin v. Anderson, *supra,* §186; 46 A.L.R.2d 103]

  (b) **Industrial or business routines:** [§192]   Because of the high degree of proof required, most cases in which habit evidence is admitted to prove that an act was done in accordance with the habit involve established business routine. *Examples:*

    1) **Letter mailing:** Proof that a company's outgoing mail is habitually deposited in a certain place, where it is picked up and carried to a mailbox by a clerk, is generally accepted as sufficient to prove the mailing of a particular letter, where there is evidence that the letter in question was deposited in the proper place. [Prudential Trust Co. v. Hayes, 142 N.E. 73 (Mass. 1924)]

    2) **Sales receipts:** Evidence that it is a store's custom to give a sales slip with each purchase is admissible to show that goods found in the defendant's possession *without* a sales slip had not been purchased from the store (*i.e.,* were stolen). [Lowe v. Inhabitants of Clinton, 136 Mass. 24 (1883)]

    3) **Use of checkbook:** The deceased's habit of paying for all purchases by check is admissible to prove that the deceased had not made a particular purchase because no check had been drawn. [Spolter v. Four-Wheel Brake Service Co., 99 Cal. App. 2d 690 (1950)]

    4) **Operation of public transportation:** Evidence as to where a bus regularly stops to pick up and discharge passengers is generally held admissible to show where the bus stopped on a particular occasion. [*See* Moffitt v. Connecticut Co., 86 A. 16 (Conn. 1913)]

    5) **Company safety rules:** The invariable custom of employees of D's garage to test brakes before renting out a car is admissible to show that the brakes were in fact tested. [Buxton v. Langan, 3 A.2d 647 (N.H. 1939)]

(2) **To show standard of care in negligence cases:** [§193]   Evidence as to custom or usage in a business or industry to which the defendant belongs

(habits of defendant and others) may be admissible as reflecting on the standard of care owed by the defendant in a negligence case. [43 A.L.R.2d 618]

    (a) **Time and location requirements:** [§194] To be relevant, there must be a showing that the custom was prevalent in the same general locality where the accident occurred and at the time it occurred.

    (b) **Custom not conclusive:** [§195] While evidence of a prevailing industry-wide custom is admissible as to the standard of care, it certainly is not conclusive. Thus, although a defendant's business activity was conducted in accordance with the industry-wide custom, the plaintiff may show that the industry standard falls below the standard required by law for the protection of the public. (*See* Torts Summary.)

    (3) **To reflect on terms of contract:** [§196] Evidence of industry custom or usage is admissible to reflect on the meaning of special terms used in a contract, or in certain cases to establish the terms. (*See* Contracts and Sale and Lease of Goods Summaries.)

F. EVIDENCE AFFECTED BY EXTRINSIC POLICIES

1. **Introduction:** [§197] In several areas, evidence that seems relevant is excluded, not because it is too prejudicial, confusing, etc., but as a means of encouraging certain kinds of conduct. In some ways, the extrinsic policies calling for exclusion of evidence in these situations are similar to the policies giving rise to privileges (*see infra,* §§554 *et seq.*). They are usually classed differently, however, since privileges are designed to protect certain kinds of communications made in the course of special confidential relationships that the state desires to encourage (*e.g.,* lawyer and client); whereas the types of evidence excluded by so-called extrinsic policies are typically actions of a party sought to be used against that party as implicit admissions of liability or guilt.

2. **Subsequent Remedial Measures**

    a. **General rule—inadmissible to show negligence:** [§198] Evidence that, following an injury to the plaintiff, the defendant made repairs or took other remedial measures is generally held not admissible to prove negligence or other culpable conduct in connection with the event. [Fed. R. Evid. 407; Ford v. Schmidt, 577 F.2d 408 (7th Cir. 1978)]

    (1) **Rationale:** The rule is justified on two grounds:

        (a) **Irrelevancy:** The subsequent repair does not logically establish prior lack of care by defendant; and

        (b) **Public policy:** Admitting such evidence would tend to discourage beneficial changes from being made following an accident. [Morse v. Minneapolis & St. Louis Railway, 16 N.W. 358 (Minn. 1883); 65 A.L.R.2d 1296]

    b. **Admissibility for other purposes:** [§199] Evidence of subsequent repairs may, however, be admitted for the following purposes:

(1) ***To impeach the defendant's witnesses as to the safety of the condition***—*e.g.,* D's engineer testifies that D's stairway was safe and proper at the time P fell; evidence that this engineer personally ordered installation of railing on stairway after the accident is admissible as tending to impeach his testimony. [Westbrooks v. Gordon H. Ball, Inc., 248 Cal. App. 2d 209 (1967)]

(2) ***To show ownership or control*** of the instrumentality causing the injury—since a stranger would hardly undertake repairs thereof. [170 A.L.R. 43]

(3) ***To show that the defendant was attempting to conceal or destroy evidence***—*e.g.,* D's repainting the fender on her car to cover up evidence of collision with P (where D denies her car struck P). [64 A.L.R.2d 1214]

(4) ***To show that precautionary measures were feasible*** (where D has denied this). [Fed. R. Evid. 407]

  c. **Admissibility in strict liability cases:** [§200] Federal Rule 407 applies in strict liability cases as well as in negligence cases. Rule 407 specifically provides that "evidence of subsequent remedial measures is not admissible to prove . . . a defect in a product, a defect in a product's design, or a need for a warning or instruction."

(1) **Compare:** Some states' rules regarding subsequent remedial measures are worded differently than Federal Rule 407. In these states, where the plaintiff is suing on a strict liability theory, evidence of subsequent repairs may be admissible as tending to show that the condition repaired was defective. [*See, e.g.,* Ault v. International Harvester Co., 13 Cal. 3d 113 (1974)]

3. **Matters Claimed as Admissions of Negligence or Liability**

  a. **Offers to compromise:** [§201] Evidence that defendant has paid or offered to pay money in settlement of a ***disputed claim*** against her (or that plaintiff has offered to accept a certain sum) is ***not*** admissible to fix liability as between the parties. (Of course, if introduced without objection, such evidence may be considered as an admission on the issue of liability; *see infra,* §294.) [Fed. R. Evid. 408; *and see* Hatfield v. Continental Imports, Inc., 578 A.2d 530 (Pa. 1990)]

(1) **Rationale:** Several theories have been used by the courts in support of this exclusionary rule [20 A.L.R.2d 291]:

  (a) **Lack of relevancy:** Offers of compromise do not necessarily reflect on liability; the offeror may merely be trying to avoid expenses of litigating (may be "buying peace").

  (b) **Danger of prejudice:** Juries may attach undue weight to such offers as indicative of liability.

  (c) **Implied agreement:** Parties impliedly agree that settlement negotiations are to be without prejudice to their positions.

  (d) **Public policy:** It is the policy of the law to encourage settlement of disputes without litigation. If either party could attempt to prove liability on the basis of offers made by the other, such settlements would be discouraged.

(2) **Statements during negotiations:** [§202]   Although the offer of compromise itself is inadmissible, some courts have taken the position that any *fact admissions* made during the course of negotiations should be received in evidence (*e.g.,* D says, "I'm sorry that I ran the red light . . . let's talk damages"). [*See* 80 A.L.R. 919]

(a) **Criticism:** This position has been repeatedly criticized as inconsistent with the rationales expressed in paragraphs (c) and (d), above.

(b) **Compare—modern trend:** [§203]   The Federal Rules and the trend of authority reject the above position and *exclude* any conduct or statement made in the course of negotiating a compromise—as well as the offer to compromise itself. [Fed. R. Evid. 408]

1) **No effect on discovery:** [§204]   Federal Rule 408 also provides (though this would probably be implied by courts anyway) that evidence "otherwise discoverable" does not become inadmissible simply because produced during the course of settlement negotiations. (*Example:* Physical evidence, otherwise discoverable in a personal injury suit, does not become inadmissible at trial simply because it was shown to the opposite party in a vain attempt to settle the case.)

(3) **Offers and statements not excluded by rule:** [§205]   Settlement offers and statements made in conjunction with offers are admissible if sufficiently probative on *some issue other than liability* for a disputed claim.

(a) **Example:** Evidence that a witness settled before trial with one of the parties may be admissible to show the witness's bias because the deal may have prejudiced the witness in favor of that party (*see infra,* §208).

(b) **Example:** Some courts go further and allow statements in a settlement negotiation to be admitted if they are inconsistent with a witness's testimony at trial, and hence can be admitted for impeachment purposes. [Davidson v. Prince, 813 P.2d 1225 (Utah 1991) (alternative holding)]

(c) **Example:** Moreover, the rule does not apply to business negotiations that are directed at something other than settlement of a disputed legal claim (*e.g.,* a merchant's routine negotiation of the terms of his lease would be admissible despite the rule).

b. **Payment of plaintiff's medical expenses:** [§206]   Evidence that the defendant paid (or offered to pay) plaintiff's medical, hospital, or similar expenses is generally held not relevant to prove the defendant liable for plaintiff's injuries. This is the "Good Samaritan rule." [Fed. R. Evid. 409; 65 A.L.R.3d 932]

(1) **Rationale:** The rationale here is the same as for offers to compromise, above, plus a concern that such payment may have been prompted solely by "humanitarian motives." [*See* Cal. Evid. Code §1152]

(2) **But note:** Unlike the situation with offers to compromise, *admissions of fact* accompanying offers to pay medical expenses *are admissible* under the Federal Rules. [*See* Fed. R. Evid. 409, note]

c. **Defendant's settlement with third person:** [§207] A defendant's settlement with another person, on a claim arising out of the same incident, is excluded for the above reasons, and because it might raise too many collateral issues. [20 A.L.R.2d 304]

    (1) **Exception:** [§208] Where the third person appears as a witness for the defendant, courts may permit cross-examination as to the settlement, to show possible bias or prejudice (*see infra,* §§1056-1063).

d. **Failure to meet professional or company standards**

    (1) **Violations of company rules:** [§209] In an action against an employer based on the alleged negligence of an employee (respondeat superior), evidence that the employee violated a company rule is generally held admissible. The courts view the employer's own rules as an implied admission of the standard of care required, so that an inference of negligence flows from the employee's violation thereof. [50 A.L.R.2d 27]

        (a) **Minority view:** [§210] A minority of courts are contra, asserting that the logical relevancy of such evidence is doubtful because the company rule may set a higher standard of care than the law requires. Hence, the probative value of the evidence is offset by the possible prejudicial effect. [*See* Hoffman v. Cedar Rapids & M.C. Railway, 139 N.W. 165 (Iowa 1912)]

    (2) **Violation of professional medical standards:** [§211] Reports of medical staff committees reviewing surgeries, etc., performed in a hospital are often highly relevant as to whether particular surgeries met the standard of care required. However, discovery and use of such evidence is generally barred for policy reasons in malpractice cases. [Cal. Evid. Code §1157]

        (a) **Public policy rationale:** Constructive professional criticism would be inhibited if staff doctors knew their suggestions might be used against a colleague in a malpractice suit. (In this sense, the evidence is like evidence of subsequent precautions.)

4. **Liability Insurance:** [§212] Evidence that either party carried (or did not carry) liability insurance is inadmissible as proof of negligence or wrongdoing. [Fed. R. Evid. 411] (Although this rule is usually classed as an extrinsic policy, it more likely is simply a codification of the determination that the prejudicial effect of the evidence outweighs its probativeness.)

a. **Rationale:** Again, there are several rationales for excluding such evidence:

    (1) **Lack of relevancy:** Basically, there is very little logical relevancy; *i.e.,* the fact that the defendant carried insurance hardly tends to prove that the defendant was liable. [Roche v. Llewellyn Ironworks, 140 Cal. 63 (1903)] (As a matter of pure relevance, however, insurance coverage might show that the defendant had less motivation to be careful.)

    (2) **Prejudice:** Despite any arguable relevancy, the risk of prejudice to the defendant is very high (*i.e.,* a jury influenced by the fact that insurance coverage is available to the defendant might more readily hold the defendant

liable; the converse may be true when a jury is told that defendant is uninsured). [4 A.L.R.2d 773]

(3) **Public policy:** To admit such evidence would discourage persons from carrying insurance. (Actually, it might only encourage them to carry more.)

b. **Admissibility for other purposes:** [§213] There are numerous situations where evidence that the defendant carried liability insurance is permitted. However, in each of these situations the evidence of insurance is admitted for some reason *other than to prove the defendant liable* [Fed. R. Evid. 411]:

(1) **Incidental to admission:** [§214] Some courts would allow insurance to be mentioned incidentally as part of an admission of fault. (Witness testifies to overhearing defendant say at scene of accident, "Don't worry . . . I am insured.") [4 A.L.R.2d 781] Other courts would redact the reference to insurance, at least if it were possible to do so without making the statement misleading or confusing. [Cameron v. Columbia Builders, Inc., 320 P.2d 251 (Or. 1958)]

(2) **Proof of ownership:** [§215] Terms of insurance may be held admissible if there is a dispute as to ownership or control of the vehicle involved in an accident or as to agency or employment of the person covered by the policy. [Dobbins v. Crain Bros., Inc., 432 F. Supp. 1060 (W.D. Pa. 1976); 4 A.L.R.2d 776]

(3) **Proof of bias:** [§216] The existence of insurance coverage may also be brought out on cross-examination of a witness for possible bias (*e.g.,* asking the defendant's medical witness whether her fees for testifying are being paid by an insurance company). [Charter v. Chleborad, 551 F.2d 246 (8th Cir. 1977); 4 A.L.R.2d 779; *compare* Posttape Associates v. Eastman Kodak Co., 537 F.2d 751 (3d Cir. 1976)—regarding question of whether trade custom limited damages for defective film to replacement cost, P's purchase of insurance indemnifying against defective film admissible]

(4) **Selection of jurors:** [§217] Insurance is frequently mentioned on voir dire examination of jurors to determine if any may be prejudiced by reason of relationship or prior dealings with an insurance carrier.

5. **Guilty Pleas:** [§218] As to the admissibility in subsequent civil or criminal proceedings of a guilty plea (or offer to plead guilty) made in a prior criminal case, *see infra,* §§311-313.

6. **Statements Made During Plea Bargaining:** [§219] Federal Rule of Evidence 410 provides that statements made during plea bargaining with a prosecuting attorney are not admissible. (*Rationale:* The rulemakers wanted to facilitate plea bargaining.) The force of the rule, however, is diminished by two matters: First, it only applies to statements made during plea bargaining with an *attorney for the government*, not to plea bargaining with law enforcement investigators. Second, the Supreme Court has held that the protection of the rule can be waived. [United States v. Mezzanatto, 513 U.S. 196 (1995)] Hence, the prosecutor who wishes to avoid the rule can ask that defendants sign a form waiving its protection as a condition of plea bargaining.

 **LAW SUMMARIES**

Evidence	Inadmissible	Admissible
Subsequent Remedial Measures	To prove negligence, culpable conduct, a defect in a product or its design, or a need for a warning or instruction	For other purposes, *e.g.,* to impeach defendant's witnesses as to the safety of the condition, to prove ownership or control, to prove defendant was attempting to conceal or destroy evidence, or to prove precautionary measures were feasible
Offers to Compromise	To prove liability of a disputed claim	For other purposes, *e.g.,* to show the bias of a witness
Offers to Pay and Payment of Medical Expenses	To prove liability for injuries	For all other purposes (Admissions of fact accompanying an offer to pay medical expenses are admissible)
Liability Insurance	To prove negligence or wrongdoing	For other purposes, *e.g.,* as part of an admission, to prove ownership or control, to prove bias, or on voir dire examination of jurors to determine prejudice
Withdrawn Guilty Pleas and Offers to Plead Guilty	Against the defendant who made the plea or offer	Against another person, or where defendant opens door by alluding to subject
Statements Made During Plea Bargaining	Against a defendant who made statements during plea bargaining to a government attorney	Against another person, or against defendant who made plea bargaining statements to police (not prosecutor)

V. THE HEARSAY RULE AND ITS EXCEPTIONS

chapter approach

The rule against hearsay is an important rule for trial lawyers. It also is a favorite of evidence professors, and questions calling for the application of the rule frequently appear on evidence exams. Thus, it is important for you to have a thorough knowledge of the rule and its exceptions and exemptions. In approaching a hearsay question, you should ask two questions:

1. ***Is the statement offered to prove the truth of the matter asserted?*** If so, it is hearsay, but if the statement is offered for a purpose ***other than proving its truth***, it is ***not*** hearsay. [Fed. R. Evid. 801(c)]

   Approach this first question by asking about the relevancy of the statement: Is the statement ***relevant for any purpose that does not require accepting the truth of the matter asserted?*** For example, a statement that a man hurt someone might be relevant both to show its truth (the man in fact hurt someone) and for some other purpose (the hearer of the statement was put in fear of the man). The statement would be hearsay for the first purpose, but not for the second. If the statement is offered for the second purpose (to show the hearer's fear of the man), the judge would weigh its probative value for the permitted purpose against the danger that the jury would use it prejudicially for the forbidden purpose. If the judge decides to admit the statement, she should instruct the jury about the limited purpose for which it has been admitted, telling the jurors not to consider the statement for the truth of the matter asserted.

2. ***If the statement is hearsay*** (offered to prove the truth of the matter asserted), ***is it nonetheless admissible under an exception or exemption to the hearsay rule?*** For example, suppose that an out-of-court declarant exclaimed, "He's the one who did it!" and the exclamation is offered to prove that the defendant in fact "did it." The statement is offered to prove its truth, and therefore it is hearsay, but it may be admissible under the exception to the hearsay rule for excited utterances.

   Note that at common law, all statements offered to prove their truth were hearsay, and the question of the admissibility of such statements turned on whether they fell within an "exception." Confusingly, the Federal Rules provide that some statements are not hearsay even if they are offered to prove their truth. [*See* Fed. R. Evid. 801(d)] For example, if the plaintiff in a personal injury case offers evidence at trial that at the scene of the accident the defendant said, "It's all my fault," although the statement by the defendant is offered to prove the truth of the matter asserted, it still is not hearsay under the Federal Rules because it is offered as the admission of a party-opponent. [*See* Fed. R. Evid. 801(d)(2)(A)] This special Federal Rules category of statements offered for their truth but still deemed not to be hearsay has come to be known as the ***"exemptions"*** to the hearsay rule, whereas the rules admitting statements that are deemed to be hearsay are known as the ***"exceptions"*** to the hearsay rule.

   Finally, when analyzing hearsay issues, pay close attention to the facts of the question because they may suggest possible exceptions (*e.g.,* a victim who makes a statement and then dies suggests a dying declaration, an employee who "routinely makes reports of this kind as part of her job" suggests a business records exception, and a witness who "exclaimed" or "shouted" something may have made an excited utterance). Be sure however that all the technical requirements of an exception are met before deciding that the exception does in fact apply.

A. INTRODUCTION [§220]

A witness's testimony may be based on: (i) the witness's personal (direct) knowledge of the facts involved; (ii) her opinions, conclusions, or estimates about those facts; or (iii) reports of the facts obtained by the witness from other persons or sources. Testimony based on the witness's personal (direct) knowledge is generally admissible if relevant, while testimony embracing the witness's opinions, conclusions, or estimates often is not (*see infra,* §§869 *et seq.*). The witness's testimony based on the ***reports of others*** may be "hearsay." Hearsay evidence is sometimes admissible, sometimes not.

B. GENERAL NATURE OF HEARSAY [§221]

The hearsay rule or, more precisely, the rule against hearsay, is easy enough to state in a general way: If evidence is "hearsay," it is ***prima facie*** inadmissible. [Fed. R. Evid. 802; United States v. Check, 582 F.2d 668 (2d Cir. 1978)] However, the rule is not always easy to apply. The problems involved are: (i) determining whether particular evidence constitutes hearsay; and (ii) if it does, whether it may nonetheless be admissible under some exception to the basic rule.

1. **Definition of "Hearsay":** [§222]   The authorities have expressed divergent views on what constitutes "hearsay":

   a. **Federal Rules' assertion-centered definition:** [§223]   "Hearsay is a statement, other than one made by the declarant while testifying at the trial or hearing, offered in evidence to prove the truth of the matter asserted." [Fed. R. Evid. 801(c)] A majority of states use this definition of hearsay.

      (1) **"Statement" defined:** [§224]   A hearsay "statement" may consist of any of the following, if offered to prove the truth thereof [Fed. R. Evid. 801(a)]:

         (a) **Oral statements:** A witness offers testimony about statements made either by the witness or someone else outside of court;

         (b) **Writings (as currently rather broadly defined):** A witness offers any document, etc., written or prepared by the witness or someone else; or

         (c) **Assertive conduct:** A witness offers testimony as to how the witness or someone else acted outside of court, where the conduct was intended by the actor as a substitute for words (*see* additional discussion *infra,* §247).

   b. **Morgan's declarant-centered definition:** [§225]   "Hearsay" is "evidence of words or conduct outside of court, assertive or nonassertive, which is offered to prove the truth of the facts therein, or that the declarant believed them to be true . . . *i.e.,* such evidence as requires the trier of fact to treat the out-of-court declarant as if he or she were in court giving testimony on the facts in issue."

APPROACH TO HEARSAY

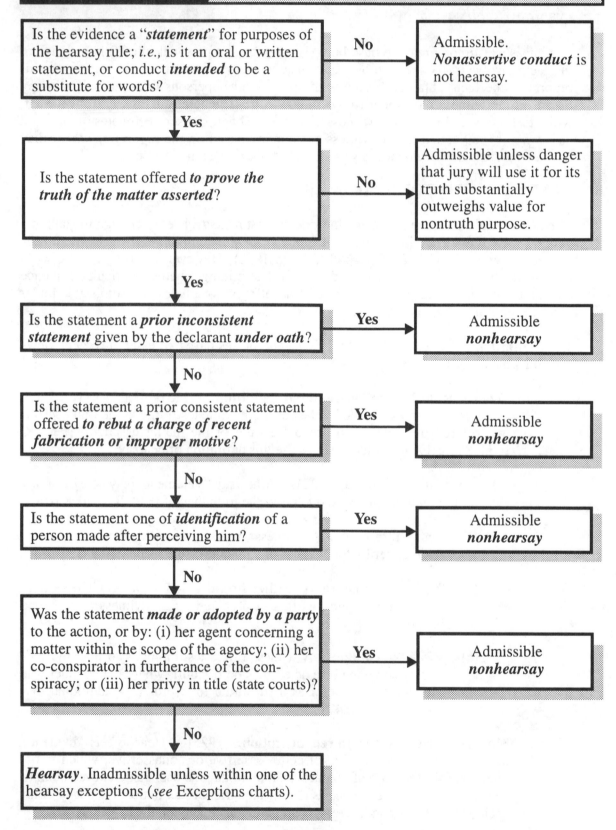

Is the evidence a "*statement*" for purposes of the hearsay rule; *i.e.,* is it an oral or written statement, or conduct *intended* to be a substitute for words? — **No** → Admissible. *Nonassertive conduct* is not hearsay.

Yes ↓

Is the statement offered *to prove the truth of the matter asserted*? — **No** → Admissible unless danger that jury will use it for its truth substantially outweighs value for nontruth purpose.

Yes ↓

Is the statement a *prior inconsistent statement* given by the declarant *under oath*? — **Yes** → Admissible *nonhearsay*

No ↓

Is the statement a prior consistent statement offered *to rebut a charge of recent fabrication or improper motive*? — **Yes** → Admissible *nonhearsay*

No ↓

Is the statement one of *identification* of a person made after perceiving him? — **Yes** → Admissible *nonhearsay*

No ↓

Was the statement *made or adopted by a party* to the action, or by: (i) her agent concerning a matter within the scope of the agency; (ii) her co-conspirator in furtherance of the conspiracy; or (iii) her privy in title (state courts)? — **Yes** → Admissible *nonhearsay*

No ↓

Hearsay. Inadmissible unless within one of the hearsay exceptions (*see* Exceptions charts).

(1) **Note—what is included:** Under Professor Morgan's definition, all of the items mentioned in §224 above are hearsay. In *addition,* so is *non-assertive* conduct—*i.e.,* conduct *not* intended by the actor as a substitute for words but nonetheless *reflecting* the actor's state of mind (belief) (*see* further discussion below).

c. **Elements of hearsay:** [§226] Hearsay is perhaps most easily understood when defined in terms of its three essential elements. These are:

(i) *An assertion* (or conduct that *translates* into an assertion),

(ii) *Made or done* by someone *other than a testifying witness* on the stand (in other words, by an out-of-court declarant or actor), that is

(iii) *Offered* in evidence *to prove the truth* of the matter asserted.

(1) **Importance of identifying the issue:** [§227] This last element indicates that it is always crucial to inquire, "To what *issue* is the evidence being directed?" Only after this question has been answered can it be determined whether the assertions are being offered for the truth of their content. (*See* discussion of the state of mind issue, *infra,* §§236-240.)

2. **Rationale for Hearsay Rule:** [§228] Underlying the rule against hearsay are serious concerns about the *worth* (trustworthiness, reliability) of hearsay evidence. This is because such evidence (i) was *not given under oath* or solemn affirmation; and (ii) was *not subject to cross-examination* by opposing counsel to test the *perception, memory, veracity,* and *articulateness* of the out-of-court declarant or actor upon whose reliability the worth of the in-court testimony depends.

a. **Example:** A witness on the stand testifies, "Joe told me that the automobile was going 80 m.p.h." In other words, the statement by Joe—the out-of-court declarant—that the automobile was going 80 m.p.h. indicates that Joe probably really believed that it was going 80 m.p.h. Hence, the statement is offered on the theory that if Joe believed that the automobile was going 80 m.p.h., it is probably true that it was going 80 m.p.h.

b. **The problems:** However, the validity of Joe's belief, and thus of his verbalization of it, depends on a number of factors:

(1) **Perception:** Joe's perception of the speed of the automobile depends on how good Joe's eyesight was at the pertinent time, on how close he was to the automobile, on whether visibility was in any way obstructed, and on how good Joe was at estimating the speed of rapidly moving objects. This is the *perception* problem.

(2) **Memory:** Joe's memory of the speed of the automobile depends on how good Joe's recollection was when he spoke to the witness. This is the *memory* problem.

(3) **Veracity:** The veracity of Joe's statement about the speed of the automobile depends on whether Joe had any reason to lie to the witness about the speed of the automobile. This is the *veracity* or *sincerity* problem.

(4) **Articulateness or narrative ability:** Joe's articulation of the speed of the automobile depends on how good Joe was at communicating to others (specifically, to the witness) precisely what he meant. For example, did Joe say "80" or "18"? This is the *articulateness* problem.

c. **Note:** Again, it is the concerns about these problems that underlie the general rule excluding hearsay evidence. [United States v. Brown, 548 F.2d 1194 (5th Cir. 1977); *and see* Park, A Subject Matter Approach to Hearsay Reform, 86 Mich. L. Rev. 51 (1987)—contains suggestion that rule against hearsay could safely be relaxed in civil cases]

3. **Applications of Hearsay Definitions:** [§229] The following are illustrative of the problems encountered in determining what is and what is not hearsay and the distinctions under the Federal Rules and Morgan definitions, above.

a. **Statements not offered to prove their truth:** [§230] The hearsay rule is *not* applicable, under *any* definition of hearsay, where evidence of the out-of-court words or actions is offered only to show that the statement *was made* or that it had a *certain effect* on a listener or observer, rather than to prove the *truth* of the facts asserted. *Examples:*

(1) **Words legally significant in and of themselves (legally operative facts):** [§231] Where the issue is simply what words were spoken—the words themselves being in issue—evidence as to what was said is admissible. In such a case the words are offered as *legally operative facts* in the litigation (rather than as proof of the *truth* of what was said) and therefore are *not* hearsay. [Ries Biologicals, Inc. v. Bank of Santa Fe, 780 F.2d 888 (10th Cir. 1986)]

(a) **Words of offer, acceptance, rejection, etc., in contract actions:** [§232] When a suit is brought on a contract, the fact that there was an offer, acceptance, etc., can, as a practical matter, be proved *only* by evidence of the out-of-court words or conduct involved. Those words or actions are *not* offered for the truth of any facts asserted but only to demonstrate *what was said or done*; they constitute operative facts as to which the substantive law of contract attaches certain duties and responsibilities. [*See, e.g.,* Creaghe v. Iowa Home Mutual Casualty Co., 323 F.2d 981 (10th Cir. 1963)]

(b) **Words of gift, sale, or bailment:** [§233] Where a party claims to hold property by virtue of a gift, sale, or bailment, that party can testify as to the words used in the transaction—*not* to prove their truth but merely to show *what was said* (from which the court will determine the nature of the transaction).

1) **Examples:** "I hereby give you this wristwatch for your birthday" (legally operative words of gift); "I'll lend you my wristwatch" (words of loan as distinguished from either gift or sale). [*See, e.g.,* Hanson v. Johnson, 201 N.W. 322 (Minn. 1924)]

(c) **Words alleged to be defamatory:** [§234] In actions for defamation (libel or slander), plaintiff offers the words used by the defendant (*e.g.,* "P is an embezzler") only to show *what was said, not* to prove that the words spoken by the defendant were true (quite the contrary, plaintiff claims those words were false). [*See* Strahorn, A Reconsideration of the Hearsay Rule and Admissions, 85 U. Pa. L. Rev. 484 (1937)]

   (d) **Words alleged to be deceitful:** [§235] Likewise, in a fraud action, plaintiff offers the out-of-court statement made to her solely to prove *what was said, not* that it was true.

(2) **Words offered to show effect on hearer or reader:** [§236] Evidence of a statement made to a person, or within his hearing, may be offered to show his state of mind in the sense that he had *notice, knowledge, motive, good faith, duress, probable cause,* etc., or that he had *acquired information* that had a bearing on his *subsequent conduct*. In such a case, the statement is not subject to attack as hearsay because the words are offered simply to show their *effect* on the hearer or reader or the circumstantially significant state of the hearer's *knowledge*, rather than to prove the truth of the matter asserted. [United States v. Rubin, *supra,* §36; *compare* State v. English, 159 S.E. 318 (N.C. 1931)—wrongly decided]

   (a) **Words of notice or warning:** [§237] Words offered to prove that notice or warning was given and received are not hearsay.

      1) **Example:** In landlord-tenant litigation, where Landlord is trying to prove that she gave Tenant oral notice to quit the premises, evidence of Landlord's out-of-court statements to Tenant is admissible to prove that Tenant received the requisite *notice*.

      2) **Example:** In an action against a grocery store for negligence, evidence that an employee yelled, "Please don't step in that ketchup!" to the plaintiff is admissible to show that the plaintiff had notice of the danger. [Safeway Stores, Inc. v. Combs, 273 F.2d 295 (5th Cir. 1960)]

      3) **Example:** Similarly, evidence of complaints to defendant that its parking lot pavement was slippery when wet is admissible on the issue of defendant's notice or knowledge of the danger. [Vinyard v. Vinyard Funeral Home, Inc., 435 S.W.2d 392 (Mo. 1968)]

   (b) **Inflammatory or accusatory words:** [§238] Words offered to prove *anger* or other *motive*, thus reflecting on the hearer's or reader's *later conduct* are not hearsay (*e.g.,* testimony that X had threatened to report D to federal authorities offered to show likelihood that D was motivated to assault X). [United States v. Cline, 570 F.2d 731 (8th Cir. 1978)]

   (c) **Words of good faith:** [§239] Words offered only to prove that the hearer's or reader's subsequent conduct was in good faith are not hearsay (*e.g.,* advice received by a taxpayer at a tax protester's meeting not hearsay in prosecution for filing false witholding forms). [United States v. Wellendorf, 574 F.2d 1289 (5th Cir. 1978)]

(3) **Words offered as circumstantial evidence of declarant's state of mind:** [§240] Statements that circumstantially or indirectly reveal the declarant's state of mind are *not* hearsay under the Federal Rules. However, they are under Morgan's declarant-centered definition of hearsay. This point is not one of great significance since, alternatively, statements as to declarant's state of mind are generally admissible under the "state of mind" exception to the hearsay rule. (*See infra,* §§423-432.)

(a) **Example:** The assertion by a woman, "My husband is a liar and a thief," while inadmissible to prove the truth of the matter asserted, is admissible to show the declarant's state of mind regarding her husband (that she disliked him).

(b) **Example:** Where the declarant's sanity is in issue, his statement, "I am the Prince of Denmark" is not hearsay when offered as circumstantial evidence of the declarant's insanity.

(c) **Example:** Statements made by an automobile driver before an accident that his brakes were defective would be admissible as circumstantial evidence of the declarant's knowledge of the defect.

(d) **Example:** Words revealing the declarant's possession of circumstantially significant knowledge of unique facts—*e.g.,* facts that could be known only to a person who had observed an object (gun) or place (interior of child-abuser's house)—are admissible. [United States v. Muscato, 534 F. Supp. 969 (E.D.N.Y. 1982)]

(e) **Example:** Where the issue is whether D was using a house to conduct unlawful bookmaking operations by telephone, evidence of incoming telephone calls from unidentified persons seeking to place bets has been held admissible to show the character of the activities in which D was involved by inference from the implied beliefs of the callers. [United States v. Zenni, 492 F. Supp. 464 (E.D. Ky. 1980); People v. Barnhart, 66 Cal. App. 2d 714 (1944); State v. Tolisano, 70 A.2d 118 (Conn. 1949)]

(4) **Prior statements by witness affecting credibility**

(a) **General rule:** [§241] Evidence of a witness's prior statements affecting her credibility (*i.e.,* prior inconsistent statements offered to impeach credibility, or prior consistent statements offered to rehabilitate) are not hearsay since they are not offered as substantive evidence in support of any fact issue (*i.e.,* they are not offered to establish the truth of their assertions). The fact that the witness made different statements at different times detracts from the witness's credibility, regardless of which statement is true.

1) **Compare:** If such statements *were* to be offered as substantive evidence, most courts *would* treat them as hearsay. However, the California Evidence Code provides that a witness's prior inconsistent statement may be used substantively for the truth of what it asserts. [Cal. Evid. Code §1235]

(b) **Federal Rule:** [§242]   Under the Federal Rules of Evidence, a restricted class of prior statements by a witness is received as *nonhearsay* (and thus as *substantive proof*): (i) prior inconsistent statements that were made by the witness while testifying **under oath** at some prior trial or hearing (including a grand jury investigation), or in a deposition; (ii) prior consistent statements, **not** under oath, offered to rebut an express or implied charge against the witness that her direct testimony is a recent fabrication; and (iii) prior identifications of a **person** (but not, apparently, of an object or thing). [Fed. R. Evid. 801(d)(1)(A), (B), (C); *and see infra,* §§258-260]

1) **Limited admissibility for impeachment purposes:** [§243] Even if a prior inconsistent statement does not fall within the requirements of Federal Rule 801(d)(1)(A), it still will be admissible under the Federal Rules when offered for impeachment purposes. When offered solely to impeach a witness, the statement is not offered for the truth of the matter asserted and hence is not hearsay within the meaning of the definition in Federal Rule 801(c).

a) **Example:** If an investigator took a statement from a witness who told the investigator that the accident victim was jaywalking, and the witness later testified that the victim was crossing in the crosswalk, the prior inconsistent statement would be admissible to impeach the witness. It, however, would not qualify under Federal Rule 801(d)(1)(A) to be admitted as substantive evidence because it was not made under oath at a prior trial or hearing, or in a deposition.

b) **Instruction to jury:** [§244]   If a statement is admissible only to impeach a witness, the judge will instruct the jury to consider the statement only for its bearing on credibility, and not for the truth of the matter asserted therein.

b. **Assertions as to declarant's state of mind:** [§245]   Under either definition of hearsay, a direct out-of-court assertion by the declarant as to her state of mind (*e.g.,* "I hate Fred" or "I intend to go to New York") is hearsay. The reason is that the trier of fact must determine the truth of the assertion in order to determine the declarant's state of mind; the assertion would have no probative value as to the declarant's state of mind had it been feigned or made as a joke.

(1) **May come in under hearsay exception:** [§246]   Even though hearsay, such statements are usually admissible under the hearsay *exception* for declarations of state of mind (*see infra,* §§423 *et seq.*).

c. **Conduct—assertive and nonassertive**

(1) **Assertive conduct:** [§247]   As previously indicated, under either definition of hearsay, evidence of out-of-court *conduct* that was *intended* as a substitute for words (*i.e.,* assertive conduct) is hearsay when offered to prove the truth of what was intended to be asserted. In other words, actions that are the *equivalent of words* are treated as hearsay if the *words* would be hearsay. [Fed. R. Evid. 801(a)]

(a) **Examples:** Declarant (actor) shakes her head from side to side in answer to a question as a substitute for saying the word "No"; victim points at a suspect in a police lineup as a substitute for saying the words, "That's the man who did it"; statement made by a deaf person in sign language. Such conduct, intended to be assertive and simply a *substitute* for words, is hearsay. [United States v. Ross, 321 F.2d 61 (2d Cir. 1963); *and see* United States *ex rel.* Carter Equipment Co. v. H. R. Morgan, Inc., 544 F.2d 1271 (5th Cir. 1977)—initialing invoices to identify job to which they pertained]

(2) **Nonassertive conduct:** [§248] The authorities take divergent views of the hearsay status of a person's out-of-court conduct where the conduct was *not* intended as a substitute for words but nonetheless is probative of state of mind. Although such conduct is termed "nonassertive," it *is*—by a process of translation or inference—assertive; it simply was not consciously *intended* to be assertive by the actor.

(a) **Examples**

1) **Conduct manifesting person's consciousness of guilt or fault** [§249]

a) X's flight from arrest may not be *intended* by her to reflect on her guilt of the crime for which she is being sought, but such nonassertive conduct may nonetheless be considered to reflect an awareness of guilt.

b) X's silence in response to accusatory statements of fault at the scene of an automobile accident may not be intended by her as an admission of negligence but may nonetheless be treated as such. (If X is a *party* to the resulting lawsuit, her silence may constitute an implied admission and be receivable—either as nonhearsay in federal practice, or under an exception to the hearsay rule in state jurisdictions; *see infra*, §320.) *See also* silence as hearsay, below.

2) **Conduct by third persons as evidencing their belief as to a party's condition** [§250]

a) The manner in which a person *is treated* by family, friends, or associates, although perhaps not intended by them as a direct expression of their opinion about the person's sanity, may be considered as nonassertive conduct reflecting their belief.

b) The fact that an institution did not segregate a prosecuting witness as was usually done with those having a venereal disease is nonassertive conduct manifesting the belief of the staff that she did not have a venereal disease. [*See* People v. Bush, 133 N.E. 201 (Ill. 1921)]

3) **Conduct manifesting third person's state of mind or condition:** [§251] Where the issue is whether the deceased killed

himself or was murdered by the defendant, evidence of prior suicide attempts by the deceased is nonassertive conduct evidencing the deceased's state of mind.

4) **Silence:** [§252]   Even the complete absence of words or actions may pose hearsay problems. For example, in P's suit for injuries suffered in a fall down D's stairway, the testimony of a tenant that no one had ever complained of defects in the stairs was nonassertive conduct offered by D to prove that the stairs were safe. [Menard v. Cashman, 55 A.2d 156 (N.H. 1947)]

(b) **Assertion-centered (Federal Rules) view:** [§253]   Nonassertive conduct is *not* treated as hearsay and hence *is admissible* not only to show the declarant's state of mind but also to prove the truth of the matter asserted. Two reasons are given: (i) there is no need to worry about the declarant's veracity because the conduct, not having been consciously assertive, did not involve *veracity*; and (ii) there is an assurance of trustworthiness—*i.e.,* the notion that a person's actions speak louder than words. [*See* Fed. R. Evid. 801(a), note]

(c) **Declarant-centered (Morgan) view:** [§254]   Nonassertive conduct *is* hearsay where it is offered as proof of some fact; it is an implied assertion of the actor's *beliefs* regarding such fact and hence is just as objectionable as an express assertion. [*See* Finman, Implied Assertions as Hearsay; Some Criticism of the Uniform Rules of Evidence, 14 Stan. L. Rev. 682 (1962)]

1) **Example:** In the landmark case excluding nonassertive conduct as hearsay, the issue was whether a testator, Marsden, was mentally competent when he made his will. The devisee sought to introduce three letters addressed to Marsden that had requested him to do things that only a mentally competent person could accomplish. Although the letters did not directly and deliberately assert the matter in issue (*i.e.,* Marsden's mental condition), they were nonassertive conduct on the part of the writers *treating* him as competent and thereby evidencing their *belief* in his sanity. However, the court refused to admit the letters on the ground that as nonassertive conduct they constituted hearsay (despite the fact that such hearsay may have been highly reliable and probative on the point). [Wright v. Doe d. Tatham, 7 Ad. & El. 313 (1837)]

2) **Example:** Similarly, in the case where D offered testimony of the lack of complaints of others to prove that a dangerous condition did not exist, the trial judge excluded the testimony as hearsay. The absence of out-of-court statements was held to involve the same risks or dangers that affect out-of-court statements: perception, memory, etc. [Menard v. Cashman, *supra*]

a) **Note:** Possible relevance problems are posed by the situation in *Menard*. Perhaps others simply did not have a chance to see or encounter the defect alleged by P, or perhaps they were injured but did not bother to complain. [*See* Rathbun v. Humphrey, 113 N.E.2d 877 (Ohio 1953)]

3) **Admissibility within hearsay exception:** [§255]   Again, even where this sort of evidence is hearsay, it is often admissible under the state of mind exception to the hearsay rule, *see infra,* §423.

d. **Nonhuman evidence:** [§256]   Testimony by a witness as to "statements" made by nonhuman declarants (*e.g.,* machines, bloodhounds, etc.) does *not* violate the rule against hearsay.

(1) **Examples:** Witness on the stand testifies that the radar equipment "said" that D was driving at 90 m.p.h.; that the parking meter "said" that D's allotted time had expired; that the computer printout "said" that D's bank balance was $30.

(2) **Rationale—veracity problem absent:** The law permits so-called nonhuman evidence on the ground that machines and animals, unlike humans, lack a conscious motivation to tell falsehoods, and because the workings of machines (including their accuracy and reliability) can be explained by human witnesses who are then subject to cross-examination by opposing counsel. [City of Webster Groves v. Quick, 323 S.W.2d 386 (Mo. 1959); Buck v. State, 138 P.2d 115 (Okla. 1943)]

C. STATEMENTS EXEMPTED FROM HEARSAY RULE BY THE FEDERAL RULES OF EVIDENCE

1. **Types of Evidence Exempted:** [§257]   Federal Rule 801(d) *exempts* from the rule against hearsay several categories of statements which are not to be considered hearsay at all, even if offered to prove the truth of their assertions:

a. **Prior inconsistent statement of a witness:** [§258]   If the prior inconsistent statement was made *under oath* and *in a proceeding*, it is not hearsay. (Thus, in federal practice, such statements are no longer usable solely for impeachment purposes.) A "proceeding" includes a prior trial, a preliminary hearing, a deposition, and grand jury testimony. [Fed. R. Evid. 801(d)(1)(A); United States v. Coran, 589 F.2d 70 (1st Cir. 1978)]

b. **Prior consistent statement of a witness:** [§259]   Whether under oath or not, a prior consistent statement, when offered to rebut an express or implied charge of recent fabrication or improper influence or motive on the part of the witness, is not hearsay. [Fed. R. Evid. 801(d)(1)(B); Baker v. Elcona Homes Corp., 588 F.2d 551 (6th Cir. 1978)]

c. **Witness's prior statement identifying a person:** [§260]   A prior identification is not hearsay. [Fed. R. Evid. 801(d)(1)(C)] The Supreme Court has held that neither the Confrontation Clause nor Federal Rule 802 is violated by the admission of a prior out-of-court identification statement of a witness who, although subject to cross-examination, is unable because of memory loss to explain the basis for the identification. [United States v. Owens, 484 U.S. 554 (1988)]

d. **Admissions by a party-opponent:** [§261]   Admissions were previously treated under an *exception* to the rule against hearsay (*see infra,* §§295-298). Under the Federal Rules, an admission is not hearsay. [Fed. R. Evid. 801(d)(2); United States v. Moskowitz, 581 F.2d 14 (2d Cir. 1978)]

2. **Use as Substantive Evidence:** [§262]   Since the above four categories are exempted from the operation of the hearsay rule, evidence falling into one of them is usable—*if relevant*—as *substantive* evidence without having to refer to any possible exception to the rule. [Waltz, *The Federal Rules of Evidence: An Analysis,* 124-128 (1975)]

D. ADMISSIBLE HEARSAY—THE SO-CALLED EXCEPTIONS TO THE HEARSAY RULE

1. **Introduction:** [§263]   As noted above, there are many situations in which evidence, although hearsay, is held admissible. In these situations, the public policies rejecting hearsay evidence are simply outweighed by other policies favoring its admission.

a. **Rationale—necessity and trustworthiness:** There is no single theory or rationale that will explain all of the exceptions below or harmonize one with another. However, Wigmore, by classifying former testimony and admissions as nonhearsay, found in every recognized exception the following elements: (i) some *necessity* for using the hearsay evidence (usually the death or unavailability of the declarant); and (ii) something in its content or in the circumstances of its utterance that serves to guarantee its *trustworthiness*.

(1) **Compare:** Similarly, Morgan observed: "The test of admissibility should be whether the hearsay is such that the trier can put a *reasonably accurate value* upon it *as evidence* of the matter it is offered to prove, and whether direct testimony of the declarant is unavailable or if available, is likely to be less reliable."

b. **Scope of exceptions:** [§264]   The number of exceptions to the hearsay rule is by no means fixed or rigid. New exceptions continue to be created by statute or case law, reflecting the ever-increasing awareness that hearsay evidence can be valuable, and, in certain situations, may even be the best evidence available.

(1) **Note:** The Federal Rules of Evidence list over 25 separate "exceptions" to the hearsay rule—plus a separate residual or "catch-all" exception for matters not covered in the specific exceptions (*see infra,* §540). [Fed. R. Evid. 803, 804(b), 807]

c. **Limitation against hearsay on hearsay:** [§265]   Extrajudicial words or conduct that merely *repeats or incorporates other* hearsay is called "hearsay on hearsay" or "totem pole" hearsay. Such hearsay is admissible only where *each part* of the statement falls within one of the exceptions to the hearsay rule. [Fed. R. Evid. 805] If one part of the statement is inadmissible, the entire statement must be excluded.

(1) **Example:** A business record containing the entry "Telephone call received from X saying his wife was leaving for Brazil" is *not* admissible as proof that X's wife left for Brazil. Even if the record itself is otherwise

admissible under the "business records exception" (*see infra*, §443), it is excluded here because the entrant had no personal knowledge of the facts, but was merely relying on the inadmissible, out-of-court declaration of another party, X.

d. **Right to challenge credibility of hearsay declarant:** [§266]   Where hearsay evidence is held admissible under one of the exceptions, courts generally allow the adverse party to challenge the credibility of the hearsay declarant. This is true whether or not the hearsay declarant is present in court. [Carver v. United States, 164 U.S. 694 (1897)]

(1) **Types of evidence admissible:** [§267]   Thus, the party against whom hearsay is admitted is allowed to prove that the hearsay declarant has a reputation for untruthfulness, has made ***prior or subsequent*** inconsistent statements, etc. [Fed. R. Evid. 806—allowing same for vicarious admissions]

(a) **Note:** Where credibility is attacked by proof of a prior inconsistent statement, most courts do not require that a foundation be laid (*i.e.,* that the declarant be given an opportunity to explain or deny the statement; *see infra,* §§1066-1080). [Fed. R. Evid. 806]

(b) **And note:** The inconsistent statements are ***not*** hearsay because they are not offered for the truth thereof, but only to impeach credibility by demonstrating inconsistency. [Lewis v. Insurance Co. of North America, 416 F.2d 1077 (5th Cir. 1969)]

(2) **Cross-examination of witness-declarant:** [§268]   Where the hearsay declarant is ***in court***, most courts permit the party against whom the hearsay evidence has been admitted to call and examine the declarant regarding the hearsay statement ***as if under cross-examination***; *i.e.,* the party can use leading and suggestive questions in examining. [Fed. R. Evid. 806]

2. **Former Testimony:** [§269]   "Former testimony" refers to transcripts of testimony given by a witness at some former deposition, hearing, or trial, in the same or another case.

a. **Hearsay status**

(1) **Minority view:** [§270]   The minority view (supported by Wigmore, section 1370) holds that a report of testimony given under oath in a prior trial is ***not*** hearsay, and hence is admissible, at least where the declarant is no longer available to testify. The rationale is that the former testimony was subject to cross-examination in the previous trial, and so the chief purpose of the hearsay rule is satisfied.

(2) **Majority view:** [§271]   Most courts today are ***contra***, holding reports of prior testimony to be hearsay, but recognizing that they are admissible under an ***exception*** to the hearsay rule. [Fed. R. Evid. 804(b)(1); State v. Dick, 271 N.E.2d 797 (Ohio 1971)]

b. **Requirements for admissibility—in general:** [§272]   Under the majority view, a report of a witness's testimony in a prior trial is admissible in the present proceedings, as an exception to the hearsay rule, if there is:

(i)   Sufficient *identity of parties*;

(ii) Sufficient *identity of issues*; and

(iii) Sufficient *unavailability* of that witness in the present proceedings.

Each of these requirements is developed below.

(1) **Form of proof:** [§273]   The usual method of proving the testimony in the prior trial is by a certified transcript of those proceedings, unless there has been a stipulation. However, where a transcript is not available, proof may be established by the testimony of the presiding judge or any other reliable person in attendance at the prior proceedings, either from his personal recollection or from notes he may have taken. [State v. Ortego, 157 P.2d 320 (Wash. 1945)]

(2) **What type of proceeding must the prior trial be?** [§274]   The proceeding can be judicial, legislative, administrative, etc. The only requirements are that the proceeding must have (i) involved testimony given *under oath*, and (ii) afforded the *opportunity for cross-examination*.

(a) **Note:** Because the cross-examination element is absent, coroner's inquests, grand jury hearings, etc., do *not* qualify; hence, certified transcripts of testimony in such proceedings are generally not admissible. [People v. Lint, 182 Cal. App. 2d 402 (1960)]

c. **Requirement of identity of parties**

(1) **Traditional view:** [§275]   The traditional view is quite narrow and requires *complete identity* between the parties; *i.e.,* both of the present parties (the proponent of the evidence and the adversary) must have been parties to the former action for the testimony to be admissible. [Bulk Transportation, Inc. v. Louisiana Public Service Commission, 209 So. 2d 4 (La. 1968)]

(a) **Effect of additional parties:** [§276]   However, as long as both present parties were parties to the former action, most courts treat the fact that there were *additional* parties in the former proceeding (or in the present trial) as immaterial. The testimony can still be received.

1) **Effect of change in counsel:** [§277]   Similarly, the fact that there has been a change in counsel between the first and second litigations has no effect on the application of this exception. [United States v. Amaya, 533 F.2d 188 (5th Cir. 1976)]

(b) **Privity:** [§278]   A number of courts have relaxed the "100% identity" requirement where a present party is a "privy in interest" to a former party (*e.g.,* successor in interest). [United States v. 205.03 Acres of Land, 251 F. Supp. 866 (W.D. Pa. 1966)]

1) **Rationale:** In such a case, the testimony is admissible because the former party had the same motive and interest to cross-examine that the present party has. [United States v. Wingate,

520 F.2d 309 (2d Cir. 1975), *cert. denied,* 423 U.S. 1074 (1976)]

(2) **Modern trend:** [§279]   The modern trend of authority in the states (but not in federal practice) is to reject the "identity of parties" requirement in favor of Wigmore's looser test of *identity of interest and motive.* Under this test, a report of testimony given in a prior trial is admissible wherever the adverse party in the former trial had an *opportunity* and similar *motive* to cross-examine as does the adverse party in the present proceeding. [Cal. Evid. Code §1291(a)(2)]

   (a) **Example—similar motive:** Testimony given in a former trial against a guarantor of note has been held admissible in a subsequent action against the principal maker of the note. [Cox v. Selover, 213 N.W. 902 (Minn. 1927)]

   (b) **Example—similar motive:** Testimony of defendant in a previous suit by Husband for loss of Wife's services was admitted against Wife in a separate action for her own injury resulting from the same accident. [Bartlett v. Kansas City Public Service Co., 100 S.W.2d 740 (Mo. 1942)]

(3) **Federal Rules approach:** [§280]   Under the Federal Rules, a witness's recorded testimony from some earlier trial, deposition, or proceeding is admissible only if the party against whom it is now being offered (i) was a *party* to the earlier trial or proceeding (or a predecessor in interest if a civil action); (ii) had *an opportunity to examine* the witness at that time; *and* (iii) had a similar *motive* to develop the witness's testimony (by direct or cross-examination) as that which he now has. [Fed. R. Evid. 804(b)(1)]

   (a) **Rationale:** The rationale for this more restricted approach is that it may be unfair to impose upon the party against whom such hearsay is offered the responsibility for the matter on which the witness was examined by some *other party* in some earlier proceeding.

   (b) **"Predecessor in interest":** [§281]   In civil actions, some courts evade the "same party or predecessor in interest" requirement by treating parties who had a similar interest as the present party as "predecessors in interest." [*See, e.g.,* Lloyd v. American Export Lines, Inc., 580 F.2d 1179 (3d Cir. 1978)] But a more traditional court is likely to restrict the concept of "predecessor" to someone from whom the present party *received the interest, title, or obligation* that is the subject of the present litigation. For example, a prior owner of real property is the "predecessor" of the person to whom the property was sold. Other examples of predecessor-successor relationships include testator and heir, principal and surety, and donor and donee.

   (c) **"Similar motive":** [§282]   The fact that the same parties were involved and had an opportunity to conduct cross-examination or its equivalent at the time of the prior testimony does not necessarily satisfy the "similar motive" requirement. For example, the defense in a criminal case may not take advantage of the former testimony exception to introduce the former testimony of a witness who exculpated the defendant during grand jury testimony. A prosecutor questioning a witness before the grand jury is motivated by different goals than a prosecutor at trial. At the grand jury stage a prosecutor might try to discover information from the witness without tipping the government's hand, while at trial a prosecutor might go all out to impeach the witness. [*See* United States v. Salerno, 505 U.S. 317 (1992)]

d. **Requirement of identity of issues:** [§283]   The issues in both trials do not have to be identical but they must at least be *substantially the same*; they must relate to the same general subject matter so as to assure the same scope of cross-examination. [United States v. Wingate, *supra*, §278]

   (1) **Comment:** Modern statutes do not state this as a separate requirement since it is inherent in the requirement that the witness was subject to cross-examination in the prior proceeding by a party whose *motive and interest* were the same as in the present proceeding. [Fed. R. Evid. 804(b)(1)]

e. **Requirement of unavailability of witness who testified at first trial:** [§284] For the former testimony to be admissible, it must be shown that the witness who gave the testimony in the earlier trial or proceeding is "unavailable" to testify as a witness in the present trial. In civil cases, and probably in criminal cases, the following grounds of "unavailability" are generally accepted [Fed. R. Evid. 804(a)]:

   (1) **Death of witness:** [§285]   Death is the ultimate unavailability.

   (2) **Physical incapacity:** [§286]   Competent proof that the witness who testified in the earlier trial is now too ill or infirm to testify establishes "unavailability." (Some courts require a showing that the physical incapacity is *permanent*, on the theory that otherwise the trial can simply be postponed.)

   (3) **Mental incapacity:** [§287]   Supervening *mental* illness or infirmity is treated the same as physical illness.

   (4) **Absence:** [§288]   A showing that the witness who testified in the earlier trial is absent and that the proponent of the witness's statement has been unable to procure the witness's testimony also establishes "unavailability."

      (a) **Example:** This covers the situation where the witness has left the jurisdiction and is therefore beyond the subpoena power of the court. It also covers the situation where the witness's present whereabouts are simply *unknown* despite reasonably diligent efforts to locate him. [*See* United States v. Hayes, 535 F.2d 479 (8th Cir. 1976); United States v. Guillette, 547 F.2d 743 (2d Cir. 1976)]

      (b) **Note:** Where the witness's whereabouts are *known*, some states require a further showing that the witness's *deposition* was sought but could not be obtained. [Burton v. Oldfield, 79 S.E.2d 660 (Va. 1954)]

1) **Federal Rules:** The Federal Rules do *not* require this, the theory being that a deposition is not necessarily more reliable than the testimony already recorded under oath in the earlier proceeding. [Fed. R. Evid. 804(a)(5)] *But note*: The Federal Rules *do* require such a showing where a witness's prior statements are sought to be admitted under the dying declaration, declaration against interest, or family history exception (*see infra*, §§375, 401, 507).

(5) **Inability or refusal to testify:** [§289]   Unavailability warranting the use of prior testimony may also be established by a showing that the *testimony* of the witness is unavailable, even though the witness herself is physically present at the trial. [United States v. Appollo, 490 F.2d 361 (5th Cir. 1974)] *Examples:*

(a) **Testimony privileged:** [§290]   The witness now asserts some legal privilege concerning the subject matter of her prior testimony, and the court upholds the witness's claim of privilege.

(b) **Refusal to testify:** [§291]   The witness persists in refusing to testify concerning the subject matter of her earlier testimony despite the court's order to testify. (Of course, the witness may be held in contempt of court.)

(c) **Lack of memory:** [§292]   The witness claims a lack of memory concerning the subject matter of her earlier testimony. [United States v. Collins, 478 F.2d 837 (5th Cir. 1973)]

(6) **Limitation—unavailability contrived:** [§293]   In no event will a witness be deemed unavailable if the witness's absence is due to *connivance with the proponent*. A party cannot arrange a declarant's disappearance in order to use the declarant's prior recorded testimony. [Fed. R. Evid. 804(a)]

3. **Admissions**

a. **In general**

(1) **Definitions:** [§294]   An admission is any extrajudicial statement or conduct by a *party* to the present litigation (not a nonparty witness) that is inconsistent with a position the party presently takes. It does not have to be an admission "against interest"; it may even be partially self-serving. The only requirement is that it turns out to be *contrary* to the party's *present position*. [People v. Gould, 54 Cal. 2d 621 (1960)]

(2) **Hearsay status:** [§295]   Is this really an *exception* to the hearsay rule? Or are admissions not hearsay at all?

(a) **Traditional classification—admissions are an exception to the hearsay rule:** [§296]   The traditional view is that admissions are an exception to the hearsay rule. The rule allowing admissions into evidence can be justified on the grounds that admissions are normally reliable and that the opponent usually has the opportunity to take the stand and explain the admission if it is inaccurate. Although the Federal Rules classify admissions as nonhearsay (*see* below), California and a number of other states continue to treat admissions as an "exception" instead of an "exemption" to the hearsay rule. [*See, e.g.,* Cal. Evid. Code §1220] Lawyers in all jurisdictions still use the word "exception" when referring to the admissions rule.

(b) **Federal Rules classification—admissions are not hearsay:** [§297] The Federal Rules exempt admissions of a party-opponent from the hearsay rule, deeming them *not to be hearsay* even if they are offered for the truth of the matter asserted. The Advisory Committee to the Federal Rules thought that this classification was appropriate because "no guarantee of trustworthiness is required in the case of an admission," and an admission's "admissibility in evidence is the result of the adversary system rather than satisfaction of the conditions of the hearsay rule." [Fed. R. Evid. 801(d)(2), note] Apparently the Advisory Committee reasoned that statements must be trustworthy to qualify for treatment under an exception to the hearsay rule, but admissions are not required to be trustworthy; therefore, admissions do not fall under an exception to the hearsay rule. However, we want to provide that admissions of a party-opponent are admissible, and so they are classified as *nonhearsay*.

1) **"Adversary system" rationale:** [§298] The Advisory Committee's brief reference to the "adversary system" rationale of the admissions rule is apparently a reference to the idea, advanced by evidence scholars such as Chaffee, Morgan, and McCormick, that admissions are admissible because it is not considered appropriate for the opponent to question her own trustworthiness— "whatever you say can be used against you." The purpose of the adversary system is not only to find truth, but also to satisfy the parties and the public. The idea that it is not fair to conceal the fact that a party previously said something that is inconsistent with that party's position in the present litigation is deeply rooted in evidence law.

(3) **No requirement of personal knowledge:** [§299] A party's admission will be competent evidence against that party even though she did not actually have personal knowledge of the facts admitted. [Mahlandt v. Wild Canid Survival & Research Center, Inc., 588 F.2d 626 (8th Cir. 1978)]

(4) **Opinion:** [§300] By the same token, an admission may, according to most courts, be based on the admitter's personal *opinion* or *conclusion* (*e.g.,* "It was all my fault").

(5) **Effect of duress, force**

(a) **Former view:** [§301] Many of the older decisions held that the fact that an admission had been obtained through duress, threats, etc., merely affected the weight of the evidence but that the admission could still be shown.

(b) **Modern trend:** [§302]   However, the strong trend of modern authority is contra: Admissions as well as confessions (*infra*) cannot be used in evidence if involuntarily given. Hence, admissions extracted through any form of duress, or even through trick, may be held inadmissible. [Cal. Evid. Code §1204]

1) **Note:** This is a *constitutional* requirement in *criminal* cases (*see infra*, §§358-373).

b. **Judicial admissions:** [§303]   Courts are frequently called upon to determine the effect of admissions made in the course of litigation, either by a party or by an attorney acting on the party's behalf.

(1) **Admissions in pleadings:** [§304]   A party may be bound by statements in pleadings prepared and filed by the party's attorney, whether or not she had personal knowledge of them. The effect given to such admissions depends upon the type of pleading.

(a) **Current pleadings in present case:** [§305]   Admissions contained in such pleadings, if not withdrawn by amendment, are *conclusive* as to the pleader; they cannot be controverted.

1) **Rationale:** If the pleadings had no binding effect, they would serve no purpose in defining and narrowing the controversy.

2) **Amendments:** [§306]   A party who wishes to controvert allegations in her own pleadings must, therefore, seek leave to *amend* the pleadings. Amendment is freely granted under the Federal Rules of Civil Procedure unless the opponent has been prejudiced by reliance on the original version. [Fed. R. Civ. P. 15(b)]

(b) **Superseded or amended pleadings in present case:** [§307]   Admissions contained in superseded pleadings are generally treated only as evidence; they are competent proof against the admitter, but are *not* binding (*i.e.,* they can be explained by showing mistake, lack of authority of attorney, etc.).

1) **Minority view:** [§308]   Some courts do not permit admissions in superseded pleadings as affirmative evidence; they can be used *solely* for *impeachment* purposes as "prior inconsistent statements."

(c) **Pleadings in prior civil case:** [§309]   Admissions contained in a pleading in some prior civil case are admissible as evidence but are not conclusive and hence may be explained. [Annot., 90 A.L.R. 1397]

(d) **Pleadings in prior criminal case**

1) **Nolo contendere or "no contest":** [§310]   Where permitted, this plea does not concede guilt; hence it *cannot* be used as an admission. [Fed. R. Evid. 410(2)]

2) **Guilty plea:** [§311]   Where the defendant enters a plea of guilty in a criminal case, this plea may be introduced against the defendant as an admission in a subsequent civil or criminal proceeding involving the same act. But it is *not* conclusive; the defendant may explain the circumstances surrounding the plea, and such explanation goes to the weight of the evidence. [Teitelbaum Furs, Inc. v. Dominion Insurance Co., 58 Cal. 2d 601 (1962)]

   a) **Guilty plea withdrawn before trial:** [§312]   However, most jurisdictions provide that a *withdrawn* guilty plea is *not admissible* against the accused in his subsequent criminal prosecution. [Fed. R. Evid. 410(1); People v. Wells, 256 Cal. App. 2d 463 (1967)]

      1/ **Modern view:** The modern view extends this rule and provides for the exclusion of a withdrawn guilty plea in *any* later civil or criminal proceeding. [Fed. R. Evid. 410; Cal. Evid. Code §1153]

      2/ **Rationale:** The fact that the trial judge allowed the plea to be withdrawn indicates that it is not a reliable admission. Whatever evidentiary value it would have is offset by its probable prejudicial effect.

   b) **Offer to plead guilty:** [§313]   An unaccepted offer to plead guilty is excluded under the same rationale applicable to offers to compromise in civil cases (*see supra,* §201). [Fed. R. Evid. 410]

   c) **Damaging statements made in connection with plea:** [§314]   Damaging statements made by the accused in connection with a withdrawn plea (or a plea or offer to plead nolo contendere, above) are generally inadmissible in any subsequent proceeding against the accused. [Fed. R. Evid. 410; Fed. R. Crim. P. 11(e)(6)] On statements made during plea bargaining, *see supra,* §219.

      1/ **Limited exception for perjury proceeding:** [§315] However, in federal courts such statements are admissible against the accused in a separate proceeding for *perjury* or false statement, if they were made under oath, on the record, and in the presence of counsel.

3) **Judgment of conviction:** [§316]   As to the admissibility of a *judgment* of conviction, *see infra,* §§483-488.

(2) **Stipulations by counsel:** [§317]   In courtroom appearances, an attorney is the agent of the client. Hence, a stipulation (agreement) entered into by counsel *in open court* is conclusive as to the client and cannot

later be controverted. If entered into by mistake, the relief sought must be a setting aside of the stipulation. [Berry v. Chaplin, 74 Cal. App. 2d 652 (1946)]

    (a) **Compare:** Stipulations made by counsel *outside* court are binding on clients only as to matters within the scope of the counsel's authority (*e.g.,* matters of procedure). An attorney outside the court does not have any inherent authority to stipulate away essential rights of the client without the client's consent.

c. **Admissions by conduct—implied admissions:** [§318]   In certain instances a party's conduct furnishes the basis for inferring an admission, even if the party clearly did not intend it as such.

    (1) **Hearsay status:** [§319]   The cases usually involve *nonassertive conduct* (*see supra,* §§248-255). In those jurisdictions that treat nonassertive conduct as hearsay, this "admission exception" to the hearsay rule is of vital importance. But in jurisdictions where nonassertive conduct is not hearsay at all (*e.g.,* Federal Rules), such evidence is admissible without the need for any exception.

    (2) **Admission by silence**

        (a) **Rule:** [§320]   If a party fails to respond or makes an evasive reply to accusatory statements made to the party or in his hearing, and a reasonable person in such position would have unequivocally denied such accusations, the party's silence or evasion may be considered an implied admission. Or as stated in the Federal Rules, the silent party is held to have "manifested an adoption or belief" in the truth of the statement made by the other person. [Fed. R. Evid. 801(d)(2)(B)]

        (b) **Requirements:** [§321]   Before silence can be held as an implied admission of the charges made against a party, the following elements must be present:

            1) **Statement heard and understood:** [§322]   The party must have been present and *capable of hearing and understanding the accusations*.

            2) **Capable of denying:** [§323]   The party must have been physically and mentally *able to deny*.

            3) **Motive to deny:** [§324]   The party must have had the *opportunity and motive* to deny; *i.e.,* a reasonable person would have denied the accusatory statement under the particular circumstances. This is the difficult element to establish.

                a) **Example:** D's silence in the face of a belligerent accusation by Y at the scene of the accident that "It was all your fault!" may or may not constitute an admission by silence; *e.g.,* if D can show that her silence was motivated by a reasonable fear of violence, it will not constitute an implied admission of guilt.

b) **Failure to reply to written communication:** [§325]   A person's failure to reply to a letter or other written communication could conceivably constitute an implied admission, at least where it would be *reasonable to expect* a denial if the written statements were untrue. [*See* Annot., 55 A.L.R. 406]

1/   **But note:** Correspondence is not answered for many reasons, and no admission by silence will be found if there is some other reason for the failure to respond, or if the circumstances are such that the recipient would normally not bother to reply. "Otherwise, the whole world would be at the mercy of letter writers." [Wigmore, §1073]

(c) **Criminal cases:** [§326]   Suppose the accused in a criminal case remained silent (or was evasive) in the face of charges hurled at him by investigators or police officers ("You killed X!") or implicating statements made by accomplices. Can the accused's silence be used as an implied admission of guilt?

1) **Former rule:** [§327]   Some of the older decisions held that the accused's silence under such circumstances constituted an *implied admission* of the charge except where it was otherwise reasonably explainable under the circumstances—*e.g.,* as an attempt to follow advice given by counsel, to exercise the privilege against self-incrimination, etc. [Annot., 77 A.L.R. 2d 463]

2) **Modern constitutional limitations:** [§328]   However, the modern rule is that the failure of a person in custody to respond to police accusations cannot be used against the accused as an implied admission of the accusations. This follows from the Supreme Court decisions requiring the police affirmatively to warn an accused of the constitutional *privilege against self-incrimination*, which includes the right to remain silent, to confer with counsel, etc. (*See* Criminal Procedure Summary.)

3) **Charges made by persons other than police:** [§329]   It is not yet clear, however, whether the same result would follow where the accusation was made by someone other than a police officer, *e.g.,* when a witness or accomplice points at the defendant and says, "That's the man who killed X!"

a) **Note:** If the accusation was made *in front* of a police officer, and certainly if it was made while the defendant was in custody, it would seem that defendant's silence should be treated substantially the same as if the charge were made by the police.

(3) **Admissions by conduct other than silence:** [§330]   Various kinds of conduct other than silence may be held to manifest an awareness of liability or guilt.

(a) **Examples:** Attempts to conceal or destroy damaging evidence, attempts to bribe the arresting officer or witnesses, attempts to improperly influence jurors, flight from the scene of the crime, assumption of a false name, attempts to resist arrest, escape from custody, and perhaps even attempts to commit suicide—all may be held to reflect the actor's awareness of guilt or liability.

(b) **Public policy limitations:** [§331]   However, certain types of conduct, which might otherwise be regarded as admissions, are excluded because of public policy factors. *Examples:*

1) *Offers of compromise* in civil cases (*see supra,* §§201-205);

2) *Offers to plead guilty* in criminal cases (*see supra,* §313);

3) *Evidence of subsequent remedial measures* (*see supra,* §§198-200).

d. **Adoptive admissions:** [§332]   A party may by words or other conduct voluntarily *adopt* or *ratify* the statement of another, and if such statement is inconsistent with the position the party takes at trial, this "adoptive admission" is receivable against him. [Fed. R. Evid. 801(d)(2)(B); *and see* State v. Carlson, 808 P.2d 1002 (Or. 1991)—issue of adoption is preliminary question of fact for trial judge]

(1) **Requirement of voluntariness:** [§333]   The adoption must be *voluntary*. Thus, where a party annexes the reports of others (*e.g.,* doctor's report, police report) to an insurance claim, as *required* by the *insurance company*, this *cannot* be construed as an admission; there is not a sufficient voluntary "adoption" of the information in furnishing *required* papers. [58 A.L.R.2d 449]

(2) **Requirement of knowledge:** [§334]   Usually, the party must be shown to have *knowledge* of what the other person said. [*See* White Industries v. Cessna Aircraft Co., 611 F. Supp. 1049 (W.D. Mo. 1985)] But this is not always essential; *e.g.,* "X is a reliable person and knows what she is talking about" might be considered an adoptive admission of X's statements.

e. **Vicarious admissions:** [§335]   Under certain circumstances, admissions made by third persons may be *imputed* to a party and be admissible as affirmative evidence against that party.

(1) **Admissions by agents and employees:** [§336]   As already discussed, admissions made by an attorney in the course of litigation may be binding on the attorney's client as "judicial admissions." Statements made by other kinds of agents and employees may also be held binding on their employers, where the following elements are established [*see, e.g.,* Hitchman Coal & Coke Co. v. Mitchell, 245 U.S. 229 (1917)]:

(a) **Independent proof of agency and authority:** [§337]   The traditional rule, which is still followed in some states, is that the existence of the agency and the agent's authority must be independently proved, *i.e.,* by evidence *other than* the hearsay statement of the supposed agent. [Annot., 3 A.L.R.2d 598; Ellis v. Kneifl, 834 F.2d 128 (8th Cir. 1987)] *But note:* Federal Rule 801(d)(2) provides that the contents of the hearsay statement *"shall be considered but are not alone sufficient"* to establish the existence of the agency or the agent's authority.

(b) **Current matters:** [§338]   The facts admitted must relate to current matters, rather than past history.

(c) **Statements within scope of agency:** [§339]   The statements must be made within the scope of the agent's authority or employment.

 1) **Authorized statements:** [§340]   Clearly, any statement made by an agent who has authority (express or implied) to speak on behalf of the principal, regarding the subject of the statement, is admissible against the principal. [Fed. R. Evid. 801(d)(2)(C)]

 a) **Note:** The authority of certain kinds of employees to speak for their employers may be presumed. Thus, a store manager may be presumed to have authority from the owner of the store to make representations to customers regarding the store's merchandising policy. [Steinhorst v. H.C. Prange Co., 180 N.W.2d 525 (Wis. 1970)]

 b) **And note:** Experts employed by a party have been held to be agents with authority to make statements for purposes of Federal Rule 801(d)(2)(C). [*See* Collins v. Wayne Corp., 621 F.2d 777 (5th Cir. 1980)—deposition testimony of expert admissible against party hiring him]

 c) **Compare—government agents:** Courts are split as to whether statements by government agents are admissible against the government. [*Compare* United States v. Kampiles, 609 F.2d 1233 (7th Cir. 1979)—CIA employee's statements *not* statements of government as government agents disinterested in outcome of trial—*with* United States v. Morgan, 581 F.2d 933 (D.C. Cir. 1978)—statements in sworn government affidavit admissible as admissions against government]

 2) **Unauthorized statements:** [§341]   The more common situation, however, involves the admissibility of some statement made by the employee or agent during the course of the job, but *not* authorized by the employer (*e.g.,* statement by employee-driver involved in traffic accident, "I ran the red light," sought to be admitted in action against employer). [Rudzinski v. Warner Theatres, Inc., 114 N.W.2d 466 (Wis. 1962)]

 a) **Traditional view:** [§342]   The traditional view is that such statements are *not* admissible against the employer.

 b) **Modern trend (Federal Rules):** [§343]   However, recognizing the evidentiary value of such statements, the modern trend is to admit against the employer statements by an agent "concerning a matter within the scope of his agency or employment, made during the existence of the relationship." [Fed. R. Evid. 801(d)(2)(D)]

1/ **Compare—California:** California Evidence Code section 1224 on its face appears to follow the current trend. It provides that whenever the liability of a party (*e.g.*, employer) is "based in whole or in part upon the liability, obligation or duty of the declarant (*e.g.*, employee) . . . evidence of a statement made by the declarant is as admissible against the party as it would be if offered in an action against the declarant." However, the California Supreme Court has held that the statute is *not* applicable to the usual respondeat superior case. [Markley v. Beagle, 66 Cal. 2d 951 (1967)]

(2) **Admissions by co-conspirators**

(a) **Requirements for admission:** [§344] Damaging statements made by one co-conspirator may be admissible against the others, provided that the following elements are present:

1) **Conspiracy established:** [§345] The conspiracy in which the defendant was involved must be established. Evidence upon which a determination of existence of a conspiracy may be based includes the following:

a) **Traditional rule:** [§346] The traditional and majority view has been that the conspiracy must be established prima facie by *independent* evidence (other than the co-conspirator's statement(s) in question).

b) **Federal Rule:** [§347] Given Federal Rule 104(a)'s provision that a court, in determining preliminary questions of admissibility, "is not bound by the rules of evidence" (except those relating to privileges), a trial court, in determining preliminarily whether a conspiracy existed, is free to examine—among other things—the co-conspirator statements in question. [Bourjaily v. United States, *supra,* §74] The Supreme Court codified the *Bourjaily* rule in Federal Rule 801(d)(2), which provides that the co-conspirator's statements must be considered but are not alone sufficient to establish the existence of a conspiracy.

2) **Statement made during conspiracy:** [§348] The statement itself must have been made *during* the conspiracy (*i.e.,* before the crime was completed or before the declarant withdrew from the conspiracy).

3) **In furtherance of conspiracy:** [§349] Finally, the statement must have been made *"in furtherance of"* the conspiracy (*i.e.,*

it relates to the effort to accomplish the illegal objective and is not merely narrative in nature). [Fed. R. Evid. 801(d)(2)(E); *and see* United States v. Doerr, 886 F.2d 944 (7th Cir. 1989)]

(b) **Application:** [§350]   Under these requirements, incriminating statements made by one of the conspirators *after* commission of the planned offense are generally held inadmissible. [Krulewitch v. United States, 336 U.S. 440 (1949)] (Of course, the declarant can still be called as a witness at trial.)

　　1) **Compare:** Such statements may be admitted, however, where made during, and in furtherance of, a *continuing* conspiracy. (The key question thus may be, "Was there one continuous conspiracy, or a number of separate conspiracies?")

(c) **Constitutional considerations:** [§351]   Use of a hearsay statement falling within the co-conspirator exception does not violate the accused's right of confrontation—even though there is no opportunity for cross-examination—if circumstances indicate the reliability of the statement. [Dutton v. Evans, 400 U.S. 74 (1970)] If the jurisdiction's co-conspirator exception has the same requirements as the federal rule, then reliability is presumed without more because the rule is "firmly rooted." [Bourjaily v. United States, *supra*]

　　1) **Note:** The Confrontation Clause does *not* require the government to show, as a condition for admissibility of a co-conspirator's out-of-court statement, that the co-conspirator is unavailable to testify. [United States v. Inadi, 475 U.S. 387 (1986); *and see infra,* §550]

(3) **Admissions by "privies" (predecessors in interest, joint obligors, etc.):** [§352]   Suppose that X, a property owner, made a statement about limits on her ownership rights—"Jones has an easement across my land." She then sold the property to Y. A third party sues Y, and seeks to introduce into evidence the statement of X as an admission of a party. X is not a party, but she is the predecessor in interest of a party. Many jurisdictions would admit the statement of a predecessor in title against the successor in interest. [Cal. Evid. Code §1224] Similarly, where several parties have joint rights or obligations, many courts hold the declarations of one admissible against the others. [Cal. Evid. Code §1224] Some jurisdictions take a similar approach to statements by a decedent during her lifetime acknowledging an indebtedness, offered against the decedent's estate [Cal. Evid. Code §1224] or a concession of contributory negligence by a decedent offered against heirs who have instituted a wrongful death action arising out of the event that was the subject of the statement [Cal. Evid. Code §§1226-1227].

(a) **Restrictive Federal Rule on admissions by "privies":** [§353]   Federal Rule 801(d)(2) makes no provision for receiving admissions by predecessors in interest or other "privies." [*See* McCormick on Evidence §260 (Practitioner's 4th ed. 1992)] These statements are not admissible under Federal Rule 801(d)(2), though they will often be admissible under some other rule. For example, the statement "Jones has an easement across my land" would be admissible under Federal Rule 804(b)(3) as a statement against interest if the declarant were unavailable for testimony. As a last resort, the residual or "catch-all" exception to the hearsay rule (*see infra*, §540) may come to the rescue. [*See* Huff v. White Motor Corp., 609 F.2d 286 (7th Cir. 1979)—statement of wrongful death decedent indicating that accident caused by decedent's catching pants on fire with cigarette not admissible against heirs as admission, but nonetheless admissible under residual exception because reliable]

4. Confessions

a **Definition:** [§354]   A confession is a direct acknowledgment of *criminal guilt* by an accused. By the very force of this definition, a confession goes beyond an admission—which at most is only a statement tending to prove guilt but of itself insufficient to authorize a conviction. [Waltz, *Criminal Evidence* 222 (2d ed. 1983)] (And, of course, an admission may have nothing to do with criminal liability; it may relate to an exclusively civil matter; *see supra.*)

(1) **Note:** A confession must admit *all* elements of the crime. Thus, "I confess I killed him, but it was self-defense," is not a confession in that it leaves open the question of a *defense*. The statement could be used, however, as an admission if the accused subsequently denied the act of killing.

b. **Hearsay status**

(1) **Federal Rules:** [§355]   Admissions and confessions are *not* hearsay under the Federal Rules (*see supra*, §261).

(2) **Traditional view:** [§356]   The traditional view is that an extrajudicial confession is hearsay since it is offered to prove the truth of the matter confessed. However, its probative value outweighs any hearsay objection, and hence it is admissible under a long-recognized *exception* to the hearsay rule.

c. **Corpus delicti must first be proved:** [§357]   Proof of the accused's confession cannot be received until the corpus delicti (*i.e.,* body or substance) of the crime has been proved by *other* evidence. (This is not a rule of evidence; it is a rule of substantive law. *See* Criminal Procedure Summary.)

d. **Confession must be voluntary:** [§358]   The principal safeguard governing confessions is that the voluntariness of the confession must always first be determined on voir dire examination—*before evidence of the confession can be received*. The burden is on the prosecution to show this; otherwise, the defendant's confession cannot be used.

(1) **Constitutional rule:** [§359]   The exclusion of coerced confessions is a rule of constitutional law. The Fifth Amendment and due process of law forbid the use of such evidence in either federal or state proceedings. [Brown v. Mississippi, 297 U.S. 278 (1936); *and see* Criminal Procedure Summary]

(2) **What constitutes "voluntariness":** [§360]   What constitutes "voluntariness" is a mixed question of fact and law, turning on whether the confession was the product of a *free and rational choice* by the accused, as disclosed by the "totality of circumstances" surrounding the confession. [Clewis v. Texas, 386 U.S. 707 (1967)]

    (a) **Factors usually considered:** [§361]   The factors usually considered in determining the voluntariness of a confession are the accused's age, intelligence, and experience; his mental and physical condition; methods used by the police in obtaining the confession (*e.g.,* physical or mental duress to accused or family, promises of leniency, trickery, or deception); length and conditions of interrogation, etc.

(3) **Procedure for determining voluntariness**

    (a) **Preliminary fact question decided by judge:** [§362]   The trial judge *must* make the determination as to the voluntariness of the confession. The judge *cannot* admit the confession into evidence and leave it to the jury to decide whether it was voluntary, because of the potential prejudice from the contents of an involuntary confession. [Jackson v. Denno, *supra,* §68]

    (b) **Jury excluded during hearing on voluntariness:** [§363]   The trial judge's determination must be made *outside the presence of the jury*. [Fed. R. Evid. 104(c)]

    (c) **Burden of proof as to voluntariness:** [§364]   As indicated above, the *prosecution* always bears the burden of proving that the accused's confession was voluntarily made.

    (d) **Quantum of proof required:** [§365]   The trial judge need only determine that the confession was voluntary by a *preponderance* of the evidence. Proof "beyond a reasonable doubt" is *not* required. [Lego v. Twomey, 404 U.S. 477 (1972)]

    (e) **Effect of judge's ruling on voluntariness:** [§366]   If the trial judge determines that the confession was involuntary, it must be excluded. If the judge determines that it was voluntary, either of the following procedures is constitutionally permissible. [Lego v. Twomey, *supra*]

        1) **Orthodox rule:** [§367]   Once admitted as voluntary, the jury cannot reconsider the issue; the jury's only function is to determine the weight and credibility of the confession. [Fed. R. Evid. 405]

        2) **Massachusetts rule:** [§368]   At the defendant's request, the jury must reconsider the voluntariness of the confession; it can then disregard it as "involuntary" despite the trial judge's determination.

e. **Even voluntary confessions must be excluded if obtained in violation of accused's constitutional rights:** [§369]   This topic is discussed in detail in the

Criminal Procedure Summary. Suffice it to note here that even a duress-free confession by the accused cannot be introduced against the accused *as proof of guilt* if it was obtained as follows:

(1) **Accused not advised of *Miranda* rights:** [§370] Even a voluntary confession cannot be admitted unless it appears that before it was made, the police affirmatively advised the accused of his constitutional rights, as required by *Miranda v. Arizona,* 384 U.S. 436 (1966).

(2) **Accused illegally arrested:** [§371] Even a voluntary confession must be excluded if it is the "fruit" of an unlawful arrest. [Wong Sun v. United States, 371 U.S. 471 (1963)]

(3) **Accused denied speedy arraignment:** [§372] In *federal* courts, as a matter of judicial policy (not constitutionally required), confessions may be inadmissible if obtained while an arrestee is being held in violation of the speedy arraignment provisions of the Federal Rules of Criminal Procedure [*McNabb-Mallory* Rule], but this rule has been limited by subsequent legislation and is not applicable in state courts. (*See* Criminal Procedure Summary.)

(4) **Compare—use of confession to impeach:** [§373] If a confession is shown to be involuntary, it is deemed *untrustworthy* and hence cannot be used for *any* purpose (either to prove guilt or to impeach the accused who testifies at trial). On the other hand, a confession obtained in violation of the *Miranda* rule is not necessarily untrustworthy. It cannot be used as substantive proof of guilt, but it *can be used to impeach* the accused if she takes the witness stand at trial and tells a different story. *Rationale:* The mere fact that the accused's constitutional rights were violated is not a shield for the accused to commit perjury at the time of trial. [Harris v. New York, 401 U.S. 222 (1971); *and see* Criminal Procedure Summary]

5. **Declarations Against Interest:** [§374] A hearsay statement may be received in evidence if: (i) the person who made the statement is *not a party to the action*, and is now *unavailable* to testify (thus establishing the *necessity* factor); and (ii) the statement was sufficiently *against important interests* of the declarant *when made* so that a reasonable person in the same position would not have made the statement unless she believed it to be true (thus establishing the *trustworthiness* factor). [Fed. R. Evid. 804(b)(3); *and see* Chambers v. Mississippi, 410 U.S. 284 (1973)]

a. **Requirements for admissibility**

(1) **Declarant now unavailable:** [§375] The declarant, a nonparty, must be *unavailable* to testify at the time of trial. [Vaccaro v. Alcoa Steamship Co., 405 F.2d 1133 (2d Cir. 1968); Goff v. State, 496 P.2d 160 (Nev. 1972)]

(a) **"Unavailable":** The declarant's unavailability is generally determined in accordance with the rules dealing with the "former testimony" exception (*see supra,* §§284-293).

(b) **Note:** In many states and under the *Federal Rules*, a mere showing that the declarant is absent or beyond the subpoena power of the court is *not* enough to establish unavailability as a witness; there must be a showing that the declarant's testimony could not be obtained by *deposition* or similar means. [Fed. R. Evid. 804(a)(5)]

(2) **Perception and knowledge at time of declaration:** [§376]   The declarant must have had the usual qualifications of an ordinary witness at the time of the declaration, and "particular, personal knowledge of the facts." Courts generally *refuse* to allow statements based only on the declarant's *opinions* or *estimates* as to the facts (*e.g.,* "I must have been driving too fast"). [Gichner v. Antonio Troiano Tile & Marble Co., 410 F.2d 238 (D.C. Cir. 1969); Carpenter v. Davis, 435 S.W.2d 382 (Mo. 1968)]

(3) **"Against interest":** [§377]   The facts, to the declarant's knowledge, must be to the declarant's *immediate* prejudice at the time of the declaration, and the prejudice must be *substantial*. [*See* United States v. Woolbright, 831 F.2d 1390 (8th Cir. 1987)] There is a split of authority over *what sort of interest* must be affected. [United States v. Pena, 527 F.2d 1356 (5th Cir.), *cert. denied,* 426 U.S. 949 (1976)]

(a) **Pecuniary or proprietary interest:** [§378]   According to the present weight of state case authority, a statement against interest only falls within the exception if it is against the declarant's pecuniary (*financial*—usually restricted to a liquidated sum) or proprietary (*property*) interest. The prejudice to such interest must be *immediate* and *substantial*, and the declarant must then be *aware* that it is.

1) **Example—proprietary interest:** Declarations by a decedent landowner acknowledging the rights or interests of *another* in her land (*e.g.,* an easement, life estate, etc.) are admissible as declarations against the decedent's *proprietary* interest. [Grissom v. Bunch, 301 S.W.2d 462 (Ark. 1957)]

2) **Example—pecuniary interest:** Acknowledgments by a decedent of an *indebtedness*, or receipt of *payment* of a debt, are admissible as declarations against the declarant's *pecuniary* interest. [Egbert v. Egbert, 132 N.E.2d 910 (Ind. 1956)]

a) **But note:** A statement, "I owe X $1,000," is against the declarant's interest only if X's claim against the declarant is for $1,000 or less. If X's claim against the declarant were for *more* than $1,000, the admission of indebtedness of a lesser amount would *not* be against the declarant's interest.

3) **Civil liability to another:** [§379]   The *Federal Rules* specifically provide that a statement is against interest if it would tend to subject the declarant to *civil* liability to another person. [Fed. R. Evid. 804(b)(3)] Some state courts simply treat such statements as falling within the contrary-to-pecuniary-interest category. [Hileman v. Northwest Engineering Co., 346 F.2d 668 (6th Cir. 1965)]

a) **Note:** It is *not* necessary that the declarant's remarks constitute an out-and-out admission of liability. It is enough that they provide an important link in a chain of evidence that subjects the declarant to liability.

4) **Invalidating own claim:** [§380] The *Federal Rules* also specifically provide that a statement is against the declarant's interest if it would "render invalid a claim by him against another," *e.g.,* admission of contributory negligence. [Fed. R. Evid. 804(b)(3)] Again, most courts treat such statements as falling within the contrary-to-pecuniary-interest category. [Annot., 114 A.L.R. 921]

(b) **Criminal liability**

1) **Traditional view—declarations inadmissible:** [§381] Many state courts do ***not*** admit declarations that subject the declarant to criminal liability out of concern that this would encourage perjured testimony in criminal cases (*e.g.,* the accused would defend by bringing in witnesses to testify that someone else admitted to having committed the crime). [*See* Chambers v. Mississippi, 410 U.S. 284 (1973)]

a) **But note:** Some criminal acts will expose the actor to civil liability as well (*e.g.,* theft). In such a case, the declaration admitting the criminal act could be held admissible under the civil liability interest category above. [Annot., 162 A.L.R. 446]

2) **Modern trend and Federal Rules:** [§382] The preferred view and trend of authority ***admits*** declarations that expose the declarant to criminal liability. [People v. Spriggs, 60 Cal. 2d 868 (1964); State v. Leong, 465 P.2d 560 (Hawaii 1970); People v. Edwards, 242 N.W.2d 739 (Mich. 1976)] However, statements offered by a criminal defendant ***to show her own innocence*** (by proof of out-of-court declarations by a third person admitting the crime charged) are admissible only if there are "***corroborating circumstances*** that clearly indicate the trustworthiness of the statement." [Fed. R. Evid. 804(b)(3); Commonwealth v. Hackett, 307 A.2d 334 (Pa. 1973); United States v. Barret, 539 F.2d 244 (1st Cir. 1976)]

a) **Rationale:** The corroboration requirement in connection with exculpatory statements is intended to overcome the concern about perjured testimony noted above. The corroboration ***cannot*** come solely from the testimony of the accused. [Alexander v. State, 449 P.2d 153 (Nev. 1968)]

b) **Note:** Some states are more liberal and do ***not*** require separate corroboration, if the declarant's statements admitting the crime are clothed with sufficient indicia of reliability. [Cal. Evid. Code §1230]

c) **And note:** Some circuits also require corroboration for inculpatory statements of third parties offered ***against*** the defendant by the prosecution—even though the danger of perjury is less obvious here. [*See, e.g.,* United States v. Riley, 657 F.2d 1377 (8th Cir. 1981); *and see* United States v. Sarmiento-Perez, 633 F.2d 1092 (5th Cir. 1980), *cert. denied,* 459 U.S. 834 (1982)—inculpatory statement must satisfy more restrictive interpretation of "against interest" requirement than exculpatory statement]

3) **Constitutional limitation—fair trial:** [§383] As a constitutional matter, a state *cannot*, by applying its "penal interest" limitation, exclude as hearsay evidence the fact that a third person has confessed to the crime with which an accused is charged —at least where such evidence is crucial to the defense and bears reasonable indicia of trustworthiness. To apply the penal interest limitation would deprive the accused of the *fair trial* guaranteed by the Fourteenth Amendment Due Process Clause. [Chambers v. Mississippi, *supra,* §381]

(c) **Social disgrace:** [§384] A *few* states hold admissible declarations that create a risk of making the declarant "an object of *hatred, ridicule or social disgrace* in the community." [Cal. Evid. Code §1230; Kans. Civ. Proc. Code §60-460(j); Nev. Rev. Stat. §51.345; N.J. Evid. Rule 63(10); N.M. Stat. Ann. §20-4-804(b)(4); Utah Rule of Evid. 63(10); Wis. Stat. Ann. §908.045(4); First National Bank v. Osborne, 503 P.2d 440 (Utah 1972)]

1) **Criticism:** This extension has been criticized on the ground that the category is *too vague* to be meaningful and hence is *lacking in sufficient assurances of reliability*.

(4) **Prejudice known or apparent:** [§385] The declarant must have *known*, or have been *chargeable with knowledge*, that the facts stated were so far contrary to her interest *"that a reasonable person in the declarant's position would not have made the statement unless believing it to be true."* [Fed. R. Evid. 804(b)(3)]

(5) **No motive to falsify:** [§386] There must be nothing to indicate that the declarant had some motive to *falsify*. [G.M. McKelvey Co. v. General Casualty Co. of America, 142 N.E.2d 854 (Ohio 1957)]

b. **Declaration must be offered in its disserving aspect:** [§387] Statements may be self-serving in one aspect and disserving in another. If so, it must appear that the declaration is being offered in evidence with respect to its *disserving* aspect—*i.e.,* for a purpose to the prejudice of the declarant. [Wigmore, §1464; Williamson v. United States, 512 U.S. 594 (1994)]

(1) **Example:** Suppose that Declarant X tells a police officer, "I was delivering the cocaine for Z." Depending on the circumstances, the part of the statement that incriminates Z may be either: (i) self-serving, if X believes that by implicating Z he will curry favor with the police and receive leniency in the case pending against him; (ii) neutral, if X neither helps nor hurts himself by implicating Z; or (iii) disserving, if X's knowledge of Z's activities incriminates X further by showing his insider knowledge of a criminal conspiracy.

c. **Distinguish declarations against interest from admissions:** [§388]   A declaration against interest is distinguished from an admission in the following ways:

(1) *A declaration against interest can be a statement by a third party*—it need not be a statement by a party to the litigation, as with admissions.

(2) *"Unavailability" is required* to lay the foundation for a declaration against interest, but not for an admission.

(3) *A declaration against interest must be based on the personal knowledge* of the declarant; an admission need not.

(4) *A declaration against interest must be "against interest" when made;* an admission need only be inconsistent with the present position taken by the admitter.

gilbert LAW SUMMARIES	**DECLARATIONS AGAINST INTEREST VS. ADMISSIONS**	
	Declaration Against Interest	**Admission by Party-Opponent**
Must statement have been made by a party?	No	Yes (and offered by opposing party)
Must declarant now be unavailable?	Yes	No
Must declarant have had personal knowledge of facts?	Yes	No
Must statement have been against interest when made?	Yes	No

6. **Dying Declarations:** [§389]   A victim's dying declarations about the cause or circumstances of his impending death are admissible as an exception to the hearsay rule. [Fed. R. Evid. 804(b)(2)]

a. **Rationale:** The victim's death often supplies the *necessity* element; particularly in homicide cases, notions of justice command that a killer should not be able to seal the victim's mouth by a criminal act. The *trustworthiness* element is supplied by fear of death. [Shepard v. United States, 290 U.S. 96 (1933)]

b. **Type of action in which admissible**

(1) **Traditional view:** [§390]   According to the traditional view, dying declarations are admissible *only* in *homicide* cases, and not in any other criminal actions or in civil actions. [Annot., 47 A.L.R.2d 526]

(a) **Note:** In homicide cases, the declarations are admissible on behalf of either the defendant or the prosecution.

(2) **Federal Rules:** [§391]   The Federal Rules expand the traditional view somewhat, *permitting* dying declarations in *civil actions generally*, but in *no* criminal case other than homicide. [Fed. R. Evid. 804(b)(2); Cummings v. Illinois Central Railroad, 260 S.W.2d 111 (Mo. 1954)]

(a) **Rationale for limiting use:** Dying declarations are not the most reliable form of hearsay. The expansion of a dubious exception to civil actions is justified on the theory that the stakes in a civil case do not involve death or imprisonment. [Commonwealth v. Smith, 314 A.2d 224 (Pa. 1973)]

(3) **Minority view:** [§392]   Some states go further and admit dying declarations in *all* actions and proceedings, civil and criminal, finding no logic in the "homicide cases only" limitation. [*See, e.g.,* Cal. Evid. Code §1242]

c. **Requirements for admissibility**

(1) **Victim's statement:** [§393]   The dying declaration must be that of the *victim*, not some third person. Thus, the deathbed confession of a third person that *she* killed the victim is excluded under this exception, although in some jurisdictions it might qualify as a declaration against interest (*see supra*).

(2) **Sense of impending death:** [§394]   The declaration must have been made by the victim while believing that his death was *imminent*. [Fed. R. Evid. 804(b)(2); Soles v. State, *supra,* §67]

(a) **Comment:** Some courts underscore this requirement by saying that the declarant must have *abandoned all hope of recovery*, must have been *conscious*, and must have believed that his death was *immediately* imminent—*i.e.,* "near and certain." [Shepard v. United States, *supra,* §389]

(b) **But note:** The death need not take place *immediately* after the statement is made (*see* below).

(3) **Percipient witness:** [§395]   The victim must have had the usual capacities of a witness at the time of the declaration—*i.e.,* the capacity to perceive, to relate facts, and to recognize the obligation to tell the truth. [Annot., 86 A.L.R.2d 905]

(a) **Lack of religious belief:** [§396]   The victim's *lack of religious belief* goes only to the *weight* of the declaration—*not* to its admissibility.

(4) **Facts related to cause of death:** [§397]   The declaration must be: (i) as to *facts* and (ii) related to the *cause* or *circumstances* of what the victim believed to be his impending death. [Fed. R. Evid. 804(b)(2)]

(a) **Opinion:** [§398]   Thus, a declaration that is a mere *opinion* by the declarant is inadmissible ("I think D poisoned me"). [Shepard v.

United States, *supra*; Miller v. Goodwin & Beevers, 439 S.W.2d 308 (Ark. 1969)]

(b) **Self-serving:** [§399]   However, the fact that the declaration is self-serving is no bar to admissibility (*e.g.,* fatally injured motorist states that other driver ran the red light).

(5) **Death required:** [§400]   In some state jurisdictions, the declarant must have actually *died* by the time the evidence is offered. However, there is no fixed time period within which the death must have taken place, as long as it appears that the declarant had the requisite fear of impending death when he made the statement. Hence, statements have been admitted even where death took place months later.

(a) **Federal Rules—unavailability sufficient:** [§401]   The Federal Rules are *contra*. As long as the statement was made while the victim *believed* death was imminent, the victim need *not* have actually died. It is sufficient that he is *otherwise unavailable* at the time of trial. [*See* Fed. R. Evid. 804(b)(2), note] (However, if the victim does not testify at the trial, the proponent will have to show why the victim's testimony could not have been obtained by *deposition* or similar means.) [Fed. R. Evid. 804(a)(5)]

d. **Rebuttal and impeachment:** [§402]   Once admitted, the declaration is subject to all the objections and grounds for impeachment that could be asserted if the declarant were on the stand testifying. Thus, the declaration can be impeached by showing that the declarant had *withheld relevant facts* or had made *prior inconsistent statements*, by proof of the declarant's *lack of perceptive capacity* as to the facts, or by *evidence of facts to the contrary*.

7. **Excited Utterances:** [§403]   Statements of any person (participant or observer) made at the time of some *exciting* event, and under the *stimulus* of its excitement, may be admissible. [Fed. R. Evid. 803(2)]

a. **Requirements for admissibility**

(1) **Startling event:** [§404]   There must be an *occurrence* that is startling enough to produce *shock* and *excitement* in the observer.

(a) **Note:** The occurrence of the event can be shown by the declaration itself if the surrounding facts and circumstances impart a reasonable measure of *corroboration* (*e.g.,* P is discovered sprawled at bottom of staircase and says, "I just fell down the stairs!").

(2) **Excitement:** [§405]   The statement must be made while the observer was *under the stress* of the nervous shock and excitement; it must be spontaneous, with no time for deliberation or calculated misstatement.

(a) **Time of statement:** There is no mechanical test, but courts usually limit admissibility to statements made soon after the event because of the requirement that the declarant still be under the stress of excitement caused by the event. [*Compare* McCurdy v. Greyhound Corp., 346 F.2d 224 (3d Cir. 1965), *with* State v. Martineau, 324

A.2d 718 (N.H. 1974)—two or three hour lapse in rape case; Johnson v. Ohls, 457 P.2d 194 (Wash. 1969)—one hour lapse in personal injury case involving infant; *and* Cestero v. Ferrara, 273 A.2d 761 (N.J. 1971)—a lapse of uncertain duration where the declarant was unconscious from the time of the exciting event (an automobile accident) to the time of her statement]

(b) **Comment:** In any event, the more composed and detailed the statement, the less likely it will be found to have been spontaneous.

(3) **Statement related to event:** [§406]   The Federal Rules and many state jurisdictions hold that the spontaneous exclamation must pertain to the exciting event. [Fed. R. Evid. 803(2); *and see* Anders v. Nash, 180 S.E.2d 878 (S.C. 1971)] However, at least one jurisdiction has construed this requirement broadly, allowing the admission of a declarant's statement indicating that he was acting within the scope of his employment at the time of the accident, even though this fact did not bear directly on the cause of the accident. [Murphy Auto Parts Co. v. Ball, 249 F.2d 508 (D.C. Cir.), *cert. denied,* 355 U.S. 932 (1958)]

b. **Types of statements admissible**

(1) **Opinions:** [§407]   There is a split of authority on the admissibility of excited utterances that do relate to the facts, but are in the form of declarant's opinion (*e.g.,* "D was going too fast!"). [Montesi v. State, 417 S.W.2d 554 (Tenn. 1967)]

(a) **Note:** Some courts will allow statements of the observer's opinion, as long as it is the *kind* of opinion that could reasonably be made under the circumstances.

(b) **But note:** However, a number of courts are *contra* and will not permit opinion declarations, particularly where they fix blame or responsibility. [Annot., 53 A.L.R.2d 1287]

(2) **Acknowledgments of fault:** [§408]   An acknowledgment of fault (even though opinion) is generally admitted if otherwise within the exception.

(3) **Self-serving statement:** [§409]   Conversely, the fact that the statement is self-serving does *not* bar its use if the conditions for admissibility are otherwise met (*e.g.,* D's statement immediately after killing X that "I had to shoot him; he was coming after me with his knife!").

c. **Declarant:** [§410]   There is *no* requirement as to competency, unavailability, or even identification of the declarant.

(1) **Competency:** [§411]   The age of the declarant is generally immaterial. The declarant need not have been old enough to understand the meaning of an oath, or the importance of telling the truth. Indeed, the declarant need *not* be a competent witness at the time of trial. All that is required is that the declarant have had personal knowledge of the facts (*i.e.,* was a percipient witness), the powers of perception and recollection, and the ability to utter almost instinctive exclamations. [Annot., 83 A.L.R.2d 1368]

    (2) **Identity:** [§412]   The declarant **need not be identified**, as long as his existence and personal observation of the facts are established by inference from the circumstances (*e.g.,* W testifies, "I heard someone yell, 'Look out!'"). The lack of the declarant's identity goes only to the **weight** of the declaration, **not** to its admissibility. [*See* Miller v. Keating, 754 F.2d 507 (3d Cir. 1985)]

    (3) **Personal observation:** [§413]   But where the witness testifies, "I heard someone (unidentified) at the scene of the accident say that D's car ran the red light," this is **not** admissible because there is no showing that the unidentified "someone" was a percipient witness to the accident. [Carney v. Pennsylvania Railroad, 240 A.2d 71 (Pa. 1968)]

  d. **Scope of exception:** [§414]   Note that the excited utterance doctrine allows proof of certain out-of-court declarations that do not meet the test of other exceptions.

    (1) **Example:** An agent's admission of fault, inadmissible as a vicarious admission against the employer because it is outside the scope of the agent's authority or employment (*supra,* §§335-343), may nevertheless qualify as an excited utterance. [Murphy Auto Parts Co. v. Ball, *supra,* §406]

    (2) **Example:** A statement by the victim of a homicide, **inadmissible** as a **dying declaration** because it was not made under any sense of impending death, may still be **sufficiently spontaneous** to be received as an **excited utterance**.

8. **Declarations of Present Sense Impressions:** [§415]   The Federal Rules and some state jurisdictions have adopted a separate exception to the hearsay rule for statements made by a person while perceiving an event or condition (even though not "exciting") and that **describe or explain** the event or condition. [Fed. R. Evid. 803(1); *and see* Waltz, The Present Sense Impression Exception to the Rule Against Hearsay: Origins and Attributes, 66 Iowa L. Rev. 869 (1981)]

  a. **Examples:** Where the driver of a car states, "I can't seem to turn the wheel," and the statement is offered to show the driver's conduct in driving the car, the statement is admissible. [Annot., 163 A.L.R. 38] Similarly where a bystander states, "That driver looks like he's been drinking," and the statement is offered to show the condition of the driver subsequently involved in a traffic accident, this statement too is admissible. [Houston Oxygen Co. v. Davis, 161 S.W.2d 474 (Tex. 1942)]

  b. **Rationale:** The **spontaneity** and contemporaneity of the statement are deemed to be assurances of its trustworthiness, and the words used are regarded as the best evidence of the then-existing sense impression experienced by the observer. [*See* Tampa Electric Co. v. Getrost, 10 So. 2d 83 (Fla. 1942); Commonwealth v. Coleman, 326 A.2d 387 (Pa. 1974)] Thus it has been held that the spontaneity requirement forecloses introduction of an expert's out-of-court statement of opinion based on training and experience; it is not sufficiently "instinctive." [Lira v. Albert Einstein Medical Center, 559 A.2d 550 (Pa. 1989)]

c.   **Requirements for admissibility**

(1)   **Declarant:** [§416]   As with the excited utterance exception, above, there is *no* requirement that the declarant be unavailable or even identified. There also is no requirement that the accuracy of the declaration be corroborated by the testimony of an equally percipient witness, although such corroboration would obviously enhance the declaration's evidentiary weight. [*See* Booth v. State, 508 A.2d 976 (Md. 1986); State v. Jones, 532 A.2d 169 (Md. 1987)]

(2)   **Time uttered:** [§417]   Most courts that recognize this exception require that the declaration be made *while* the observer was engaged in the conduct or perceiving the event that the statement is offered to explain. This is to assure the spontaneity and accuracy of the observer's present sense impression.

(a)   **Compare—Federal Rule:** Federal Rule 803(1) expands this requirement, however, admitting statements made either while the declarant was perceiving an event or condition or *immediately thereafter*—thus *perhaps* covering the case where a witness makes a report of an accident or crime very shortly after its commission (*i.e.,* after any excitement has worn off so that it cannot come in as an excited utterance; *see* above).

(b)   **But note:** Congress rejected a proposed exception for statements of *recent* sense impression, indicating an insistence on contemporaneity.

9.   **Declarations of Physical Condition ("State of Body" Cases)**

a.   **Present condition:** [§418]   Where a person's *physical* condition at a specified time is in issue, that person's spontaneous statements *made at that time* are admissible to prove the condition. [Fed. R. Evid. 803(3)]

(1)   **Example:** Where the issue is the extent of P's injuries in a traffic collision, P's statements at and after the collision as to how she feels are admissible to prove same. [Murray v. Foster, 180 N.E.2d 311 (Mass. 1962)]

(2)   **Type of condition:** [§419]   Some courts limit admissibility to declarations of present *pain* and will not allow statements as to other present bodily conditions (*e.g.,* pregnancy, impotency, visual defects, etc.), fearing less spontaneity than in the pain cases. [*See* Annot., 90 A.L.R.2d 1071] The Federal Rules, however, admit statements as to *any* sensation or bodily condition, and this is believed to be the better view.

b.   **Past condition**

(1)   **Traditional view—inadmissible:** [§420]   Prior to the Federal Rules, most courts did *not* admit evidence of a person's out-of-court statements as to how she felt in the *past* (*e.g.,* "I was in terrible pain last Thursday"). The rationale is that with the passage of time there is too great a likelihood of inaccuracy, falsification, etc. [*See* Meaney v. United States, 112 F.2d 538 (2d Cir. 1940), per L. Hand, J.]

(a) **Note:** In most cases, even statements made by an injured person to her doctor as to how she *previously* felt are *not* admissible (whereas *present* body pains *would* be).

(b) **Compare:** Statements made by a person to a doctor as to past conditions may be admissible to this extent: If the doctor is called to testify as an *expert witness*, the doctor may, in stating the *facts upon which her expert opinion is based*, include statements by the patient as to some past condition. [Annot., 130 A.L.R. 977; *see infra,* §§897-906]

(2) **Federal Rules:** [§421]   The Federal Rules have *rejected* the limitation against statements of past physical condition and allow such statements where they are *made to a physician or other medical personnel for the purpose of medical diagnosis or treatment*. [Fed. R. Evid. 803(4)]

(a) **Comment:** This is believed to be the better view. Even though lacking in spontaneity, such statements are usually reliable because it is thought that patients generally tell their doctors the truth about their symptoms—present or past.

(b) **But note—limitation:** The Federal Rules allow statements of past physical condition to be admitted *only* when made for the purpose of diagnosis or treatment. For example, a statement of past physical condition made to a forensic expert (not for diagnosis or treatment) is inadmissible because the declarant may have a motive to lie.

(3) **Intermediate view:** [§422]   Section 1251 of the California Evidence Code provides that a declarant's statements as to her *"state of mind, emotion, or physical sensation"* at some prior time *are* admissible, where such condition is itself at issue. The statements may have been *made to anyone* (*i.e.,* not limited to statements made to doctors). The only limitations are that the declarant now be *unavailable* to testify and that no circumstances indicate the statements' lack of trustworthiness. [Cal. Evid. Code §1252; as to definition of "unavailable," *see supra,* §§284-293]

10. **Declarations of Mental Condition ("State of Mind" Cases):** [§423]   As already discussed, a direct assertion by a declarant of his state of mind (*e.g.,* "I hate Fred") is generally recognized to be hearsay. However, an *indirect* assertion (*e.g.,* "Fred is a liar" to show declarant's dislike of Fred) is *not* hearsay under the Federal Rules truth-of-the-matter-asserted definition, although it *is* under the Morgan declarant-centered definition. The state of mind exception was developed to allow admission of indirect assertions of intent in states following the Morgan view, and of direct assertions of intent under both views.

a. **Declarations as to present mental or emotional state:** [§424]   Whenever a person's state of mind at a particular time is itself in issue (*e.g.,* did D intentionally strike Fred? or did H convey his property to W to defraud his creditors?), that person's declarations as to his state of mind *at the time in question* are admissible, provided they are made under circumstances indicating sincerity. [Fed. R. Evid. 803(3)]

(1) **Rationale:** Such declarations have some degree of spontaneity ("trustworthiness" element), and may be the best evidence of the declarant's

state of mind ("necessity" element). Because the declarant knows his own state of mind, there is no need to check perception, and since the statement is of *present* (then-existing) state of mind, there is no need to check the declarant's memory. [*See* Shepard v. United States, *supra,* §398]

(2) **Application:** [§425]   The exception is broad enough to cover any declaration as to a person's intent, motive, plan, emotions (love, hate, fear), confusion, knowledge, or other mental state. [Ebasco Services, Inc. v. Pennsylvania Power & Light Co., 460 F. Supp. 163 (E.D. Pa. 1978)]

   (a) **Example:** A person's statement, "I intend to send X some money," is admissible to show her intention toward X. [United States v. Annunziato, 293 F.2d 373 (3d Cir.), *cert. denied,* 368 U.S. 919 (1961)]

   (b) **Example:** Testator's statements of love and affection toward a beneficiary are admissible in a will contest case as evidence of the desire to make a valid gift to that beneficiary. [Annot., 79 A.L.R. 1447]

   (c) **Example:** A person's statements as to where he intends to make his home are admissible to establish his domicile. [Smith v. Smith, 70 A.2d 630 (Pa. 1950); Doern v. Crawford, 153 N.W.2d 58 (Wis. 1967)]

b. **Declarations of present intent as evidence to show subsequent conduct:** [§426]   A person's out-of-court declarations of state of mind may be admissible not only as proof of the person's state of mind at the time the statements were made (above), but also to show the *probability* that he committed some subsequent act pursuant to that declared state of mind. [Fed. R. Evid. 803(3)]

   (1) **Examples**

      (a) **Plans to travel:** Letters written by X stating that X was planning to go to Colorado were admissible as proof that X had in fact gone there. [Mutual Life Insurance Co. v. Hillmon, 145 U.S. 285 (1892)—leading case]

      (b) **Intent to commit suicide:** Declarations by a deceased of an intent to commit suicide (or of prior acts of attempted suicide) are admissible where the issue is whether the deceased took her own life or was murdered. [Annot., 93 A.L.R. 426]

         1) **Compare:** Where the declaration might be used in a backward-looking way to prejudicially implicate another person, the declaration is inadmissible. Thus, in *Shepard v. United States, supra,* H had been convicted of murdering W despite his defense that she had taken her own life. The trial court had allowed into evidence statements made by W before her death that "H poisoned me!" The Supreme Court reversed, holding the accusation inadmissible as a dying declaration (no fear of impending death, *supra,* §394), and also inadmissible as negativing her intent to commit suicide. The statement was deemed so *prejudicial* as to

H that the jury could not have been capable of considering it only to negative her claimed suicide intent.

(c) **Intent to harm:** Declarations of intention to frame, kill, or attack another are admissible to prove that the declarant did in fact commit the act, and did so intentionally.

   1) **Note:** Such declarations may also be used to show their *effect* on a third person in whose presence they were made. (As such, they are nonhearsay; *see supra*, §236.)

   2) **Example:** In a homicide case, evidence of threats that the deceased (X) had made to D ("I'm going to kill you!") are admissible as circumstantial evidence that D's killing of X was in self-defense. The statements tend to show *both* that X had been the aggressor and also that D was in reasonable fear of attack.

(2) **Limitations respecting conduct of third persons:** [§427]   Extrajudicial statements made by a declarant as to his state of mind cannot be used to implicate or reflect upon the probable conduct of a *third person*. [Johnson v. Chrans, 844 F.2d 482 (7th Cir. 1988); United States v. Mangan, 575 F.2d 32 (2d Cir. 1978)]

   (a) **Example:** D's statement that he and X are planning to commit a crime is by itself insufficient to prove that X was involved and is inadmissible hearsay as to X. [*See* Shepard v. United States, *supra*]

   (b) **Example:** A homicide victim's statement to a friend, shortly before her death, "I know he [the husband] is going to kill me," is inadmissible hearsay in a murder prosecution against the husband. The victim's state of mind was not in issue, and the statement was irrelevant as to the husband's state of mind or to explain his conduct.

   (c) **Compare:** California has held that the statement of the deceased, "I am going out with Frank tonight," was admissible against the defendant, Frank. [People v. Alcalde, 24 Cal. 2d 177 (1944); *and see* United States v. Pheaster, 544 F.2d 353 (9th Cir. 1976)]

c. **Declarations as to past state of mind:** [§428]   Courts hesitate to receive extrajudicial declarations of intent to show the declarant's state of mind at a time when she committed some *past* act—*i.e., past* state of mind (*e.g.,* "I didn't mean to hit him"—offered to show lack of intent at time of alleged battery). Such declarations involve danger of defects in *memory* and other hearsay difficulties.

(1) **Exceptions:** [§429]   Nevertheless, there are a few situations in which such declarations as to *past* state of mind *are* admitted:

   (a) **Will cases:** [§430]   Where the issue relates to the execution, revocation, or interpretation of a decedent's will, courts admit evidence of declarations by the testator, made both before *and after* the execution of the will, to reflect on testamentary intent, state of mind, undue influence, etc., at the time the will was made. [Annot., 62 A.L.R.2d 855; Fed. R. Evid. 803(3)]

    (b) **Delivery of deed cases:** [§431] Similarly, many courts admit evidence of declarations by the grantor of a deed, made both before **and after** the alleged delivery of the deed to the grantee, to reflect on whether the grantor intended the deed to have immediate effect (or only to take effect after his death, etc., in which case there is no valid delivery). (*See* Property Summary.)

(2) **Minority view:** [§432] Note again the unique position taken by California Evidence Code section 1251: Where the declarant is now unavailable, his extrajudicial statements as to his "state of mind, emotion, or physical sensation," either at the time he made the statement **or at any prior time** are admissible where such factors are in issue and where nothing indicates the statements are untrustworthy (*see supra,* §422).

11. **Past Recollection Recorded:** [§433] "Past recollection recorded" is frequently confused with the doctrine of "refreshing recollection" (*see infra,* §964), and so is often discussed in connection with techniques of direct and cross-examination. In fact, past recollection recorded is simply an **exception** to the hearsay rule that allows in evidence a writing made (or adopted) by the witness on the stand where the witness now has **insufficient memory** to testify fully and accurately to the facts contained therein. [Fed. R. Evid. 803(5)]

    a. **Rationale:** Since the witness-declarant lacks sufficient memory to testify, the only choice is to admit the hearsay written statement or do without the witness's evidence entirely (*"necessity"* element). Also, problems of memory and sincerity are minimized because the statement was written or adopted at a time when it was fresh in the witness's memory, and the declarant is generally on the witness stand and available for cross-examination (*"reliability"* element).

    b. **Requirements:** [§434] The requirements for admissibility under this exception are:

        (i) The document was **prepared** or **adopted** by the witness;

        (ii) Such preparation or adoption occurred when the matter described was **fresh in the witness's memory**;

        (iii) The document **correctly reflects** what was remembered when it was made;

        (iv) The witness has **insufficient recollection** to testify fully and accurately about the matter; and

        (v) The document is the **authentic memorandum** which has not been **tampered with**.

[*See* Fed. R. Evid. 803(5); United States v. Edwards, 539 F.2d 689 (9th Cir. 1976)]

(1) **Source of record**

    (a) **Writing "adopted" by witness:** [§435] Some jurisdictions require that the witness have written the statement. However, the ***modern trend*** is to hold that the document is admissible—regardless of who prepared it—if the witness read the document when the event was fresh in her memory, knew then that the document was correct, and therefore "adopted" the document as a record of the event. [Fed. R. Evid. 803(5)]

    (b) **Writing prepared at direction of witness:** [§436] Some courts allow admission of a written statement that was neither prepared nor adopted by the witness, provided it was prepared "under the witness's direction." [*See, e.g.,* Cal. Evid. Code §1237]

        1) **Laying the foundation:** [§437] The witness must still testify that she correctly told the writer what to write down when it was fresh in her memory. In addition, the ***writer*** must then testify that he wrote down correctly what the witness had said. However, the witness need not actually have seen the document.

        2) **Federal Rules:** [§438] Where the witness did not adopt the statement written by another, the Federal Rules treat the document as hearsay on hearsay. The document would probably still be admissible, however, as past recollection recorded of the writer (the written statement) of a present sense impression (of the person who dictated the memorandum). [*See* Fed. R. Evd. 803(1)]

(2) **Witness's inability to testify:** [§439] Before any document will be admitted as past recollection recorded, the witness's memory must be examined to ensure that she is unable to testify fully and accurately about the matter, but a total lapse of memory is not necessary. [United States v. Williams, 571 F.2d 344 (6th Cir. 1978)] Such examination is accomplished by attempting to revive the witness's present memory of the past event (*see* "refreshing recollection," *infra,* §§963-974).

(3) **Compare—business records exception:** [§440] For the past recollection recorded exception, the document need ***not*** be prepared in the regular course of some business; this hearsay exception is distinct from the business records exception (below).

c. **Admissibility of the writing itself:** [§441] The general view is that although a document is admissible as past recollection recorded, it cannot be seen by the jury (except at the request of the adversary party); juries give too much credence to documents, and the documents are considered inferior to the testimony of a witness who remembers the event in issue. Thus, in a jury trial the witness and counsel are limited to reading from the document.

12. Business Records

a. **"Parties' shop-book doctrine":** [§442]   At early common law, in a suit by a creditor against a debtor, the creditor, being a party, was *incompetent* to testify in his own behalf (*see infra,* §812). To prevent the debtor from evading the debt altogether, an exception was developed allowing use of the creditor's business records—"shop-books"—to prove the debt (the "necessity" element is at work here). The requirements were:

(1) *Such records were admissible only where the party had kept his own records* (no clerk or bookkeeper could testify);

(2) *In addition, the records had to have been entered in a regularly kept business journal,* the shopkeeper had to *authenticate* the records under oath, and the shopkeeper had to be shown to have a *reputation for keeping good records*; and

(3) *The transactions involved had to be on credit*—not cash sales.

b. **"Regular course of business doctrine":** [§443]   As the complexity of business increased, the common law rule was expanded to allow into evidence many of the business entries that were inadmissible under the "parties' shop-book doctrine," above. The Uniform Business Records as Evidence Act was adopted in most states as a codification of the later common law rule. More recently, the same principles have been incorporated, and expanded somewhat, in the Federal Rules and similar state codes.

(1) **Rationale:** The gist of this doctrine is that business records should be admissible, despite the hearsay rule, where the *sources of information, and the method and time of preparation, indicate their trustworthiness*.

(2) **Requirements for admissibility**

(a) **Entry in "regular course of business":** [§444]   The record must be written and made in the course of a *regularly conducted business activity*. This requirement encompasses (i) the types of activities that may be "business" activities; (ii) the necessity of the entrant being under a duty to make the entries; and (iii) the requirement that the records relate to the primary business (*see* below).

1) **"Business" activity:** [§445]   Most statutes define "business" quite broadly. Under Federal Rule 803(6), the definition includes every "business, institution, association, profession, occupation, and calling of every kind, *whether or not conducted for profit.*"

a) **Note:** This definition is broad enough to cover the records of many organizations that are not regarded as "businesses" in the normal sense—*e.g.,* hospitals, churches, schools, etc.

2) **"Regular course of" business:** [§446]   To assure trustworthiness, it must appear that the records in question were prepared in the regular course of the business activity involved, *and* that it was the regular practice to make the particular record or entry in question. [Fed. R. Evid. 803(6); Pulkrabek,

Inc. v. Yamaha International Corp., 261 N.W.2d 657 (N.D. 1977)—records made during winding up of business will not qualify]

a) **Entrant under duty to record:** [§447] It must appear that the entry was made by someone whose duty it was to make such entries as part of his employment. Thus, records kept as a hobby or "unofficially" do not qualify.

b) **Records related to primary business:** [§448] It must also appear that the records in question are of a type customarily maintained by the organization as part of its *primary* activities.

1/ **Hospital records:** [§449] It is for this reason that entries in hospital records are generally held admissible only to the extent that they are reasonably related to the diagnosis and treatment of patients' conditions. [United States v. Sackett, 598 F.2d 739 (2d Cir. 1979)] Entries not so related are *excluded*.

a/ **Example:** Entries in hospital records of statements made by the patient as to who hit him may be held unrelated to the patient's treatment, and hence inadmissible. [Kelly v. Sheehan, 259 A.2d 605 (Conn. 1968)]

b/ **Compare:** Statements as to the *cause* of injury may or may not be so related (sometimes the cause of an injury *is* relevant to diagnosis and treatment—*e.g.,* electric shock, etc.).

c/ **Note:** A *portion* of a business record may be held admissible, while other portions are excluded.

2/ **Accident reports:** [§450] Along the same lines, it has been held that accident reports prepared by railroad personnel, even though required by company rules or governmental regulations, are not admissible under the business records exception. Such reports are prepared in *anticipation of possible litigation*, and railroading—not litigating—is the *primary business* of the railroad. [Palmer v. Hoffman, 318 U.S. 109 (1943)]

a/ **By whom offered:** [§451] A number of cases have interpreted *Palmer v. Hoffman, supra,* as excluding the report *only* where it is sought to be introduced on *behalf* of the party whose personnel prepared it (in which case there are obvious concerns as to its self-serving nature). These decisions hold that where the report is being offered *against* the company or employer, accident reports prepared by an employee in accordance with company rules are *admissible*; *i.e.,* they are sufficiently "in the regular course of" the *business* activity. [Leon v. Penn Central Co., 428 F.2d 528 (7th Cir. 1970)—injured party's offered report by railroad engineer to show railroad's negligence held admissible; United States v. Smith, 521 F.2d 957 (D.C. Cir. 1975)—police report offered by *accused* admissible]

b/ **Federal Rule:** [§452]   The Federal Rules partially codify *Palmer v. Hoffman, supra,* by providing for the exclusion of business records where the *source* of the information, or other circumstances, indicate a lack of trustworthiness. [Fed. R. Evid. 803(6)]

3/ **Law enforcement records:** [§453]   When a police record is offered against the accused in a criminal case, the adversarial atmosphere in which the record was created detracts from its trustworthiness. Congress manifested its concern about the dangers of police records by prohibiting their use against the accused under the public records exception. [*See* Fed. R. Evid. 803(8); *and see infra,* §§476-480] Because of trustworthiness dangers, such records are normally also inadmissible when offered against the accused under the business records exception. [*See* United States v. Oates, 560 F.2d 45 (2d Cir. 1977)]

(b) **Form of records:** [§454]   Generally, the records being offered must be the *original entries* (or at least the first *permanent* entries, as where the original entries were mere scraps or memos). The *Federal Rules* expand this requirement to include records in *any* form, as long as made in the regular course of business. [Fed. R. Evid. 803(6)]

1) **Example—computer printouts:** Thus, where business records have been stored on magnetic tape for use in electronic computing equipment, and the original entries are destroyed, the printout sheets from the computer *are* admissible under the business records exception. [United States v. Russo, 480 F.2d 1228 (6th Cir. 1973)] Some courts require a more comprehensive foundation to be laid before admitting these records; accuracy of information sources and of computer procedures must be demonstrated. [United States v. Scholle, 553 F.2d 1109 (8th Cir. 1977)] Other courts allow the evidence to be received on the same foundation as a traditional paper record. [*See* Peritz, Computer Data and Reliability: A Call for Authentication of Business Records Under the Federal Rules of Evidence, 80 Nw. U. L. Rev. 956 (1986)]

2) **Example—summaries:** Sometimes even records that were not made in the "regular course of" business may be admissible if they are the best way of presenting the facts; *e.g.*, where the underlying records are so voluminous that they would confuse rather than aid the trier of fact, *summaries or compilations* thereof may be admitted even though they were made specially for litigation rather than in the "regular course of" business. [Fed. R. Evid. 1006; *and see infra*, §1206]

(c) **Contents of entry**

1) **Facts vs. opinion**

a) **Traditional rule—facts only:** [§455] The traditional rule is that only statements of *fact* in business records are admissible. Statements of opinion, even though made in the regular course of business (*e.g.*, medical diagnoses by a doctor), are not. [New York Life Insurance Co. v. Taylor, 147 F.2d 297 (D.C. Cir. 1945); *and see* Cal. Evid. Code §1271]

b) **Modern trend (Federal Rules):** [§456] The modern trend, however, allows into evidence entries of "acts, events, conditions, *opinions, or diagnoses*" as long as they were made in the regular course of business. [Fed. R. Evid. 803(6); Smith v. Universal Services, Inc., 454 F.2d 154 (5th Cir. 1972); United States v. Calvert, 523 F.2d 895 (8th Cir. 1975)]

2) **Source of information:** [§457] The entry must consist of matters that were either: (i) within the *personal knowledge* of the *entrant*; or (ii) *transmitted* to the entrant by someone who was under a *business duty* to report such matters to the entrant and who had *firsthand knowledge* of the facts. [Annot., 69 A.L.R.2d 1148]

a) **Example:** Hence, safety reports, police reports, etc., based on the firsthand knowledge of the reporting officer are admissible. But such reports based solely on the statements of *bystanders* to the officer (no business duty to report) are not. [Johnson v. Lutz, 253 N.Y. 124 (1930); Rosario v. Amalgamated Ladies Garment Cutters Union, 605 F.2d 1228 (2d Cir. 1979)]

b) **Compare:** On the other hand, many *third persons* in a business organization may be under a duty to report matters to the record keeper; *e.g.*, sales personnel, timekeepers, plant guards, etc. Hence, entries based on their reports (business duty to report) *are* admissible. [United States v. Lange, 466 F.2d 1021 (9th Cir. 1972)] Indeed, admissibility may be found where the employee of one business entity prepares a record that is then transmitted to and kept by a separate business entity, at least if this was part of a continuing contractual relationship between the entities.

[*See* White Industries v. Cessna Aircraft Co., 611 F. Supp. 1049 (W.D. Mo. 1985)]

(d) **Time of entry:** [§458]   The entry must have been made at or near the time of the transaction—*i.e.,* while the entrant's knowledge of the matter was still fresh. [Fed. R. Evid. 803(6); United States v. Kim, 595 F.2d 755 (D.C. Cir. 1979)]

(e) **Availability of entrant**

   1) **Traditional view—"unavailability" required:** [§459]   For the record itself to be admissible, the traditional view is that the entrant must be unavailable to testify as a witness. The early cases required that the entrant be dead, insane, ill, etc., but more recent cases recognize *practical* unavailability as well: entrant out of state, claiming privilege, or where it appears that even if the entrant testified he probably could not add anything to the credibility or completeness of the records as they stand (*e.g.,* bank clerk who debited and credited account).

   2) **Modern rules—unavailability requirement eliminated:** [§460] Modern rules have *eliminated* the requirement of unavailability altogether. [Fed. R. Evid. 803(6)] It is for the court to decide whether the record itself is sufficiently trustworthy, regardless of any testimony the entrant might give.

      a) **Rationale:** The law today recognizes that there is a tremendous division of labor in record-keeping in large business organizations and that it would unduly burden the party who prepared the record to produce as a witness every entrant involved in the making of the record. [Fed. R. Evid. 803(6), note]

   3) **Constitutional issue—criminal cases:** [§461]   It is not settled whether use of business records in a criminal case violates the accused's *confrontation rights* where the entrant fails to testify. Does use of such records deny the accused the right to confront and cross-examine the witnesses against him where the entrant is not produced at the time of trial? Some cases have permitted such evidence [People v. Kirtdoll, 217 N.W.2d 37 (Mich. 1974)]; whereas others have not [United States v. Strauss, 452 F.2d 375 (7th Cir. 1971), *cert. denied,* 405 U.S. 989 (1972)]. The Supreme Court may ultimately have to decide the issue.

(f) **Records authenticated:** [§462]   To "authenticate" means the *custodian* of the records "or *other qualified witness*" (not necessarily the original entrant) must appear in court, identify the records, and testify as to their mode of preparation and safekeeping. [Fed. R. Evid. 803(6); United States v. Reese, 561 F.2d 894 (D.C. Cir. 1977); United States v. Rappy, 157 F.2d 964 (2d Cir. 1946)—mere possession by the witness of a purported copy is not enough]

1) **Authentication by affidavit:** [§463]   Some states permit the custodian to authenticate business records by *affidavit* (instead of appearing in court) if the business or organization involved *is not a party* to the suit. [Cal. Evid. Code §1560]

2) **Limitation—trustworthiness:** [§464]   Regardless of compliance with the foregoing requirements, the trial court has the inherent power to exclude any business entry "where the source of the information or the method or circumstances of preparation indicate *lack of trustworthiness*." [Fed. R. Evid. 803(6)]

c. **Business records as evidence of absence of any entry**

(1) **At common law:** [§465]   Business entries were permitted only to prove the facts *contained therein*. It was *not* permissible to use a record for *negative* purposes—*i.e.*, to show that no transaction had been made because the record contained no such entry. [L.J. Brosius & Co. v. First National Bank, 174 P. 269 (Okla. 1916)]

(2) **Modern view:** [§466]   The modern view provides that properly authenticated business records *can* be used to prove "the occurrence *or nonoccurrence* of a transaction" as long as it can be shown that it was the *regular practice* of the organization to record all such transactions. [Fed. R. Evid. 803(7); United States v. DeGeorgia, 420 F.2d 889 (9th Cir. 1969); Podvin v. Eickhorst, 128 N.W.2d 523 (Mich. 1964); Commerce Union Bank v. Horton, 475 S.W.2d 660 (Tenn. 1972)]

13. **Official Records:** [§467]   Statements and documents prepared by a public official in the performance of official duties are admissible under various exceptions to the hearsay rule. [Fed. R. Evid. 803(8)-(10), (14)] (In most instances, they could also come in under the business records exception; *see* above.) [*See also* LaPorte v. United States, 300 F.2d 878 (2d Cir. 1962)]

a. **Rationale:** Public officers would frequently have to leave their jobs to appear in court and testify as to acts done in their official capacity, and since the public officer is under a duty to record properly, the records are probably reliable. [Chesapeake & Delaware Canal Co. v. United States, 250 U.S. 123 (1919)]

b. **Requirements for admissibility**

(1) **Duty to record:** [§468]   The record must be prepared by a public employee acting within the scope of her official duties; *i.e.*, there must be a *duty to record* the facts involved.

(a) **Recorded private documents:** [§469]   Where private documents (deeds, mortgages, etc.) are filed for recording in a public office, the recorder is under a duty to record same. By such recordation the documents *become* public records admissible under this exception. [Fed. R. Evid. 803(14)]

1) **Note:** As with public records generally, recorded private documents are usually proved by *certified copies*. [Fed. R. Evid. 902] The recorder's certification, however, establishes only the

fact of recording, not the *genuineness* of the document or its contents. (But, in many states, a presumption of genuineness attaches to recorded documents; *see infra*, §§1178-1184.)

(b) **Records need not be open to public inspection:** [§470]   The fact that a document is not open for public *inspection* (*e.g.,* government personnel records) does not prevent it from being a "public record" within the meaning of this exception. [People v. Nisonoff, 293 N.Y. 597 (1944)]

   1) **But note:** There is some authority to the contrary, on the theory that unless public inspection is afforded, the *trustworthiness* element may be lacking. [Cushing v. Nantasket Beach Railroad, 9 N.E. 22 (Mass. 1886)]

(2) **Personal knowledge of entrant generally required:** [§471]   To assure trustworthiness, the record must be based on the official's firsthand knowledge of the *facts* recorded, as opposed to the official's mere *opinions or conclusions* or reports to the official by *others*. [Love v. Common School District No. 28, 391 P.2d 152 (Kan. 1964)]

   (a) **Example:** A medical examiner's autopsy report showing cause of death as "bullet penetrated brain; probable suicide"; "bullet penetrated brain" is admissible as within the *personal knowledge* of the reporting officer, but in many jurisdictions the entry "probable suicide" would not be admissible because the coroner would have no *firsthand knowledge* of how the fatal wound was inflicted. [Backstrom v. New York Life Insurance Co., 236 N.W. 708 (Minn. 1931)]

(3) **Exceptions to personal knowledge requirement:** [§472]   Modern rules have relaxed the personal knowledge requirement as to certain kinds of official records:

   (a) **Vital statistics:** [§473]   Records of birth, death, or marriage are admissible although based on reports by others (doctors, ministers, parents). The theory is that such events are required by law to be reported *as they happen*, thus assuring trustworthiness. [Fed. R. Evid. 803(9)]

      1) **Compare—census reports:** But census reports are usually admissible for *statistical* purposes only and *not* for the truth of the data reported (*e.g.,* the age or marital status of a person as reported to the census taker). *Rationale:* Although census information is required by law to be reported, the reports are of *past* events and hence not as accurate.

   (b) **Agency operations:** [§474]   Records as to the activities or functions of the agency itself are admissible even though not entirely based on personal knowledge of the reporting officer—*e.g.,* records of receipts and disbursements of government monies. [Fed. R. Evid. 803(8)(A)]

(c) **Matters required to be reported:** [§475]   Likewise, all matters that a governmental agency is required by law to observe and report on (*e.g.*, weather records) are admissible. [Fed. R. Evid. 803(8)(B)]

1) **Limitation—in criminal cases:** [§476]   But this exception does *not* permit the use in criminal cases of matters "observed" by police officers or other law enforcement personnel. [Fed. R. Evid. 803(8)(B)]

a) **Nonadversarial reports:** [§477]   Several circuits allow admission of reports of the observations of law enforcement officers against criminal defendants where the reports were of "routine, nonadversarial matters." [United States v. Puente, 826 F.2d 1415 (5th Cir. 1987)—Treasury Enforcement Communication Data System computer data admissible to prove the defendant's auto crossed border from Mexico on particular date; United States v. Grady, 544 F.2d 598 (2d Cir. 1976)—Irish police weapons inventory admissible to prove that specified weapons were found in Northern Ireland]

(d) **Factual findings made pursuant to investigation:** [§478]   One of the far-reaching features of the federal public records exception is that it admits "factual findings resulting from an investigation made pursuant to authority granted by law." [Fed. R. Evid. 803(8)(C)] The fact that the public official considered hearsay reports from persons who were not public officials in making the findings does not prevent the record from being received under the exception. Thus, for example, in an action against an employer for discriminatory employment practices, an investigation report prepared by an Equal Employment Opportunity Commission investigator would be admissible. Similarly, the report of a military investigator about the cause of an aircraft crash is admissible, both for its narrow factual findings and for its broader fact-based conclusion that the probable cause of the accident was pilot error. [*See* Beech Aircraft Corp. v. Rainey, 488 U.S. 153 (1988)]

1) **Limitation—trustworthiness:** [§479]   The Federal Rule provides, however, that the findings should be excluded if the opponent demonstrates that the "sources of information or the circumstances indicate lack of trustworthiness." [Fed. R. Evid. 803(8)(C)]

2) **Limitation—in criminal cases:** [§480]   The Federal Rule also provides that findings resulting from an investigation may not be used *against the accused* in a criminal case (though if offered by the accused they are admissible against the government). [Fed. R. Evid. 803(8)(C)]

c. **Public records as evidence of absence of an entry:** [§481]   A certificate from the custodian of the public record that certain records are *not* on file in her office is admissible to prove that the matter has not been reported or recorded; if it is the kind of matter as to which reports are regularly made by the agency involved, this may reflect on whether the matter has in fact occurred. [Fed. R. Evid. 803(10); Chesapeake & Delaware Canal Co. v. United States, *supra*, §467; United States v. Lee, 589 F.2d 980 (2d Cir. 1979)]

14. **Judgments:** [§482]   A certified copy of a judgment of any court of record is always admissible proof that such judgment has been entered. The problem is to what extent the *facts adjudicated* in the former proceeding are competent proof of the facts in the *present* case.

   a. **Judgment of prior criminal conviction:** [§483]   The authorities are widely split as to the admissibility of a criminal conviction in a subsequent action involving the same facts upon which the conviction was based. *Example:* D is convicted of drunk driving. The injured party later sues D for damages and seeks to introduce the record of D's criminal conviction to establish liability. What ruling? (Keep in mind that if D had *pleaded guilty* to the crime, her *plea* would be admissible as a party admission, *see supra*, §311.)

      (1) **Traditional view excludes:** [§484]   The traditional view is that the conviction is not admissible in any civil suit. It is deemed inadmissible hearsay and merely a record of the criminal jury's *opinion* as to D's guilt. [Brooks v. State, 291 N.E.2d 559 (Ind. 1973)]

      (2) **Modern trend admits:** [§485]   However, the modern trend of authority *favors* the admission of the criminal conviction in a later *civil* case. [Weichhand v. Garlinger, 447 S.W.2d 606 (Ky. 1969); Burd v. Sussex Mutual Insurance Co., 267 A.2d 7 (N.J. 1970)]

         (a) **Rationale:** In the criminal case, D's guilt had to be established "beyond a reasonable doubt"—a burden of persuasion heavier than that required in civil proceedings. [Schindler v. Royal Insurance Co., 258 N.Y. 310 (1932)]

      (3) **Federal Rules:** [§486]   The Federal Rules specifically provide that judgments of criminal convictions are admissible in civil actions to *prove "any fact essential to sustain the judgment,"* but limit the admissibility of judgments to felony convictions (crimes punishable by death or imprisonment in excess of one year). The Federal Rules allow such evidence in criminal actions when it is offered *against* the government by a defendant and when it is offered *by* the government against a defendant who was the *subject* of the prior conviction. [Fed. R. Evid. 803(22); Lloyd v. American Export Lines, Inc., *supra*, §281]

         (a) **Rationale:** The reason for the felony limitation expressed in a number of state decisions is that many times persons accused of misdemeanors (particularly traffic offenses) may choose, for the sake of sheer convenience, not to defend against the charge. [Gray v. Grayson, 414 P.2d 228 (N.M. 1966)]

         (b) **Note:** The criminal judgment is not admissible if based on a plea of *nolo contendere*, reflecting the policy of encouraging this plea.

(c) **And note:** The criminal judgment need not be *final* in the sense that the pendency of an appeal does *not* affect its admissibility.

(4) **Evidentiary effect of conviction:** [§487] The courts permitting the use of records of prior criminal convictions are not in agreement as to the evidentiary *effect* of the conviction: Does it conclusively establish the facts, or is the defendant permitted to offer counterevidence?

(a) **Majority view:** Most courts treat the conviction *merely as evidence, not* conclusive as to the facts. *Rationale:* The criminal conviction is *not* res judicata because the requisite identity of parties does not exist. (It was State vs. D in the criminal case; here it is P vs. D, and there is no privity between the State and P.) [Schindler v. Royal Insurance Co., *supra*]

(b) **Minority view:** A few states take the position that the criminal conviction is entitled to the *res judicata effect of collateral estoppel*, and therefore the criminal conviction is *conclusive* against D as to the facts upon which it is based. [Emich Motors Corp. v. General Motors Corp., 340 U.S. 558 (1950)] But even states following this view do not apply it to convictions for misdemeanor traffic violations. [*See* Cal. Veh. Code §40834]

(5) **Constitutional limitation:** [§488] Even courts permitting evidence of prior convictions in both civil and criminal actions would *not* permit the government to use the conviction of some *third person* to *implicate* the accused in a criminal case. (*Example:* In a prosecution for receiving stolen property, a judgment of conviction of a third person for theft is *not* admissible to prove that goods were, in fact, stolen.) [Fed. R. Evid. 803(22)]

(a) **Rationale:** Admitting the conviction of a third person would deprive the accused of *the right of confrontation* as to an essential element of the charge against him.

(b) **But note:** However, the government may use the record of conviction for witness impeachment purposes (*see infra,* §1012).

b. **Judgment of prior acquittal:** [§489] The exclusionary rule is still strictly applied to records of prior acquittals of crime. The fact that the defendant has been acquitted of criminal conduct based on the very facts that are the subject of later civil proceedings *cannot* be shown. [United States v. Viserto, 596 F.2d 531 (2d Cir. 1979)]

(1) **Rationale:** The criminal acquittal may establish only that the prosecution did not prove the defendant guilty "beyond a reasonable doubt" to the satisfaction of the jurors. This high degree of evidentiary proof is not required in civil cases (*see* above). [United States v. National Association of Real Estate Boards, 339 U.S. 485 (1950)]

(2) **Application:** Thus, a judgment of acquittal of crime does not in itself bar other types of actions or proceedings against the accused, either by the injured party *or even by the State*. Thus, the acquittal of an attorney

on an embezzlement charge does not prevent disbarment proceedings against her by the State Bar, even if the issues in both proceedings are identical.

c. **Judgment in former civil case:** [§490]   A former civil judgment conclusively determines the rights of the parties thereto as between *themselves* under principles of res judicata. However, a hearsay problem arises when the judgment is sought to be introduced by (or against) a *stranger* to the original proceedings.

   (1) **Inadmissible in criminal cases:** [§491]   The civil judgment is clearly inadmissible in subsequent *criminal* proceedings because of the differing standards of proof (*see* above).

   (2) **Generally inadmissible in civil cases:** [§492]   The civil judgment is also generally inadmissible when asserted by a stranger in subsequent civil proceedings—*unless* the issues are so alike that the principles of *collateral estoppel* apply. (*See* Civil Procedure Summary.)

     (a) **But note—default judgments:** If the judgment had been obtained by *default*, it probably *would* be admissible as an *implied admission* (by silence) to the charging statements in the complaint. [Wigmore, §1066; *and see supra*, §§320-325]

   (3) **Statutory exceptions:** [§493]   Certain exceptions are provided by statute to the general rule of inadmissibility:

     (a) **Final judgment against third persons:** [§494]   It is provided by statute in some states that when the liability, obligation, or duty of a *third person* is in issue in a civil action (between two other persons), evidence of a final judgment against that person is admissible. [Cal. Evid. Code §1302] *Example:* In an action against a guarantor or surety, the judgment obtained against the principal (establishing the debt) may be shown.

     (b) **Enforcement of indemnity agreements:** [§495]   Likewise a person seeking to enforce an *indemnity* agreement may introduce a prior judgment against himself to prove that he has been held liable on the underlying obligation and therefore has the right to enforce the indemnity agreement. [Cal. Evid. Code §1301]

     (c) **Proof of personal matters:** [§496]   Under the Federal Rules, a prior civil judgment is admissible as proof of *matters of personal, family, or general history, or boundaries of land,* wherever such matters are provable by reputation evidence (*see* below). (*Example:* P may prove his citizenship by a judgment establishing that P's parents were citizens.) [Fed. R. Evid. 803(23)]

15. **Declarations Concerning Family History ("Pedigree"):** [§497]   Whenever *family relationships* are in issue (*e.g.,* in inheritance contests), it is often necessary to rely on hearsay to prove the various births, deaths, marriages, etc., that establish the relationships. The hearsay may consist of entries in family Bibles or other ancient

writings (*see infra,* §§528-530); reputation in the family (*see infra,* §§517-520); judgments (above); or out-of-court declarations by family members. [Lewis v. Marshall, 30 U.S. 469 (1831); Rhoades v. Bussinger, 53 A.2d 419 (Md. 1947)]

a. **Cases in which admissible:** [§498] The early cases (and English view) held that declarations concerning pedigree were admissible *only* in controversies involving *inheritance or legitimacy—i.e.,* where pedigree was directly in issue. However, the clear weight of authority today is that such evidence is admissible *whenever relevant*—in any kind of case or proceeding in which the issue arises. [Wigmore, §1530; Fed. R. Evid. 804(b)(4)]

    (1) **Rationale for admissibility:** Because issues of pedigree frequently involve facts many years old, the persons having firsthand knowledge of the facts have usually long since died (giving rise to the *"necessity"* element). And the reliability of such evidence is safeguarded by the requirement (below) that the hearsay statement must have been made *before* the controversy arose (*"trustworthiness"* element).

b. **Declarations by family member whose relationship is in issue:** [§499] Wherever the hearsay declarant's *own* birth, adoption, marriage, divorce, or other fact of family history is in issue, evidence of the declarant's statements concerning such matters are admissible *if the declarant is unavailable* to testify. [Fed. R. Evid. 804(b)(4)(A)]

    (1) **Firsthand knowledge unnecessary:** [§500] It is *not* required that the declarant's statements be based on *firsthand* knowledge; indeed, it may be *impossible* for the declarant to have such knowledge—*e.g.,* where and when declarant was born, who his parents were, etc. The declarant may be relying on hearsay evidence from other family members or reputation evidence as to aspects of his own background.

c. **Declarations by other family members:** [§501] Extrajudicial statements by one family member concerning the personal history (including death) of *another* family member are admissible to prove the relationship in question, under the following conditions:

    (1) **Declarant must be member of family in question**

        (a) **Majority requires blood or marital relationship:** [§502] Most courts require that the declarant be related by *blood or marriage* to the family whose history or relationship is involved. [Aaholm v. People, 211 N.Y. 406 (1914)]

            1) **"By marriage":** [§503] A relative "by marriage" means a *spouse*; it does *not* extend to the spouse's family (in-laws).

            2) **"By blood":** [§504] A "blood" relationship need not be a *legitimate* one; *i.e.,* an illegitimate child may qualify as a "family member" for this purpose. [Wigmore, §1491]

        (b) **Federal Rules include intimate associate:** [§505] The Federal Rules and the modern trend broaden the definition of "family member" to include any person "so *intimately associated* with the other's family as to be likely to have accurate information concerning the matter declared." [Fed. R. Evid. 804(b)(4)(B)]

    1)   **Example:** Included in the "intimate association" class are in-laws, housekeeper, family doctor, close friends, etc. [Annot., 15 A.L.R.2d 1412]

(2) **Proof requirement:** [§506]   There must be some *independent* proof of the declarant's relationship to the family in question; *i.e.,* there must be at least some "slight" evidence *in addition to the declarant's own assertions* as to such relationship. [Aaholm v. People, *supra*]

    (a) **Note:** Some courts extend this to require "slight" independent proof of relationship with the particular *claimant* as well. [Hankins v. United States, 67 F.2d 317 (5th Cir. 1933)]

(3) **Declarant unavailable:** [§507]   The traditional rule is that the declarant must be *dead*; but modern cases probably would recognize *insanity* or *illness* as well. The Federal Rules broaden "unavailability" to include *practical* unavailability (declarant out of jurisdiction, claiming privilege, etc.); *see supra,* §§284-293.

    (a) **Note:** Under the Federal Rules, if the declarant is merely *absent* at the time of trial, there must be some showing why his testimony could not have been obtained by *deposition or other similar means* (*see supra,* §288).

(4) **Declaration concerns "matter of family history":** [§508]   The declaration must pertain to facts of family history: births, deaths, marriages, divorces, ancestry, paternity, legitimation, etc.

    (a) **"Nonpedigree declarations":** [§509]   Statements by a declarant that he had *no* children (or other relatives) are also admissible. [*In re* Morgan's Estate, 203 Cal. 569 (1928)]

(5) **Source of declarant's knowledge:** [§510]   It is *not* required that the declarant have personal knowledge of the facts involved; declarant may be relying on his knowledge of family reputation (*see* below).

    (a) **Modern view:** Under modern rules, the declarant's statement may even be based on the *hearsay* declarations of *some other* family member (*e.g.,* "I heard my father say that P was his brother"). [Eisenlord v. Clum, 126 N.Y. 552 (1891)] Of course, such testimony would be admissible only if *both* declarants were now unavailable to testify; *see* above.

    (b) **Note:** Where the declarant's statements are based on knowledge other than his own, testimony as to the statements is really "hearsay on hearsay," but it is permissible if *both* hearsay statements qualify under this exception.

(6) **Declaration made "ante litem motam":** [§511]   In most states, it must appear that the declaration was made *before any controversy arose* (whether the controversy had ripened into a lawsuit or not) and without

any apparent motive to fabricate—*i.e.,* under circumstances assuring its trustworthiness.

    (a) **Note:** The Federal Rules drop this requirement, the theory being that pendency of litigation goes more to the *weight* than the *admissibility* of the evidence. [Fed R. Evid. 804(b)(4)]

16. **Records to Prove "Pedigree":** [§512]   Miscellaneous exceptions are recognized for various types of "pedigree" records that have inherent safeguards of accuracy and reliability:

    a. **Family records:** [§513]   Entries in family Bibles or other family books or charts or on family monuments or gravestones, and inscriptions on family photographs, wedding rings and the like are admissible as proof of *any matter of family history.* As long as properly authenticated (*infra,* §§529-530), these records are admissible proof of the facts recited, even though there is usually no proof as to who made the original entry or notation. [Fed. R. Evid. 803(13); Annot., 29 A.L.R. 372]

        (1) **Rationale:** If the entry was known to members of the family, it is assumed that they would have corrected or repudiated any errors in it ("trustworthiness" element). The unknown and probably undiscoverable identity of the entrant supplies the "necessity" factor.

        (2) **Unavailability of entrant:** [§514]   Some courts refuse to admit such records if the actual entrant (declarant) is *available.* [People v. Mayne, 118 Cal. 516 (1897); *but see* Fed. R. Evid. 803(13)—contra]

    b. **Church records:** [§515]   Most jurisdictions will also admit regularly kept records of a religious organization to establish any fact of family history (births, deaths, marriages, etc.). [Fed. R. Evid. 803(11)] (*Note:* This rule is *broader* than the typical business records or public records exception because it is *not* required that the entrant be shown to have had personal knowledge of the facts.)

        (1) **Marriage and baptismal certificates:** [§516]   Such records made by a member of the clergy authorized by a religious organization to perform such sacraments are also generally accepted as evidence of the facts therein recited. [Fed. R. Evid. 803(12)]

17. **Reputation Evidence:** [§517]   Several different types of reputation evidence may come in as exceptions to the hearsay rule:

    a. **Family reputation concerning pedigree:** [§518]   Common tradition or reputation in a family may be shown in proof of any matter of family history. [Fed. R. Evid. 803(19)]

        (1) **Rationale:** Indeed, as pointed out above, most declarations regarding pedigree are based on family reputation. A person's statements even as to her own age, birthdate, birthplace, and relationship to others are usually based on reputation in that person's family, rather than on personal knowledge.

    b. **Community reputation concerning pedigree**

        (1) **General view:** [§519]   Insofar as questions of pedigree are concerned, the weight of authority allows neighborhood or community reputation as

evidence *only* of *marriage*. [*See* Wigmore, §1602] (Some states go a little further and also allow it as evidence of birth, death, or divorce.) [Cal. Evid. Code §1314]

(2) **Federal Rules:** [§520]   However, the Federal Rules have adopted the more liberal position that community reputation may be admissible evidence to prove *any matter* of personal or family history. [Fed. R. Evid. 803(19)]

c. **Community reputation concerning character:** [§521]   As discussed previously, whenever a person's character is in issue, it is usually proved by testimony of witnesses as to that person's reputation in the community for the character trait in issue. [Fed. R. Evid. 803(20)] (*See* detailed discussion of character evidence, *supra,* §§119-184.)

d. **Community reputation concerning land boundaries:** [§522]   Community reputation is also generally held admissible in disputes concerning ***boundaries*** of public or private lands in the community. [Fed. R. Evid. 803(20)]

(1) **Limited to boundary disputes:** [§523]   Note that this exception is limited to ***boundary line*** disputes. It does ***not*** permit ***title*** to land to be proved by reputation evidence.

(2) **Reputation must precede dispute:** [§524]   It must always appear that the reputation arose ***ante litem motam***—*i.e.,* before any controversy pertaining to boundaries arose.

(a) **Additional limitation:** Some states impose the arbitrary limitation that the facts in dispute and the reputation concerning them must be at least *30* years old.

(3) **Comment:** [§525]   Where such evidence is admitted, it generally comes in through the testimony of elderly witnesses recalling statements of other elderly persons since deceased—again, an example of permissible "hearsay on hearsay."

e. **Community reputation concerning matters of general history:** [§526]   Community reputation is likewise held admissible to prove any matter of "general history" in the community (*e.g.,* the date of a hurricane long past). [Fed. R. Evid. 803(20)]

(1) **Methods of proof:** [§527]   Such reputation may be established either by ***testimony*** of witnesses or by ***accepted historical works*** (judicial notice).

18. **Ancient Documents Affecting Property:** [§528]   Declarations contained in ancient deeds, mortgages, wills, or other property-disposing documents are generally held admissible as evidence of the facts recited therein—provided the recitals were relevant to the purpose of the writing, and subsequent dealings with the property have been ***consistent*** with the facts recited. [Perry v. Parker, 141 A.2d 883 (N.H. 1958)]

a. **Authentication**

(1) **Traditional view:** [§529]   For a document to be accepted as genuine within the meaning of this exception, it must first be shown that the

document is at least **30 years old**; is **"fair on its face"** (free from suspicious appearances); **has been in proper custody**; and **has been accepted as true** by persons having an interest in the property. [Wilson v. Snow, 228 U.S. 217 (1913); Cal. Evid. Code §1331]

(2) **Modern trend (Federal Rules):** [§530]   The Federal Rules have liberalized considerably the authentication requirements for ancient documents. The Rules provide for the admissibility of:

(a) **Statements in any document in existence 20 years** or more, whose authenticity is established. [Fed. R. Evid. 803(16); Dartez v. Fibreboard Corp., 765 F.2d 456 (5th Cir. 1985)—proponent must show where documents were found]

(b) **Statements in any deed, will, etc., that relate to the purpose of the document** (disposing of any interest in property), **regardless of how long the document has been in existence**, unless "dealings with the property since the document was made have been inconsistent with the truth of the statement or the purport of the document." [Fed. R. Evid. 803(15)]

19. Learned Treatises

a. **Common law:** [§531]   Under the majority view at common law, a learned treatise is **not** admissible as substantive evidence, but can be used to cross-examine an opponent's expert (*i.e.*, to impeach) so long as it is not used for the truth of the matter asserted. For example, if the opponent's expert testified that she relied on Dr. X's treatise in forming her opinion, the cross-examiner could bring out that Dr. X's treatise actually reached a conclusion opposite from the opinion of the witness. This use of a treatise does not require a hearsay exception because the credibility of the witness is impeached without using the treatise for the truth of what it asserts.

b. **Federal Rules:** [§532]   The Federal Rules create a true hearsay exception for learned treatises. A treatise **is** admissible as **substantive evidence** and may be admitted either to **support or attack** the opinion of an expert once the treatise has been shown to be **reliable**. [Fed. R. Evid. 803(18)]

(1) **Note:** Under both the common law and Federal Rules, the pertinent statements are **read into evidence**, but the book is **not** admitted as an exhibit; admitting the work as an exhibit and allowing the jury to take it to the jury room would invite uninformed jury research not subject to adversarial protections.

c. **Statutory changes:** [§533]   A *few* states have more liberal rules. California recognizes a hearsay exception for "historical works, books of science or art, and published maps or charts, made by persons indifferent between the parties." [Cal. Evid. Code §1341] However, the statute is narrowly construed so as to exclude any controversial works, and particularly medical texts.

Former Testimony	Statement made ***under oath*** in same or at other proceeding at which the party against whom it is offered had ***motive and opportunity to develop testimony***.
Declaration Against Interest	Statement against declarant's ***pecuniary, proprietary, or penal interest when made***.
Dying Declaration	Statement made while declarant ***believed death was imminent, concerning the cause*** or ***circumstances*** of the impending death.
Excited Utterance	Statement made while ***under stress of excitement of startling event***.
Present Sense Impression	Statement made ***concurrently with perception*** of event described.
Physical Condition (State of Body)	Statement made to ***medical personnel*** for the purpose of diagnosis or treatment.
Mental Condition (State of Mind)	Statement of ***then-existing state of mind, emotion, sensation, or physical condition***. (Usually introduced to establish ***intent***. Admissible when state of mind is a material issue or to show subsequent acts of declarant.)
Past Recollection Recorded	***Writing by witness who cannot now remember*** the facts, made while the facts were fresh in her mind.
Business Records	Writing made in the ***regular course of business***, consisting of matters within the ***personal knowledge*** of one with a ***business duty*** to record. Lack of such writing may be used to show nonoccurrence of event.
Official Records	Records and reports of ***public agencies*** regarding their activities, and records of ***births, deaths, marriages***, etc. Absence of public record is admissible to show nonexistence of matter.
Judgment	A judgment of a ***prior felony conviction*** is admissible in a civil case to prove any fact essential to the judgment. In a criminal case, it may be used by the government for this purpose only against the accused.
Declaration of Family History	Statement of personal or family history (*e.g.*, birth, death, marriage) ***made by family member*** or one intimately associated with the family.
Records to Prove "Pedigree"	Statements of fact found in ***family Bibles, jewelry engravings, tombstones, etc.*** or regularly kept records of religious organizations.
Reputation	Reputation evidence concerning a person's ***character*** or ***personal or family history***, land ***boundaries***, or a community's ***general history***.
Ancient Documents	Documents ***20 years old*** or more.
Learned Treatises	Statements from ***authoritative works*** admitted if called to attention of expert witness and ***established as reliable*** authority.
Residual "Catch-All" Exception	Necessary statement with circumstantial ***guarantees of trustworthiness*** comparable to those of the above exceptions.

20. **Other Exceptions:** [§534]   The above enumeration of exceptions to the hearsay rule is not all-inclusive.

    a.   **Various other exceptions provided in the Federal Rules and other statutes**

        (1) **Market reports, etc.:** [§535]   Published quotations and compilations of information generally used and relied upon by persons in a particular occupation are admissible under a special exception to the hearsay rule (*e.g.,* commodity market reports, stock market quotes, mortality tables, cost of living indexes, etc.). [Fed. R. Evid. 803(17); Fraser-Smith Co. v. Chicago Rock Island & Pacific Railway, 435 F.2d 1396 (7th Cir. 1971); Casey v. Phillips Pipeline Co., 431 P.2d 518 (Kan. 1967)]

        (2) **Prior consistent and inconsistent statements of witness testifying:** [§536]   In a number of jurisdictions, a special exception allows evidence of prior consistent or inconsistent statements by a witness as substantive evidence (not merely to impeach or rehabilitate credibility; *see infra,* §§1081-1087).

        (3) **Affidavits:** [§537]   Special statutes permit the use of affidavits in lieu of testimony in various proceedings—*e.g.,* as proof of service of process [Fed. R. Crim. P. 4(g)], or in support of a motion for summary judgment [Fed. R. Crim. P. 56].

        (4) **Depositions and discovery:** [§538]   Answers given by a party in depositions and discovery proceedings are admissible as substantive evidence against that party. [Fed. R. Crim. P. 32]

        (5) **Forfeiture by wrongdoing:** [§539]   Hearsay is admissible against a party who has engaged or acquiesced in wrongdoing that was intended to, and did, procure the declarant's unavailability as a witness. [Fed. R. Evid. 804(b)(6)] For example, if the judge determines that the defendant murdered the declarant to prevent the declarant from testifying, the declarant's hearsay statements are admissible against the defendant.

    b.   **"Catch-all" exception under Federal Rules:** [§540]   In addition to specific hearsay exceptions, the Federal Rules create a residual or "catch-all" exception to allow other kinds of hearsay that meet the same standards of *"necessity" and "trustworthiness"* as required for the listed exceptions. [Fed. R. Evid. 807; United States v. Carlson, 547 F.2d 1346 (8th Cir. 1976)]

        (1) **Requirements**

            (a) **"Trustworthiness" factor:** [§541]   To be admissible under the catch-all exception, the hearsay must first of all have "circumstantial guarantees of trustworthiness" that are equivalent to those of the other hearsay exceptions. [*See* United States v. Love, 592 F.2d 1022 (8th Cir. 1979)]

            (b) **"Necessity" factor:** [§542]   Secondly, the hearsay must: (i) be offered as evidence of a *material* fact (which probably simply means "important," "consequential," or "central"); (ii) be *more probative* of that fact than any other evidence that the proponent could reasonably produce; *and* (iii) serve the *"interests of justice"* by its admission. [United States v. Lyon, 567 F.2d 777 (8th Cir. 1977)]

OUT-OF-COURT STATEMENTS ADMISSIBLE UNDER FEDERAL RULES

NONHEARSAY

HEARSAY EXCEPTIONS

Unavailability Required

Availability Immaterial

NONHEARSAY

1. Nonassertive Conduct

2. Statement Not Offered for Its Truth

3. Prior Inconsistent Statement Made Under Oath

4. Prior Consistent Statement Offered to Rebut Charge of Recent Fabrication

5. Prior Statement of Identification

6. Admission of Party-Opponent (including vicarious admission); Confession

Unavailability Required

1. Former Testimony

2. Declaration Against Interest

3. Dying Declaration

4. Declaration of Family History

Availability Immaterial

1. Excited Utterance

2. Present Sense Impression

3. Physical Condition (State of Body)

4. Mental Condition (State of Mind)

5. Past Recollection Recorded

6. Business Records

7. Official Records

8. Judgments

9. Records to Prove "Pedigree"

10. Reputation

11. Ancient Documents

12. Learned Treatises

(c) **Fairness to adversary:** [§543]   Finally, the proponent must give *notice to the adverse party* in advance of trial as to the nature of the hearsay (including the name and address of the declarant), to afford the opponent an opportunity to rebut. [Fed. R. Evid. 807; United States v. Davis, 571 F.2d 1354 (5th Cir. 1978)] But some federal courts have relaxed this rule to permit notice in the midst of trial. [United States v. Iaconetti, 540 F.2d 574 (2d Cir. 1976), *cert. denied,* 429 U.S. 1041 (1977)]

(d) **"Near miss" doctrine:** [§544]   Where evidence is of a type covered by a specific hearsay exception but fails to meet the exact standards for the exception, the near miss doctrine would block its admissibility under Rule 807. However, one court has distinguished between well-defined hearsay categories (*e.g.,* learned treatises) and "amorphous" categories (*e.g.,* business records or present sense impressions), *rejecting* application of the near miss doctrine to the amorphous categories lest the residual clause be negated entirely. [Zenith Radio Corp. v. Matsushita Electric Industrial Co., 505 F. Supp. 1190 (E.D. Pa. 1980)]

(2) **Criticism:** [§545]   Some commentators have criticized the catch-all provision as creating a general open-ended exception that permits the judge to admit any kind of hearsay she wants. [*See, e.g.,* Waltz & Beckley, The Exception for Great Hearsay: Some Concerned Comments, 1 Amer. J. Tr. Advocacy 123 (1977); United States v. Barnes, 586 F.2d 1052 (5th Cir. 1978)]

E.   HEARSAY AND THE RIGHT TO CONFRONTATION [§546]

In *criminal cases*, if a hearsay objection fails, the defendant sometimes has a fallback objection based on the *Confrontation Clause* of the Sixth Amendment. The Clause provides: "In all criminal prosecutions, the accused shall enjoy the right . . . to be confronted with the witnesses against him. . . ." When hearsay is used in lieu of live testimony, the defendant can argue that the hearsay declarant was a "witness" and that the defendant was deprived of the right "to be confronted." The Confrontation Clause, however, has never been interpreted to exclude all hearsay, but only hearsay considered especially dubious, dangerous, or unnecessary. Many of the most celebrated cases have been ones in which hearsay admitted in a state trial under a state law hearsay exception (perhaps a novel or broad one) has been challenged in federal court.

1.   **Two-Pronged Test of *Ohio v. Roberts*:** [§547]   The United States Supreme Court decisions on the scope of the Confrontation Clause have wavered between broad and narrow. In *Ohio v. Roberts,* 448 U.S. 56 (1980), the Court announced a broad two-pronged test for deciding whether the admission of hearsay violates the Confrontation Clause. The first prong, the *unavailability prong*, of the *Roberts* test requires that the prosecution produce the hearsay declarant or demonstrate that the declarant is unavailable. The second prong, the *reliability prong*, requires that the hearsay possess sufficient indicia of trustworthiness. Both prongs have to be satisfied before hearsay can be admitted over a Confrontation Clause challenge.

a.   **"Fine print" of *Roberts*:** The *Roberts* case itself contained qualifying language indicating that the two requirements might not be applied strictly in all cases. The Court indicated that the unavailability requirement would not apply in unusual cases where the utility of confrontation is remote. The Court further indicated that the reliability requirement would be automatically satisfied without any need for a particularized showing of trustworthiness if the hearsay falls under a *"firmly rooted"* exception to the hearsay rule. In the case of "firmly rooted" exceptions, courts are invited to take advantage of past wisdom and deem the evidence sufficiently reliable without making further inquiry. Only in cases of novel exceptions—*e.g.,* exceptions modeled on the federal "catch-all" exception—would the prosecution be required to make a specific showing that under the conditions of the particular case the hearsay is reliable. In subsequent cases, the Supreme Court has sometimes used the "fine print" of *Roberts* to water down its impact as precedent.

2. **Application of Confrontation Clause to Particular Types of Hearsay:** [§548] The question of whether the Confrontation Clause poses an obstacle to the admission of evidence differs depending on the hearsay exception that the prosecution relies on in offering the evidence. The Supreme Court has addressed several types of hearsay:

a. **Former testimony:** [§549] *Ohio v. Roberts* was a case in which the evidence offered was former testimony—*i.e.,* testimony given by a witness during the preliminary hearing in the case, later offered against the defendant at trial when the witness became unavailable. The Supreme Court's view of the scope of the precedent established by *Roberts* has wavered, and thus the *Roberts* two-pronged analysis may apply only to former testimony cases like *Roberts.* [*See* United States v. Inadi, *supra,* §351; *and see* White v. Illinois, 502 U.S. 346 (1992)—majority's language indicated that Roberts applied only to former testimony cases; *but see* Idaho v. Wright, 497 U.S. 805 (1990)—Court applied the Roberts precedent more broadly (*see* below)]

b. **Co-conspirator's statements:** [§550] The Supreme Court has held that no showing of unavailability need be made when a statement of a co-conspirator is offered against the defendant. [United States v. Inadi, *supra*] It also has held that no particularized showing of trustworthiness need be made when the prosecution offers a statement of a co-conspirator against the defendant because the co-conspirator's exception is "firmly rooted." [Bourjaily v. United States, *supra,* §351] Thus, for practical purposes, the Confrontation Clause does not pose any barrier to the admission of statements of co-conspirators so long as they are offered under an exception similar to the federal hearsay exception.

c. **Statements offered under "catch-all" exceptions:** [§551] In *Idaho v. Wright, supra,* the Court examined a child's statement concerning sexual abuse offered under a state court version of the "catch-all" or residual exception. Although the Court assumed the child to be unavailable, it nevertheless held that because the catch-all exception was not "firmly rooted," the statement was not admissible in the absence of a *particularized showing of trustworthiness*. The only evidence on trustworthiness that could be used was evidence of the circumstances surrounding the making of the statement, not other evidence corroborating the hearsay declarant's story. That meant in *Wright* that in evaluating the trustworthiness of the statement by the child about sexual abuse, physical evidence of abuse could not be used to show the trustworthiness for purposes of satisfying the Confrontation Clause.

d. **Excited utterances; statements for medical treatment:** [§552]   In *White v. Illinois, supra,* the defendant challenged the admission of statements by a child implicating him in sexual abuse. The child was not shown to be unavailable for testimony. The Court excused the prosecution from making such a showing, indicating that the unavailability prong of *Roberts* did not apply beyond the narrow facts of *Roberts* (*i.e.,* beyond situations in which the prosecution was offering former testimony as evidence). The Court also stated that the hearsay exceptions for excited utterances and statements for medical treatment were "firmly rooted" and that "where proffered hearsay has sufficient guarantees of reliability to come within a firmly rooted exception to the hearsay rule, the Confrontation Clause is satisfied."

e. **Confessions by accomplices—declarations against interest:** [§553]   In *Bruton v. United States,* 391 U.S. 123 (1968), the Court held that the Confrontation Clause prohibited using against the defendant the confession of an accomplice that he and the defendant had committed the crime. The Court also held that an instruction telling the jury only to use the confession against the person making it and not against the defendant was not sufficient to protect the defendant. If, however, the part of an accomplice's confession or other out-of-court statement that incriminates the defendant itself falls under a "firmly rooted" hearsay exception, then it will be admissible against the defendant under that exception. Some courts have considered declarations against penal interest to be "firmly rooted," even though the common law hearsay exception for declarations against interest does not cover declarations against penal interest (*see supra,* §378).

gilbert LAW SUMMARIES — CONFRONTATION CLAUSE ANALYSIS OF HEARSAY STATEMENTS

Type of Hearsay	Showing of Unavailability	Showing of Reliability/ Trustworthiness
Former Testimony	Required	Required
Co-Conspirator's Statement	Not Required	Not Required
Statement Admitted Under Catch-All Exception	Undecided	Required
Excited Utterance; Statement for Medical Treatment	Not Required	Not Required

VI. PRIVILEGE

chapter approach

Use of a privilege may be another way that relevant evidence is excluded. Questions of privilege usually reveal themselves by mention of the particular groups in the relationships covered by privileges (*e.g.*, attorneys, physicians, spouses, etc.). Where you see such groups, ask:

1. Was there a *confidential communication* of the type protected?

2. Is one of the *exceptions* to the privilege rule applicable?

3. Has the privilege been *waived* or otherwise lost?

A. INTRODUCTION

1. **"Privilege" Defined:** [§554] A privilege is a rule of law that, to protect a particular relationship or interest, either permits a witness to refrain from giving testimony he otherwise could be compelled to give, or permits someone, usually one of the parties, to prevent the witness from revealing certain information.

    a. **Enforcement of confidentiality:** [§555] A privilege can be viewed as simply one method of enforcing the broad legal guarantee of confidentiality or privacy that encourages certain relationships. This guarantee is enforceable in some contexts by a client's suit for malpractice against an overtalkative attorney, doctor, or the like, or perhaps by an injunction to prohibit disclosure. Privileges enforce the promised confidentiality by keeping confidential material out of evidence.

    b. **Strict construction of privileges:** [§556] Each recognized privilege reflects a public policy determination that the protection of the particular relationship or interest involved is more important than the testimony that the witness might otherwise give. However, since privileges operate to "shut off the light" on otherwise competent testimony, many courts construe them narrowly and give them limited application.

2. **Origin of Privileges:** [§557] Many recognized privileges developed at early common law, although several (*e.g.*, for journalists, physicians, psychotherapists, etc.) are of relatively recent statutory origin.

    a. **Majority view—judicial expansion allowed:** [§558] In most states, the rules of privileges are subject to judicial expansion, as are other common law principles. The Federal Rules (below) adopt this approach, by providing that federal courts shall interpret the common law privileges "in the light of reason and experience." [Fed. R. Evid. 501; *and see* United States v. Allery, 526 F.2d 1362 (8th Cir. 1975)]

    b. **Minority rule—no new privileges:** [§559] In some states, only those privileges set forth by statute are recognized, thus precluding judicial recognition of new privileges. [*See, e.g.*, Cal. Evid. Code §911]

3. **In Federal Courts:** [§560]   The Federal Rules contain no specific privilege provisions. Rather, they provide that federal courts shall apply the rules of privilege developed at common law, except that they must look to state rules of privilege in diversity cases. [Fed. R. Evid. 501; Richards of Rockford, Inc. v. Pacific Gas & Electric Co., 71 F.R.D. 388 (2d Cir. 1976)]

   a. **Federal question cases:** [§561]   The reason for Congress's failure to develop statutory rules of privilege in federal question cases was its inability to agree on specific rules for such cases. It concluded that the issues were not sufficiently defined for rules to be fixed in advance and that such rules would be better left to common law development by the courts. [Lewis v. Radcliff Materials, Inc., 74 F.R.D. 102 (5th Cir. 1977)]

   b. **Diversity cases:** [§562]   The rationale for having state law govern in diversity cases is that a witness's ability to testify may often affect the outcome of the case, and therefore should be governed by state law whenever it otherwise provides the rule of decision (as it does in diversity jurisdiction cases). The rule thus discourages *"forum shopping"* between the federal and state courts. (*See* discussion of the *Erie* doctrine in Civil Procedure Summary.) [Republic Gear Co. v. Borg-Warner Corp., 381 F.2d 551 (5th Cir. 1967); *and see* Scott v. McDonald, 70 F.R.D. 568 (2d Cir. 1976)]

B.   GENERAL PRINCIPLES APPLICABLE TO ALL PRIVILEGES

1. **Who May Assert Privilege—In General**

   a. **Holder of privilege:** [§563]   A privilege is *personal* in nature; *i.e.*, it can be claimed only by the *"holder"*—the person whose interest or relationship is sought to be protected (client, patient, etc.). If the privilege is held *jointly* by two or more persons, *each* of them can claim the privilege.

   b. **Authorized persons:** [§564]   A privilege may also be asserted by a person authorized to do so on behalf of the holder.

      (1) **Example:** If the holder is legally incompetent, her guardian can assert (or waive) the privilege. Similarly, since privileges generally "survive" the death of the holder, they can be asserted (or waived) by the holder's executor or administrator.

         (a) **Exceptions:** There are some exceptions, however; *e.g.*, the privilege to withhold confidential communications between spouses terminates in some states on the death of either spouse, and some states provide that privileges do not survive the winding up of the holder's estate.

      (2) **Note:** The person with whom the confidence was shared may, in certain cases, claim the privilege on behalf of the holder (*e.g.*, attorney is authorized to assert client's privilege in the latter's absence; *see infra*, §587).

   c. **Absence of holder—court or other party may assert:** [§565]   Although a privilege is personal, if neither the holder of the privilege (nor anyone entitled to assert it for her) is present when the testimony is sought to be introduced, then the court on its own motion, or the motion of any party, must exclude the testimony subject to the claim of privilege. [Cal. Evid. Code §916] However, if the privilege is erroneously ignored, only the holder has the right to claim error.

    d.   **Persons to whom privileged communications made:** [§566] In some cases, the person to whom the privileged statements were made may assert the privilege for an absent holder as long as the holder is *alive* and has not *waived* the privilege. For example, an attorney to whom confidential communications were made may assert the privilege on behalf of an absent, living client.

2.   **Requirement of Confidentiality—Presumption:** [§567] Where a communication is claimed to be privileged, it must always be shown that it was made in *confidence*. Note, however, that many states recognize a *presumption* that disclosures made in the course of a *privileged relationship* (*i.e.*, between attorney and client, etc.) were made in confidence. [*See, e.g.*, Cal. Evid. Code §917]

3.   **Effect of Claiming Privilege:** [§568] Most courts today recognize that no inference should be drawn from the fact that a witness has claimed a privilege, either during the present trial or on any previous occasion.

    a.   **Argument to jury prohibited:** [§569] Accordingly, neither counsel nor the trial judge may make any comment or argument to the jury based on such claim of privilege (*e.g.*, the prosecution may not argue, "If the defendant didn't confess to his attorney, why did he object when I attempted to call the attorney as a witness?"). [Cal. Evid. Code §913]

        (1) **Rationale:** To permit such argument would undermine the privilege.

        (2) **Constitutional implications:** The rule is of constitutional dimension where the privilege claimed is against self-incrimination (*see infra*, §583).

    b.   **Instruction to jury:** [§570] If the party against whom the adverse inference might be drawn so requests, the trial judge must instruct the jury not to draw any inference from the fact that a witness has exercised a privilege.

        (1) **But note:** Such a request is not always made; often that party will not want to call any further attention to the situation.

4.   **Waiver:** [§571] Waiver of particular privileges is discussed in detail below. However, the following types of waiver are applicable to all privileges.

    a.   **By failure to object:** [§572] As with other exclusionary rules of evidence, privileges are deemed waived if not raised by *appropriate and timely objection* when the testimony is first offered.

        (1) **Specific objection:** [§573] As noted *supra* (§§39-43), the objection must be specific; the general objection "incompetent, irrelevant, and immaterial" will not suffice. [People v. Rulia Singh, 182 Cal. 457 (1920)]

    b.   **By consent:** [§574] Moreover, a person entitled to claim a privilege may waive it by consent. Such consent may be manifested by:

(1) *Failure to claim the privilege* where the holder has the legal standing and opportunity to claim the privilege;

(2) *Voluntary disclosure by the holder* (or by anyone if with the holder's consent) of all or a significant part of the privileged matter—except where the disclosure is itself privileged (*e.g.*, D tells a priest what D previously told her attorney) [*See* Cal. Evid. Code §912; Velsicol Chemical Corp. v. Parsons, 561 F.2d 671 (7th Cir. 1977)]; or

(3) *Contractual provision* waiving in advance the right to claim the privilege (*e.g.*, as a condition of receiving disability or life insurance, the insured often must agree to waive the physician-patient privilege should any litigation on the policy become necessary).

c. **Compare—no waiver**

(1) **Privilege erroneously denied:** [§575] However, there is no waiver where the disclosure was compelled erroneously or made without opportunity for the holder to claim the privilege. Hence, evidence obtained in an earlier trial or proceeding in which the witness's claim of privilege was erroneously denied cannot be used in a later trial. [Cal. Evid. Code §919]

(2) **Joint holders:** [§576] Where a privilege is held jointly (*e.g.*, two persons consult a lawyer together), a waiver of the privilege by one holder does not affect the right of the other to claim the privilege. [Cal. Evid. Code §912(c)]

(3) **Wrongful disclosure:** [§577] Where someone wrongfully discloses privileged information without the holder's consent, there is no waiver. Hence, even if the privileged material becomes public knowledge because of the disclosing party's wrongful act, the holder will be protected from the additional injury of having the information revealed in court.

5. **Effect of Eavesdroppers**

a. **Traditional view—testimony allowed:** [§578] The traditional view is that an eavesdropper can testify to what he has overheard—whether or not such overhearing was due to the carelessness of the communicating parties. [63 A.L.R. 107; *and see* United States v. Landof, 591 F.2d 36 (9th Cir. 1978)]

(1) **Rationale:** Some courts rationalize their admission of eavesdropper testimony on the theory that the holder of the privilege was responsible for taking precautions to safeguard the confidentiality of the communications, and therefore must be deemed to have *"waived"* the privilege. Other courts regard privilege simply as a method of silencing particular people (such as one's attorney or physician), and hence do not apply the prohibition on testifying to eavesdroppers.

(2) **Limitations:** [§579] Statutory and constitutional limitations applicable to wiretapping and illegal searches may prevent testimony from a police

officer, or person working in conjunction with the police, who used electronic or other improper means to eavesdrop on a confidential communication. This is true even where there is no privilege. (*See* Criminal Procedure Summary.)

b.   **Modern trend contra:** [§580]   A significant number of modern cases and statutes assert that as long as the holder of the privilege was not *negligent* (*i.e.*, had no reasonable basis to believe that the communication would be overheard), there is *no "waiver"* of the privilege and hence the eavesdropper is not permitted to testify. [*See, e.g.*, Cal. Evid. Code §954]

6. **Appeal of Erroneous Rulings on Privilege**

a.   **Disclosure erroneously compelled:** [§581]   The prevailing view is that only the *holder* of the privilege—whose confidence has been violated—has a right to complain where disclosure of the privileged matter was (i) compelled erroneously or (ii) made without opportunity to claim the privilege.

(1)   **Effect:** A party may predicate error on the court's ruling admitting the privileged information only if the party is the holder of the privilege; *i.e.*, violation of a *third person's* privilege is not grounds for appeal by either of the parties. [Cal. Evid. Code §918]

b.   **Privilege erroneously sustained:** [§582]   Of course, if a claim of privilege by any person is erroneously *sustained* (*i.e.*, the evidence is excluded), the losing party can *always* base an appeal on that ground. [McCormick, §73]

7. **Constitutional Limitations on Claim of Privilege:** [§583]   In a criminal case, a claim of privilege may be denied if its exercise would deprive the accused of the right to present her defense.

a.   **Rationale:** Policy considerations supporting the privilege may be held outweighed by the accused's constitutional right to present a defense under the Sixth and Fourteenth Amendments.

b.   **Example:** D was charged with murdering his wife, W. D's defense was insanity, which he sought to prove by calling the marriage counselor whom he and W had consulted shortly before her death. *Held:* The counselor was compelled to testify notwithstanding a statutory privilege for marriage counselors. [State v. Roma, 357 A.2d 37 (N.J. 1926)]

(1)   **Note:** How an individual's constitutional rights affect a claim of privilege is still a developing area of the law, and many jurisdictions would handle the above case simply by saying that the wife's privilege *died* with her and that the husband could waive his own privilege (*see infra*, §695).

(2)   **Comment:** A harder question would arise if D attempted to subpoena the attorney of a person *unrelated* to the legal proceedings to show that this person had confessed committing the crime to the attorney. It is possible that the attorney-client privilege would *not* apply in this case. However, cases on this issue are not numerous because serious hearsay problems generally exclude such evidence.

C. SPECIFIC PRIVILEGES

1. **Attorney-Client Privilege:** [§584]   The attorney-client privilege is the oldest privilege recognized at common law. The purpose of the privilege, of course, is to encourage full disclosure by a client to her attorney of all pertinent matters, so as to further the administration of justice. A high percentage of all privilege cases deal with the attorney-client privilege.

   a. **Rule:** [§585]   A client, whether or not a party to the litigation, has a privilege to refuse to disclose, and to prevent her attorney or anyone else from disclosing, any confidential communication made between the client and the attorney related to the rendering of legal services. [Cal. Evid. Code §954]

   b. **Actions in which assertable:** [§586]   The privilege is generally recognized in all actions, civil and criminal (although a few states limit it to criminal).

   c. **Who may assert:** [§587]   The privilege clearly belongs to the *client*, not the attorney (although the attorney is authorized to assert it on behalf of the client in the latter's absence).

      (1) **Client waiver:** [§588]   Therefore, if the client consents (or waives the privilege), the attorney may not withhold the communication; the attorney has no privilege. [United States v. Juarez, 573 F.2d 267 (5th Cir. 1978)]

      (2) **Client deceased or incompetent:** [§589]   If the client is deceased, the privilege may be asserted (or waived) by the client's executor or administrator, and if the client is incompetent, by the client's guardian or conservator. [Cal. Evid. Code §953]

      (3) **Improper disclosure by attorney:** [§590]   Since the privilege belongs to the client, improper disclosures by the attorney do *not* "waive" the privilege. The client can still prevent not only the attorney, but any person to whom the attorney has revealed the privileged information from testifying (assuming such statements could overcome the hearsay rule).

   d. **Requirements:** [§591]   Case law has developed strict and exacting requirements as to when the privilege can be claimed. The burden is on the holder to show that these requirements have been met.

      (1) **Client:** [§592]   There must have been a client who directly, or through an authorized representative, consulted a lawyer for the purpose of securing legal advice. The client may be a natural person, corporation, association, or public or private entity. [Cal. Evid. Code §951]

         (a) **Corporate client:** [§593]   Where the client is a corporation or other entity that can communicate only through its officers or employees, it becomes necessary to determine whose communications will be deemed protected by the privilege.

            1) **Statements of corporate officials and employees:** [§594]   Until recently, authorities were split on the matter of whose statements were protected by the privilege. Some cases held

that only statements of **high corporate officials** belonging to the *"control group"* of the corporation were protected. [City of Philadelphia v. Westinghouse, 210 F. Supp. 483 (E.D. Pa. 1962)] Other courts held that the statements of a somewhat **broader** group of corporate officers were protected. [Diversified Industries, Inc. v. Meredith, 572 F.2d 596 (8th Cir. 1978)]

a) **Modern rule:** [§595]   The United States Supreme Court has **rejected** the "control group" test and held that the privilege protects the statements of **any** corporate officials or employees made to counseling attorneys as long as the officials or employees are **authorized** or **directed** by the corporation to make such communications. [Upjohn Co. v. United States, 449 U.S. 383 (1981)]

1/ **Rationale:** This broader rule is based on the notion that certain information necessary for adequate legal advice may be possessed by employees outside the "control group."

2) **Employee's statement outside scope of duties:** [§596]   Where the employee gives an **ordinary** witness statement—*i.e.*, one which the scope of the job does not require the employee to prepare—to the corporation's attorney (or an investigator acting on the attorney's behalf) such statement is **not** privileged—even if the employer has asked (or required) the witness-employee to make the statement. [D.I. Chadbourne, Inc. v. Superior Court, 60 Cal. 2d 723 (1964)]

3) **Privilege is corporation's, not employee's:** [§597]   Where the employee communicates with the corporation's counsel in a **representative** rather than personal capacity, the privilege is the **corporation's**, not the individual employee's. [*In re* Grand Jury Proceedings (Jackier), 434 F. Supp. 648 (E.D. Mich. 1977)]

(2) **Attorney:** [§598]   The second requirement for the attorney-client privilege is that the communication must have been made to a **member of the Bar**, or to a subordinate (*e.g.*, a secretary, law clerk, etc.) for transmission to the lawyer.

(a) **Note:** Under the better view, it is sufficient if the communication is made to a person the client reasonably believes is a lawyer—even though in fact the person is not. [*But see* Dabney v. Investment Corp. of America, 82 F.R.D. 464 (E.D. Pa. 1979)—unsupervised law student, no privilege]

(3) **Professional consultation:** [§599]   The communication must have been made to the attorney in his legal capacity, and for the purpose of securing a legal opinion or legal services. Thus, the privilege does not apply to communications made while consulting a lawyer to obtain accounting services, etc. [Clayton v. Canida, 223 S.W.2d 264 (Tex. 1949)] Nor does the privilege apply to communications made while consulting an attorney for **business** advice, as distinguished from **legal** advice.

(a) **Actual employment not necessary:** [§600]   Any communications made in *consulting* the attorney are privileged, even if the attorney later declines the case or the client decides against hiring that attorney.

(4) **Communication:** [§601]   Another requirement is that there must have been a "communication"—an expression intended to convey a *specific meaning*—between client and attorney. Such communications include disclosures made by the client to the attorney, as well as the attorney's legal opinion and advice to the client based thereon. [Cal. Evid. Code §952]

(a) **Observations not privileged:** [§602]   An attorney's *observations* of the client's mental or physical condition, etc., are not within the privilege because no *communication* is involved. [Oliver v. Warren, 16 Cal. App. 164 (1911)]

1) **Minority view:** [§603]   *A minority of cases are contra*, holding that any knowledge gained by the attorney is privileged—whether a communication from the client or the attorney's own observation of the client's condition. [Taylor v. Sheldon, 173 N.E.2d 892 (Ohio 1961)]

(b) **Identity not privileged:** [§604]   Ordinarily, the identity of the client is not a "communication" and hence not privileged; *i.e.*, the attorney can be compelled to identify whom he represents. [114 A.L.R. 1321]

1) **But note:** Where the only purpose of identification would be to prove guilt of the client in the very matter on which the attorney is employed, then the privilege may apply. [Baird v. Koerner, 279 F.2d 623 (9th Cir. 1960)—attorney privileged to refuse to identify client upon whose behalf he had paid delinquent taxes to government; government demanded identity of taxpayer, obviously wishing to audit his tax return]

(c) **Fact of consultation not privileged:** [§605]   The fact that a client obtained a lawyer is not itself privileged.

1) **Compare:** However, the retention of a lawyer by a client at a late hour immediately after a crime was discovered has been held inadmissible—not because privileged, but because admission of this evidence would interfere with the client's Sixth Amendment right to counsel. [United States v. Liddy, 509 F.2d 428 (D.C. Cir. 1974)]

(d) **Documents**

1) **Preexisting documents:** [§606]   Preexisting books, records, and papers turned over by the client to the attorney do not become privileged merely because they are given to provide the attorney with information. Nor is there a privilege where the attorney is merely to act as custodian of such documents. [Collette v. Sarrasin, 184 Cal. 283 (1920)]

2) **Documents prepared by client:** [§607]   Where a document is prepared by the client *for the purpose* of giving an attorney information, that document will be privileged.

   a) **Information in document:** [§608]   The information in the document will also be privileged as long as that information comes from the document. If the information is derived from any other source, the fact that it is also contained in the document prepared for and given to the attorney does not make it privileged.

   b) **Other real evidence not privileged:** [§609]   Other real evidence (*e.g.*, a suspected murder weapon) is not a "communication"; hence the attorney can be forced to turn it over. (Under some circumstances, an attorney may have an ethical obligation to turn over such evidence. *See* Legal Ethics Summary.)

3) **Documents prepared by attorney:** [§610]   Documents, correspondence, or other items prepared by the attorney for her own use (research memos, witness statements, etc.) are *not* protected by the attorney-client privilege because they are not "communications" to or from the client.

   a) **Work product:** [§611]   However, it is recognized that the attorney has a right of privacy as to her "work product"; hence, even though not privileged per se, such items are not subject to discovery by the adversary unless "good cause" is first shown—*i.e.*, a qualified protection exists. [Hickman v. Taylor, 329 U.S. 495 (1947); *and see* Civil Procedure Summary]

   b) **Privileged information protected:** [§612]   Of course, if such documents contain privileged information, those parts will be privileged.

(e) **Fee information not privileged:** [§613]   The amount of fees, and the facts regarding payment thereof, ordinarily are not "communications" and so are not privileged. [United States v. Pape, 144 F.2d 778 (2d Cir. 1944)]

(5) **Confidential:** [§614]   The last requirement for the privilege is that the communication must have been made *outside the presence of strangers* and have seemed of a type reasonably *expected* to be kept secret.

(a) **Presumption of confidentiality:** [§615]   In many states, a presumption exists that *any* communication between attorney and client was made in confidence. [*See, e.g.*, Cal. Evid. Code §917]

(b) **Presence of persons furthering client's interest:** [§616]   Statements made in front of *third persons* whose presence is *reasonably necessary* to the consultation (*e.g.*, client's spouse, parent, business associate, or joint client) are still treated as "confidential." [Cal. Evid. Code §952]

(c) **Eavesdroppers:** [§617] For effect of eavesdroppers, *see supra*, §§578-580.

(d) **Communications through agents:** [§618] Communications made to third persons are "confidential" if reasonably required for the purpose of transmitting information between lawyer and client. *Examples:*

1) **Secretary, messenger, interpreter:** Statements transmitted by the attorney's secretary or by a messenger of the client; or communication through an interpreter (as where the client does not speak English, or a case involving a document in a foreign language) are confidential.

2) **Accountant:** Likewise, information transmitted to an attorney by the client's accountant or tax adviser (in a sense acting as interpreters of the client's records or business problems) is confidential. [United States v. Kovel, 296 F.2d 918 (2d Cir. 1961)]

3) **Physician:** Where an attorney employs a physician to examine the client, the physician's report may *not* be privileged under the physician-patient privilege because no treatment is contemplated (*see infra*, §641). But if the examination is required to enable the client to *communicate her condition* to the attorney, the attorney-client privilege applies. The doctor is deemed the agent of the client to interpret and communicate the client's condition to the attorney. [Edney v. Smith, 425 F. Supp. 1038 (E.D.N.Y. 1976); City & County of San Francisco v. Superior Court, 37 Cal. 2d 227 (1951)]

4) **Liability insurance company:** A client's liability insurance company (indemnifying her from liability to others) and its employees (*e.g.*, investigators) are generally deemed the client's agents for purposes of "communicating" with the attorneys defending the client in a liability action. (But the number of hands through which the communication may travel without losing confidentiality depends on the reason and the facts of the particular case.) [People v. Alotes, 60 Cal. 2d 723 (1964)]

5) **Another lawyer:** Similarly, communications made by the client or the client's lawyer to a lawyer representing another "in a matter of common interest" are generally held privileged. This covers, for example, communications among counsel representing co-plaintiffs or co-defendants in the same litigation.

e. **Exceptions:** [§619] There are various situations in which, for overriding policy reasons, the attorney-client privilege is held *"waived"* or simply not applicable.

(1) **Communications of proposed fraud or crime:** [§620] No privilege exists for communications made to enable the client (or attorney) to perpetrate a proposed crime or fraud. Hence, while communications made after the wrongful act are privileged, those made beforehand (in contemplation of the fraud or crime) are not. [United States v. Hodge and Zweig, 548 F.2d 1347 (9th Cir. 1977); Cal. Evid. Code §956]

(a) **Rationale:** The privilege exists to enable an accused to defend herself as to past acts—not to assist her in future crimes.

(b) **Compare—past crime:** [§621]   Where a client admits to an attorney that she is guilty of a crime, but nonetheless wishes the attorney to defend her, the admission is privileged.

    1)   According to the weight of authority, such privilege is *not* lost even if the defendant tells the attorney that she plans to commit the crime of *perjury* in maintaining her innocence of the past crime.

    2)   However, the attorney in this situation has a duty to *disassociate* from the client if possible. (In most such cases withdrawal is not possible, either because the judge will not allow substitution of another attorney—who would have the same problem— or because the attorney is a public defender required to defend indigent defendants.)

    3)   If the attorney is told *before* being retained that the client expects to commit perjury, the attorney has a duty not to take the case.

(c) **In camera disclosure:** [§622]   Often it is necessary for a trial court to know the contents of a communication in order to ascertain whether it was made in furtherance of a future crime or fraud. The fact that a party claims that a document or other communication is privileged does not conclusively make the communication privileged. If the party seeking discovery of the communication makes a preliminary showing of a good faith reason to believe that the communication was made in furtherance of a crime or fraud, the trial court has the authority to examine the contents of the communication *in camera* (privately) to determine whether it was made in furtherance of a crime or fraud. [United States v. Zolin, 491 U.S. 554 (1989)]

    1)   **Example:** One party claims that letters the other party sent to her attorney were sent in furtherance of a crime or fraud. The party resisting discovery of the letters claims that they are privileged. In this case, the court can examine the communications in camera to determine if they are privileged.

(2) **Communications to attorney representing joint clients:** [§623]   Where the attorney is the legal adviser of both parties to a transaction, communications from either client relating to a matter of common interest are not privileged from disclosure in later litigation between those clients. [141 A.L.R. 553] Of course, the communications would still be privileged as to any *third party*. [Doll v. Loesel, 136 A. 796 (Pa. 1927); Cal. Evid. Code §912]

(3) **Breach of duty by lawyer or client:** [§624]   If an issue is raised as to the attorney's breach of duty to a client (claims of malpractice, etc.), or

by the client to the attorney (nonpayment of fees), the attorney may testify as to the relevant communications between himself and the client. [Cal. Evid. Code §958]

(a) **Application:** This exception applies in litigation between the attorney and client, or involving any third party, in which the attorney's breach of duty is claimed (*e.g.*, P sues Attorney on contract that Attorney claims to have executed solely on behalf of Client). [Pacific Telephone & Telegraph Co. v. Fink, 141 Cal. App. 2d 332 (1956)]

(4) **Communications in connection with decedent's will:** [§625] As already indicated, the attorney-client privilege survives the death of the client; her personal representative may assert the privilege (*see supra*, §589). However, the privilege is held not applicable in certain cases involving the decedent's will.

(a) **Attorney as subscribing witness:** [§626] A client who requested the attorney to witness the will is deemed thereby to "waive" the privilege as to any testimony necessary to establish the will. The attorney thus can testify to all of the facts and circumstances surrounding the execution of the will, including the decedent's statements of intent and competence at the time of execution, but *not* to other communications **unrelated** to being an attesting witness. [Bradway v. Thompson, 214 S.W. 27 (Ark. 1919); Cal. Evid. Code §959]

1) **Compare:** Under some rules, this exception is expanded to include any deed, conveyance, or other document executed by the decedent during her lifetime to which the attorney was an attesting witness. [*See* Cal. Evid. Code §960]

(b) **Litigation among heirs:** [§627] Moreover, it is generally held that the privilege does *not* apply in will contests, petitions to determine heirship, or other controversies among parties all claiming as heirs of the client-testator. In such cases, the parties are all deemed *"in privity"* with the decedent, so that there is no unauthorized disclosure in permitting the attorney to testify as to the decedent's declarations. [Cal. Evid. Code §957]

1) **Rationale:** The theory in will contests is that the client would have wanted her intention to govern and hence would have authorized the attorney to testify.

2) **Note:** Similarly, even where there is no will, the law *fictionalizes* that the deceased client would have wanted all facts known so that proper disposition under the law could be made.

(5) **Public officials:** [§628] In response to Watergate, the Uniform Rules of Evidence were amended to *limit* the attorney-client privilege to *private affairs*. Uniform Rule 802(c)(6) provides that there is no privilege as to communications made by a public official to counsel on matters of public interest except where there is a showing that disclosure would *"seriously impair"* the functioning of some governmental agency or proceeding.

(a) **Note:** Whether the courts would generally follow this provision as a matter of common law is not clear.

(b) **And note:** Even if the attorney-client privilege does not apply, there may be other governmental privileges that do.

(c) **Application:** For a celebrated and controversial federal case concerning a public official and the attorney-client privilege, *see In re Grand Jury Subpoena Duces Tecum*, 112 F.3d 910 (8th Cir.), *cert. denied*, 117 S. Ct. 2482 (1997)—court agreed with Special Prosecutor that privilege does not cover consultation of public official with government attorney where information is sought by grand jury.

2. **Physician-Patient Privilege:** [§629]   The physician-patient privilege is statutory in origin and was not recognized at common law. It is based on the policy of encouraging full disclosure between physician and patient, so as to aid in the effective treatment of illness. [47 Cal. L. Rev. 783 (1959)]

   a. **Rule:** [§630]   A patient, whether or not a party to the action, has a privilege to refuse to disclose, and to prevent his physician from disclosing, any information acquired by the physician in confidence while attending the patient. [Cal. Evid. Code §994]

   b. **Actions in which assertable:** [§631]   Most states permit the assertion of the privilege in *civil actions* only. [7 A.L.R.3d 1458; *and see* Cal. Evid. Code §998]

   c. **Who may assert:** [§632]   The privilege clearly belongs to the ***patient***, not the physician, and the physician may thus be compelled to testify if the patient has waived the privilege. [Cal. Evid. Code §993]

      (1) **Patient not present:** [§633]   In most states, if the patient is not present, the doctor is authorized (and is ethically obligated) to assert the privilege on the patient's behalf. [*See, e.g.*, Cal. Evid. Code §995]

      (2) **Patient incompetent or deceased:** [§634]   If the patient is incompetent, the privilege may be asserted by the patient's guardian; or if the patient is deceased, it may be asserted by his personal representative (*see supra*, §564).

   d. **Requirements:** [§635]   The following must be established to justify assertion of the privilege:

      (1) **Physician:** [§636]   Some cases hold that the privilege does not apply if the "physician" is not licensed to practice. However, the better view is that the privilege applies if the patient reasonably believes that the person he is consulting is a licensed physician. [Arizona & New Mexico Railway v. Clark, 207 F. 817 (9th Cir. 1913); Cal. Evid. Code §990]

      (2) **Subject matter:** [§637]   The privilege applies not only to "communications" between doctor and patient, but to any information obtained by the doctor in the course of examination or treatment which would normally be regarded as confidential. [Cal. Evid. Code §992]

(a) **Tests, X-rays:** [§638]   The privilege would thus cover the results of laboratory tests, X-rays, etc.

(b) **Advice, diagnosis:** [§639]   The privilege also covers advice given by the physician to the patient, as well as the doctor's diagnosis and opinions based upon the examination (whether or not communicated to the patient).

(c) **Incidental information:** [§640]   However, incidental information obtained in the course of treatment—name and address of patient, occupation, age, fees, dates of treatment, etc.—would probably *not* be privileged, because this information is not normally regarded as confidential. [79 A.L.R. 1131]

(3) **Professional consultation:** [§641]   In most states, the privilege applies only to information obtained by a physician in the course of *consultation* for the purpose of *obtaining treatment*.

(a) **Example:** When a doctor is appointed by the court, or an adverse party, to make an examination or diagnosis as the basis for testimony in court (no treatment for patient intended), there is no privilege. [107 A.L.R. 1495] The same is true where the doctor is employed by the patient's attorney. (But here, the report may be privileged under the attorney-client privilege, *see supra*, §§584 *et seq.*)

(b) **Example:** Likewise, examinations for life insurance are not privileged. [McGinty v. Brotherhood of Railway Trainmen, 164 N.W. 249 (Wis. 1917)]

(c) **But note:** Some states do extend the privilege to information obtained in consultation for treatment "or diagnosis." [*See, e.g.,* Cal. Evid. Code §991]

e. **Exceptions:** [§642]   As indicated above, the privilege is generally limited to civil actions. Its principal application is in domestic relations cases. Most other civil actions are treated as "exceptions" to which the privilege does not apply:

(1) **Personal injury suit by patient:** [§643]   No privilege may be claimed in a personal injury suit brought by the patient (or in a wrongful death action brought by the patient's estate). [Cal. Evid. Code §996]

(a) **Rationale:** The whole purpose of the privilege is to preclude humiliation, which might be caused by disclosure of the patient's condition. If the patient (or the patient's estate) places such matters in issue, the purpose does not apply.

(b) **Note—extension of exception:** Some states extend this exception to any case in which the patient, or anyone claiming through the patient, tenders an issue as to the patient's condition—*e.g.*, including workers' compensation proceedings and claims on life insurance contracts on patient's life. [*See, e.g.,* Cal. Evid. Code §996]

(2) **Competency, guardianship, and commitment proceedings:** [§644] The privilege does not apply in competency, guardianship, or commitment proceedings affecting the patient. [*See* Cal. Evid. Code §§1004-1005]

(3) **Deceased patient:** [§645] The privilege does not apply in contests involving the patient's will. Nor does it apply in any action involving the validity of a deed or conveyance executed by the now-deceased patient or concerning the decedent's intentions with regard thereto, nor in any proceeding in which all parties are claiming through the deceased patient. [Cal. Evid. Code §1000]

(4) **Malpractice cases:** [§646] The patient cannot assert the privilege to prevent the physician from testifying in any case in which the patient has asserted a claim against the doctor for breach of duty arising from the physician-patient relationship. [Cal. Evid. Code §1001]

(5) **Illegal purpose:** [§647] Also, no privilege exists where the services of the physician were sought to assist anyone to plan or commit a crime or tort. [Cal. Evid. Code §997]

   (a) **Note:** This exception is *broader* than the "crime or fraud" exception to the attorney-client privilege (*see supra*, §620).

(6) **Comment on exceptions:** [§648] Note that the many restrictions on the physician-patient privilege—particularly those making it inapplicable to criminal proceedings and plaintiffs in personal injury actions—leave a relatively narrow field where the privilege might be applicable.

   (a) **Application:** One of the most common applications is in cases where the plaintiff wishes to *tender an issue* about the *defendant's physical condition* (*e.g.*, "the defendant's eyesight was so bad that his mere driving was negligence").

   (b) **Compare:** However, some states allow the judge discretion to hold the privilege inapplicable even in this type of case. [*See, e.g.*, Cal. Evid. Code §999]

f. **Waiver**

(1) **By contract:** [§649] Contractual provisions waiving the privilege in any litigation arising under the contract (often found in insurance applications) are usually upheld. But such waivers are strictly construed. [54 A.L.R. 412]

(2) **By calling physician to testify:** [§650] The patient's calling the doctor as a witness obviously constitutes a waiver. [158 A.L.R. 215]

   (a) **Complete waiver:** [§651] The patient cannot claim the privilege as to certain examinations and call the doctor to testify only with regard to other examinations; calling the doctor as a witness waives the privilege *entirely*. [Lissak v. Crocker Estate Co., 119 Cal. 442 (1897)]

(3) **By patient testifying:** [§652]   Likewise, it is generally held that a patient who testifies as to a consultation with a doctor can be cross-examined thereon. The *doctor* may also then be compelled to testify. [114 A.L.R. 798]

    (a) **Note:** There is a split of authority as to whether the patient's testimony as to his mere physical condition (without mentioning the privileged communication with the doctor) constitutes a waiver. [*See* 25 A.L.R.3d 1401]

(4) **By making disclosures to third persons:** [§653]   Where the communication is made in the presence of *unnecessary* third persons, the privilege is waived entirely so that anyone present can testify. [*See* 25 A.L.R.3d 1401]

    (a) **Compare:** But disclosure by the physician to subordinates or to consultants working on the case does not destroy the privilege; the patient can prevent them from testifying. [Ostrowski v. Mockridge, 65 N.W.2d 185 (Minn. 1954)]

    (b) **Note:** Similarly, disclosure of privileged information to a health care plan for billing and payment purposes is not a waiver of the privilege. [BlueCross v. Superior Court, 61 Cal. App. 3d 798 (1976)]

    (c) **But note:** A number of cases have held that nurses, interns, or doctors on the staff of a hospital to which the patient has been sent by his physician may testify as to information taken from the hospital records—on the basis that such personnel are not "attending" the patient. [169 A.L.R. 678; Frederick v. Federal Life Insurance Co., 13 Cal. App. 2d 585 (1936)]

3. **Psychotherapist-Patient Privilege:** [§654]   Most American jurisdictions recognize a psychotherapist-patient privilege, on the rationale that full disclosure between psychotherapist and patient is necessary for the treatment of mental and emotional illnesses. [*See* Cal. Evid. Code §1010; *and see* Jaffee v. Redmond, 518 U.S. 1 (1996)]

    a. **Rule:** [§655]   A patient can refuse to disclose confidential communications between the patient and a psychotherapist made for the purpose of diagnosing or treating his mental or emotional condition. The patient also can prevent testimony by the psychotherapist or by any other person participating in such diagnosis or treatment under the psychotherapist's direction—*e.g.*, members of the patient's family or possibly members of therapy groups. [Cal. Evid. Code §1014; *and see* Ellis v. Ellis, 472 S.W.2d 741 (Tenn. 1971)]

    b. **Actions in which assertable:** [§656]   The privilege applies to *any litigation*—civil or criminal (whereas the physician-patient privilege is generally recognized only in civil proceedings). Also, it applies whether or not the patient is a party to such proceedings.

    c. **Who may assert:** [§657]   The privilege belongs to the *patient* (not the psychotherapist). However, if the patient is absent, the psychotherapist can assert it on the patient's behalf. [Cal. Evid. Code §1015]

(1) **Patient deceased or incompetent:** [§658]   If the patient is dead or incompetent, the privilege can be asserted by the patient's executor or guardian, etc.

(2) **"Psychotherapist":** [§659]   The "psychotherapist" need not be a licensed physician; the privilege applies to certified psychologists [Cal. Evid. Code §1010] and, in many jurisdictions, to other therapists—*e.g.*, to psychiatric social workers [*see* Jaffee v. Redmond, *supra*].

d. **Exceptions:** [§660]   The psychotherapist privilege is broader than the physician privilege; *i.e.*, fewer exceptions are recognized.

  (1) **Commitment proceedings against patient:** [§661]   If the psychotherapist has determined that the patient is in need of hospitalization for mental illness, she may testify. [Cal. Evid. Code §1024—this exception limited to cases where patient is dangerous to himself or others]

  (2) **Court-ordered examinations:** [§662]   Communications by the patient in the course of a court-ordered mental examination are *not* privileged.

  (3) **Mental condition in issue:** [§663]   Whenever the *patient* has placed his mental condition in issue—*e.g.*, by claiming insanity as a defense in a criminal case, or by suing for damages due to traumatic neurosis—the patient *cannot* assert the privilege. [Cal. Evid. Code §1016]

    (a) **But note:** The waiver of privilege in these cases is *sharply confined* to the particular aspects of the patient's mental condition *brought into issue*.

    (b) **Extent of waiver:** Courts disagree as to whether the waiver in such cases extends to communications made to any psychiatrist or just to those the defendant calls to testify.

    (c) **Unresolved issue:** Some defendants have argued that communications made to psychiatrists consulted before trial fall within the attorney-client privilege and are not waived even upon production of the psychiatrist as a defense expert. This question is unresolved.

e. **Limitation—danger to third persons:** [§664]   Several courts have held that where the patient confides an intent to harm a third person, the danger of violence may justify the psychotherapist in warning the *third person* of the threat. Indeed, *failure* to do so may render the psychotherapist *civilly liable* for any harm inflicted by the patient (*see* Torts Summary). [Tarasoff v. Regents of University of California, 17 Cal. 3d 425 (1976)]

f. **Compare—federal privilege:** [§665]   In *Jaffee v. Redmond, supra*, the Supreme Court recognized a federal privilege for confidential communications between a therapist and her patient.

  (1) **Not a balancing test:** [§666]   The *Jaffee* Court decided *not* to adopt a balancing test approach that would give trial judges discretion to weigh privacy interests against probative value. It opted for the greater certainty of a categorical privilege. The Court indicated, however, that there would

be situations in which the privilege would not apply—*e.g.*, where a serious threat of harm to the patient or others can be averted only by the therapist's disclosure. It thus left the door open to judicial creation of exceptions to the privilege, such as the California exceptions discussed above.

    (2) **Applicable to social workers:** [§667] Stating that the privilege should extend to therapy available to those of modest means, the *Jaffee* Court applied the privilege to protect confidences given to a *licensed social worker* who provided therapeutic counseling.

4. Sexual Assault Victim-Counselor Privilege: [§668] A number of states have statutorily enacted a privilege to protect confidential communications between a sexual assault victim and a person engaged in sexual assault counselling, even though that person is not a physician or psychotherapist. [*See, e.g.,* Cal. Evid. Code §§1035 *et seq.*]

5. Privilege (and Competency) Based on the Marital Relationship: [§669] There are *two* marital exclusionary rules:

    (i) The rule prohibiting either spouse from *testifying* for or against the other; and

    (ii) The rule prohibiting either spouse from *revealing confidential communications* from the other during the marriage.

In either situation, the interest protected is the *marital relationship* and therefore a *valid marriage* must *always* be shown to exist. [Lutwak v. United States, 344 U.S. 604 (1953)—no privilege protects sham or void marriages]

    a. **Privilege not to testify against spouse**

        (1) **Statement of rule**

            (a) **Common law (incompetency):** [§670] At common law, either spouse was *disqualified* (incompetent) to testify for or against the other in any civil or criminal action in which the other spouse was a party.

                1) **Rationale:** To permit a spouse to testify *for* the other would be to foster biased or perjured testimony. To allow a spouse to testify *against* the other would jeopardize the marriage.

            (b) **Modern law (privilege)**

                1) **Testimony for spouse:** [§671] The great majority of states have *rejected* the common law rule above, to the extent of *permitting* either spouse to testify for the other, in either civil or criminal proceedings to which the other is a party. [8 Stan. L. Rev. 423 (1956)]

                    a) **Rationale:** Since a party is now recognized to be competent as a witness, the party's spouse is likewise competent.

                2) **Testimony against spouse—spousal immunity**

    a)   **In civil cases:** [§672]   Likewise, in most jurisdictions either spouse can be compelled to testify against the other in a civil case. [*But see* Cal. Evid. Code §970—contra]

    b)   **In criminal cases:** [§673]   In federal court, the common law rule has been modified. In a criminal case, a spouse may testify against the other spouse (except as to confidential communications, *infra*, §§686 *et seq.*), with or without the consent of the other spouse. The federal courts view the privilege as belonging to the witness-spouse, and thus the witness-spouse can neither be compelled to testify nor foreclosed from testifying. [Trammel v. United States, 445 U.S. 40 (1980)]

(2)   **Basis for exclusion:** [§674]   Technically, this so-called husband-wife privilege is not a privilege at all, since it does not protect confidential communications. Rather, it is an incompetency of one spouse to testify against the other. The testimony is excluded because of the potential danger to the marital relationship (*e.g.*, if one spouse's testimony sent the other to prison, there would likely be resentment which might endanger the future of the marriage).

(3)   **What is excluded:** [§675]   The privilege not only prevents the witness-spouse from testifying in the present proceeding, but also excludes any record of the spouse's testimony given in any other (unprivileged) proceeding. (*Example:* Where W was compelled to testify against H in a civil case, a transcript of that testimony is inadmissible against H in a criminal case.)

(4)   **Who may assert:** [§676]   Traditionally, decisions have held that the privilege belongs only to the party-spouse, and therefore the witness-spouse may be compelled to testify if the party-spouse fails to raise (or is barred from raising) the objection. However in *Trammel, supra*, the United States Supreme Court held that in federal court, the ***witness-spouse*** alone has the privilege to testify or to refuse to testify. (A few states had adopted this position prior to *Trammel*. [*See, e.g.*, Cal. Evid. Code §970])

(5)   **Duration:** [§677]   The privilege may be asserted only ***during the marriage***. It terminates upon divorce or annulment, in which event either former spouse can be compelled to testify against the other (even as to matters that occurred during the marriage).

    (a)   **Marrying the witness:** [§678]   In most states, an accused can effectively "seal the lips" of a witness by marrying the witness! As long as a valid marriage is in existence at the time of trial, the witness-spouse cannot be compelled to testify—even where the crime charged is against the witness's person, and even though the marriage was entered into for the express purpose of suppressing the testimony. [11 A.L.R.2d 649]

    (b)   **Marriage must be valid:** [§679]   However, if the marriage is not valid (*e.g.*, is a fraud), the privilege will not be recognized. [United States v. Apodaca, 522 F.2d 568 (10th Cir. 1975); *and see* United

States v. Lustig, 555 F.2d 737 (9th Cir. 1977)—common law marriage]

(6) **Exceptions:** [§680]   There is no privilege in the following cases, all of which involve situations where the marriage is (or should be) past saving:

(a) **Crimes against the person or property of other spouse:** [§681] Where crimes against the person or property of the other spouse are committed during the marriage (as well as crimes against a third person in the course of committing such a crime), there is no privilege. [8 Wigmore, §2239] (Bigamy and adultery are included. [*See* Cal. Evid. Code §972])

(b) **Crimes against the children:** [§682]   There is no privilege in cases involving crimes against the children of either spouse (including failure to support and child abuse). [United States v. Allery, *supra*, §558]

(c) **Certain statutory offenses:** [§683]   There is also no privilege regarding certain statutory offenses (*e.g.*, importing aliens for prostitution; transporting females across state lines for immoral purposes).

1) **Example:** In a prosecution for violation of the Mann Act (H taking W across state lines to have her engage in prostitution), W can be forced to testify against H. The purpose of the Mann Act (to protect women) would be defeated if H could induce W (his victim) not to testify against him. [Wyatt v. United States, 362 U.S. 525 (1960)]

(d) **Other exceptions:** [§684]   In the minority of states that hold the privilege applicable in civil actions as well as criminal, certain *additional* exceptions are recognized:

1) *Civil action or proceeding instituted by one spouse against the other* (*e.g.*, divorce) or the other's estate;

2) *Proceedings to determine the mental competency of either spouse* (guardianship, conservatorship, etc.); or

3) *Juvenile proceedings involving their children.* [*See* Cal. Evid. Code §972]

(7) **Waiver:** [§685]   Remember that if specific objection is not made by the spouse entitled to assert the privilege, it is waived (*see supra*, §§572-573).

b. **Privilege for confidential marital communications:** [§686]   The second marital exclusionary rule is the common law rule, still in effect in most states, that either spouse can refuse to disclose, or can prevent another from disclosing, *"confidential communications"* made between the spouses during their marriage. [Hopkins v. Grimshaw, 165 U.S. 342 (1897); Cal. Evid. Code §980]

(1) **Rationale:** This exclusionary rule is clearly a matter of privilege, and not incompetency. Reliable as the testimony may be, it is suppressed as a matter of public policy to encourage trust and confidence between spouses.

(2) **What is privileged:** [§687]   The privilege applies only to confidential communications—*i.e.*, some sort of expression from one spouse to the other intended to convey a message.

    (a) **Meaning of "confidential":** [§688]   The communication must be made out of the presence of third parties, and it must concern a matter that the communicating spouse would probably desire to be kept secret.

        1) **Presumption of confidentiality:** [§689]   A communication made between spouses is generally ***presumed*** to have been intended as confidential. The party objecting to the claim of privilege has the burden of showing that it was not. [Blau v. United States, 340 U.S. 332 (1951); Cal. Evid. Code §917]

    (b) **Observations by spouse not privileged:** [§690]   No privilege applies as to either spouse's ***observations*** as to the physical or mental condition, actions, or conduct of the other spouse, because no "communication" is involved. [United States v. Bolzer, 556 F.2d 948 (9th Cir. 1977)] Note that it is not clear, however, whether a wife would be permitted to testify as to a mark on her husband's chest which she saw in the bedroom when he removed his shirt. This would seem to involve a ***reliance*** by the husband upon marital privacy.

        1) **Nonverbal communications:** [§691]   The cases are split as to nonverbal conduct intended to be private and confidential. *Example:* W sees H bring home stolen loot and hide it in their basement. A number of courts hold that this is in effect a "communication" by H, and hence privileged; but an equal number of courts are contra. [10 A.L.R.2d 1385]

(3) **Actions in which assertable:** [§692]   The marital communications privilege may be asserted in ***any*** action, civil or criminal; it is not limited to actions in which the other spouse is a party. *Example:* If W is called as a witness in litigation between P and D, H may appear and assert the privilege to prevent W from revealing any of his confidences—even if W ***wants*** to testify.

    (a) **Constitutional limitation in criminal cases:** [§693]   Some courts hold that the marital communications privilege must give way where it would interfere with an accused's constitutional right to confront (cross-examine) the witnesses against him in a criminal case. Under this approach, the defense is entitled to introduce evidence of confidential communications between the accused and his spouse—or between other spouses—where necessary to effectively cross-examine the prosecution's witness.

        1) **Example:** Prosecution called X as witness against D in murder trial; X testified that D murdered victim. D held entitled to call X's wife to testify that X admitted to her that it was he, not D, who killed victim.

(4) **Who may assert:** [§694]   The confidential communications privilege belongs to *both spouses*; *i.e.*, either spouse may assert it to avoid giving testimony or to preclude testimony by the other. [Luick v. Arends, 132 N.W. 353 (N.D. 1911)]

    (a) **Effect of death or incompetency:** [§695]   A guardian of an incompetent spouse may claim the privilege on behalf of that spouse. However, unlike other privileges, *no one* can assert the privilege for a *deceased spouse*; it can be claimed *only* by or on behalf of the *surviving spouse*.

(5) **Duration:** [§696]   The prevailing rule is that a confidential communication made during marriage is privileged *forever*—*i.e.*, even after the marriage has been terminated (by death, divorce, etc.). [Cal. Evid. Code §980]

    (a) **Criticism:** The rule has been criticized by some writers (Wigmore) on the ground that the need for secrecy of such communications terminates when the marriage ends.

    (b) **Support:** On the other hand, a promise of permanent confidentiality may be especially important if the communications are made while the marriage is in serious trouble in an effort to save the marriage.

(6) **Exceptions—same as for privilege not to testify against spouse:** [§697]   The exceptions to the marital communications privilege are basically the same as those recognized under the rule prohibiting a witness-spouse from testifying for or against a party-spouse (*see supra*, §§680 *et seq.*). [Cal. Evid. Code §984]

    (a) **Crime against spouse or child:** [§698]   Thus where the defendant is charged with a crime against his spouse or child, he can defend himself by introducing evidence of communications with his spouse, and the spouse has no privilege to withhold such information. [Cal. Evid. Code §985]

    (b) **Furtherance of crime or fraud:** [§699]   In addition, the marital communications privilege does not apply where the communication is made "to enable or aid anyone to commit or plan to commit a crime or fraud." [Cal. Evid. Code §981; United States v. Mendoza, 574 F.2d 1373 (5th Cir. 1978)]

(7) **Waiver:** [§700]   Again, the privilege is waived unless a *specific and timely objection* is made by the spouse or spouses entitled to assert it.

    (a) **Voluntary disclosure:** [§701]   The voluntary disclosure to a third person waives the privilege as to the disclosing spouse. However, the other spouse can still claim the privilege. [Cal. Evid. Code §912(a)]

    (b) **Compare—mutual promises not to waive privilege:** [§702]   Where both spouses made communications in confidence to a marriage counselor, with the understanding that the counselor would not be called as a witness, it was held there was no waiver of the privilege; the parties' mutual promises to refrain from calling the counselor as a witness were held enforceable. [Simrin v. Simrin, 233 Cal. App. 2d 90 (1965)]

Spousal Immunity*	Confidential Marital Communications
One spouse *cannot be compelled to testify* against the other spouse in any *criminal* proceeding.	*Confidential communications* (those made out of presence of third parties and intended to be secret) are privileged. The privilege applies in both *civil and criminal* proceedings.
Only the *witness-spouse* may invoke spousal immunity.	*Both spouses* have the privilege not to disclose, and to prevent the other from disclosing, a confidential marital communication.
The privilege can be claimed *only during marriage*, but covers information learned before and during the marriage. *Based on federal law	The privilege *survives the marriage*, but covers only statements made during marriage.

6. **Clergy-Penitent Privilege:** [§703] Like the physician-patient privilege, the clergy-penitent privilege is a wholly statutory privilege, not recognized at common law. However, it is recognized today in a majority of the states. [22 A.L.R.2d 1152; Cal. Evid. Code §1030]

   a. **Rule:** [§704] A person may refuse to disclose (and may prevent the clergy member from disclosing) any confidential communication that the person made to a member of the clergy who was acting in a professional capacity as spiritual adviser. [Cal. Evid. Code §1033]

   b. **Actions in which assertable:** [§705] The privilege applies in *all* actions (civil and criminal) and *regardless* of whether the penitent (the person making the communication) is a *party* to such actions.

   c. **Communications covered:** [§706] In some states, the privilege is limited to "confessions" (*i.e.*, to persons whose religious practices involve confessions). However, most states extend the privilege to any *"penitential communication"*—i.e., any disclosures made in the course of religious practice or consultation which the member of the clergy would be expected to keep secret. [*See* Cal. Evid. Code §1034; *and see In re* Verplank, 329 F. Supp. 433 (C.D. Cal. 1971)—clergyman who ran draft counseling service held entitled to assert privilege as to records of persons he was counseling]

      (1) **Note:** Only *communications* are privileged, not observations by the member of the clergy.

d. **Who may assert:** [§707] The *minority view* is that the privilege belongs to the *penitent*, and he alone (or his estate, etc.) can assert it (although in the penitent's absence, the clergy member can assert the privilege on the penitent's behalf). [*See* Cal. Evid. Code §1033]

(1) **Compare:** However, the *majority view* extends the privilege to the clergy member as well so that the member of the clergy can refuse to testify even if the penitent wants the clergy member to do so. [*See* Cal. Evid. Code §1034] *Rationale:* Tenets of religious faith often require the clergy to maintain secrecy, regardless of the penitent's wishes.

7. **Official Information Privilege:** [§708] Although the official information privilege stems from the common law, it has been expanded under modern practice and is growing in importance due to the increasing role of governmental activities.

a. **Rule:** [§709] If disclosure is specifically forbidden by federal or state law, the privilege is absolute. Otherwise, the government has a privilege to refuse disclosure of official information (and to prevent any other person from disclosing such information) only on a showing that such disclosure is *contrary to public interest*. [Cal. Evid. Code §1040]

b. **Information covered**

(1) **State secrets:** [§710] "State secrets" come within this privilege—*i.e.*, information the disclosure of which might be detrimental to national defense or international relations.

(2) **Internal affairs information:** [§711] Likewise, any confidential "official information" that relates to the internal affairs of government (state or federal) may be privileged if the trial judge determines that the public interest in preserving confidentiality outweighs the necessity for disclosure—a discretionary determination in each case. [Cal. Evid. Code §1040(b)(2)]

(a) **Example:** Reports of law enforcement agencies, personnel review boards, licensing boards, grand jury proceedings, etc., are privileged if disclosure would reveal information that would undermine public safety, cause embarrassment or scandal, etc. [36 A.L.R.2d 1318]

(3) **Presidential communications:** [§712] The Supreme Court has recognized the existence of an executive privilege protecting confidential presidential communications. This privilege is *absolute* where the communications relate to *military, diplomatic, or national security* secrets. Other communications, however, are only *presumptively* privileged and must yield to a demonstrated specific need for essential evidence in a criminal trial. [United States v. Nixon, 417 U.S. 683 (1974)]

(a) **Civil proceedings:** [§713] Whether disclosure of presidential communications would ever be required in civil proceedings is an open question.

(b) **Government officials:** [§714]   Lower courts have recognized executive privilege as applicable to confidential communications by agency heads and other top policy-making officials of government.

c. **Determination of claim:** [§715]   Claims of privilege by public officers frequently raise a difficult procedural problem: How does the trial court determine if the matter is a "state secret," etc. (or whether the public interest would be adversely affected by disclosure) without requiring such disclosure?

   (1) **In camera disclosure:** [§716]   The trial judge has wide discretion here and generally will require an "off the record" (in camera) disclosure so that she can make a ruling. But there may be national security cases in which even this "off the record" disclosure would be improper. [*See* 70 Harv. L. Rev. 935 (1957)]

   (2) **Complex cases:** [§717]   In some cases, the details of the material presented for the trial judge may be so complex and specialized that the trial judge is unable to determine to what extent the material should be considered a state or military secret. In such cases, the trial judge must use discretion in balancing the need for confidentiality versus disclosure.

      (a) **Example:** In the only Supreme Court case on point, the Court held that a trial judge should have upheld the privilege where the Secretary of the Air Force filed an affidavit that the material constituted a military secret, and it was conceded that the material concerned electronic gear on an Air Force plane during the Cold War. [United States v. Reynolds, 345 U.S. 1 (1953)]

d. **Effect of sustaining claim**

   (1) **In criminal cases:** [§718]   If the government as prosecutor asserts the official information privilege, thereby depriving the defendant of material evidence, the trial judge may have to dismiss the prosecution.

   (2) **In civil cases:** [§719]   The effect of the government's assertion of privilege varies in civil cases:

      (a) *Where the government is the plaintiff* in a civil case and deprives the defendant of material evidence, most courts hold that the trial judge may make *any* order that the *interest of justice requires*—including striking testimony, declaring a mistrial, or finding against the government.

      (b) *Similarly, where the government asserts the privilege on cross-examination of its own witness*, the trial judge may strike the witness's testimony and perhaps declare a mistrial.

      (c) *But where the government is the defendant* in a civil case, it apparently has as much right as any other litigant to withhold privileged information and may not be penalized therefor.

8. **Identity of Police Informer Privilege:** [§720]   To protect confidential informers, the police are privileged to refuse to disclose the identity of the informer who gave

them the information that led to the arrest and prosecution of the accused. [Cal. Evid. Code §1041]

    a.   **Rationale:** The theory is that this policy will encourage citizens to come forward with information concerning the commission of crimes.

    b.   **Effect of invoking privilege in criminal cases:** [§721]   However, the court must dismiss (or make findings of fact adverse to the prosecution) whenever invoking the privilege impairs the accused's constitutional right to a *fair trial*. [United States v. Fatico, 441 F. Supp. 1285 (E.D.N.Y. 1977), *rev'd*, 579 F.2d 707 (2d Cir. 1978)]

        (1)   **Where informer may be material witness:** [§722]   Whenever it appears that the informer could be a material witness on the issue of the defendant's guilt, the informer's identity *must* be disclosed (or the charges against the defendant must be *dismissed*). [Roviaro v. United States, 353 U.S. 53 (1957)—federal agents testified they saw D sell narcotics to their paid informer, "John Doe," but refused to disclose the informer's real name; conviction *reversed* because informer was present at commission of crime, and hence might have *material evidence* which would exonerate D]

            (a)   **Note:** Any *doubt* as to whether the informer *is* a material witness must be resolved in the *accused's* favor. The defendant need establish only a *"reasonable probability"* that the informer might have evidence that could exonerate him. [Honore v. Superior Court, 70 Cal. 2d 162 (1969)—"reasonable possibility" sufficient]

        (2)   **Information establishing probable cause:** [§723]   More frequently, however, the informer was *not* an actual witness to the crime, but merely *supplied leads* to the police upon which they based their investigation, and upon which they relied as "probable cause" to arrest defendant or search defendant's property (*e.g.*, informer reports that defendant is in possession of a stolen car, but does not claim to have been present when car was stolen). In this situation, failure to identify the informer does not *per se* interfere with the defendant's constitutional right to a fair trial or the right to confront and cross-examine the witnesses against the defendant. [McCray v. Illinois, 386 U.S. 300 (1967)]

            (a)   **Reliable informer need not be identified:** [§724]   As long as the judge is satisfied with the informer's reliability, the defendant cannot attack the legality of the arrest or search (so as to exclude evidence obtained thereby) on the ground that the police refuse to disclose the informer's identity. [Cal. Evid. Code §1042; *and see* Criminal Procedure Summary]

            (b)   **In camera disclosure:** [§725]   A judge who is not satisfied with the informer's reliability may require the informer's identity to be disclosed in camera. [*See* United States v. Jackson, 384 F.2d 825 (3d Cir. 1967)]

    c.   **Civil cases:** [§726]   The government's informer privilege applies in civil cases as well. Indeed, it is stronger in civil cases since there is no interference with an accused's confrontation rights. [Westinghouse Electric Corp. v. City of Burlington, 351 F.2d 762 (D.C. Cir. 1965)]

d. **Duration of privilege:** [§727]   The informer's privilege disappears once the informer's identity has been revealed.

e. **Probable cause hearings:** [§728]   Courts differ as to whether police officers must reveal the informer's identity to the trial judge when probable cause to search or to arrest is based on information given by the informer. [*Compare* McCray v. Illinois, *supra*—not necessary to reveal where court convinced that officers relied on credible information provided by reliable informant—*with* United States v. Tucker, 380 F.2d 206 (2d Cir. 1967); *and* United States v. Commission, 429 F.2d 834 (2d Cir. 1970)—disclosure necessary where information constitutes "'the essence or core or main bulk' of the evidence brought forth which would otherwise establish probable cause"]

9. **News Reporter's Privilege:** [§729]   The news reporter's privilege did not exist at common law. However, in recent years a substantial minority of states have enacted statutes protecting a journalist's right to withhold the sources of stories. In addition, there appears to be some constitutional protection in this area.

a. **Constitutional privilege?** [§730]   The "freedom of press" guaranteed by the First Amendment assures a reporter of some sort of constitutional protection in gathering news and safeguarding sources. However, the scope of such protection has not yet been resolved.

(1) **Grand jury appearance mandatory:** [§731]   The Supreme Court has clearly ruled that a journalist, like any other citizen, must appear in response to subpoenas issued by a court or grand jury, and must answer all questions relevant to a grand jury's investigation. [Branzburg v. Hayes, 408 U.S. 665 (1972)]

(2) **Revelation of sources:** [§732]   The Court has indicated that a reporter *must* answer all questions asked in *other* kinds of judicial proceedings— *i.e.*, civil cases. [Herbert v. Lando, 441 U.S. 153 (1979)—journalists' thoughts and opinions not privileged in defamation action in which plaintiff required to prove actual malice]

(a) **Qualified privilege:** [§733]   A majority of the Court in *Branzburg* implied that there is some sort of *qualified privilege* in other kinds of judicial proceedings safeguarding the sources of a reporter's stories. Whatever privilege exists, however, was held *not* to shield a reporter who witnessed a crime from testifying in a criminal prosecution as to what he saw (*i.e.*, identifying the criminal). Any "free press" claims in such a case were held outweighed by the needs of law enforcement.

(b) **Elements of privilege:** [§734]   Some courts have interpreted *Branzburg* as shielding a reporter from having to disclose information obtained in gathering the news, unless the following elements are established: (i) the information sought is *relevant to the litigation*; (ii) *no alternative sources* of discovering this information exist; and (iii) a *"compelling state interest"* requires disclosure (*i.e.*, it is essential to the judicial process). [Gilbert v. Allied Chemical Corp., 411 F. Supp. 505 (E.D. Va. 1976)]

1) **Example:** Where all attorneys in a criminal case were under oath not to divulge certain testimony, a reporter who conceded that he obtained the testimony from one of the attorneys and published it could not withhold the name of the attorney who had furnished it. In this case, the defendant's right to a fair trial (without adverse publicity), plus the court's obligation to enforce its orders, outweighed the reporter's First Amendment privilege. (This was true despite a state statute making contempt inapplicable against a news reporter for failing to reveal sources.) [Farr v. Pitchess, 522 F.2d 464 (9th Cir. 1975)]

(c) **Other courts—no privilege:** [§735]   However, not all courts agree with this reading of *Branzburg*. Some interpret the case as requiring reporters not only to appear, but also to answer *all* relevant inquiries in *any* judicial proceeding. [*See* Dow Jones v. Superior Court, 303 N.E.2d 847 (Mass. 1973)]

b. **Statutory privilege:** [§736]   Apart from constitutional protection, a substantial minority of states have *statutes* that give a news publisher, editor, or reporter a privilege to withhold the source of any information published. [102 A.L.R. 771]

(1) **Immunity from contempt rather than privilege:** [§737]   Some statutes merely grant journalists an immunity from *contempt*, rather than a *legal privilege*. Thus, other sanctions might be imposed against a journalist who refuses to disclose a source (*e.g.*, if newspaper sued for libel, editor could not be adjudged guilty of contempt for refusing to disclose source of story, but her answer might be stricken and a default judgment taken against her). [*See, e.g.*, Cal. Evid. Code §1070]

(2) **Privilege (immunity)—generally absolute:** [§738]   Where recognized, the statutory privilege (or contempt immunity) is generally *absolute*; the reason for the reporter's refusal to disclose is immaterial.

(a) **But note—some statutes are contra:** [§739]   Some statutes hold that the privilege does not exist where the interest in maintaining confidentiality of news sources is *outweighed* by the *need* for the testimony. [*See In re* Goodfader's Appeal, 367 P.2d 472 (Hawaii 1961)]

(3) **Scope of privilege (immunity)**

(a) **Majority—source only:** [§740]   Most statutes protect only the *sources* of the journalist's stories. [102 A.L.R. 771]

b) **Minority—any information:** [§741]   A few statutes go further and protect *any* information obtained by a journalist while employed as such—regardless of whether the information was ever actually *published*, and regardless of whether the journalist is *still employed* as such when asked to testify. [Cal. Evid. Code §1070]

10. **Other Privileges:** [§742] Other privileges that have received recognition are:

    a. **Political vote:** [§743] Except where the *legality* of such vote is in issue, any witness has the privilege to refuse to disclose how he voted. [Cal. Evid. Code §1050]

    b. **Trade secrets:** [§744] The owner of a trade secret may refuse to disclose it, unless nondisclosure will tend to conceal *fraud* or work an *injustice*. [Cal. Evid. Code §1060]

        (1) **Discretion of trial court:** [§745] Whether the matter is a "trade secret" and whether its nondisclosure might "work an injustice" are matters that rest within the *discretion* of the trial court.

        (2) **Difference of opinion:** [§746] Some courts do not recognize a trade secret *privilege* at all, but rather treat the area as a *balancing* of the "holder's" competitive interest with the materiality of the evidence. [*See, e.g.*, Natta v. Zletz, 405 F.2d 99 (7th Cir. 1968)]

            (a) **Note:** The balance is sometimes struck by admitting the evidence but limiting access to it. [*See, e.g.*, Natta v. Zletz, *supra*]

    c. **Statutory privilege for required reports:** [§747] Whenever a statute requires the filing of information with a government agency, and at the same time provides that the information shall not be disclosed by the agency, the party filing the report has a *privilege* to refuse to disclose (and to prevent anyone else from disclosing) what the party has filed. This does not mean, however, that a federal court *must* honor a state statutory privilege in a *federal criminal case*. [*In re* Grand Jury Impaneled January 21, 1975, 541 F.2d 373 (3d Cir. 1976)]

        (1) **Examples:** The privilege applies to information given under statutes requiring filing of tax returns, motor vehicle accident reports, census reports, etc., containing prohibitions against disclosure.

            (a) **Tax returns:** A number of courts have held tax returns privileged even in the absence of statute. *Rationale:* This is to encourage full and truthful declarations to the taxing authorities. [70 A.L.R.2d 240]

        (2) **Limitations:** [§748] In no event, however, does this privilege apply in actions involving perjury or false statements made in the report or return filed or other failure to comply with the law in question.

    d. **Accountant-client:** [§749] A privilege for accountant-client, similar in scope to the attorney-client privilege, is recognized in a few states. [*See, e.g.*, Colo. Rev. Stat. §154-1-7(7)]

    e. **Parent-child:** [§750] A few opinions recognize the existence of a parent-child privilege. [*See In re* Grand Jury Proceedings (Witnesses Mary Agosto *et al.*), 553 F. Supp. 1298 (D. Nev. 1983)]

11. Privilege Against Self-Incrimination

a. **In general:** [§751]   The Fifth Amendment to the United States Constitution provides that "[n]o person . . . shall be compelled in any criminal case to be a witness against himself." (Similar provisions are contained in most state constitutions. [*See, e.g.,* Cal. Const. art. I, §13])

   (1) **Applies in both federal and state proceedings:** [§752]   The Fifth Amendment prohibition is directly applicable to proceedings in the federal courts, and is made applicable to state court proceedings, as well, through the Fourteenth Amendment Due Process Clause. [Malloy v. Hogan, 378 U.S. 1 (1964); *and see* Constitutional Law Summary]

   (2) **Dual effect of privilege:** [§753]   The privilege has a twofold operation:

   (a) **Privilege of witness:** [§754]   Any witness has the privilege to refuse to answer any question whose answer might incriminate her.

   (b) **Privilege of accused:** [§755]   A defendant in a criminal proceeding has the privilege to refuse to testify at all—*i.e.,* to refuse even to take the witness stand.

b. **Privilege of every witness not to answer incriminating questions:** [§756]   Every witness has a privilege to refuse to answer incriminating questions. [Cal. Evid. Code §940]

   (1) **What is protected:** [§757]   Note that this privilege is a very different kind of privilege from the usual privilege which safeguards confidential communications. Here the privilege protects what is in the mind of a particular individual—*i.e.,* certain information that she knows which might incriminate her.

   (2) **Purposes of privilege:** [§758]   The privilege is to protect the dignity of the individual in contests with the government; to prevent the government from being able to enforce its laws completely at the expense of the rights and privacy of the citizen (on the theory that this would merely lead to more and more laws invading such rights); and to prevent repetition of historical experiences where incriminating questions were used to root out political and religious dissent (*e.g.,* the Star Chamber).

   (3) **Proceedings in which privilege applicable:** [§759]   The privilege may be claimed by a witness in any proceeding in which the witness's appearance and testimony are compelled (usually by subpoena with a threat of contempt for refusal to answer questions)—*i.e.,* in criminal or civil actions, grand jury proceedings, legislative investigations, administrative proceedings, etc. [38 A.L.R 2d 225]

   (a) **Rationale:** Even though the words of the Constitution make the privilege applicable only "in any criminal case," if the testimony could be extorted in a legislative hearing, it could later be used as an *admission* in a subsequent criminal case.

   (b) **Informal situations:** [§760]   The privilege against self-incrimination also applies when the witness is in *police custody*, even though there is no formal method of punishment for refusal to answer.

1) *Miranda* **decision:** [§761]   In *Miranda v. Arizona, supra,* §370, the Supreme Court held that the informal pressures on an individual in police custody were at least the equivalent of the formal pressures in the above proceedings and hence that the privilege was at least as necessary. (*See* Criminal Procedure Summary.)

(4) **Who may claim privilege:** [§762]   Only *natural persons* can claim the privilege against self-incrimination. Neither a corporation nor a partnership can claim this privilege in its own right. [Soft Lite Lens Co. v. United States, 321 U.S. 707 (1944)]

    (a) **But note:** An officer of the corporation, or a partner of the partnership, may be entitled to assert the privilege if a question would tend to incriminate that person as well as the business entity. [Bellis v. United States, 417 U.S. 85 (1974); 52 A.L.R.3d 636]

(5) **What constitutes being compelled to testify?** [§763]   The modern view is that the Fifth Amendment applies to any form of *"testimonial"* compulsion.

    (a) **Production of records**

        1) **Former law:** [§764]   At one time it was widely held that an individual's *private papers*, even those existing prior to the proceedings and nontestimonial in nature, were within the privilege against self-incrimination (*e.g.*, private financial records and diaries).

        2) **Present law:** [§765]   Recent Supreme Court cases have made clear that *private financial records* are *no longer* protected by the privilege against self-incrimination. Although protection of *diaries* has not yet been resolved, the modern trend seems to view them also as *not within* the privilege.

            a) **Authentication of records:** [§766]   However, the witness cannot be compelled to identify nonprivileged documents or records if the *identification itself* might be *incriminatory*.

            b) **Effect of immunity:** [§767]   Similarly, where a witness is required to produce private papers, *the fact of such production*, as evidence that the witness has identified the papers, may be protected by a grant of use immunity. [United States v. Doe, 465 U.S. 605 (1984)—financial records of sole proprietorship outside privilege, but act of production must be protected through grant of use immunity as to production itself]

(6) **Meaning of incriminating question:** [§768]   A question is incriminating if the answer would directly or indirectly tie the witness to the *commission of any crime*, or would furnish a *lead* to evidence upon which a criminal prosecution against the witness might be based. The answer need not prove *guilt*. It is sufficient that it might be a *link* in a chain of

evidence against the witness. [Hoffman v. United States, 341 U.S. 479 (1951)]

(a) **Criminal liability essential:** [§769]   The privilege cannot be claimed to avoid answering questions that would merely expose the witness to *civil liability* or *public disgrace*, rather than criminal prosecution. [Wigmore, §2254]

1) **Forfeiture proceedings:** [§770]   But a witness can claim the privilege to avoid forfeiture of her property resulting from involvement with criminal activities (*e.g.*, in proceedings to forfeit an automobile used to transport narcotics). Such penalty is regarded as criminal in nature. [United States v. U.S. Coin & Currency, 401 U.S. 715 (1971)]

(b) **Federal or state prosecution:** [§771]   The privilege applies to protect against *any* criminal prosecution. Thus, a witness in federal court may not be compelled to give testimony that might subject her to prosecution under federal law, or the law of any state. Likewise, a state court may not compel a witness to give testimony subjecting her to prosecution under the laws of that state or any sister state, or under federal law. [Murphy v. Waterfront Commission, 378 U.S. 52 (1964)]

(c) **Determination of incriminating character:** [§772]   It is up to the trial court to determine whether a direct answer to the question could implicate the witness.

1) **Nature of question determinative:** [§773]   The judge must make this determination from the question itself; he may *not* require the witness to disclose any information in order to rule on the claim of privilege. [Cal. Evid. Code §915]

2) **Certainty of prosecution not necessary:** [§774]   In addition, it need not appear certain that an answer would subject the witness to prosecution, nor that, if prosecuted, the witness would likely be convicted. Once the point is reached where reasonable judicial imagination can take over, the witness may remain silent. [Prudhomme v. Superior Court, 2 Cal. 3d 320 (1970)]

3) **Doubtful cases—privilege favored:** [§775]   Any doubts must be resolved by upholding the claim of privilege. The court must exclude the evidence "unless it clearly appears that the proffered evidence cannot possibly have a tendency to incriminate the witness." [Mason v. United States, 244 U.S. 362 (1917); Cal. Evid. Code §404]

a) **Forced testimony rare:** [§776]   Thus, it is very rare that a witness will be forced to testify on grounds that the claim of privilege is unfounded. (Even where the statute of limitations has run on the specific crime to which the testimony relates, there might be a continuing conspiracy; similarly, the fact that double jeopardy protects the witness from prosecution for a particular crime does not mean that crime might not be a link in a chain of evidence connecting the witness to another crime.)

    b) **Compare—immunity or waiver:** [§777] As a result, where the privilege is disallowed it is usually either because immunity has been given or because the privilege has been waived (below).

(d) **No privilege where prosecution barred:** [§778] The privilege is available only when there is a legal possibility of criminal prosecution. If the witness is permanently immune from such prosecution, she cannot assert this privilege.

    1) **By limitations or jeopardy:** [§779] Thus, a witness may be compelled to testify where the *statute of limitations has run* on a crime, or the witness has been *acquitted* of the crime and is protected by the bar of double jeopardy.

    2) **By grant of immunity:** [§780] Likewise, there is no privilege where the witness has been granted *immunity* from prosecution.

        a) **How grant made:** [§781] The witness must be *granted* immunity by the court after claiming the privilege. Immunity does not attach merely because the witness has given self-incriminatory testimony.

        b) **Transactional immunity:** [§782] Until fairly recently, it was held that the only kind of immunity grant broad enough to require a witness to testify as to incriminating matters was "transactional immunity." This kind of immunity prevented the witness from being prosecuted for any crime *related* to the transaction she was being compelled to testify about.

        c) **Use immunity:** [§783] Recently, however, the Supreme Court has held that the government need only grant use immunity—*i.e.*, a guarantee that neither the compelled testimony, nor leads or evidence derived therefrom, could be used against the witness in a subsequent prosecution. Under this type of immunity, the witness *could* still be prosecuted for events *related* to the transactions about which she testified as long as no evidence *derived* from such testimony was used. [Kastigar v. United States, 406 U.S. 441 (1972)]

            1/ **Note:** Determining whether evidence used by the government in a subsequent prosecution was *derived* from the witness's testimony or from an independent source can often be quite difficult. Some courts have held that the government must meet a high burden of proof that its evidence was *not* derived from the witness's compelled testimony.

    d)   **No immunity for perjury or false statement:** [§784]   The witness may be prosecuted for perjury based on false statements made while testifying under a grant of transactional or use immunity. [18 U.S.C. §6002] In such prosecution, both the false statements which are the offense itself and relevant true statements made under the grant of immunity are admissible. [United States v. Apfelbaum, 445 U.S. 115 (1980)]

(7) Waiver of privilege: [§785]   The privilege belongs to the *witness*; no *party* can assert it on her behalf. If the witness fails to assert it at the time the incriminating question is *asked*, the privilege is *waived*. [United States v. Murdock, 284 U.S. 141 (1931)]

    (a)   **Waiver by partial disclosure:** [§786]   By testifying as to *any of the facts* pertaining to a criminal transaction, the witness waives the privilege, and may then be compelled to testify as to *all* of the facts involved. [147 A.L.R. 255]

        1)   **Rationale:** The witness need not have spoken at all; but having *chosen* to tell part of the story, it would be an injustice to allow the witness not to tell all.

        2)   **When waiver effective:** [§787]   The waiver is said to occur when the witness *first* admits any incriminating fact as to which she otherwise could not have been compelled to testify. [United States v. Costello, 198 F.2d 200 (2d Cir. 1952)]

        3)   **Compare—testimony in former proceeding:** [§788]   The fact that a witness has testified fully in a *different* proceeding is generally *not* held to be a waiver of the privilege in a subsequent proceeding.

            a)   **Rationale:** The former testimony might be discounted on some ground (*e.g.*, mental incompetency or coercion) so that the subsequent testimony could become the link in the chain of evidence necessary to convict her.

        4)   **Compare—testimony in same proceeding:** [§789]   Generally, testimony by a nonparty witness constitutes a waiver of the privilege in the same proceeding. However, even in the same proceeding, a nonparty witness may not waive the Fifth Amendment privilege where her original testimony was nonincriminating and wholly unrelated to the criminality that her subsequent testimony would tend to subject her to. This rule recognizes that, as with separate proceedings, a witness in the same proceeding can be subjected to dramatically different circumstances surrounding her testimony. [People v. Bagby, 65 N.Y.2d 410 (1985)]

(b) **No duty to warn:** [§790]   A witness is presumed to know the privilege. Accordingly, most courts hold that there is no duty on the part of the judge, or any party, to warn or advise the witness regarding the privilege. [79 A.L.R.2d 643]

   1) **Special circumstances:** [§791]   However, some courts indicate that there may be such a duty under special circumstances—*e.g.*, grand jury investigations where the witness is not permitted to have the assistance of counsel, or where the witness is a minor, illiterate, etc.

   2) **Police custody:** [§792]   Because of the special circumstances existing when an accused is in police custody, the *Miranda* rule requires that a warning be given before any questioning takes place. (*See* Criminal Procedure Summary.)

(8) **No comment on claim of privilege:** [§793]   No adverse inference can be drawn from the fact that a witness has claimed the privilege—regardless of whether the witness is a party to the action.

   (a) **Rationale:** Allowing inferences to be drawn from the exercise of the privilege would undermine the privilege and prevent its exercise. In addition, some commentators feel that the inference of guilt from invocation of the privilege is not strong but is likely to be overestimated by the jury.

   (b) **Compare—parties in civil cases:** Some jurisdictions do allow an inference to be drawn against a party in a civil case who has pleaded the privilege because that party has withheld relevant evidence by pleading the privilege.

   (c) **Compare—nonparties in civil cases:** Some jurisdictions also allow an inference to be drawn against a party in a civil case from the invocation of the privilege by a nonparty witness employee of the defendant on the ground that the probative value of the evidence in a civil case is not offset by the prejudice that would be engendered nor the lesser constitutional interests involved. [Brinks v. New York, 717 F.2d 700 (2d Cir. 1983)]

c. **Privilege of accused not to testify at all:** [§794]   As previously indicated, the accused in a criminal proceeding may refuse to testify at all. [Cal. Evid. Code §930]

(1) **Purpose of privilege:** [§795]   The privilege is to protect the accused against the possible adverse reaction a jury might have if the prosecutor could call the accused as a witness and ask incriminating questions which the accused would then have to refuse to answer.

(2) **Proceedings in which not applicable:** [§796]   The privilege (to refuse to take the stand) does *not* apply where the person is not an "accused"—*i.e.*, where no criminal prosecution is involved. (However, the privilege of any witness to refuse to answer incriminating questions is still applicable; *see supra*, §§756 *et seq.*)

(a) **Example:** Thus, in *grand jury* proceedings and hearings before *legislative investigating committees* or *administrative bodies* (including disciplinary proceedings), a witness may not refuse to take the stand at all. [38 A.L.R.2d 225; 24 A.L.R. 863]

(3) **What constitutes compulsion of accused:** [§797]   As indicated *supra*, §765, an individual's *private records* and *documents* are *no longer protected* under the privilege as testimonial compulsion.

(a) **Seizure of accused's records:** [§798]   Thus, where the accused's records are seized pursuant to a proper search warrant, any incriminating statement contained therein may be used against the accused. Since the writings were made *voluntarily*, and the accused was not *required* to produce them, there is no testimonial compulsion in violation of the privilege. [United States v. Doe, *supra*, §767]

(b) **Production by third person:** [§799]   The privilege is also inapplicable where the witness's incriminating records are in the possession of some *third person* (*e.g.*, an accountant). The third person *can* be compelled to produce the records—again on grounds that there is no *compulsion* of the accused. [Couch v. United States, 409 U.S. 322 (1973)] Likewise, the witness's *attorney* may be required to produce records in his possession *unless* the papers are protected by virtue of the *attorney-client privilege*. [Fisher v. United States, 425 U.S. 391 (1976)]

(c) **Physical examinations:** [§800]   Along the same lines, the accused can be compelled to submit to *reasonable* examinations of her person; appear in a *lineup*; speak for *voice identification*; and give *physical evidence*—*e.g.*, blood samples, urine samples, fingerprints, and handwriting specimens. [Gilbert v. California, 388 U.S. 263 (1967)]

1) **Rationale:** Such evidence is not testimonial in the sense that the defendant has no control over the results of such an examination and because it is not investigating defendant's thoughts or memory.

2) **Limitation:** [§801]   However, the Fourth Amendment requires that the taking of samples (blood, urine, etc.) must be accomplished without unreasonable force and by competent medical personnel (if a medical procedure is required). [Schmerber v. California, 384 U.S. 757 (1966)]

(d) **Photographs, recordings, etc.:** [§802]   Motion pictures and sound recordings of an accused's voluntary conduct at the scene of the crime or elsewhere are also admissible on grounds that they are not *"testimony"* of the accused. [State v. Strickland, 168 S.E.2d 697 (N.C. 1969)]

(4) **Waiver of privilege by the accused**

(a) **By testifying at trial:** [§803]   An accused *waives* the privilege to refuse to testify by *taking the stand* in her own defense. Thereafter, the accused can be compelled to answer *all* relevant inquiries about the charge (to the extent of permissible cross-examination), including matters that go to *impeachment*. [Johnson v. United States, 318 U.S. 189 (1943)]

(b) **No waiver by testimony on preliminary fact question:** [§804]   The accused may testify at a hearing on a preliminary fact question (*e.g.,* the "voluntariness" of the confession, or the circumstances surrounding an allegedly illegal search) without surrendering the privilege to refuse to testify *at trial*. [Fed. R. Evid. 104(d); Simmons v. United States, 390 U.S. 777 (1968)]

1) **Procedural matters:** [§805]   Such preliminary fact questions may be litigated in a *pretrial hearing* (motion to suppress evidence), or during the trial itself. If done *at trial*, the accused is entitled to have the jury excused during her testimony to prevent any adverse inference from her failure to testify on other matters. [Fed. R. Evid. 104(c)]

2) **Admissibility of testimony:** [§806]   To protect the Fifth Amendment privilege, any admissions or statements made by the accused while testifying on the preliminary fact question are inadmissible at the accused's trial as substantive evidence of guilt. [Simmons v. United States, *supra*]

a) **Compare—impeachment:** [§807]   However, an accused who chooses to testify in her own defense waives the privilege (above), and any conflicting testimony given by her during the preliminary fact hearing may be used to impeach her testimony at trial. [*See* Harris v. New York, 401 U.S. 222 (1971); *and see* Criminal Procedure Summary]

(c) **No waiver by testimony in prior trial or proceeding:** [§808] Similarly, an accused cannot be compelled to testify at trial even though she gave testimony in a previous trial for the same offense, or in a grand jury hearing. Since the privilege applies, no comment may be made to the jury thereon (*see* below).

(d) **Waiver of witness privilege by accused taking stand?** [§809]   As discussed above, an accused waives the privilege to refuse to testify by taking the witness stand in her own defense at trial (*e.g.,* to give an alibi). But courts are in disagreement as to whether the accused, by testifying in her own defense at trial, also waives the privilege of an ordinary witness not to answer questions that might tend to incriminate her as to other crimes.

1) **Example:** D is charged with bank robbery; D takes the witness stand to offer an alibi that she was out of town at the time of the crime. The prosecution seeks to rebut D's alibi defense by cross-examining her to show that she was involved in several other criminal acts locally at the same time.

PRIVILEGE AGAINST SELF-INCRIMINATION

	Privilege Not to Answer Incriminating Questions	**Privilege Not to Testify**
Who May Assert Privilege?	*Every witness* has a privilege to refuse to answer incriminating questions.	A *criminal accused* may refuse to testify at all (*i.e.,* not take the stand at trial).
When May Privilege Be Asserted?	Privilege may be asserted in *any proceeding when the witness's appearance and testimony are compelled* (*e.g.,* in criminal and civil cases and grand jury proceedings).	Privilege may be asserted *only when the person to testify is an "accused"* (*i.e.,* when criminal prosecution is involved).
Who Determines Applicability of Privilege?	*Court* determines whether privilege applies—whether a direct answer to question asked implicates witness. (Privilege favored)	*Accused* determines if she will testify.
How Is Privilege Waived?	Privilege waived by witness *failing to assert* it at time incriminating question is asked or by *partial disclosure*.	Privilege waived by accused *taking the stand* in own defense (no waiver though when accused testifies as to preliminary fact questions).

a) *Some courts hold that by taking the stand at all, an accused surrenders all privilege* ("throws away the shield"). The accused, after taking the stand, may thereafter be compelled to answer questions tending to incriminate her as to other crimes, as well as the crime charged, as long as the questions are within the permissible scope of cross-examination. [People v. Redmond, 265 App. Div. 307 (1942)]

b) *More courts, however, are to the contrary*, holding that the accused cannot be compelled to answer questions relating to other crimes on the ground that this in effect would permit impeachment by showing collateral misconduct. [*See* Johnson v. United States, *supra*, §803; *and see infra*, §1088]

　　1/ Since *Johnson* was decided **before** the privilege was held applicable to the states, it is not clear whether this particular rule is of constitutional dimension and thus binding upon the state courts.

(5) **Inference or comment on assertion of privilege:** [§810]   An accused's failure to take the witness stand in her own defense is tantamount to a claim of the privilege. As a matter of constitutional right, no adverse inference of guilt can be drawn from the accused's assertion of the privilege. Consequently, a prosecutor is not permitted to make any direct comment or argument to the jury suggesting defendant's guilt on the basis of her refusal to testify. [Griffin v. California, 380 U.S. 609 (1965)]

(a) **But note:** This does not prevent the prosecutor from commenting on the accused's failure to prevent evidence to support an alibi, or refusal to submit to reasonable tests or examinations which would have been admissible on the issue of guilt (*e.g.*, blood and urine samples, *see supra*, §800). (*See* further discussion in Criminal Procedure Summary.)

VII. COMPETENCY TO TESTIFY

chapter approach

Quite frankly, rules as to competency rarely arise in either litigation or examination questions. In litigation, they do not arise because the areas on which there are rules—*e.g.,* testimony of judges and jurors—very rarely arise in a practical context. In examination questions, these rules do not arise primarily because the overwhelming number of reasons why a witness was incompetent to testify have now been repealed by statute. However, a general exposure to these issues is useful.

A. GENERAL RULES OF COMPETENCY [§811]

At one time, competency meant simply compliance with the rules of evidence. As a result, hearsay evidence, though relevant, was "incompetent." Now, competency almost always means the *willingness* of the court to *hear evidence* from a *particular* witness.

1. **Common Law:** [§812]   At common law, there were a number of grounds upon which a person could be disqualified from giving testimony: having a financial interest in the outcome of the suit (the parties), being married to a party, having a lack of religious belief, having been convicted of a felony, or due to race, infancy, or mental derangement.

2. **Modern Law:** [§813]   Under the modern trend, *any* person may testify as a witness, subject mostly to reasonable rules as to *physical* and *mental* qualifications. However, the *weight* of the witness's testimony may be affected by various factors (*e.g.,* financial interest, felony conviction, etc.).

3. **Federal Rules—*Erie* Doctrine:** [§814]   The Federal Rules adopt the trend toward abolition of rigid grounds for disqualification, except where the case turns on *state law* (*e.g.,* diversity jurisdiction cases), in which case the competency of a witness must be determined in accordance with the *state law*. [Fed. R. Evid. 601; Super Valu Stores v. First National Bank, 463 F. Supp. 1183 (M.D. Ga. 1979)]

B. SPECIFIC RULES AFFECTING COMPETENCY

1. **Competency as Affected by Physical and Mental Qualifications**

    a. **Requirements:** [§815]   To be competent to testify, a witness must meet the following requirements [Cal. Evid. Code §§701, 702]:

    (1) **Ability to communicate:** [§816]   The witness must be capable of *expressing* himself so as to be understood by the jury—either directly or through an interpreter. Where the witness testifies through an interpreter, it must be shown that the interpreter is qualified in the foreign language in question and is *under oath* to make a true translation. [Fed. R. Evid. 604]

    (2) **Personal knowledge:** [§817]   A witness, other than an expert, may not testify as to matters about which he is not found to have personal knowledge. [Fed. R. Evid. 602; *and see infra,* §829]

(3) **Obligation of truthfulness:** [§818]   The witness must be capable of *understanding* the duty to tell the truth.

(4) **Time of competency:** [§819]   The above requirements refer to the condition of the witness *at the time he is called to testify*. Thus, the fact that a witness's recollection vanished *after* the event in question, but was restored *prior* to trial (*e.g.*, by a memory-refreshing writing), does *not* render him incompetent as a witness. [Kline v. Ford Motor Co., 523 F.2d 1067 (9th Cir. 1975)]

b. **Preliminary fact determination:** [§820]   The witness's competency is a preliminary fact question that the trial judge must determine *before* the witness is permitted to testify. However, since the requirements for competency of witnesses are less stringent today than in the past, the court's decision on this type of issue has been held to require less evidence than for other preliminary questions.

c. **Application of requirements**

(1) **Children:** [§821]   A child of any age may be permitted to testify as long as the trial judge is satisfied that the child possesses the ability to *observe*, *recollect*, and *communicate*. [Pocatello v. United States, 394 F.2d 115 (9th Cir. 1968)] It is not uncommon for courts to allow testimony of children as young as four years old.

(a) **State statutes:** [§822]   Some state statutes raise a presumption that children over a certain age (*e.g.*, 10 years) are competent, while the competency of younger children must be determined by the trial court. [159 A.L.R. 1102]

(2) **Mental incompetents:** [§823]   Mental unsoundness does not per se disqualify a witness. It must be of such degree that the person's ability to perceive, recall, and testify are so impaired that the witness's testimony is worthless. [United States v. Roach, 590 F.2d 181 (5th Cir. 1979)]

(a) **Commitment:** [§824]   In many states, a commitment or adjudication of insanity or mental incompetency raises a presumption that the witness is disqualified to testify. [*See, e.g., In re* Waite's Guardianship, 14 Cal. 2d 727 (1939)]

(3) **Criminals:** [§825]   Even a convicted felon may give testimony (the common law is contra). The fact of the conviction, however, may serve as a basis for *impeachment* (*see infra*, §1015); *i.e.*, the conviction may affect the weight of the felon's testimony, but not its admissibility. [United States v. Mills, 597 F.2d 693 (9th Cir. 1979)]

(4) **Atheists:** [§826]   Under modern law, a lack of religious belief has *no effect* on a witness's competency. Nor may it be considered as affecting credibility (*i.e.*, it does not affect either the admissibility or weight of the testimony). [Fed. R. Evid. 610]

(5) **Narcotics addiction:** [§827]   The fact that a witness is addicted to narcotics does not affect the witness's competency, but it may affect her credibility. [United States v. Jackson, 576 F.2d 46 (5th Cir. 1978)]

    d.   **Waiver—failure to object:** [§828]   A ground for disqualifying the witness must be raised by timely objection in the trial court or it is waived—*i.e.,* the testimony may be considered by the jury and may serve as evidence to support the verdict or judgment on appeal. [Pocatello v. United States, *supra*]

2.   **Competency as Affected by Lack of Personal Knowledge:** [§829]   Witnesses (other than expert witnesses) are not competent to testify unless they have personal knowledge of the facts they relate. Such knowledge must be garnered through the witness's senses (typically sight or hearing).

    a.   **Comparison with hearsay rule:** [§830]   Often the difference between testimony being objectionable as hearsay or for lack of personal knowledge is purely a formal one.

       (1)   **Example—no personal knowledge:** If the witness wishes to testify, "I did not see or hear the accident, but I know that the blue car went through the red light," the witness would be incompetent because of lack of personal knowledge.

       (2)   **Example—hearsay:** But if the witness wishes to testify, "I did not see, hear, or otherwise sense the accident, but X told me that he saw it and that the blue car went through the red light," the testimony would be hearsay.

    b.   **Personal knowledge as jury question:** [§831]   Personal knowledge is a matter to be determined by the jury, subject only to the judge's finding that there is sufficient evidence from which the jury could decide that the witness did have personal knowledge.

       (1)   **Sense perception usually sufficient:** [§832]   Typically, the witness's own statement that she saw or heard the accident will be enough to justify a jury finding of personal knowledge, and hence will allow admissibility of the witness's testimony about the matters in dispute. The opposing party can, of course, attempt to convince the jury that the witness lacked such perception—*e.g.,* was miles away at the time—and hence that the testimony should be ignored.

3.   **Competency as Affected by Connection with the Tribunal**

    a.   **Judge as witness:** [§833]   A judge is not disqualified as a witness merely by virtue of judicial office. Judges may be subpoenaed or appear voluntarily to testify just as any other person. However, serious problems of possible *prejudice* arise where a judge takes the witness stand in the very case over which he is *presiding*.

       (1)   **Majority view—judicial discretion:** [§834]   Most decisions have left the matter to the *trial court's discretion*; *i.e.,* it is up to the judge to determine whether being called as a witness might deprive either party of a fair trial (so that a mistrial or substitution of judges would be in order). [157 A.L.R. 315]

(2) **Statutory changes—objection required:** [§835] Some statutes provide that the trial judge cannot testify if *either party objects*. [*See, e.g.,* Cal. Evid. Code §703—objection results in automatic mistrial to protect objecting party]

(3) **Federal Rules—absolute disqualification:** [§836] Under the Federal Rules, *no objection* is necessary. The presiding trial judge is *absolutely incompetent* to testify. [Fed. R. Evid. 605; United States v. Alberico, 453 F. Supp. 178 (D. Colo. 1977)]

(4) **Law clerks:** [§837] Some courts have extended the policy behind Federal Rule 605 to bar the use of a judge's law clerk as a witness or other source of evidence. [Kennedy v. Great Atlantic & Pacific Tea Co., 551 F.2d 593 (5th Cir. 1977); Price Brothers Co. v. Philadelphia Great Corp., 629 F.2d 444 (6th Cir. 1980)—nonjury case remanded where judge sent his law clerk to examine the site at issue]

b. **Juror as witness**

(1) **Traditional rule—juror competent:** [§838] The traditional and *prevailing rule* is that a juror is competent to testify in the case in which he is *serving*. (Of course, instances in which a juror will be called as an ordinary witness are rare since voir dire will generally reveal that a juror has knowledge of the facts or parties.) [Phillips v. Van Horn, 68 N.W. 452 (Iowa 1896)]

(2) **Modern rule—objection disqualifies:** [§839] However, the modern rule is that a juror cannot testify (or give an affidavit) if *either party objects*. [Fed. R. Evid. 606]

(a) **Presence of jury:** [§840] Under this rule, the opposing party must be afforded the opportunity to object to such testimony *outside the presence of the jury* to avoid jury prejudice. [Fed. R. Evid. 606(a)]

(3) **Testimony as to jury deliberations:** [§841] Unlike the issue of whether the judge or juror may serve as a witness in the trial itself, a question that often arises is the extent to which jurors are permitted to testify in *post-verdict* proceedings for the purpose of *attacking* or *supporting* the jury verdict. There is a wide *split of authority* on this issue:

(a) **Traditional view:** [§842] Traditionally, jurors were *incompetent* to testify at all; *i.e.,* a juror was *never* allowed to "impeach his own verdict."

1) **Rationale:** Courts felt they would have to overturn far too many verdicts if they actually found out what happened in the jury room. As a result, they shut off what would usually be the only source of information as to jury misconduct.

2) **Compare—testimony of court official:** [§843] However, by treating juror testimony as an issue of the *juror's competency* to testify, courts did not foreclose the ability of a *court official*

who had *improperly* listened to the jury deliberations and had heard evidence of jury misconduct to testify to such misconduct to overturn the verdict.

(b) **Federal Rules:** [§844]   Under the Federal Rules, juror testimony (or affidavits) is admissible *only* to show any outside influences improperly brought to bear on any member of the jury (*e.g.,* threats to family) or "extraneous prejudicial information improperly brought to the jury's attention" (*e.g.,* news releases). [Fed. R. Evid. 606(b); United States v. Marques, 600 F.2d 742 (9th Cir. 1979)]

   1) **Comment:** The Rules have been criticized as not allowing evidence of misconduct in the jury room between the jurors (*e.g.,* personal threats by one juror against another which caused return of the particular verdict). [*See, e.g.,* Simmons First National Bank v. Ford Motor Co., 88 F.R.D. 344 (E.D. Ark. 1980)]

   2) **Mental competence; drug and alcohol abuse:** [§845]   One court has found that a juror's statements that he had heard voices and vibrations during the trial and during jury deliberations warranted an evidentiary hearing on competency, at which the defendant could cross-examine. [Sullivan v. Fogg, 613 F.2d 465 (2d Cir. 1980)] But the Supreme Court has held that juror testimony concerning drug and alcohol abuse during deliberations is inadmissible in federal courts. [Tanner v. United States, 483 U.S. 107 (1987)]

   3) **Racial prejudice:** [§846]   Generally, allegations of racial prejudice will not support inquiry; however, strong evidence of prejudice, or that the juror lied on voir dire about his prejudice, may mandate a hearing based on outside influences affecting fundamental fairness.

(c) **Modern trend:** [§847]   The modern trend is to allow a wider latitude of *juror testimony*, but to restrict the grounds on which jury verdicts may be overturned.

   1) **Example:** A few states go much further than the Federal Rules and permit jurors to testify as to "any fact or event" that occurred, inside or outside the jury room, that improperly influenced their verdict—*e.g.,* drunkenness, verdicts by lot, etc. [*See, e.g.,* Cal. Evid. Code §1150]

c. **Attorney as witness:** [§848]   An attorney is a competent witness, even in the trial in which she is involved.

(1) **Witness for client:** [§849]   However, an attorney who is called as a witness for a client (except as to purely formal matters—*e.g.,* attestation of documents), may be violating professional ethics standards if she continues to handle the case since such might give the appearance that the attorney was being paid a professional fee for favorable testimony. Some

courts refuse to let an attorney who has testified as a witness argue the case to the jury. [*See* Bickford v. John E. Mitchell Co., 595 F.2d 540 (10th Cir. 1979); *and see* Legal Ethics Summary]

(2) **Witness against client:** [§850]   Where the attorney is called as a witness against the client, the issue of the attorney-client privilege may be raised (*see supra,* §§584 *et seq.*).

4. Competency as Affected by Interest

a.   **Common law rule—parties incompetent:** [§851]   As previously noted, at common law, a party to a civil action was ordinarily incompetent to testify therein, the rationale being that a party was too "interested" to give reliable testimony.

(1) **Other persons disqualified:** [§852]   The same rationale disqualified all other persons who had a "certain, immediate, and legal interest" in the outcome—*e.g.,* partners, assignors, and even those merely liable for the costs of the litigation.

(2) **Effect of rule:** [§853]   Frequently, the effect of the rule was to preclude a party from litigating a valid claim since the party might be the only one who could prove his case. (The rule also had the counterbalancing effect that a party could not be forced to testify against himself; *see supra,* §§751 *et seq.*)

(3) **Statutory abolition:** [§854]   Modern statutes have done away with the common law rule against party testimony. The sole remaining exceptions are the "dead man statutes" discussed below.

b.   **"Dead man statutes":** [§855]   Many states still have "dead man statutes." These statutes, and the case law interpreting them, vary widely from state to state.

(1) **Example—dead man statute:** A fairly typical dead man statute might read as follows: "In a claim or demand against a decedent's estate, the party seeking to enforce such claim and/or his assignor or the person for whose benefit the action is brought, is incompetent to testify as to any matter or fact occurring before the death of such deceased person." [Ladd, The Dead Man Statute: Some Further Observations and a Legislative Proposal, 26 Iowa L. Rev. 207 (1941)]

(a) **Note:** Rather than preventing the party from testifying as to any fact occurring before the death of the deceased opponent, dead man statutes often prevent the party from testifying as to "any conversation" or "any transaction" with the deceased opponent.

(2) **Rationale:** Since death has closed the decedent's mouth, the law will "even things up" by closing the claimant's.

(3) **Criticisms:** [§856]   Dead man statutes have been strongly criticized on several grounds:

(a) **Survivor unable to prove claim:** As a practical matter, the survivor is rendered helpless in many cases. If he trusted the decedent, and therefore did not insist on written evidence or an outside witness, there is no way the survivor can enforce the claim against the decedent's estate.

(b) **Estate not always disadvantaged:** Furthermore, the decedent's death does not always put the estate at a testimonial disadvantage. There are many cases in which the decedent may have had no personal knowledge of the facts involved (*e.g.*, where the plaintiff sues the decedent's estate for injuries caused by the decedent's employee or servant).

(4) **Application of dead man statutes:** [§857] Because of the frequent unfairness involved, dead man statutes are *narrowly construed*.

   (a) **Only money judgments:** [§858] Thus, the language "claim or demand" is construed to mean only debts and demands upon which a money judgment is sought. [45 A.L.R. 1477]

   1) **Example:** The dead man statute therefore is not applicable in a suit for specific performance, in quiet title actions, in an action to enforce a trust, or in an action to enforce a contract to bequeath or devise property in return for personal services to decedent. [54 A.L.R.2d 1103]

   2) **Compare:** But where the plaintiff is seeking both specific performance and/or money damages, the courts usually hold the statute applicable; *i.e.,* it is enough that money damages constitute even part of the claim.

   (b) **Only actions against estate:** [§859] For the statute to apply, the action must be "against the estate."

   1) **Example:** The statute does not apply in an action against a partnership of which decedent was a member even though the estate might ultimately be liable. Nor does it apply in an action *by the estate*. If the executor sues, the defendant may testify (but not on any cross-demand against the estate).

   (c) **Only immediate beneficiary disqualified:** [§860] Only a person for whose immediate benefit the action is brought is disqualified from testifying.

   1) **Example:** A shareholder of a corporation has been held competent to testify on a claim by her corporation against a decedent's estate. The shareholder's benefit from the claim is held to be indirect, even where she is the sole shareholder. [163 A.L.R. 1215]

(5) **Waiver of statute:** [§861] Dead man statutes may be effectively waived by the executor or administrator of the estate. A "waiver" will be found in *either* of the following circumstances:

(a) **Consent:** [§862]   The executor or administrator consents or *fails to object* to the introduction of evidence or testimony that falls within the statutory prohibition. [159 A.L.R. 411]

(b) **Claimant called as witness:** [§863]   Similarly, there is a waiver if the executor or administrator calls the *claimant as a witness*—whether or not the claimant is asked questions as to "facts or matters occurring before the decedent's death." [159 A.L.R. 421]

   1) **Note:** Some cases have found a waiver where the executor merely takes a *pretrial deposition* from the plaintiff—whether or not the deposition is *actually* used at the trial! Other courts are contra, however. [Wittbrot v. Anderson, 262 F. Supp. 10 (W.D. Mich. 1966)]

   2) **And note:** *Cross-examining* the claimant as to any matters involved in the claim is, of course, a waiver.

(6) **Statutory changes—abolition:** [§864]   The criticisms noted above and general dissatisfaction with the operation of dead man statutes have resulted in the *abolition* of such statutes in an increasing number of states. [*See, e.g.,* Cal. Evid. Code §1261; *and see* Kirk v. Marquis, 391 A.2d 335 (Me. 1978)]

   (a) **Federal Rules:** [§865]   The Federal Rules follow this approach in nondiversity cases. [Fed. R. Evid. 601, note; *and see supra,* §814]

   (b) **Exception to hearsay rule:** [§866]   To offset the supposed inequality of allowing the claimant to testify while the decedent cannot, some states that have abolished dead man statutes have created a *special exception* to the hearsay rule: The decedent's estate may introduce oral or written statements made by the decedent prior to death as to matters of *recent, firsthand knowledge*. (Of course if such hearsay is helpful to the claimant, he may introduce it as an admission as well.) [*See* Cal. Evid. Code §1261]

5. **Competency as Affected by Marital Relationship:** [§867]   In certain cases, the common law rule rendering spouses incompetent to testify against each other has been retained. These are discussed in detail *supra,* §§669 *et seq.,* in connection with the *marital privilege*.

VIII. OPINION EVIDENCE AND EXPERT WITNESSES

chapter approach

The opinion rules and the rules as to expert testimony are very important in the trial of a case, but they do not appear very often on exam questions. If opinion issues do arise on your exam, remember:

1. The admissibility of a lay opinion is generally within the discretion of the trial judge; that is, the opinion may be allowed if it is based on the *witness's perception* and is *helpful* to the fact finder.

2. The rules as to expert testimony, although extremely important, usually depend on modern science or are held to be within the trial judge's discretion. Admission of the expert's opinion depends on: (i) whether the specific knowledge is *helpful*; (ii) whether the witness is *qualified as an expert*; (iii) whether the opinion has a *proper basis*; and in some jurisdictions, (iv) whether the expert possesses a *reasonable degree of certainty* as to her opinion.

A. INTRODUCTION

1. **Definition of "Opinion":** [§868]   An opinion is an *inference* or *conclusion* drawn from facts observed.

2. **The "Opinion Rule"**

   a. **Background:** [§869]   The rule in England through the eighteenth century was that opinion testimony was excluded to the extent that it was not based upon *personal (firsthand) knowledge*. [3 Weinstein & Berger, Evidence ¶701[01] (1976)] This rule was expanded by American courts, which attempted to exclude *all* inferences, conclusions, and opinions and to admit only "*facts*." [*See* United States v. Alexander, 415 F.2d 1352 (7th Cir. 1969), *cert. denied,* 397 U.S. 1014 (1970); *and see* 7 Wigmore, §1917]

   b. **Current "opinion rule":** [§870]   Despite the frequent difficulty in distinguishing between fact and opinion, American courts still adhere to the general rule that a nonexpert called to the stand to give *direct evidence* (*i.e,* firsthand or "eyewitness" testimony) is *restricted* to describing relevant *facts* about which the witness has *knowledge*. The witness ordinarily *cannot* state *opinions* and *conclusions drawn* from his observations. [*See* Randolph v. Collectramatic, Inc., 590 F.2d 844 (10th Cir. 1979)]

      (1) **Rationale:** Factual conclusions that are within the comprehension of the average layperson should be left to the jury—which supposedly is composed of average laypersons. If the jury can just as well arrive at its *own* conclusions by adding together the factual components provided by the witnesses, there is no *need* for the witnesses to inject their own conclusions. [King & Pillinger, *Opinion Evidence in Illinois* 7 (1942)]

(2) **Exceptions to opinion rule**

(a) **Nonexpert witnesses:** [§871]   Despite the general rule, nonexpert witnesses are allowed to give opinion testimony in two kinds of situations:

    1) *When no better evidence can reasonably be obtained* of facts that the witness *personally observed* [United States v. Schneiderman, 106 F. Supp. 892 (S.D. Cal. 1952)]; *and*

    2) *When it is next to impossible for the lay witness to express the matter in any other way* [*see infra*, §882; *and see* Ladd, Expert Testimony, 5 Vand. L. Rev. 414 (1952)].

(b) **Expert witnesses:** [§872]   Opinion testimony by expert witnesses may be considered an *exception* to the general rule against opinion testimony, or it can simply be said to lie *outside* the general rule against opinion testimony by *nonexpert* witnesses. [*See, e.g.,* Fed. R. Evid. 702] Experts are allowed to give opinion testimony because they possess training, knowledge, and skill in drawing conclusions from certain sorts of information or data that lay fact finders (nonexperts) do not possess. Experts may give opinion testimony only in areas in which the trier of fact cannot draw *unassisted conclusions* (*see* below).

B.   OPINION TESTIMONY BY NONEXPERT WITNESSES

1. **Nonexpert Opinions that Are Excluded:** [§873]   In accordance with the opinion rule, above, there are many matters upon which the opinions of laypersons are inadmissible. The most common examples of such matters are those involving legal conclusions rather than factual observations.

    a. **Standard of care:** [§874]   Witnesses are ordinarily not allowed to express their opinions concerning "negligence" or "fault." Nor are they permitted to testify whether they would have acted as the defendant did.

    b. **Cause of accident:** [§875]   Where an accident or occurrence is of a type such that expert or specialized knowledge is usually required to determine its cause, nonexpert testimony is impermissible. [Duntley v. Inman, Poulsen & Co., 70 P. 529 (Or. 1902)]

    (1) **Exception—common incidents:** [§876]   On the other hand, where the accident or occurrence is of a sort about which laypersons commonly form accurate opinions, a lay witness can properly give an opinion as to causation based on observation of the event. [Schmidt v. Chapman, 131 N.W.2d 352 (Wis. 1964)]

    (2) **Difficult cases:** [§877]   There are some difficult in-between cases— *e.g.,* whether driver's speed "caused him to lose control" of vehicle. The only satisfactory approach is to determine whether the witness's opinion represents the best way of making the matter understandable to the trier of fact. [Annot., 38 A.L.R.2d 13]

c. **Contracts and the like:** [§878]   The existence or nonexistence of contractual or other similar relationships is ultimately a question of law, and a witness is consequently not permitted to testify thereto (*e.g.,* "I did not enter into a contract with P"). This is true whether or not the witness was a party to the asserted contract. [*See, e.g.,* Briney v. Tri-State Mutual Grain Dealers Fire Insurance Co., 117 N.W.2d 889 (Iowa 1962); Federal Underwriters' Exchange v. Cost, 123 S.W.2d 332 (Tex. 1938)]

(1) **Procedure for examination:** [§879]   The proper mode of examination would be to ask the witness what was said by each of the negotiating parties—unless, of course, the alleged contract was in writing, in which case the writing is the best evidence of its existence and terms (*see infra,* §1190).

d. **Agency or authorization:** [§880]   A witness is ordinarily not permitted to testify to her own agency or authority to act for another since the existence and scope of agency authority is ultimately a question of law.

2. **Exceptions to Opinion Rule:** [§881]   Despite the general rule, in a number of situations, statements constituting opinions or conclusions by nonexpert witness *are* admissible.

a. **Requirements for admissibility:** [§882]   As indicated above, the modern approach is that conclusions and opinions by nonexpert witnesses are inadmissible except when they are derived from the witness's personal observation of the facts in dispute and when, from the nature of those facts, no better evidence of them can reasonably be obtained. [United States v. Schneiderman, *supra,* §871] Thus, before a nonexpert witness's opinion is admissible, the trial court must be satisfied that [Fed. R. Evid. 701]:

(1) *The witness's opinion is "rationally based on the perception of the witness"* (*i.e.,* the witness personally observed that about which he has an opinion) [*see* United States v. Jackson, 569 F.2d 1003 (7th Cir. 1978)]; and

(2) *The opinion is "helpful to a clear understanding* of his testimony or the determination of a fact in issue."

(a) **Note:** This generally means that the subject matter of the witness's opinion is something about which normal persons commonly (regularly) form opinions (*e.g.,* size, speed, smell, sound, etc.), and that testimony in the form of an opinion is the **clearest, most understandable way** of getting the matter to the jury (*e.g.,* testifying that a person appeared "drunk" may be a clearer way of conveying his appearance to the jury than describing details about his speech, breath, etc.). [United States v. Thomas, 571 F.2d 285 (5th Cir. 1978)]

b. **Examples**

(1) **Matters of taste, smell, and appearance:** [§883]   A nonexpert witness may state an opinion about matters of appearance, smell, or taste. [People v. Reed, 164 N.E. 847 (Ill. 1928)—"It smelled like dynamite"; Wood v. United States, 361 F.2d 802 (8th Cir. 1966)—"I saw grease and blood on the accused's shirt"]

(2) **Identity:** [§884]   A witness's opinion about the identity of another is admissible; indeed, it is often the *only* adequate way of conveying identification.

    (a) **Example:** W can testify that accused "looks like" the person who committed the crime, or that "I recognize his voice," or "it sounded like his footsteps." [United States v. Butcher, 557 F.2d 666 (9th Cir. 1977)]

    (b) **Note:** An opinion concerning identity need *not* be absolutely positive; lack of positiveness simply affects the *weight* of the testimony.

(3) **Mental condition:** [§885]   The opinion of a nonexpert witness is often admissible on the issue of the *sanity* or other mental state of a close acquaintance. [Annot., 40 A.L.R.2d 15]

    (a) **Example:** Where the validity of a *writing* is in dispute, the subscribing witness can give an opinion concerning the *sanity* of the signer at the *time of execution*. [Annot., 155 A.L.R. 281; *and see* John Hancock Mutual Life Insurance Co. v. Dutton, 585 F.2d 1289 (5th Cir. 1978)]

    (b) **Compare:** But an *opinion* as to whether the decedent seemed to be under the "undue influence" of another is improper. This is because sanity is a conclusion which *normal persons* can regularly draw but "undue influence" is a *legal conclusion*. [*See* 29 Cal. L. Rev. 430 (1941)]

(4) **Physical condition:** [§886]   A witness can give an opinion in describing the apparent *physical condition* of another including the other's apparent age, health, or pain. Words such as "nervous," "drunk," etc., are permitted because the person's condition may be difficult to describe by any language *other* than this sort of *verbal "shorthand."* [United States v. Mastberg, 503 F.2d 465 (9th Cir. 1974)]

(5) **Value (by owner):** [§887]   Proof of *ownership* of property for a reasonable length of time usually qualifies the witness to give an estimate as to its value. [McInnis & Co. v. Western Tractor & Equipment Co., 410 P.2d 908 (Wash. 1966)]

(6) **Dimensions, etc.:** [§888]   Estimates of any measurement or dimension are usually admissible where they will assist the trier of fact in its determination—*e.g.,* size, speed, weight, color, quantity, time, etc. [Waltz, *Introduction to Criminal Evidence* 305-307 (3d ed. 1991)]

    (a) **Example:** Thus, a witness who had even a *glimpse* of D's passing automobile may be allowed to give an opinion as to its *speed*. The brevity of the period of observation usually goes to the *weight* and not to the *admissibility* of the testimony. [*See, e.g.,* Patton v. Henrikson, 380 P.2d 916 (Nev. 1963); Smith v. Hill, 381 P.2d 868 (Okla. 1963)]

(7) **Handwriting:** [§889]   The opinion of a lay witness is admissible to identify handwriting as that of a certain person if the witness is shown to be sufficiently familiar with that person's handwriting. [Fed. R. Evid. 901(b)(2); Annot., 128 A.L.R. 1329]

    (a) **Compare:** However, the general rule is that a nonexpert *cannot* base an opinion on a *comparison* of handwriting samples. In the absence of familiarity with the particular person's handwriting, expert testimony would be required (*see* below).

  (8) **Collateral matters:** [§890] Courts generally have discretion to admit opinion evidence bearing on matters ***not directly in issue*** in order to save time.

gilbert LAW SUMMARIES	**EXAMPLES OF ADMISSIBLE OPINIONS OF LAY WITNESSES**
1. *Matters of Taste, Smell, and Appearance*	"He smelled of alcohol." *or* "She had a tattoo on her ankle."
2. *Identity*	"It sounded like Mark."
3. *Mental Condition*	"He was acting crazy." *or* "She was angry."
4. *Physical Condition*	"He was about 80 years old." *or* "She was slurring her words and couldn't walk straight. She was drunk."
5. *Value of Property*	"My house is worth $150,000."
6. *Speed of Moving Vehicle*	"The truck was going very fast" or (if experienced in estimating rates of speed), "The truck was going at least 60 miles per hour."
7. *Handwriting*	"That's Fran's handwriting."

C. OPINION TESTIMONY BY EXPERT WITNESSES

1. **Requirements for Admissibility—In General:** [§891] An expert can testify to an opinion or inference if the following five conditions are met.

    a. **Specialized knowledge helpful to fact finder:** [§892] The opinions or inferences offered by the expert must depend on special knowledge, skill, experience, or training not within the ordinary experience of lay jurors, so that the witness's testimony will be of assistance to the trier of fact in understanding the evidence or determining some issue. [United States v. Fosher, 590 F.2d 381 (1st Cir. 1979); Meeropol v. Nizer, 417 F. Supp. 1201 (S.D.N.Y. 1976); People v. Crooks, 250 Cal. App. 2d 788 (1967)]

b. **Witness specially qualified:** [§893] The witness must be qualified as an expert—by reason of some special knowledge, skill, experience, or training in the pertinent field.

c. **Proper basis for opinion:** [§894] The witness's opinion must be based on matters upon which other experts in the pertinent field reasonably rely in forming opinions about the subject in issue. [*See* Fed. R. Evid. 702-703; United States v. Watson, 587 F.2d 365 (7th Cir. 1978)] Although Rule 703 could be construed to allow an expert witness to rely on the credibility of another witness in forming an opinion, one prominent court has held that this sort of reliance is *not* permissible. [*See* United States v. Scop, 846 F.2d 135 (2d Cir. 1988)—in securities fraud case expert impermissibly relied on credibility of other witnesses in forming opinion]

d. **Underlying data revealed or available:** [§895] At common law, it was generally necessary that the witness *first* describe the matters or data on which her opinion or inference is based or testify in response to a *hypothetical question* setting forth such matters or data. [Ingram v. McCruston, 134 S.E.2d 705 (N.C. 1964)] Many states still require disclosure before testimony (*see infra,* §§907-913).

e. **Reasonable degree of certainty:** [§896] In some jurisdictions, but by no means all, it must be established that the expert witness possesses "a reasonable degree of certainty (probability)" regarding her opinion or inference. [*Compare* State v. Mitchell, 390 A.2d 495 (Me. 1978)—"high probability" sufficient]

2. **Sources of Expert Witness's Data:** [§897] As suggested by the analysis above, the opinion of an expert witness may be drawn from one of the following four sources:

    a. **Opinion based on facts personally observed:** [§898] The expert witness can express an opinion or conclusion based on facts personally observed (*e.g.,* a treating physician may render a diagnosis on the basis of data clinically observed).

        (1) **Facts communicated by others:** [§899] An expert can also take into account facts communicated to her by others (*e.g.,* the treating physician can base her diagnosis in part on the report of another physician or an X-ray technician; a tax expert can base an opinion on an audit performed by another).

        (2) **Admissibility of source material:** [§900] Furthermore, if the data on which the expert bases her opinion or inference is of a type reasonably relied on by experts in forming opinions or inferences on the particular subject, the data need not itself be *independently* admissible in evidence (*see* below). [Fed. R. Evid. 702-703; United States v. Mills, 434 F.2d 266 (8th Cir. 1970), *cert. denied,* 401 U.S. 925 (1971); State v. Rupp, 586 P.2d 1302 (Ariz. 1978)]

(a) **But note:** The trend is to hold that such data does not itself constitute affirmative evidence and is received only to show the bases of an expert's testimony. [*See* Paddack v. Dave Christensen, Inc., 745 F.2d 1254 (9th Cir. 1985); Carlson, Collision Course in Expert Testimony: Limitations on Affirmative Introduction of Underlying Data, 36 U. Fla. L. Rev. 234 (1984)]

(b) **And note:** To use data as a basis for an expert's opinion, some courts apply a reasonableness or reliance test for expert testimony based on inadmissible hearsay. [*See, e.g.,* Zenith Radio Corp. v. Matsushita Electric Industrial Co., *supra,* §544] However, one commentator has argued that an independent look at the trustworthiness of the underlying data frustrates the very exception Rule 703 was designed to create. [Weinstein, *Evidence* ¶703[03], pp. 703-718 (Supp. 1982); *compare In re* Agent Orange Product Liability Litigation, 611 F. Supp. 1223 (E.D.N.Y. 1985) (per Weinstein, J.)]

b. **Opinion based on evidence adduced during trial:** [§901]   An expert witness who has been present in the courtroom can also base an opinion on the evidence adduced during trial, as long as the witness does not usurp the role of the jury by resolving credibility conflicts. [*See* Waltz, *Introduction to Criminal Evidence* 315 (3d ed. 1991); Kale v. Douthitt, 274 F.2d 476 (4th Cir. 1960)]

c. **Opinion based on hypothetical question:** [§902]   An expert witness can base an opinion on data transmitted to her by means of a *hypothetical question* drawn from the evidence adduced at trial. [*See* Fed. R. Evid. 705]

d. **Opinion based on data conveyed by counsel or others:** [§903]   Under Federal Rule 703, the expert can also base her opinion on data presented by counsel or others *outside of court.*

(1) **Opinion based on inadmissible evidence:** [§904]   Again, the data presented need not be *independently* admissible in evidence as long as it is "of a type reasonably relied on by experts in the particular field in forming opinions or inferences upon the subject." Thus, the physician-expert may base an opinion, at least in part, on information gleaned from texts and learned journals and consultations with other experts. [United States v. Golden, 532 F.2d 1244 (9th Cir. 1976)] And a handwriting expert can base an opinion on writing exemplars which, because of prejudicial content, are inadmissible. [United States v. Shields, 573 F.2d 18 (10th Cir. 1978)] Note, however, that some *state jurisdictions* hold that an expert's testimony must reveal that data relied upon *would be admissible* if appropriate sponsoring witnesses were produced. [*See, e.g.,* Department of Youth Services v. A Juvenile, 499 N.E.2d 812 (Mass. 1986)]

(a) **Opinion based on opinion of another:** [§905]   Most courts will permit an expert witness to ground an opinion in whole or in part on the opinions of *other experts* in the same field regardless of whether those opinions are themselves in evidence. However, it must be *customary* within the witness's discipline to rely on the opinions of others in forming a personal conclusion. [Jenkins v. United States, 307 F.2d 637 (D.C. Cir. 1962)]

(b) **Opinion based on learned treatises:** [§906]   Under the Federal Rules, when an expert witness has relied on statements in learned treatises (scientific texts) during direct examination or they have been brought to her attention during cross-examination, those statements can be read into evidence, either by the party calling the witness or by the cross-examiner. [Fed. R. Evid. 803(18)] However, it must be demonstrated in some acceptable fashion that the treatise is recognized as *authoritative*. The statements then are usable as *substantive evidence* and not merely for impeachment of an adverse witness.

3. **Disclosure of Bases for Expert Opinion:** [§907]   Unless the expert witness can be shown to have *personally* observed the pertinent facts (*e.g.*, the treating physician mentioned above), many state courts require the expert to *disclose* the data relied upon in forming the opinion *before* stating that opinion.

   a. **State court procedures**

      (1) **Testimony heard in court:** [§908]   As suggested above, the expert can be asked if she was in the courtroom and heard the facts developed in previous testimony. Following an affirmative response, the expert will simply be asked whether her opinion is based on the data described in that testimony.

      (2) **Hypothetical question:** [§909]   Alternatively, a hypothetical question can be posed to the expert. (In many states this is the *only* way expert testimony can be elicited. [*See* Annot., 56 A.L.R.3d 300; Cal. Evid. Code §802, comment])

         (a) **Definition:** [§910]   A hypothetical question is one that asks the expert witness to *assume as true* various data that examining counsel believes he has proved (or will be able to prove) concerning the condition in question and then asks the expert to state an opinion based on the assumed data.

            1) **Note on completeness:** [§911]   Some state courts require that the hypothetical question include "every material fact," and not just those that support the conclusion that the expert will express. [*See, e.g.,* Ames & Webb, Inc. v. Commercial Laundry Co., 33 S.E.2d 547 (Va. 1963)] However, the modern trend is to reject this requirement as unnecessarily cumbersome, confusing, and time-consuming. Facts that support a *contrary* conclusion can be brought out on cross-examination. [Fed. R. Evid. 705; Vermont Food Industries, Inc. v. Ralston Purina Co., 514 F.2d 456 (2d Cir. 1975)]

         (b) **Assumed facts must be of record:** [§912]   The facts assumed must be in the trial record when the hypothetical question is asked, or else examining counsel must indicate to the court that evidence of those facts will be produced in due course. Some courts would require an offer of proof. [*See, e.g.,* Takoma Park Bank v. Abbott, 19 A.2d 169 (Md. 1941)]

(c) **Criticisms of approach:** [§913] Hypothetical questions are frequently awkward and confusing to jurors. They are fraught with possibilities of error and can be inordinately time-consuming. Moreover, they are almost invariably tedious for the jury to hear.

b. **Federal approach:** [§914] Recognizing the criticisms of the hypothetical question, Federal Rule 705 would permit examining counsel to ask the expert for an opinion and then immediately allow the opposing side to cross-examine, without any disclosure of the data underlying the opinion (unless the trial court requires advance disclosure). [Vermont Food Industries, Inc. v. Ralston Purina Co., *supra*]

(1) **Criticism:** The federal approach may not always be a satisfactory procedure for the cross-examiner since (unless there has been exhaustive pretrial discovery) the cross-examiner may not know how to begin getting at the facts behind the opinion.

(2) **Effect of Federal Rule:** As a practical matter, trial lawyers are unlikely to abandon the hypothetical question even though Federal Rule 705 permits them to do so, if only because the hypothetical question allows counsel to sum up the evidence in advance of closing arguments. However, Federal Rule 705 probably forecloses a reversal on appeal based on a claim that opposing counsel's hypothetical question was incomplete (*i.e.,* did not include the underlying facts or data) by in effect placing on the cross-examiner the burden of eliciting any missing data. [*See* Waltz, *The New Federal Rules of Evidence: An Analysis* 112-113 (2d ed. 1975)]

4. **Qualifications of Expert Witness:** [§915] Before a witness is permitted to give an opinion as an expert, counsel must satisfy the trial judge that the witness possesses some special knowledge, skill, or experience that qualifies her to render the opinion. [Fed. R. Evid. 702; Knight v. Otis Elevator Co., 596 F.2d 84 (3d Cir. 1979)]

a. **Qualifying questions:** [§916] Preliminary information as to the witness's qualifications is elicited by examining counsel with what are referred to as "qualifying questions." [*See* Waltz & Inbau, *Medical Jurisprudence* 371 (1971)]

b. **Qualifying factors:** [§917] Among the factors usually raised by the qualifying questions and considered in deciding whether a witness is "qualified" are: (i) education and training; (ii) experience; (iii) familiarity with authoritative references in the field; and (iv) membership in professional associations.

c. **Requirement of expertise:** [§918] Technical expertise is not always essential. *Any* special experience, etc., can qualify a person to give an expert opinion.

(1) **Example:** An F.B.I. agent was held qualified as an expert on the mechanics of "numbers" games. [Moore v. United States, 394 F.2d 818 (5th Cir. 1968)]

(2) **Example:** A *convicted burglar* can testify to the utility to burglars of such tools as crowbars, gloves, wires, etc. [State v. Briner, 255 N.W.2d 422 (Neb. 1977)]

(3) **Example:** A drug user and dealer was sufficiently experienced to give an opinion that a substance was heroin [United States v. Atkins, 473 F.2d 308 (8th Cir. 1973)]; a heavy user of LSD was allowed to give an opinion that a pill given to and consumed by him contained LSD [State v. Johnson, 196 N.W.2d 717 (Wis. 1972)]; a narcotics agent could testify from visual examination that a substance was cocaine [United States v. Bermudez, 526 F.2d 89 (2d Cir. 1975)]; and a user could testify that marijuana came from Colombia [United States v. Johnson, 575 F.2d 1347 (5th Cir. 1978)].

(4) **Compare:** But a *prosecutor* is *not* qualified to give an expert opinion that a book's dominant theme is prurient and offensive to contemporary community standards. [State v. Watson, 414 P.2d 337 (Or. 1966)]

(5) **And note:** A *police officer* is *not* qualified to express expert opinion as to vehicular speed on the basis of skid marks and damage to vehicles, since this requires *knowledge* of *physics* and *mechanics*. [Deaver v. Hickox, 224 N.E.2d 468 (Ill. 1967)] *But note:* An experienced police officer can testify to the effect of alcohol on a person's ability to safely operate a motor vehicle. [Marr v. State, 741 P.2d 844 (Okla. 1987)]

5. **Subject Matter of Opinion:** [§919]   The expert witness can testify only to matters embraced by her field of expertise and about which people lacking the witness's special knowledge are uninformed.

   a. **Opinion on "ultimate issue"**

      (1) **Traditional rule prohibits:** [§920]   In times past, an expert would not be permitted to render an opinion on the *"ultimate issue"* in the case (*e.g.,* whether an operation was "necessary" or whether a bridge was "properly constructed"), since this would *"invade the province of the jury."*

      (2) **Modern trend admits:** [§921]   However, the modern trend *repudiates* so ambiguous a limitation. Testimony in the form of an expert opinion is *not* objectionable because it *embraces* the ultimate issue or issues to be decided by the trier of fact. [Fed. R. Evid. 704(a); United States v. Scavo, 593 F.2d 837 (8th Cir. 1979)]

      (3) **Unhelpful opinions excluded:** [§922]   Nevertheless, testimony on an ultimate issue may still be excluded if it embraces a *conclusion of law*, or *is unhelpful* [Fed. R. Evid. 702], *prejudicial*, or a *waste of time* [Fed. R. Evid. 403]. Thus, opinions going directly to innocence or guilt are likely to be excluded in criminal cases. [*See, e.g.,* State v. Odom, 560 A.2d 1198 (N.J. 1989); United States v. Guterriez, 576 F.2d 269 (10th Cir. 1978)]

         (a) **Note—criminal defendant's mental state:** An expert witness testifying to the mental state or condition of a defendant in a criminal case may *not* state an opinion or inference as to whether defendant had the mental state or condition constituting an *element* of the crime charged or of a defense thereto. Such ultimate issues are matters for the trier of fact alone. [Fed. R. Evid. 704(b)] Thus, an expert may testify that the defendant suffered from a mental disease or defect and can describe the characteristics of such a condition, but cannot offer a conclusion as to whether the condition rendered the defendant incapable of appreciating the nature and quality or wrongfulness of her acts. (Some courts draw a fine semantic line: The **defense** can ask whether a particular psychiatric condition would prevent the defendant from **understanding** the nature and quality of her acts, but **cannot** call for an ultimate legal conclusion regarding **culpability**. [United States v. Kristiansen, 901 F.2d 1463 (8th Cir. 1990)]) Likewise, where the defense of entrapment is raised, an expert is precluded from offering an opinion that the defendant lacked the predisposition to commit a law violation. [*See* United States v. Prickett, 604 F. Supp. 407 (S.D. Ohio 1985); *and see* United States v. Esch, 832 F.2d 531 (10th Cir. 1987)]

b. **Opinions on matters as to which jurors uninformed:** [§923]   Whenever some **special knowledge** or **training** is required to render an opinion on a matter at issue, expert testimony is proper to aid the jurors in reaching their verdict. Examples include:

(1) **Causation:** Expert testimony regarding causation of an accident or occurrence is proper.

(2) **Sanity:** Expert opinion concerning a person's sanity may be received even when sanity constitutes the ultimate issue—*e.g.,* in will contests, guardianship proceedings, and other civil cases. (In criminal cases in which insanity is asserted as a defense, *see* above note. Keep in mind that **nonexpert** (lay) opinion is also admissible on this issue; *see supra,* §885.)

(3) **Handwriting:** A handwriting expert may testify that two writings were probably prepared by the same person. [United States v. Spencer, 439 F.2d 1047 (2d Cir. 1971)] And handwriting, fingerprints, blood groupings, DNA, etc., may be received to establish identification even where identification is the ultimate issue, as it often is in criminal cases. (Again, remember that **nonexpert** (lay) opinion is also admissible; *see supra,* §889.)

(4) **Property values:** Experts (*e.g.,* realtors) can give testimony as to property values. (A **nonexpert**—the property owner—may also be permitted to give valuation testimony; *see supra,* §887.)

(5) **Identity:** Photo comparison experts can give opinions as to the identity of the person in a photograph. [United States v. Sellers, 566 F.2d 884 (4th Cir. 1977)]

c. **Opinions on matters as to which jurors competent:** [§924]   As was indicated *supra,* §§919-922, expert testimony is usually considered improper—or at least unnecessary—when the jurors are competent to draw their own conclusions on the issue. Thus, expert opinion is **not** allowed on the issues of "**fault**," "**negligence**," or "**guilt**" because these are conclusions that jurors are competent to draw from the facts presented in evidence.

(1) **Example:** Opinions that a dip in a highway was a "dangerous condition" or that the plaintiff was driving "too fast for highway conditions" were improper since these were inferences jurors could readily draw from facts in evidence. [Wilkerson v. City of El Monte, 17 Cal. App. 2d 615 (1936); *and see* Stoler v. Penn Central Transportation Co., 583 F.2d 896 (6th Cir. 1978)—expert not permitted to testify that railroad crossing was "extra-hazardous"]

(2) **Example:** In a medical malpractice case an expert can testify about the standard of care, but *not* whether defendant physician was "negligent." The jury is capable of determining whether defendant's conduct measured up to the applicable standard. [Clifford-Jacobs Forging Co. v. Industrial Commission, 166 N.E.2d 582 (Ill. 1960)]

6. **Effect of Expert Opinion**

   a. **General rule—jury can disregard:** [§925]   It is generally held that jurors are *not bound* to accept expert opinion even when it is uncontradicted by other evidence. *Rationale:* An expert's opinion is no better than the reasons and data on which it is based, and the trier of fact may decide to disagree with or disbelieve the reasons or data presented by the expert witness.

   b. **Limitation—uncontroverted expert opinion:** [§926]   On the other hand, it is frequently said that jurors cannot arbitrarily disregard uncontroverted expert opinion and substitute their own opinions on matters about which laypersons are *not qualified* to render valid opinions. Accordingly, a verdict arrived at in this manner must be set aside as unsupported by the evidence. [Krause v. Apodaca, 186 Cal. App. 2d 413 (1960)—uncontroverted expert opinion on origin of fire binding on trier of fact]

7. **Cross-Examination and Impeachment of Expert Witnesses:** [§927]   An expert witness can be cross-examined to the same extent as any other witness and can be impeached on the same grounds (*infra,* §§1003 *et seq.*), *plus* the following:

   a. **Lack of expert qualifications:** [§928]   The cross-examiner is free to show, either by cross-examination or independent (extrinsic) evidence, that the witness *lacks* the qualifications she claimed to have on direct examination, or that those qualifications do not make the witness a *true expert* in the field in which she claims expertise.

      (1) **Voir dire procedure:** [§929]   Many jurisdictions will permit adverse counsel to engage in a limited cross-examination immediately following the proponent's qualifying questions for the purpose of testing a witness's qualifications as an expert.

   b. **Prior inconsistent opinions:** [§930]   Cross-examination may reveal that the expert previously expressed a *different* opinion in the *present* case. Note, however, that most courts refuse to allow impeachment on differing conclusions arrived at in *other* cases, regardless of how similar they might be.

   c. **Altering facts of hypothetical question:** [§931]   The facts of any hypothetical question put to the expert on direct examination can, on cross-examination, be *altered* or *withdrawn*, and counsel can then inquire whether, on the basis of the altered hypothetical, the expert would change her opinion. Facts can also be *added* to the hypothetical question if the trial record reflects them or counsel represents that they will be elicited.

d. **Showing compensation received:** [§932] The expert may be cross-examined about the compensation and expenses she is receiving in connection with her reports and testimony. [*See* Cal. Evid. Code §722]

e. **Contrary views of other experts; use of scientific texts, learned treatises, and journals:** [§933] Rebuttal testimony by other experts, called by an adverse party, is of course proper. Likewise, it is permissible to show on cross-examination that pertinent texts, treatises, or articles in learned journals do not support the opinions expressed by the witness, at least if the witness stated that they were *relied on* in arriving at her opinions.

   (1) **Use of materials not relied on by expert:** [§934] A more difficult problem is whether the cross-examiner can use *other* texts, etc.—*i.e.,* ones on which the expert does *not* claim to have relied in arriving at the opinion—to controvert the witness's expert opinion.

      (a) **Some states do not allow:** [§935] Some states do not permit the cross-examiner to use other texts on the theory that some cross-examiners might attempt to use the hearsay opinions of irresponsible authors who cannot themselves be cross-examined. [*See* Cal. Evid. Code §721(b)]

      (b) **Compare—Federal Rules and many states:** [§936] The Federal Rules and many states *allow* cross-examination of an expert witness concerning contrary views expressed in *any* recognized (authoritative) scientific text, treatise, etc., regardless of whether the expert claims to have relied thereon. [Fed. R. Evid. 803(18)]

         1) **Rationale:** If courts did not allow experts to be cross-examined with authoritative texts expressing contrary views, an expert witness could *always* avoid an embarrassing cross-examination by denying that she relied on texts, etc., that are contrary to her opinion.

         2) **Safeguard on reliability:** [§937] The major safeguard under the Federal Rules is that the text, etc., must be shown to be *authoritative* and therefore reliable. If the expert denies its authoritativeness, independent evidence can be brought in (*e.g.,* the testimony of other experts), or the trial court may take judicial notice of its authoritative status. [Fed. R. Evid. 803(18); *and see infra*, §§1267 *et seq.*]

         3) **Use as substantive evidence:** [§938] In most courts, the text, etc., is admissible *solely for impeaching purposes* and not as substantive evidence of the contrary views expressed therein. [Waltz & Inbau, *Medical Jurisprudence* 85-87 (1971)]

            a) **Example:** P sued for injuries sustained in an automobile accident. On cross-examination, P's counsel asked the medical experts for the defense whether they were familiar with a specified medical treatise. Both experts agreed that the treatise was a recognized one, and one of the experts stated that he had a copy of it in his library. The treatise included expert opinion contrary to that given in the experts' testimony on direct. *Held:* The material from the treatise was admissible to **impeach** the experts, but the trial court had properly instructed the jurors **not** to consider it as **substantive evidence**. [Ruth v. Fenchel, 121 A.2d 373 (N.J. 1956)]

IX. EXAMINATION, CROSS-EXAMINATION, AND IMPEACHMENT

chapter approach

Issues regarding *direct examination* are generally not complicated. Important issues are:

1. Is the *form* of the question proper?

2. When may a party impeach his *own witness*? (Today, usually anytime.)

3. What may be done if the witness can't remember? (Consider *refreshing recollection* or *past recollection recorded*.)

The rules as to cross-examination and impeachment are extremely important, not only practically, but on examination questions. *Cross-examination* issues require consideration of:

1. Is the *form* of the question proper? (It usually is unless the question is argumentative or unintelligible.)

2. Is the *scope* of the cross-examination limited? Or has someone "opened the door" as to that matter?

3. Is the cross-examination attempting to bring out *inadmissible* impeachment or other inadmissible evidence?

Impeachment rules are quite technical, and for this reason it is quite easy for examiners to fashion questions that rely on them. In each case you must ask:

1. Precisely what is the impeaching evidence *being used for* (to rebut testimony, to show lack of knowledge or perceptive ability, or to attack credibility)?

2. If used to attack credibility, in which technical *area of impeachment* does it fall (character impeachment, showing of hostility or bias, or prior inconsistencies)?

3. Does it meet the technical *requirements* of that area of impeachment (*e.g.,* whether extrinsic evidence as well as cross-examination is permitted)?

A. FORM OF EXAMINATION [§939]

The mode and order of interrogating witnesses is a matter largely within the discretion of the trial judge. The judge is empowered to regulate the interrogation process in whatever manner is necessary to expedite the trial, to protect witnesses from harassment, and to heighten the effectiveness of the examination. [Fed. R. Evid. 611(a)]

1. **Exclusion of Witnesses:** [§940]   In most courts, the exclusion of witnesses so that they cannot hear the testimony of other witnesses is within the discretion of the trial judge. However, this discretion does not allow the judge to exclude witnesses

who are *parties* to the action (or their employee-representatives) or other "essential" witnesses.

a. **Federal Rule:** [§941]   Under the Federal Rules, the judge may—and upon the request of either party, must—order witnesses excluded during the testimony of other witnesses. But again, this does not authorize the exclusion of parties and persons whose presence is shown to be essential to the party's presentation of his case. [Fed. R. Evid. 615]

   (1) **Sanctions:** [§942]   Violation of a witness sequestration order may be enforced through a number of sanctions including refusal to allow the witness in question to testify. [*See, e.g.,* Miller v. Universal City Studios, Inc., 650 F.2d 1365 (5th Cir. 1981)—expert in civil copyright case had read daily transcript]

   (2) **Pretrial proceedings:** [§943]   Rule 1101(c) renders Rule 615 inapplicable to pretrial proceedings. However, many of the policy considerations underlying Rule 615 are applied in such proceedings.

2. **Direct Examination and Matters Incident Thereto**

a. **Form of questioning—in general:** [§944]   Testimony from a witness on direct examination is presented simply by placing the witness on the stand, swearing in the witness, and then asking the witness a series of questions. On direct examination, the examiner is usually limited to questions calling for specific responses by the witness (typically): who? where? when? how? etc. Other forms of questioning may be objectionable.

   (1) **Questions calling for conclusions:** [§945]   Except where opinion testimony is permissible (*supra,* §§871-872), questions that call for the opinion or conclusion of the witness are not allowed. Thus, "Could the defendant easily see the plaintiff in the crosswalk?" is not allowed because it calls for the witness's opinion as to what the defendant did or did not see. "Why did the defendant strike the plaintiff?" also is not allowed because it calls for a conclusion as to the defendant's state of mind.

   (2) **Repetitive questions:** [§946]   Another prohibition on direct examination is against repetitive questioning designed to bolster or emphasize what has already been established. The objection that the question has been "asked and answered" is used to limit such cumulative evidence. (Repetitive questions may be more readily permitted on cross-examination, *see infra,* §979.)

   (3) **Narrative questioning:** [§947]   Questions that allow the witness to present a narrative (*e.g.,* "Tell us everything that happened on the evening of the accident") are not permitted by many courts. The rationale is that it is too difficult to determine whether specific portions of the testimony might be objectionable before uttered. As a result, more specific questions, such as "What happened next?" are usually required.

      (a) **But note:** Some courts do permit narrative questioning; if incompetent matter is admitted as part of the free narrative, the only remedy of the adverse party is a motion to strike. [*See, e.g.,* Silva v. Dias, 46 Cal. App. 2d 662 (1941)]

(4) **Questions containing facts not in evidence:** [§948] Questions suggesting a fact to the witness that is not yet in evidence in the case are not permitted. Such "loaded" questions are misleading since they imply the existence of an *unestablished fact* (*e.g.*, "How long has it been since you stopped beating your wife?").

(5) **Leading questions:** [§949] The use of "leading questions" on direct examination is limited. [Fed. R. Evid. 611(c)]

(a) **Types of leading questions:** [§950] There are *two* types of leading questions:

(i) *Those merely leading the witness to a desired answer* (*e.g.*, "Did D stop at the stop sign?"). This type is sometimes allowed (*see* below); and

(ii) *Questions that strongly suggest a large volume of facts*, permitting the witness to affirm them with a simple "yes" answer (*e.g.*, "Did you see the car veering from side to side and silently bearing down on the defendant without lights as he was in the crosswalk?"). This type of question would *certainly* be *disallowed*.

Some judges use the rule of thumb that if a question can be answered by a simple "yes," it is leading. This is probably too simplistic a test, although it may be one indication that a question may be too *suggestive*.

(b) **When leading questions permitted:** [§951] The first type of leading question, above, may be permitted when necessary to develop the witness's testimony and where there is no real danger of *improper* suggestion. [Fed. R. Evid. 611(c)] *Examples:*

1) *Preliminary or background questioning* (setting the stage): "You are an insurance salesman, aren't you?"

2) *To jog a witness's memory* (to "refresh the recollection," *see infra*, §§964-973). [*But see* United States v. Shoupe, 548 F.2d 636 (6th Cir. 1977)—leading questions cannot be used to place inadmissible statement before jury]

3) *When dealing with a timid or confused witness*, or a *child* of tender years. [*See* United States v. Littlewind, 551 F.2d 244 (8th Cir. 1977)]

4) *When dealing with a hostile witness*. If a witness evidences pronounced hostility or bias on the witness stand, the court may permit the attorney who called the witness to interrogate by leading questions.

5) ***When examining the adverse party*** or any witness ***identified*** with the adverse party. [Fed. R. Evid. 611(c)]

    a) Either party may, of course, call the adverse party as a witness. Because the examination of an adverse party is "in the nature of ***cross-examination***" the use of leading questions is generally permitted. Indeed, under some statutes, it is a matter of right. [*See* Cal. Evid. Code §776]

    b) Under many statutes, the use of leading questions is ***extended*** to persons "***identified with***" the adverse party— *e.g.,* spouses, relatives, employees, business associates. [Fed. R. Evid. 611(e); Cal. Evid. Code §776]

    c) *Note:* Where the adverse party (or someone identified with the adverse party) is called as a witness by the other party, the adverse party's ***own*** attorney may then seek to "cross-examine," but courts normally do not permit leading questions because it is really ***not*** an adversary cross-examination. [*See* Cal. Evid. Code §776(b)(1); *compare* Morvant v. Construction Aggregates Corp., 570 F.2d 626 (6th Cir. 1978)—matter for judicial discretion]

b. **Rule against impeachment of party's own witness**

(1) **Traditional rule:** [§952]   The traditional rule is that a party is ***not*** allowed to impeach ***her "own"*** witnesses.

    (a) **Rationale:** At common law, witnesses "***belonged***" to the party first calling them; *i.e.,* a party "vouched" for the credibility of those called as witnesses and hence was ***barred*** from impeaching them.

    (b) **Exceptions:** [§953]   There are several situations in which a party is allowed to impeach a witness whom she has called:

        1) **Witness required by law:** [§954]   Where the witness is one whom the party is required by ***law*** to call to prove her case (*i.e.,* an attesting witness in a will contest), courts have uniformly ***allowed*** impeachment. Where the witness is merely one ***required*** to prove the facts of the case (*i.e.,* the only eyewitness), impeachment is generally ***not*** allowed. (Some courts are contra; *see infra*, §§959-960.)

        2) **Witness is adverse party:** [§955]   Where the party calls as a witness the ***adverse party*** (or someone ***united in interest*** with the adverse party—*e.g.,* spouse, partner, employee, etc.), the examination of such witness is "in the nature of cross-examination." Thus, most courts permit the examiner to use leading questions (above) and to impeach.

            a) **Civil cases only:** [§956]   Of course, this rule applies in civil cases only; the privilege against ***self-incrimination*** prevents the prosecution from calling the defendant as a witness in criminal cases.

3) **Witness hostile on stand; surprise testimony:** [§957]   Whenever the witness gives testimony in such a manner as to indicate hostility to the calling party, impeachment is allowed. *Examples:*

   a) *Witness shows hostility* or *animosity* to party calling him.

   b) *Witness appears to be biased* in favor of *adversary* or to have some *adverse financial interest* in the litigation (although many courts hold that mere bias or adverse interest is not enough).

   c) *Party calling the witness is legitimately surprised* by the testimony given (as where the witness had previously made inconsistent statements).

      1/   But where the witness merely testifies that she *cannot remember facts* as to which the witness had previously given statements, impeachment is not allowed because there is no inconsistency. (*But see* "refreshing recollection," *infra*, §964.)

      2/   And impeachment, as on a prior inconsistent statement, cannot be used as a mere subterfuge for getting otherwise *inadmissible* hearsay into evidence. [Whitehurst v. Wright, 592 F.2d 834 (5th Cir. 1979)]

4) **Grounds and procedure for impeachment:** [§958]   Where impeachment is allowed, the procedure and grounds are the same as on *cross-examination* (*see infra*, §§975 *et seq.*).

(2) **Criticism of rule:** [§959]   The rule limiting impeachment of one's own witness is criticized on the basis that a party does not always have a free choice as to the witnesses the party must call to prove her case (*i.e.*, the sole eyewitness to the accident), and therefore should hardly be held to "vouch" for them.

   (a) **Modern trend—abolition of rule:** [§960]   Recognizing the validity of the above criticism, the modern trend is to permit impeachment of any witness by any party. For example, the Federal Rules provide that the "credibility of a witness may be attacked by any party, including the party calling the witness." [Fed. R. Evid. 607]

      1) **But note:** Some courts will prevent a prosecutor from calling a witness solely to "impeach" the witness with evidence that would otherwise be inadmissible. For example, suppose that the prosecutor knows that the witness will exonerate the defendant, and the prosecutor calls the witness anyway in order to "impeach" the witness with an out-of-court statement made to an investigator saying that the defendant committed the crime.

In this case, the prosecutor is hoping that the jury will use the statement for a purpose forbidden by law—*i.e.,* that the jury will use the statement for the truth of what it asserts and pay no attention to a limiting instruction telling it that the statement is admissible only for the light it sheds on the credibility of the witness. In this limited situation, the prosecutor may be prevented from impeaching her own witness. [United States v. Hogan, 763 F.2d 697 (5th Cir. 1985)]

(3) **Constitutional limitation:** [§961]   Even where retained, the rule against impeaching one's own witness can never be applied in a criminal case so as to deprive the accused of a fair trial as guaranteed by the Fourteenth Amendment Due Process Clause.

(a) **Example:** D, accused of murder, called X to testify; X had previously confessed to killing the victim, but now repudiates his confession. D then attempted to impeach X by showing the prior confession. The Supreme Court held that the application of the rule against impeaching one's own witness was violative of Fourteenth Amendment due process because D's impeachment of X was crucial to his defense. [Chambers v. Mississippi, 410 U.S. 284 (1973)]

c. **Effect of uncertainty in testimony:** [§962]   Obviously, the more certain and definite the witness's testimony, the more probative value it has. However, testimony should not be rejected merely because it is couched in indefinite terms (*e.g.,* where witness testifies, "I'm not sure, but I think I saw him . . ."; or "To the best of my recollection, I believe he said . . ."). Whether the witness was merely being cautious, or actually did not know much, or was just guessing, is up to the trier of fact to decide. In other words, lack of certainty goes to the weight of the testimony but does not affect its admissibility. [Turner v. Smith's Administratrix, 222 S.W.2d 353 (Ky. 1949)]

d. **Effect of lack of memory:** [§963]   A witness who has absolutely *no recollection* regarding the matters at issue obviously is not competent to testify (*see supra,* §§815-819, 829). However, the more common situation is where the witness's memory is incomplete—*i.e.,* the witness remembers the transaction in general, but not the essential details. In such a case, the examiner may seek to aid the witness's memory on direct examination. Such revival of recollection may involve the two concepts known as *"refreshing recollection"* and *"past recollection recorded."*

(1) **Present memory revived—"refreshing recollection":** [§964]   Basically, a testifying witness may be permitted to refresh or revive her memory by referring to a writing or anything else if the witness will thereafter be able to testify from present recollection—*i.e.,* without depending on the terms of the writing, etc., to which reference is made. [125 A.L.R. 19; Baker v. State, 371 A.2d 699 (Md. 1977)]

(a) **Anything may be used:** [§965]   Note that this rule is not limited to the use of a writing. The examiner may use anything that legitimately jogs the witness's memory—*i.e.,* a picture, reference to another witness's testimony, or even a leading question ("Do you remember that . . . ?"). [Marchand v. Public Service Co., 65 A.2d 468 (N.H. 1949)]

1) **Hypnosis:** [§966]   A few courts have even allowed the use of hypnosis to refresh the witness's memory. [*See* Wyller v. Fairchild Hiller Corp., 503 F.2d 506 (9th Cir. 1974)]

   a) **Caution:** Other courts, however, have held that hypnotism is so likely to "*implant*" false memories that any witness who has been previously hypnotized for the purpose of recalling material about an event is *incompetent* to testify about such matters.

(b) **Use of writings**

1) **Laying the foundation:** [§967]   However, if a writing (or other tangible evidence) is used to refresh the witness's recollection, a proper foundation must be laid. The requirements for using a writing to refresh recollection are that:

   a) *Before reference* to the writing, the witness had some *present* memory, however defective;

   b) *After presentation* to the court and opposing counsel, the writing is *shown* to the witness; and

   c) *After reference thereto*, the witness's memory is *refreshed*, and she is able to testify *without depending* on the writing.

2) **Admissibility of writing:** [§968]   The writing need not be authentic nor made by the witness; indeed, it may have no independent relevancy. Hence, the party using it to refresh the witness's recollection does not have any absolute right to *offer* it in evidence.

   a) **Rights of adverse party:** [§969]   However, the adverse party has the right to *inspect* the document and to *introduce* any portion that *relates* to the testimony of the witness. [Fed. R. Evid. 612]

      1/ **Purpose:** The adverse party may wish to do this to show either that: (i) the witness's testimony was *limited* to just exactly what was on the writing, and that the witness thus had no real *present* memory of what she was testifying to; or (ii) the document was *false*, and that if the witness's testimony agreed with it, the testimony should be *discredited*. [125 A.L.R. 65]

      2/ **Note:** If there is a dispute as to which portions of the document properly relate to the testimony of the witness, the judge will examine the document and excise improper parts thereof (but they are preserved for appellate review). [Fed. R. Evid. 612]

3/ **And note:** Where the writing used to refresh the witness's recollection contains *privileged* material, most courts hold that divulging such material to someone not involved in the privileged relationship constitutes a *waiver* of the privilege. Thus, where a client allows his communication to an attorney to be used to refresh a witness's recollection, the document would have to be turned over to the adverse party under the above rule.

3) **Compare—showing writing to witness before witness takes stand:** [§970]   Attempting to refresh the recollection of a witness who is on the stand is certainly not as effective as conferring with the witness before she takes the stand and showing her whatever writings are involved. The witness can then testify from present recollection without reference to the documents examined before her testimony.

a) **Production of document:** [§971]   However, suppose on cross-examination the witness admits to using some document or writing to refresh recollection prior to testifying; can the cross-examiner then compel production of the writing?

1/ **Majority view:** [§972]   Most courts deny the cross-examiner any absolute right to compel production of the writing although the trial court in its discretion may order it produced. [Fed R. Evid. 612; Prucha v. M & N Modern Hydraulic Press Co., 76 F.R.D. 207 (7th Cir. 1977)—production required]

a/ **Rationale:** This rule is to prevent "fishing expeditions" as to everything the witness may have looked at while preparing her testimony, some of which may be privileged.

b/ **Note:** If the court orders production of a writing and the witness refuses to comply, the court must make whatever order "justice requires"; in criminal cases, the court must either strike the testimony of a prosecution witness or declare a mistrial. [Fed. R. Evid. 612]

2/ **Federal view—criminal cases:** [§973]   In federal criminal cases, the accused has an absolute right to compel production of any pretrial statement given by a witness who testifies against him at trial—whether or not the witness acknowledges referring to the statement before taking the stand. [Jencks v. United States, 353 U.S. 657 (1957); Fed. R. Crim. P. 26.2]

(2) **Insufficient memory—"past recollection recorded":** [§974]   Where the witness has no independent memory of the contents of a document (even after being shown the document), the witness will not be permitted to testify by relying on the writing. However, if the document meets the somewhat rigid standards of the past recollection recorded exception to the hearsay rule (*see supra,* §§433-441), the document itself may be introduced into evidence and read into the record (although it cannot be sent to the jury room).

3. Cross-Examination and Matters Incident Thereto

a. **Right of cross-examination:** [§975]   Cross-examination is the most reliable and effective way of testing the credibility and accuracy of testimony. Therefore, the right to cross-examine the opposing party's witness in any court proceeding (trial, deposition, etc.) is an essential element of due process (and, in criminal cases, a requirement of the Sixth Amendment Confrontation Clause as well). [Alford v. United States, 282 U.S. 687 (1931)]

(1) **Effect of denial of right:** [§976]   Where one side is denied the opportunity to cross-examine, by the death (or other legitimate unavailability) of a witness who has already testified for the opponent on direct, most courts require that the testimony given on direct examination be stricken— provided the unavailability of the witness is through no fault of the party seeking to cross-examine.

(a) **Note:** Likewise, all courts hold that the direct testimony will be stricken where the witness refuses to submit to cross-examination, or claims a privilege (assuming the privilege has not been waived by the witness's direct testimony; *see supra,* §574).

b. **Questions permitted on cross-examination:** [§977]   On cross-examination, a party is permitted to employ any type of question that would be proper on direct, along with certain types that would not be.

(1) **Leading questions permitted:** [§978]   Thus, a cross-examiner may use leading questions suggestive of the answer ("Isn't it true that . . ."; or "You saw him, didn't you . . ."). [Fed. R. Evid. 611(c)]

(2) **Improper questioning:** [§979]   However, certain types of questions are not permitted:

(a) **Misleading:** A question that cannot be answered without making an unintended admission. The classic example is, "Do you still beat your wife?"

(b) **Compound:** A question that requires a single answer to more than one question. *Example:* "Did you see and hear him?"

(c) **Argumentative:** A leading question that also reflects the *examiner's* interpretation of the facts. *Example:* "Why were you driving so carelessly?"

(d) **Assuming facts not in evidence:** A question that assumes that a disputed fact is true although it has not yet been affirmed by the witness. *Example:* "After he ran the stop sign, he honked his horn, didn't he?" (where the witness has not previously been asked about anyone running a stop sign).

(e) **Conclusionary:** A question that calls for an opinion or conclusion that the witness is **not qualified** or **permitted** to make. *Example:* "Did your wife understand this also?" (opinion as to wife's understanding).

(f) **Cumulative:** A question that has **already** been asked and answered. More repetition is allowed on cross-examination than on direct, but where it is apparent that the cross-examiner is not getting anywhere, the judge may disallow the question.

(g) **Harassing, embarrassing:** A trial judge has discretion to disallow cross-examination that is unduly harassing or embarrassing. [*See, e.g.,* United States v. Colyer, 571 F.2d 941 (5th Cir. 1978)—"Are you a homosexual?"]

c. **Scope of cross-examination**

(1) **Minority view—wide open:** [§980]   A minority of states retain the common law rule that a witness is a witness for **all purposes**, not just as to certain facts, and hence, may be cross-examined on **all relevant matters**, whether or not covered on or related to direct (subject only to the trial court's discretionary power to limit). [Neely v. State, 272 N.W.2d 381 (Wis. 1978)]

(2) **Minority view—intermediate position:** [§981]   A middle ground taken in a few courts is that cross-examination may cover any matters **raised on direct**, and any part of the defendant's case that is covered by his **denials** of the **plaintiff's case**; *i.e.,* the cross-examiner can go into any part of his own case, **except** affirmative defenses, cross-claims, etc. [Dietsch v. Mayberry, 47 N.E.2d 404 (Ohio 1942)]

(3) **General view—restricted scope:** [§982]   Most states (and the Federal Rules) restrict the scope of cross-examination to matters put in issue on **direct** examination, including, of course, the credibility of the witness. [Fed. R. Evid. 611(b); Cal. Evid. Code §761; United States v. Southers, 583 F.2d 1302 (5th Cir. 1978)] *Note:* Other matters are accessible by recalling the witness to the stand in one's **own** case-in-chief and inquiring into the matter on direct examination. Often there are tactical disadvantages to this because of the inability to ask leading questions of one's own witness.

(a) **What constitutes "scope of the direct":** [§983]   Most courts are liberal and allow cross-examination on any matter related to a subject testified to on direct. In other words, testimony on direct that touches on any phase of a subject "opens up the door" to thorough cross-examination as to any other phase of that subject. [*See, e.g.,* United States v. Wolfson, 573 F.2d 216 (5th Cir. 1978)]

1) **Application:** Moreover, it is generally held that cross-examination is proper to rebut not only matters actually testified to on direct, but also any *inferences* or *deductions* that may be drawn therefrom. [108 A.L.R. 160]

2) **"Rule of completeness":** [§984] Along the same lines, it is generally held that where the witness, on direct, has testified to *part* of an event or conversation, or has introduced part of a writing or document, it is proper on cross-examination to inquire into any *other* part thereof necessary to make understandable the part already introduced—*i.e.,* to dispel any misleading impressions, etc. Any objection to such cross-examination is deemed waived.

   a) **Note:** This rule extends not only to matters that are part of the same transaction, but to any other related act or event necessary to make the transaction understandable. Thus, if a witness testifies about a certain letter on direct examination, it may be proper on cross-examination to inquire about any replies to that letter or any former or later correspondence relevant to the contents of that letter.

   b) **And note:** In some jurisdictions, the "rule of completeness" is carried one step farther (at least as to documents), so that if a party on direct examination seeks to introduce only part of a writing, the other party may require introduction at the same time of any other part that in fairness ought to be considered along with it (*see infra,* §1215). [Fed. R. Evid. 106]

d. **Effect of exceeding permissible scope:** [§985] Where the scope of cross-examination is restricted (as it is in most jurisdictions, *see* above), the court may, in its discretion, permit inquiry into additional matters. However, such expanded inquiry is "in the nature of direct examination." [Fed. R. Evid. 611(b)]

(1) **Leading questions limited:** [§986] Since the expanded inquiry is in the "nature of direct examination," the cross-examiner's right to use leading questions is limited (*see supra,* §§949-951).

(2) **Right to impeach?** [§987] More importantly, in jurisdictions that retain the rule against impeaching one's own witness (*supra,* §§952-961), the cross-examiner who exceeds the permissible scope of cross-examination cannot impeach the witness with respect to such testimony; *i.e.,* the cross-examiner is deemed to "make the witness his own" with respect to questions beyond the scope of direct, and therefore is bound by the answers given.

(a) **Modern trend:** [§988] Of course, the result is contra under the modern trend allowing a party to impeach any witness, including his own. [Fed. R. Evid. 607; *and see supra,* §960] Under this approach, the cross-examiner is not bound by the witness's answers and is free to impeach or rebut.

4. **Redirect and Subsequent Examinations**

   a. **Redirect examination:** [§989] The purpose of redirect is to *explain or rebut* adverse testimony or inferences developed on cross-examination, and to *rehabilitate* a witness whose credibility has been impeached on cross-examination.

      (1) **Form of questioning:** [§990] The form of questioning allowed on redirect is the same as on direct examination (*see supra*, §§944-974).

      (2) **Scope of redirect:** [§991] Those states that limit cross-examination to the scope of the direct (*see supra*, §982) normally limit redirect to the matters covered in cross-examination.

         (a) **Example:** The party first calling the witness cannot, on redirect, ask about matters that were covered on direct examination and not gone into on cross-examination. Nor can that party ask about matters that he forgot to ask about on direct examination. The court, however, has discretion to allow the party to "reopen" the direct and go into such matters. [Johnson v. Minihan, 200 S.W.2d 334 (Mo. 1947)]

         (b) **Compare:** In courts that allow a "wide open" cross-examination (*see supra*, §980), *any* matter may likewise be inquired into on redirect, subject only to the court's power to limit the scope of the questioning.

      (3) **Rehabilitation of witness:** [§992] For a discussion of rehabilitation of witnesses, *see infra,* §§1090 *et seq.*

   b. **Recross-examination:** [§993] After redirect, the trial judge may allow *recross-examination* of the witness. The purpose is to overcome the other party's attempts to rehabilitate a witness or to rebut damaging evidence brought out on cross-examination. Such examination is generally within the trial court's discretion [Fed. R. Evid. 611(a)], although it is provided as a matter of *right* under some codes [*See* Cal. Evid. Code §763].

      (1) **Scope of recross:** [§994] The scope of recross is normally limited to matters gone into on redirect.

      (2) **Form of questioning:** [§995] The form of questioning on recross is the same as on cross-examination (*see supra*, §§975-988).

5. **Examination of Witness by Trial Judge:** [§996] Either on her own motion, or on the motion of any party, the trial judge may call any person to testify as a witness, and may interrogate such person in the same manner as any other witness in the case. [Fed. R. Evid. 614; Moore v. United States, 598 F.2d 439 (5th Cir. 1979)]

   a. **Form of interrogation:** [§997] The trial judge may use leading questions suggestive of the answers, etc. However, the examination must be *fair*, not intimidating in nature. [United States v. Latimer, 548 F.2d 311 (10th Cir. 1977)] *Either* party may cross-examine any witness called by the judge. [Fed. R. Evid. 614(a)]

b. **Objections:** [§998]   Either party may object to the judge's examination of the witness at the time of interrogation or at the next available opportunity when the jury is not present. [Fed. R. Evid. 614(c)]

c. **Expert witnesses:** [§999]   The court's power to call witnesses is most frequently illustrated in cases where the trial judge calls an expert witness to advise the court or jury on matters that are in dispute and that are the subject of conflicting testimony by the experts of the respective parties. [Fed. R. Evid. 706]

d. **Appellate review:** [§1000]   Generally, appellate courts frown on a trial judge "taking over" the conduct of the case. Although judgments are rarely reversed on this ground alone, it is not considered *proper* for a trial judge to assume direct control over the case—particularly in a jury case where the judge's questioning may give the jury the *impression* that the judge favors one side or the other.

e. **Compare—judge's right to comment on evidence:** [§1001]   Many states allow a trial judge the *discretionary* power to comment to the jury on the evidence. Although there is a strong risk of prejudice, these states permit a trial judge to express views (either during the course of trial or at the close of the case) as to the sufficiency of the evidence, the credibility of witnesses, etc.—provided the judge makes it clear that such comments are only *personal opinions*, and are *not binding* on the jurors.

(1) **Federal courts:** [§1002]   Although such practice is not specifically sanctioned in the Federal Rules of Evidence, federal courts have for a long time permitted such comment by a trial judge at the close of a case. [*See* Capital Traction Co. v. Hof, 174 U.S. 1 (1899)]

B. IMPEACHMENT AND REHABILITATION

1. **Right to Impeach:** [§1003]   To "impeach" a witness means to *discredit the witness's testimony*. Impeaching a witness is a fundamental right on cross-examination. Since the witness's credibility is always in issue, it is never beyond the permissible scope of cross-examination (*see supra*, §§975 *et seq.*).

a. **Stage of proceeding:** [§1004]   And under modern practice, impeachment is not limited to cross-examination. The old limitation against impeaching one's own witness has been abolished in many jurisdictions, so that either party may impeach any witness (*i.e.*, on direct or redirect examination). [Fed. R. Evid. 607; *and see supra*, §960]

2. **Effect of Impeachment:** [§1005]   The fact that a witness has been impeached does not mean that her testimony will be stricken or disregarded. The trial judge may properly instruct the jury to consider the witness's testimony with caution. But the jury may still choose to believe the witness despite impeachment evidence. Again, the weight and credibility of evidence is ultimately for the jury to decide. [State v. Elijah, 289 N.W. 575 (Minn. 1940)]

3. **Methods of Impeachment:** [§1006]   A witness's testimony may be discredited by the following:

a. **Contrary evidence:** [§1007]   The content of a witness's testimony may be rebutted by proof of facts contrary thereto. Such rebuttal evidence may discredit only a portion of the witness's testimony and does not necessarily affect her credibility as a witness per se.

  (1) **Requirement of relevancy:** [§1008]   Impeachment by contradictory evidence raises no evidentiary problems as long as the contradictory evidence is *relevant* to the issues in the case. Indeed, if relevant, it would not even fall within the rule against impeaching one's own witness.

   (a) **But note:** Where the contradictory testimony is not otherwise relevant to the issues in the case, the testimony may run afoul of the rule against impeachment on a collateral matter (*infra,* §1088) and of the rule against impeaching one's own witness.

b. **Evidence showing lack of knowledge or perceptive capacity:** [§1009]   A witness's credibility may also be attacked by showing that the witness had no real knowledge of the facts to which she testified, or that the witness's faculties were so much impaired (*e.g.,* witness asleep, drunk, poor vision, etc.) that it is doubtful she could have perceived those facts. Such impeachment can be made either by cross-examining the witness or introducing extrinsic evidence.

  (1) **Poor memory:** [§1010]   It is also proper to show that the witness has a poor memory of the events about which she testified. That is usually done by questioning the witness as to other related matters—the inference being that if the witness's memory of related matters is poor, her recollection of the events testified about is doubtful. [Davis v. California Powder Works, 84 Cal. 617 (1890)]

c. **Evidence attacking credibility:** [§1011]   A witness's entire testimony may be discredited because her credibility as a witness is suspect.

  (1) **What constitutes:** The facts that the law recognizes as sufficient to attack credibility are the "methods of attacking credibility" set forth below.

  (2) **How proved:** [§1012]   The grounds for attacking credibility may always be brought out by examination of the witness (getting the witness to admit facts constituting impeachment). And certain of the grounds (*e.g.,* criminal convictions) can be proved by independent (extrinsic) evidence as well (*see* below).

  (3) **Methods of attacking credibility:** [§1013]   The generally accepted methods of attacking credibility are as follows: (i) demonstrating *poor character for truthfulness*; (ii) establishing *bias* or interest; and (iii) establishing *prior inconsistent statements*. Each of these methods is discussed in detail below.

   (a) **Character impeachment:** [§1014]   Witnesses (party or nonparty) who take the stand put their character for *honesty* and *veracity* in issue; therefore, they can be impeached by evidence that their character is such that they may lie under oath. The difficult question is what evidence is admissible for this purpose.

1) **Conviction of crime:** [§1015]   The early common law rule was that a person who had been convicted of a *felony* or any *misdemeanor involving dishonesty* was incompetent to testify at all (*see supra*, §812). This rule has been abandoned, but proof of *conviction* of certain crimes may be used to *impeach* a witness. (*Note:* A mere showing of *arrest* or *indictment* is *not* enough.) [Fed. R. Evid. 609]

   a) **What crimes:** [§1016]   The courts are in disagreement as to what crimes constitute grounds for impeachment.

   1/ **Any crime:** [§1017]   A number of states admit evidence of conviction of *any* crime—felony or misdemeanor. [Coslow v. State, 177 P.2d 518 (Okla. 1947)]

   2/ **"Moral turpitude" or "infamous" crimes:** [§1018]   A few states limit impeachment to felonies and misdemeanors involving "*moral turpitude*" or "*infamous*" crimes. [State v. Jenness, 62 A.2d 867 (Me. 1948)]

   3/ **Crimes discrediting veracity:** [§1019]   Other states hold that the crime must be one that logically would *discredit* the *veracity* or *credibility* of the witness (*e.g.*, perjury, theft by false pretenses).

   4/ **Majority—felonies:** [§1020]   The probable *majority* view permits impeachment by *any felony conviction—i.e.*, without restriction as to *type*. [*See, e.g.*, Cal. Evid. Code §788] (Under this view, involuntary manslaughter, as well as perjury, is ground for impeachment.)

   5/ **Federal Rule:** [§1021] The Federal Rule straddles the fence—*i.e.*, certain convictions are automatically admissible to impeach, others are automatically excluded, and the trial judge has discretion to admit others.

   a/ **Crimes of dishonesty or false statement:** [§1022]   Under Federal Rule 609(a)(2), a conviction for a crime of "*dishonesty or false statement*" is *admissible per se*, unless it falls outside the 10-year time limit of Rule 609(b) (*see infra*, §1035). In other words, the trial judge has no authority to exclude a crime of dishonesty or false statement on the ground that it is too prejudicial. [United States v. Wong, 703 F.2d 65 (3d Cir. 1983)] Thus, a crime such as perjury or lying to a federal agent is admissible per se.

   1] **Meaning of dishonesty:** [§1023]   In ordinary life we say that stealing is "dishonest."

It is not clear, however, that stealing is "dishonest" within the meaning of Rule 609(a)(2). Some courts, relying on the legislative history of the Rule, have held that "dishonesty" refers only to *deceitful behavior*. [*See* United States v. Brackeen, 969 F.2d 827 (9th Cir. 1992) (en banc)] Under this view, crimes such as armed robbery and burglary are not necessarily "dishonest." Among the courts that have taken this approach, some look only to the definition of the crime to determine whether it is deceitful, while others are willing to look at the particular way the crime was committed. Under the latter approach, shoplifting would be deceitful if it were accomplished with the help of spoken falsehoods, but not if it were accomplished simply by grabbing and running.

b/ **Serious but "honest" crimes:** [§1024] If a crime is *punishable by more than one year*, the trial judge has the *discretion to admit* the crime (subject to the 10-year time limit, *infra*, §1035) to impeach a witness even if the crime did not involve dishonesty or false statement (*e.g.*, the trial judge could admit a prior conviction for aggravated assault or homicide to impeach the testimony of a witness). [Fed. R. Evid. 609(a)(1)]

1] **Witness—criminal accused:** [§1025] If the witness is the *accused* in a criminal case, the Federal Rules afford the accused an extra measure of protection. In such cases the crime is inadmissible *unless* the trial judge determines that the *probative value* of the evidence *outweighs* the *prejudice* to the accused. [Fed. R. Evid. 609(a)(1)]

2] **Witness—other than criminal accused:** [§1026] Prior convictions of a witness *other than a criminal accused* are governed by Federal Rule 403, not 609(a), and thus will be inadmissible *only if* the opponent shows that their *probative value* is *substantially outweighed* by the danger of *unfair prejudice*. In short, a criminal accused is afforded somewhat greater protection than other witnesses (*e.g.,* prosecution witnesses and witnesses in civil cases). If the prejudice to the accused equals or outweighs its probative value, the evidence must be excluded; but as to other witnesses, the evidence will be excluded only if the risk of prejudice substantially outweighs probative value.

c/ **Minor "honest" crimes:** [§1027] Under Federal Rule 609(a), a crime that is not a crime of dishonesty or false statement must be a serious crime in order to be eligible for admission (*see* above). Therefore, if a crime is **punishable by one year or less** and is **not** a crime of dishonesty or false statement, the trial judge has **no discretion** to admit the conviction. The judge is **required to exclude** the evidence when it is offered to impeach.

b) **Nature of conviction**

1/ **Out-of-state convictions:** [§1028] Convictions obtained in other jurisdictions are admissible to impeach. It is sufficient that the crime constituted a felony, etc., under the law of the jurisdiction where the witness was convicted. [Fed. R. Evid. 609(a)]

2/ **Juvenile adjudications:** [§1029] Juvenile offenses are generally **not** admissible for impeachment purposes. [Banas v. State, 149 N.W.2d 571 (Wis. 1966); 63 A.L.R.3d 1107]

a/ **Compare:** The Federal Rules are in accord, although in a criminal case the judge has discretion to admit evidence of juvenile offenses committed by a witness other than the accused if "necessary to a fair determination of the issue of (the accused's) guilt or innocence." [Fed. R. Evid. 609(d); *and see* Davis v. Alaska, 415 U.S. 308 (1974)]

3/ **Constitutionally defective conviction:** [§1030] Where the prior felony conviction was obtained in violation of the defendant's Sixth Amendment rights (*e.g.,* to have counsel, to confront witnesses, etc.), the conviction is invalid for all purposes and hence cannot be used for impeachment. [State v. Knapp, 509 P.2d 410 (Wash. 1973)]

4/ **Effect of appeal:** [§1031] In most jurisdictions, a conviction is admissible to impeach a witness even though the conviction is on appeal (although the pendency of the appeal may also be shown). [*See* Fed. R. Evid. 609(e)]

5/ **Effect of pardon:** [§1032]   In most states, the conviction may still be shown, even though the witness subsequently received a full pardon. [*See, e.g.,* Richards v. United States, 192 F.2d 602 (D.C. Cir. 1951)] However, the Federal Rule is contra where the pardon was based on the witness's innocence (or a showing of rehabilitation) and the witness had no subsequent felony convictions. [Fed. R. Evid. 609(c); United States v. DiNapoli, 557 F.2d 962 (2d Cir. 1977)]

6/ **Effect of remoteness, etc.**

   a/ **Traditional rule:** [§1033]   The traditional rule is that a conviction is admissible to impeach—regardless of how old or remote it is from the issue of credibility (lacking in probative value). Its remoteness is simply a factor for the jury to consider in weighing the witness's credibility. [State v. Hawthorne, 228 A.2d 682 (N.J. 1967)]

   b/ **Modern rule:** [§1034]   However, the more modern rule, and that followed by most courts today, gives the trial judge discretion to exclude convictions whenever the probative value thereof is substantially outweighed by danger of unfair prejudice. [*See* Luck v. United States, 348 F.2d 763 (D.C. Cir. 1965)]

      1] According to this view, the trial judge may choose to exclude convictions deemed "remote"—*e.g.,* because of lapse of time, changed circumstances, the nature of the offense, or other factors—where there is a risk of undue prejudice or confusion of the issues. [People v. Beagle, 6 Cal. 3d 441 (1972); Brown v. United States, 370 F.2d 242 (D.C. Cir. 1966)]

      2] Thus, a conviction of manslaughter, even though a felony, would be thought to have virtually no relation to the credibility of the witness. Yet if the witness were also the defendant, it would be highly prejudicial.

      3] Similarly, a prior felony conviction may be excluded as prejudicial if too similar to the crime presently charged, especially where there are other convictions available for impeachment purposes. [People v. Rist, 16 Cal. 3d 211 (1976)]

4] At least two cases combine to establish a five-part test for balancing probative value against prejudice under Rule 609. The five factors are: (i) the prior conviction's impeachment value; (ii) proximity in time; (iii) similarity of the acts involved; (iv) importance of defendant's testifying; and (v) the centrality of credibility as an issue. [*See* Gordon v. United States, 383 F.2d 936 (D.C. Cir. 1967); United States v. Mahone, 537 F.2d 922 (7th Cir. 1976)]

5] There exists a split of authority as to who bears the burden of proof with respect to the admissibility of the defendant's prior convictions, although most courts place it with the government. Some question exists as to where the burden falls when defendant attempts to use evidence of a prosecution witness's prior convictions. [*See, e.g.,* United States v. Cunningham, 638 F.2d 696 (4th Cir. 1981)—placing the burden on defendant] The burden should ordinarily properly fall on the objecting party.

c/ **Federal Rule:** [§1035]   Under the Federal Rules, where *more than 10 years* have passed from the date of the conviction (or the witness's release thereunder), the conviction becomes inadmissible unless: (i) the court determines that its probative value ("supported by specific facts and circumstances") *substantially outweighs* its prejudicial effect; and (ii) the party seeking to show the conviction gives *prior written notice* so that the other party will have a fair opportunity to contest its use. [Fed. R. Evid. 609(b)] The exception is to be indulged "very rarely and only in exceptional circumstances." [United States v. Bibbs, 564 F.2d 1165 (5th Cir. 1977)]

c) **Foundation and proof:** [§1036]   Evidence of the conviction may be elicited from the *witness*, or a *certified copy* of the record of conviction may be introduced directly, without any prior questioning of the witness. [Fed. R. Evid. 609(a); MacKnight v. United States, 263 F. 832 (1st Cir. 1920)]

1/ **Compare—witness denies conviction:** [§1037]   However, if the witness *denies* the conviction, there must be proof that the witness *is* the person who was convicted; some states have a *presumption* that if the witness's name and the name on the record are the same, the conviction is the witness's. [3 A.L.R.3d 965]

    2/ **What may be shown:** [§1038]   Ordinarily, only the *nature* of the offense and the *fact* of conviction can be shown—not the *details* of the crime. [United States v. Wolf, 561 F.2d 1376 (10th Cir. 1977)]

d) **Limitation—criminal cases:** [§1039]   There is a trend toward restricting impeachment by evidence of a criminal conviction in a *criminal trial* where the witness to be impeached is also the *defendant*.

    1/ **Rationale:** Here, the probative value of the conviction on the issue of the defendant's credibility is more likely to be *outweighed* by the prejudicial effect on the issue of guilt—especially where the conviction is for a *similar* crime. [*See* United States v. Hawley, 544 F.2d 50 (2d Cir. 1977)] However, the Supreme Court has held that the defendant must take the stand and testify in order to preserve for appellate review a claim of error in ruling on her pretrial assertion (*e.g.,* motion *in limine*) that the proposed impeachment on a prior conviction would be improper. [Luce v. United States, 469 U.S. 38 (1984)]

e) **Limiting instruction:** [§1040]   When a conviction is admitted for impeachment purposes only, the trial judge should instruct the jury about its limited use. For example, the judge might tell the jury that the conviction can be used only in assessing the credibility of the defendant as a witness, and not as evidence that the defendant has a propensity to commit the crime charged.

2) **Misconduct not the subject of criminal conviction:** [§1041] Various acts that are not crimes may nonetheless reflect on a witness's veracity—*e.g.,* whether the witness has defrauded others, cheated at cards, lied on other occasions, etc.—and might be a means of character impeachment.

a) **"Wide open" rule:** [§1042]   The English rule (a minority view in this country) allows inquiry into such misconduct on the theory that the entire personal history of a witness is "fair game" on cross-examination (although not through the use of extrinsic evidence).

b) **Rule of inadmissibility:** [§1043]   On the opposite side, several states *prohibit* impeachment by this kind of evidence; *i.e.,* if the past conduct does not amount to a criminal conviction, it cannot be inquired into on cross-examination (and a fortiori, it cannot be shown by extrinsic evidence). [*See, e.g.,* Cal Evid. Code §787]

Rationale: Too many collateral issues are usually involved.

c) **Majority rule—discretionary exclusion:** [§1044] However, most courts in this country permit cross-examination of the witness as to *past acts* or *conduct* if it is clearly probative of veracity and does not involve unreasonable risks of prejudice, confusion of issues, etc. Basically, the matter is left to the discretion of the trial judge. [Fed. R. Evid. 608(b)]

  1/ **How proved:** [§1045]   Note that under both the English rule and the majority rule, the cross-examiner must accept (be "bound" by) the answers given by the witness; *i.e.,* extrinsic evidence cannot be introduced to prove the past misconduct. [Fed. R. Evid. 608(b); State v. McKelvy, 574 P.2d 603 (N.M. 1978)] This is the "rule against collateral impeachment."

    a/ **Rationale:** The theory is that allowing extrinsic evidence to prove the prior misconduct would simply be wasting too much time on a collateral issue. [*See* United States v. Simmons, 444 F. Supp. 500 (E.D. Pa. 1978)]

    b/ **Exception:** [§1046]   However, where a defendant witness opens the door to the same incident on direct or gratuitously volunteers a material denial on cross, impeachment use of extrinsic evidence to contradict may be allowed. [United States v. Benedetto, 571 F.2d 1246 (2d Cir. 1978)] However, where the defendant's statement was invited by cross-examination, courts generally prohibit the use of extrinsic evidence merely to contradict.

  2/ **Limitations:** [§1047]   The witness can always invoke the privilege against *self-incrimination*, if applicable. And again, where the *defendant in a criminal case is the witness* sought to be impeached, allowing such highly prejudicial evidence to be introduced would undermine the rules preventing use of character testimony against a criminal defendant.

3) **Poor reputation for truthfulness:** [§1048]   Since the witness's credibility is always at issue, the witness may be impeached by showing that she has a poor reputation in the community for truthfulness (*see supra,* §§179-180).

a) **Applies to any witness:** [§1049]   A party who takes the witness stand in her own case thereby puts her reputation for truthfulness in issue, just as any other witness. The result is that evidence regarding this trait of the party's character may become admissible even though it would not otherwise be relevant. [United States v. Bennett, 539 F.2d 45 (10th Cir. 1976)]

b) **Type of evidence admissible:** [§1050] In accordance with the traditional rule that character is proved by reputation (*supra*, §147), the accepted method of proving the witness's character is to ask other witnesses about the witness's *reputation for truthfulness in the community or neighborhood* in which she resides.

1/ **Traditional view:** [§1051] Under the traditional view, evidence of the witness's reputation at any other place (*e.g.*, on the job) is improper. [Khan v. Zemansky, 59 Cal. App. 324 (1922)]

2/ **Modern view:** [§1052] However, the modern cases allow evidence of reputation in business circles as well as in the community. [*See, e.g.*, Hamilton v. State, 176 So. 89 (Fla. 1937)]

4) **Opinion evidence as to lack of credibility**

a) **Traditional view prohibits:** [§1053] Although a witness may be impeached by the testimony of other witnesses as to the witness's poor *reputation* for truthfulness, most courts do not allow other witnesses to testify directly as to their opinions of the witness's credibility (although the reason for this distinction is obscure). [*See, e.g.*, State v. Swenson, 382 P.2d 614 (Wash. 1963)]

b) **Modern trend permits:** [§1054] Recognizing that opinion evidence is often valuable, and that statements as to a witness's "community reputation" are often merely disguised statements of opinion, the modern trend is to *allow* evidence in the form of opinion as well as reputation. [*See* Fed. R. Evid. 608(a); Cal. Evid. Code §1100]

1/ **But note:** The admission of lay opinion testimony must be based on the other witness's *personal knowledge* of the subject witness's credibility. [*See* United States v. Mandel, 591 F.2d 1347 (4th Cir. 1979)]

c) **Expert opinion:** [§1055] Some cases allow expert testimony, usually by a psychiatrist, that certain *categories* of people are especially likely to be liars. The most common cases are those where the witness is a narcotics addict or an alcoholic.

1/ **Example:** In the trial of Alger Hiss, the defense was permitted to introduce evidence that the principal government witness was not to be believed because he was a psychopathic liar. [United States v. Hiss, 88 F. Supp. 559 (S.D.N.Y. 1950)]

(b) **Evidence showing hostility, bias, and interest:** [§1056] Besides attacking the witness's character for truthfulness, the cross-examiner may use the second method of attacking credibility—*i.e.,* impeaching a witness by showing that the witness is *biased, hostile,* or has some *interest* in the outcome of the trial giving her a motive to lie.

1) **Examples of bias or interest**

a) **Compensation for testimony:** [§1057] It is proper to ask a witness on cross-examination what *compensation,* etc., the witness has been promised for testifying. This might show that the witness is attempting to "earn" something by testifying in a particular matter.

1/ **Example:** In criminal cases, it is proper to ask prosecution witnesses on cross-examination whether there are any *charges* pending against them (or whether they are on parole or probation or awaiting sentencing), and whether they have been promised *immunity* or *leniency* on such charges.

b) **Bias of family and friends**

1/ **Family:** [§1058] It can always be shown that the witness is related to one of the parties since this at least *implies* a bias in that party's favor. Otherwise, however, evidence as to the bias, prejudice, or interest of the witness's relatives is generally *not* admissible to impeach the witness. *Rationale:* A person cannot choose relatives; hence nothing can be inferred from their biases or interests. [Templeton v. United States, 151 F.2d 706 (6th Cir. 1945)]

2/ **Friends:** [§1059] On the other hand, a person *can* choose friends and business associates, and consequently evidence of their bias or interest (brought out either by way of *cross-examination* or *extrinsic evidence*) is generally admissible for impeachment purposes. [Frost v. United States, 80 F.2d 341 (5th Cir. 1935)]

c) **Hostile statements:** [§1060] Animosity toward a party may be shown by adverse statements, or by the fact that the witness has some dispute or litigation pending against such party.

2) **How bias, interest proved:** [§1061]   The bias or adverse interest of the witness can be proved either by cross-examination of that witness or by introducing extrinsic evidence (*e.g.,* testimony of other witnesses). [State v. Elijah, *supra,* §1005]

  a) **Foundation required:** [§1062]   Most courts require that before a witness can be impeached by extrinsic evidence of bias, etc., she must first be *asked* about the facts that indicate such bias, hostility, or adverse interest. Only if the witness denies bias or adverse interest will extrinsic evidence be admissible. [87 A.L.R.2d 431]

  b) **Minority contra:** [§1063]   However, a substantial minority of courts disagree, and permit extrinsic evidence without any preliminary foundation. [87 A.L.R.2d 407]

(c) **Prior inconsistent acts or statements:** [§1064]   A third method of attacking the witness's credibility is by showing that the witness has made prior inconsistent statements regarding the matters as to which she has given testimony.

  1) **Actual inconsistency required:** [§1065]   Before a witness's prior statement can be admitted it must in fact be *inconsistent* with the witness's testimony at trial.

    a) **Example:** Thus, if the witness's only testimony is that she does not remember anything, the prior statement is inadmissible because there is nothing with which it can be inconsistent. [People v. Sam, 71 Cal. 2d 194 (1969)]

    b) **Compare:** But some cases hold that if the witness gives an evasive answer in addition to claiming no recollection, the prior statement may be admitted for impeachment purposes. [Clifton v. Ulis, 17 Cal. 3d 99 (1976)]

  2) **Laying a foundation:** [§1066]   There is a split of authority as to whether the prior inconsistent statement can be introduced directly into evidence, or whether the witness must first be asked about the statement and given an opportunity to explain the inconsistency. [*See, e.g.,* United States v. Nacrelli, 468 F. Supp. 241 (E.D. Pa. 1979)]

    a) **Traditional rule:** [§1067]   The traditional rule requires that the witness be asked about the statement before it can be introduced; *i.e.,* the cross-examiner must ask the witness whether she made the statement, giving its substance, and the time, place, and person to whom it was made.

      1/ **Example:** Typically, the witness will be asked the following types of questions in the following order:

        a/ "You have never made a statement contrary to your present testimony, have you?"

b/ "You have never told anyone that it was the defendant, not the plaintiff, who went through the red light, have you?"

c/ "You have never said to anyone, 'I saw the whole thing and the defendant went right through the red light and hit the plaintiff'?"

d/ "Specifically, on May 23, 1992, at about 7:30 p.m. in the presence of John Jones and William Smith, at the Colony Bar on Fifth Street, did you not say, 'I saw the defendant go through a red light and hit the plaintiff'?"

2/ **Rationale for traditional rule:** [§1068] The rationale for the traditional rule above is to avoid unfair surprise to the witness (and the calling party), to save time (if the witness to be impeached admits making the statement), and finally, to give the witness a chance to explain why she made the statement.

3/ **Admissibility of statement:** [§1069] Whether the statement is admissible depends on the response of the witness.

a/ *If the witness is not asked the foundational questions* on cross-examination, the prior inconsistent statement cannot be received into evidence. [United States v. DiNapoli, *supra,* §1032]

b/ *If the witness admits making the inconsistent statement* (whether or not a satisfactory explanation is provided), the witness is impeached (discredited) thereby; and in most jurisdictions the statement itself is *not* admissible as it would merely be redundant. [*See, e.g.,* State v. Buffone, 234 P. 539 (Utah 1925)]

c/ *If the witness denies the statement*, or claims not to remember it, the foundational requirement is satisfied so that the statement itself may be offered into evidence when the cross-examiner puts on his case. [State v. Miles, 436 P.2d 198 (Wash. 1968)]

d/ *If the witness refuses to answer* the foundational questions by exercising the privilege against self-incrimination, the witness cannot claim lack of opportunity to explain or deny the statement. Thus, the witness cannot use the privilege to preclude the proper laying of a foundation, thereby preventing introduction of the statement.

4/ **Criticism of rule:** [§1070]   Unfortunately, the traditional rule, if applied rigidly, is a trap for unwary lawyers who simply forget to ask the relatively unimportant foundational questions and thereby lose important evidence. Additionally, if the impeaching statement comes to light only after the witness has finished testifying, there would be no time to lay the foundation.

b) **Modern rules relax foundational requirement:** [§1071] Recognizing the validity of these criticisms, many jurisdictions today limit the foundational questions that must be asked.

1/ **Witness under subpoena:** [§1072]   Some jurisdictions provide that the foundational requirement does not apply where the witness to be impeached, though finished testifying, is nonetheless still under subpoena and can be *recalled* to explain or deny making the statement.

2/ **Discretion of judge:** [§1073]   In some jurisdictions, the judge has discretion to *ignore* the foundational requirement after balancing the importance of laying the foundation in the particular case against the disadvantage of losing the impeaching evidence.

3/ **"Interests of justice":** [§1074]   Foundational questions may also be dispensed with "where the interests of justice . . . require," as where the inconsistent statement is not discovered until after the witness has left the witness stand and cannot be recalled. [Fed. R. Evid. 613(b)]

4/ **Hearsay:** [§1075]   Likewise, the foundational requirement is dispensed with when attacking the *credibility* of a hearsay declarant. [Fed. R. Evid. 806]

5/ **Party witness:** [§1076]   Finally, when the witness whose credibility is under attack is a *party* to the action, her prior inconsistent statement constitutes an *admission* and hence is *independently* admissible. As a result, *no* foundation need be laid. [Fed. R. Evid. 613(b)]

c) **Impeaching statement in writing:** [§1077]   Where the prior inconsistent statement was written or signed by the witness, the only foundation necessary is that the witness be shown the statement and asked whether *in fact* she wrote or signed it. [United States v. Rogers, 549 F.2d 490 (8th Cir. 1976)]

1/ **Rule in *Queen Caroline's Case***: [§1078]   At one time, the witness could not be questioned about the statement at all, unless it was *first* shown to her. [Queen Caroline's Case, 129 Eng. Rep. 976 (1820)]

2/ **Abolition of rule:** [§1079]   However, the overwhelming modern trend is to repeal the rule in *Queen Caroline's Case* so that the witness may be questioned about the statement *before* being shown it.

d) **Tactical reasons for laying foundation:** [§1080]   Usually, as a tactical measure, the impeaching attorney will wish to lay a foundation for impeachment by a prior inconsistent statement even where the lack of a foundation might be excused. This procedure has the following advantages:

1/ *The witness, faced with the statement, may recant* her testimony, the inconsistent statement thereby making a much greater impression on the jury.

2/ *The witness may become so flustered* when the statement is called to her attention that the witness's credibility may be completely destroyed.

3/ *The witness's denial of having made the statement may so obviously be a lie* that her credibility will be undermined.

4/ *Finally, regardless of the witness's response,* the laying of the foundation will *focus the jury's attention* on the impeaching statement when it is introduced.

3) **Evidentiary effect of statement**

a) **Majority rule—impeachment only:** [§1081]   The traditional (and still majority) rule is that a prior inconsistent statement by the witness is *hearsay* and therefore cannot be used as *proof* of the facts contained therein (unless it qualifies under some exception to the hearsay rule). Its use is limited to *impeachment* of the witness, and the jury must be so instructed. [133 A.L.R. 1454; *and see supra*, §241]

1/ **Criticism:** [§1082]   The prior inconsistent statement may have great *probative value*—particularly when made at or about the time of the transaction in question.

b) **Minority rule—substantive proof:** [§1083]   A few jurisdictions have now rejected the above rule, and *admit* the prior inconsistent statement as *substantive proof* of the matters contained therein. [*See, e.g.,* Cal. Evid. Code §1235; State v. Jolly, 116 P.2d 686 (Mont. 1941)]

1/ **Hearsay status:** [§1084] The jurisdictions that follow this approach recognize a *special exception* to the hearsay rule for prior inconsistent statements made by witnesses who testify at trial. [*See* Cal. Evid. Code §1235; People v. Williams, 16 Cal. 3d 663 (1976)]

2/ **Rationale for admission:** Any hearsay problem is lessened because the declarant is in court and may be cross-examined with regard to the statement. Also, the prior statement will often be more accurate than in-court testimony because it was made nearer to the time of the events in question. Finally, telling the jury to consider the statement for "impeachment purposes only" is simply asking too much of the jurors. Since the jury will hear the statement anyway, the jury will almost certainly use the statement for the truth of the matter asserted and not merely for impeachment.

3/ **Significance of admission:** [§1085] Admission of the prior inconsistent statement as substantive proof may be of particular help to a party whose witness *changes* her story on the witness stand, leaving the party with no other way to prove key points in issue. Under modern statutes permitting a party to impeach his own witness (*supra,* §960), the party can introduce the prior statement made by the "turncoat" witness as *substantive* proof of the key points.

   a/ **Note:** In addition, the combination of these two rules suggests the tactical possibility that if a party has a prior statement of a witness that the witness has repudiated prior to trial, the party may call that witness, impeach the witness, and thus get the prior statement admitted as *substantive* evidence.

4/ **Constitutionality upheld:** [§1086] A prior inconsistent statement made by a witness can be used as substantive proof even against the defendant in a criminal case. As long as the witness whose prior statement is involved is present at trial and subject to cross-examination, the accused's Sixth Amendment right of confrontation is preserved. [California v. Green, 399 U.S. 149 (1970); *and see* Criminal Procedure Summary]

c) **Federal Rule:** [§1087] Under the Federal Rules, a prior inconsistent statement is in most instances admissible solely for impeachment purposes (as under the majority view, above). However, the Federal Rules recognize one limited exception: A prior inconsistent statement made by the witness while testifying ***under oath*** at some prior trial, hearing, or other proceeding is admissible nonhearsay; as such, it can be used as substantive proof of whatever was stated. [Fed. R. Evid. 801(d)(1); *and see supra,* §242]

1/ **Rationale:** As opposed to situations involving unsworn oral statements, there can be no dispute as to whether the prior statement was made; and the formal proceeding, the oath, and the opportunity for cross-examination provide additional assurances of the trustworthiness of the prior statement. [*See* United States v. Cunningham, 446 F.2d 194 (2d Cir. 1971); United States v. Castro-Ayon, 537 F.2d 1055 (9th Cir. 1976)—admitting statements made under oath at border patrol interrogation]

a/ **Note:** Some *state* courts have refused, on constitutional grounds, to allow an ***unsworn*** prior statement of a witness to be used as substantive evidence against a defendant in a criminal case.

4. **Limitation Against Impeachment on "Collateral Matters":** [§1088]   No matter what type of impeachment evidence is offered, it must be relevant to the witness's credibility or some other issue in the present litigation. Hence, there is a basic limitation against impeachment evidence on "collateral matters"—*i.e.,* matters that could not be the subject of proof independently on the impeachment. *Rationale:* The concern is for the possible confusion of issues and undue consumption of time. [State v. Larson, 253 N.W.2d 433 (N.D. 1977)]

a. **Example:** In an auto accident case, P's witness, W, testifies, "I saw the accident on my way home from church." D concedes that W was at the scene of the accident, but attempts to impeach W by showing that W actually was on his way home from a house of prostitution. This impeachment is on a "collateral" matter and hence improper—*i.e.,* W's misstating where he had been does not necessarily tend to disprove his testimony regarding what he saw.

(1) **Analysis:** Certainly the fact that W lied under oath as to one matter (where he had been) suggests that he may have lied about other matters as well (*i.e.,* what he saw). As such, it has some probative value. However, whatever value it has is simply outweighed by the potential risks of confusion of issues, consumption of time, etc.

(2) **Compare:** The result might be different if D could show that W had spent the evening drinking at a bar (reflecting on his perceptive ability), or visiting P or P's family (reflecting possible bias).

b. **Exclusion discretionary:** [§1089]   There is no rigid classification as to what is or is not "collateral." Rather, the conclusion that a matter is "collateral" (not a proper subject for impeachment) is the result of the trial court's determination that its probative value is simply outweighed by the potential risks of confusion of issues, consumption of time, etc. [Walder v. United States, 347 U.S. 52 (1954)]

(1) **Note:** As such, the rule against impeachment on "collateral" matters is just another aspect of the trial court's broad discretionary power to exclude any evidence—regardless of relevancy—which involves unreasonable risks of prejudice, surprise, confusion, etc. [Fed. R. Evid. 403; *and see supra,* §91]

5. **Rehabilitation of Witnesses:** [§1090]   When the cross-examiner has attempted to impeach a witness, the party who called the witness is allowed on redirect to attempt to "rehabilitate" (*i.e.,* to restore the witness's credibility). Although a witness is presumed to speak the truth, the impeachment puts the witness's credibility in issue so that evidence as to her credibility becomes relevant.

   a. **When allowed:** [§1091]   Note that rehabilitation of a witness is not allowed merely because there has been some contradiction or rebuttal of the witness's testimony by other witnesses. It must appear that the *witness's credibility has been attacked*. Until credibility is attacked, there is nothing to rehabilitate.

   b. **What may be shown:** [§1092]   Even after the credibility of a witness has been attacked, there are limits on the evidence that may be offered to support credibility. In general, *the support must meet the attack*. Thus, an attack using character evidence may be rebutted with character evidence, but not necessarily with evidence of a prior consistent statement (*see infra,* §1111). If the support does not meet the attack, the evidence should be excluded on grounds that its probative value is not sufficient to justify the confusion and consumption of time that would result from receiving it. [*See* Fed. R. Evid. 403]

      (1) **Rehabilitation by disproof of impeaching evidence:** [§1093]   The party supporting a witness is always permitted to show that evidence offered to impeach is untrue. For example, if the witness has been impeached with evidence that the witness had a secret financial interest in the case, the supporting party can introduce evidence disproving the existence of any such interest. Also, where the witness has been impeached with an alleged prior inconsistent statement, the supporting party can introduce testimony that the statement was never made.

      (2) **Rehabilitation by explaining impeaching evidence:** [§1094]   Witnesses who have been impeached are often allowed to give a brief explanation or excuse to diminish the force of the impeaching evidence.

         (a) **Explaining prior inconsistent statement:** [§1095]   If the witness has made a prior inconsistent statement, the witness will be allowed to give an explanation (*e.g.,* the witness might testify that the prior statement was made under pressure, or that someone else wrote the statement and the witness did not read it carefully before signing it). In fact, the party impeaching with a prior inconsistent statement *must* make sure that the witness is afforded an opportunity to "explain or deny" the statement; the impeaching party cannot decide to keep the statement a secret until the witness is unavailable and then introduce it into evidence. [Fed. R. Evid. 613(b)]

         (b) **Explaining misconduct:** [§1096]   If the witness has been impeached by cross-examination about specific acts of misconduct, the witness is always entitled to *explain* the conduct; but just as extrinsic evidence is inadmissible to prove misconduct short of conviction, so also is *extrinsic evidence inadmissible* to explain or justify such conduct.

1) **But note:** If the misconduct resulted in a criminal conviction, the law is unclear whether the witness being impeached can seek to explain or excuse the conviction (*e.g.,* by saying that he pled guilty to keep his sister from being charged). There is some authority in favor of allowing a brief explanation, though the discretion of the trial judge would probably be upheld whichever way she ruled. [*See* United States v. Crisafi, 304 F.2d 803 (2d Cir. 1962)]

(3) **Rehabilitation with character evidence**

(a) **When character evidence is permitted:** [§1097]   Favorable evidence showing the witness's good character for truthfulness may be introduced *only after the witness's character has been attacked*. [Fed. R. Evid. 608(b)] For example, if the impeaching party introduces evidence that the witness has a poor reputation for truthfulness, the supporting party may counter with evidence of good character for truthfulness.

1) **Rebuttal of misconduct evidence:** [§1098]   If the party impeaching the witness attacks character by introducing evidence that the witness has been convicted of crime or by asking the witness about specific instances of misconduct, the party supporting the witness is entitled to respond with evidence of the witness's good character for truthfulness. Note that sometimes an aggressive, hostile cross-examination that implies that the witness is lying will also be deemed to be a character attack that opens the door to support of the witness with evidence of good character.

2) **Rebuttal of bias evidence:** [§1099]   Merely showing that a witness is biased is not in itself an attack on the witness's character for truthfulness. For example, the question "You are the defendant's mother, aren't you?" seeks to impeach by showing bias, but it is not a character attack. A witness's credibility impeached in this fashion is *not* entitled to be supported by evidence of a good character for truthfulness because it would be a waste of time. But if the evidence of bias throws an evil light upon the witness's character for truthfulness, then the witness may be entitled to support his credibility with character evidence.

3) **Rebuttal of prior inconsistent statement evidence:** [§1100] Evidence that the witness made a prior inconsistent statement usually makes an implicit or explicit attack on the truthfulness of the witness, and a witness's credibility attacked in this fashion may normally be supported with evidence of good character for truthfulness. [*See* 6 A.L.R. 862]

(b) **Form of evidence—reputation, opinion, and specific acts:** [§1101] Even if character evidence is admissible to rehabilitate, there are strict limits on the form that the character evidence may take.

1) **Traditional view:** [§1102] When character evidence to support the credibility of a witness is admissible, the traditional view is that the evidence should take the form of testimony of the witness's *reputation in the community* for truthfulness. *Rationale:* Reputation testimony was thought to be more reliable than opinion testimony because it was based on community opinion, not one person's opinion.

2) **Federal Rules view:** [§1103] The Federal Rules permit a witness's credibility to be supported by *both* reputation and opinion testimony. [Fed. R. Evid. 608(a)] However, extrinsic evidence of specific acts showing character is *not* admissible since it would involve the court in time-consuming mini-trials concerning a collateral issue (the credibility of a witness). The party attempting to introduce evidence of a witness's good character must be satisfied with opinion and reputation testimony (and with cross-examining the opponent's character witnesses).

(4) **Rehabilitation with evidence of witness's prior consistent statements:** [§1104] The fact that a witness's credibility has been impeached, or even that the witness has been completely disgraced, does not automatically open the door to supporting the witness's credibility by introducing evidence of the witness's prior consistent statements. The fact that a witness said the same thing 100 times before does not justify admitting evidence of the 100 other statements unless the evidence in some way increases the likelihood of the trial testimony being true. Nevertheless, sometimes prior consistent statements are allowed to rehabilitate a witness's credibility.

(a) **Use of prior consistent statements**

1) **Prior consistent statements after attack for bias or interest:** [§1105] When a witness has been impeached with evidence of bias or interest, prior consistent statements are admissible to rehabilitate the witness only if they were made *prior to the time that the bias or interest arose*. [*See* Fed. R. Evid. 801(d)(1)(B)] This rule is sometimes known as the *premotive rule*. The Supreme Court has held that Federal Rule 801(d)(1)(B) "permits the introduction of a declarant's consistent out-of-court statements to rebut a charge of recent fabrication or improper influence or motive only when those statements were made before the charged recent fabrication or improper influence or motive." [Tome v. United States, 513 U.S. 150 (1995)]

a) **Example:** A witness in a criminal case testifies, "I bought the cocaine from the defendant." The witness herself has a criminal charge for distribution of cocaine pending against her. On cross-examination, the defense counsel seeks to show that the witness is testifying falsely in order to curry favor with the prosecution and receive leniency in the case pending against her. If the prosecution offers evidence that the witness signed a statement after being arrested saying that the defendant was the source of her cocaine, that statement would be inadmissible because the witness had the same motive to curry favor after her arrest that she has at trial. Basically, the evidence does not meet the attack and is a waste of time.

b) **Compare:** If, however, the prosecution offers testimony that, prior to being arrested, the above witness told an associate that she was obtaining her cocaine from the defendant, the consistent statement would be admissible because it occurred before the charged motive to fabricate arose.

2) **Prior consistent statements after attack with inconsistent statements:** [§1106]   A witness's credibility may be rehabilitated by admitting a prior consistent statement after the witness is impeached with a prior inconsistent statement. For example, suppose that a witness who testifies "the siren was on" is impeached with evidence that before trial he told someone that he had not heard a siren. To rehabilitate the witness, the proponent offers evidence that the witness told an investigator before trial that he had in fact heard a siren. Note that a prior consistent statement is not admissible every time an inconsistent statement has been introduced into evidence. [United States v. Quinto, 582 F.2d 224 (2d Cir. 1978)]

a) **Inadmissible when impeached witness admits making flatly inconsistent statement:** [§1107]   If the impeached witness admits making a flatly inconsistent statement, then the consistent statement does not remove the sting of the impeachment. The witness still has been shown to be unreliable by evidence that he said different things at different times. Hence, there is substantial authority that consistent statements are *not admissible* when they do not remove the taint of inconsistency.

1/ **Exception—consistent statement made before inconsistent statement:** [§1108]   If, however, the consistent statement was made before the inconsistent statement, some courts will admit it. Statements made closer in time to the relevant events are often more accurate than later statements, and the fact that the trial testimony conforms to the witness's earlier account of the relevant events helps support it. [*See* Cal. Evid. Code §791]

b) **Admissible when impeached witness denies making inconsistent statement:** [§1109]   When the witness denies making the prior inconsistent statement and the alleged consistent statement casts doubt upon whether the alleged inconsistent statement was ever made, the consistent statement should ordinarily be admitted.

    c)   **Admissible to explain inconsistent statement:** [§1110] When the consistent statement helps explain, put in context, or amplify the inconsistent statement, it should be admitted into evidence to rehabilitate the witness. [*See* United States v. Castillo, 14 F.3d 802 (2d Cir. 1994)]

  3)   **Prior consistent statements after attack on witness's character:** [§1111] Mere attack on character does not in itself open the door to introducing consistent statements of the witness. For example, if the witness testified that the defendant crossed the centerline and caused an automobile accident, and then was impeached with evidence that she had previously been convicted of perjury, evidence that she had made other statements blaming the accident on the defendant would not be admissible. They do not meet the attack and are simply a waste of time. [4 Wigmore on Evidence §1125 (Chadbourn rev. 1972)]

  4)   **Prior consistent statements after attack on witness's memory:** [§1112] Prior consistent statements are normally admissible to support a witness when there is a question about whether the witness's trial testimony is the product of a faulty memory, provided that the consistent statements were made earlier in time at a point when the witness's memory would have been fresher. Of course, the trial judge retains discretion to exclude cumulative or repetitious evidence. [140 A.L.R. 47]

(b)   **Hearsay status of prior consistent statements:** [§1113] Conceptually, there are two bases for objecting to prior consistent statements: (i) they lack probative value and are a waste of time (Rule 403 attack), and (ii) they are hearsay. The mere fact that the witness is on the stand does not in and of itself eradicate the hearsay objection, although some scholars have argued that it makes little sense to apply the hearsay rule because the opponent has the full opportunity to cross-examine the maker of the statement. Nonetheless, it remains the law that a statement made by the declarant at a place other than the hearing at which it is offered can be hearsay even if the declarant is on the stand. [*See* Fed. R. Evid. 801(c)] If a prior consistent statement is offered for the truth of what it asserts and no hearsay exception or exemption applies, then the statement must be excluded as hearsay.

  1)   **Traditional view:** [§1114] The traditional view is that when prior consistent statements are made in circumstances that give them significant probative value for purposes of rehabilitating the witness, they pass both the probative value test and the hearsay test. The prior consistent statements are not hearsay because they are not offered to prove the truth of what they assert. They are merely offered to bolster the credibility of the witness by showing that the witness has been consistent over time. Under this view, the jury should be given a limiting instruction

(quite a hard one to follow) telling it to use the statement only for its bearing on credibility, and not for the truth of the matter asserted.

2) **Federal Rules view:** [§1115] The Federal Rules of Evidence contain a special hearsay exemption for prior consistent statements. Rule 801(d)(1)(B) provides that a statement is *not hearsay* if it is "consistent with the declarant's testimony and is offered to rebut an express or implied charge against the declarant of recent fabrication or improper influence or motive." No limiting instruction is necessary when such statements are offered because the exemption allows them to be used for the truth of the matter asserted. (When a statement does not meet the requirements of Rule 801(d)(1)(B), it arguably might still be received under the traditional view if it can be offered for a purpose other than showing the truth of the matter asserted. For example, a statement offered in response to an attack on the witness's memory might be admitted on grounds that it is not being offered to show the truth of the matter asserted but merely to rebut aspersions of failing memory by showing that the witness was consistent over time.)

3) **California view:** [§1116] The California Evidence Code allows consistent statements to be admitted as substantive evidence. Consistent statements may be used to prove the truth of the matter asserted, and no limiting instruction is necessary. [Cal. Evid. Code §1236] To be admissible, however, the statements must either: (i) be offered in response to impeachment with a prior inconsistent statement, and made before the inconsistent statement; or (ii) be offered in response to a charge of recent fabrication or of influence by an improper motive, and made before the influence or motive for fabrication is alleged to have arisen. [Cal. Evid. Code §791]

(c) **Prior identification of accused:** [§1117] A frequent issue in criminal trials is whether the prosecutor can introduce evidence that the victim of the crime, or some eyewitness, was able to *identify* the accused at a police lineup, etc., shortly after the crime occurred.

1) **Witness unavailable at trial:** [§1118] If the victim or eyewitness is *unavailable* at the time of trial, such evidence is generally *excluded* as (i) inadmissible hearsay and (ii) perhaps unconstitutional because of the necessity of protecting the accused's Sixth Amendment confrontation rights.

2) **Witness available, but unable or unwilling to identify accused**

a) **Unable to identify:** [§1119] If the witness testifies at trial, but is unable to identify the accused, many courts permit the prosecutor to question the witness as to the police lineup identification for the purpose of *"refreshing the recollection"* of the witness.

1/ **Note:** This would not make the evidence of the prior identification admissible if the witness *remained* unable to make the identification. Under these circumstances, a court might well hold that the probative value of the attempted refreshing was *outweighed* by its prejudicial hearsay impact.

b) **Unwilling to identify:** [§1120]   If the witness has turned hostile and denied that the accused was the perpetrator, the identification *might* be admissible as a prior inconsistent statement in jurisdictions that allow a party to impeach his own witness. [71 A.L.R.2d 466]

c) **Note:** Some jurisdictions hold evidence of the witness's previous identification of the accused admissible as an *exception* to the hearsay rule.

3) **Witness testifies, but identification challenged:** [§1121] More frequently, however, the prior identification is offered to *bolster* the witness's courtroom identification of the accused, where the courtroom identification has been *challenged* or the witness's credibility otherwise impeached. Here, most courts *will* admit evidence of the identification at the police lineup as a prior consistent statement by the witness. [Fed. R. Evid. 801(d)(1)(C); 71 A.L.R.2d 449]

4) **Evidentiary effect**

a) **Traditional view—corroboration:** [§1122]   Most courts hold that evidence of a prior identification is admissible *solely to corroborate* a witness's in-court identification. Such evidence may *not* be used as *substantive* proof that the accused is the guilty party, out of concern that a conviction might be based solely on an out-of-court identification. [71 A.L.R.2d 463]

b) **Modern trend—substantive proof:** [§1123]   But the modern trend goes further and admits the prior identification as *substantive* proof of identity on the rationale that evidence of an identification made at or near the time of the crime is *more reliable* than any later courtroom identification (*i.e.,* accused's appearance may be changed; he may be wearing different clothing, etc.). [State v. Simmons, 385 P.2d 389 (Wash. 1963)]

1/ **Hearsay exception:** [§1124]   Some states create a special exception to the hearsay rule to allow in such evidence. [*See, e.g.,* Cal. Evid. Code §1238; N.Y. Crim. Proc. Law §393-6]

2/ **Federal Rules:** [§1125]   Under the Federal Rules, the prior identification is nonhearsay. [Fed. R. Evid. 801(d)(1)(C)]

3/ **Limitation:** [§1126] Keep in mind, however, that such evidence is admissible only if the *witness testifies* at the accused's trial (even though the witness has by then suffered a memory loss), to assure Sixth Amendment confrontation rights. [United States v. Owens, 484 U.S. 554 (1988)—nonhearsay and no violation of Confrontation Clause]

5) **Note on constitutionality of lineup:** [§1127] The issue of admissibility of the witness's prior identification arises only if the lineup or other identification was constitutionally obtained. If the lineup was unduly suggestive, or was made with insufficient attention to the accused's constitutional right of counsel, the prior identification will be inadmissible.

a) **Note:** Moreover, if the prior identification was unconstitutional, a subsequent identification at trial may be held inadmissible unless it was untainted by the prior identification. (*See* Criminal Procedure Summary.)

X. REAL, DEMONSTRATIVE, AND SCIENTIFIC EVIDENCE

chapter approach

Questions regarding real and demonstrative evidence do not show up all that often, but occasionally you will need to discuss these forms of tangible evidence.

When analyzing real evidence (the "real thing"), ask yourself:

— Can the foundation be laid that the evidence is what its proponent says it is? (This is sometimes referred to as the problem of authentication.)

— Is the evidence relevant and **not too unfairly prejudicial**? (This is generally a matter within the judge's discretion.)

And for **documentary** real evidence, consider the effects (if any) of the best evidence rule, the doctrine of completeness, and, of course, the hearsay rule.

When analyzing demonstrative evidence (a visual or audiovisual aid for the fact finder), ask yourself:

— Can the foundation be laid to show that the evidence is what its proponent says it is? (Not a distorted or fabricated representation.)

— Does the evidence help the jury? (This too is generally within the judge's discretion and raises relatively few of the kinds of issues that arise on examinations.)

A. REAL EVIDENCE

1. **In General:** [§1128]   As defined earlier, real evidence is **tangible** evidence (*e.g.,* guns, bullets, wearing apparel, contracts, etc.) presented to the trier of fact for inspection as relevant to an issue in the case.

2. **Direct vs. Circumstantial Real Evidence**

   a. **Direct evidence:** [§1129]   Real evidence may be **direct** evidence; *i.e.,* it can prove directly the fact for which it is offered.

      (1) **Example:** In a personal injury case, direct real evidence of a disfiguring injury would be an exhibition to the jury of the injury itself.

   b. **Circumstantial evidence:** [§1130]   Real evidence may also be **circumstantial**. In such case, facts about the object are proved as the basis for an inference that other facts are true.

      (1) **Example:** In a paternity case, the jury may be shown the baby and asked to compare its appearance with that of the alleged father. From the fact

that the child and alleged father look alike, the jury may then be asked to draw an inference that the parental relationship exists.

3. **Admissibility of Real Evidence:** [§1131]   Real evidence, like any other kind of evidence, must be *relevant*, must *not be hearsay* (or it must come within an exception to the hearsay rule), and must *not be privileged*. In addition, it must meet any additional requirements set by law (*e.g.*, it must not be the result of an illegal search and seizure or violate any pretrial order).

a. **Requirement of authentication:** [§1132]   The basic additional requirement for the admissibility of real evidence is that it be "*authenticated*." This requires a showing that the real evidence "is what it purports to be," or more precisely, that it is what its proponent says it is.

   (1) **Meaning of authentic:** [§1133]   Note that, in this sense, a piece of evidence may be "authentic" (*i.e.*, what it is claimed to be) even though it consists of false information.

      (a) **Example:** The falsified set of books kept by the defendant is authentic if it is introduced by the prosecution for the purpose of showing its falsity (*e.g.*, to raise an inference of the defendant's consciousness of guilt).

   (2) **Relationship to relevance:** [§1134]   Authentication may be viewed as one aspect of the problem of relevance. For example, if a knife other than the one found in the victim's body is sought to be introduced as the murder weapon, it is not only *not* authentic but, in the usual case, is simply irrelevant.

      (a) **Relevance as broader concept:** [§1135]   On the other hand, relevance of real evidence is not confined to its authenticity. Thus, the fact that a gun alleged to be owned by the defendant was authenticated as such would be irrelevant if the victim had been stabbed to death with a knife.

   (3) **Preliminary determination of authenticity:** [§1136]   The preliminary facts as to authentication, like those of relevance, are decided by the jury, not the judge.

      (a) **Judge's role:** Accordingly, the judge need only find that there is *sufficient* evidence introduced from which the jury can reasonably find that the evidence was authentic.

      (b) **Rationale:** The jury will presumably pay no attention to a contract, murder weapon, or other piece of real evidence that it finds was not authentic.

   (4) **Purposes of authentication:** [§1137]   Authentication is necessary to protect against two dangers:

      (a) *To prevent the introduction of an object different* from the one testified about; and

    (b) *To ensure that there have been no significant changes* in the object's condition.

(5) **Types of authentication**

    (a) **By testimony:** [§1138]   If the real evidence is of a type that can be readily identified by a witness, the witness's testimony will be sufficient authentication.

        1) **Example:** A witness in a murder case may testify that the instrument shown to her is the knife she found next to the body, that she recognizes it because of its peculiar markings, and that it is in the same condition as when she found it.

    (b) **Chain of custody:** [§1139]   If the real evidence is of a type that *cannot* easily be recognized or can readily be confused or tampered with, the proponent of the object must present evidence of its *chain of custody*. The proponent need not negate *all* possibilities of substitution or tampering in the chain of custody but must show that there was a *strong probability* of correct identification.

        1) **Example:** Assume that a white powder was seized from the defendant and the prosecution's chemist wishes to testify that she analyzed it and found it to be heroin. Clearly it is necessary for the prosecution to produce evidence that the white powder seized from the defendant is indeed the *same* as that analyzed by the chemist.

            a) **Procedure:** Typically authentication is done by establishing a *chain of custody:* that the seizing officer put the powder found on the defendant into an envelope; that he sealed and signed the envelope and then put it in a safe to which only he—or very few people—had the combination; that he then later took it out, noted that it appeared not to have been opened; and that he then delivered it to the chemist. The chemist may then testify that she received the particular envelope from the agent, opened it, and found therein the powder that she analyzed and about which she wishes to testify.

b. **Grounds for excluding real evidence**

(1) **Discretionary exclusion:** [§1140]   Real evidence may be (and often is) excluded on the ground that, although relevant and authentic, its *probative* value is *exceeded* by its unfairly *prejudicial* effect.

    (a) **Example:** Photographs of murder victims that the court considers too gruesome may be kept out of evidence because of their prejudicial effect.

    (b) **But note:** The trial judge's discretion is not absolute. Some appellate cases have reversed the trial judge's decision allowing unduly prejudicial material into evidence. [*See, e.g.,* Commonwealth v. Dankel, 301 A.2d 365 (Pa. 1973)]

(2) **Illegally obtained evidence:** [§1141] Most litigation over illegally seized evidence concerns real evidence (*e.g.,* drugs, weapons, bank loot, and gambling slips). If such evidence is the product of an unconstitutional search and seizure, it is inadmissible. (*See* Criminal Procedure Summary.)

4. **Particular Types of Real Evidence**

a. **Documentary evidence:** [§1142] The most common kind of real evidence is documentary evidence. Documentary evidence includes contracts, written confessions, letters, and, when otherwise admissible, books. The regular rules of evidence (*i.e.,* relevance, hearsay, privilege), of course, also apply to documents. But three special rules have particular application to documentary evidence: (i) authentication, (ii) the best evidence rule, and (iii) the doctrine of completeness. (Each of these is discussed in detail; *see infra,* §§1160, 1190, 1214.)

b. **Exhibition of injuries**

(1) **Personal injury cases:** [§1143] In a personal injury case, exhibition of the injured portion of the body constitutes real evidence. It is obviously relevant. [Yellow Cab Co. v. Henderson, 39 A.2d 546 (Md. 1944)] However, where the wound is particularly gory, or if showing the injured portion of the body would embarrass or offend the jury, the trial court in its discretion may *exclude* such evidence to avoid possible unfair prejudice. [159 A.L.R. 1410] Plaintiff must then rely on descriptive testimony.

(2) **Criminal cases:** [§1144] While weapons, bullets, etc., are generally admitted, the trial courts tend to exclude evidence that might shock or inflame the jury (*e.g.,* corpses, severed fingers, etc.). However, admitting shocking or inflammatory evidence is a matter of discretion, and where such evidence is received, the appellate courts generally sustain the trial court. [4 Stan. L. Rev. 589 (1952); *but see* People v. Gibson, 56 Cal. App. 3d 119 (1976)—prejudicial error to admit particularly gruesome pictures of victim shocking to ordinary sensibilities]

c. **Photographs, motion pictures, X-rays, tape recordings:** [§1145] All of these items fall within the definition of "real evidence."

(1) **Authentication:** [§1146] Since all of the above are merely reproductions, they must be authenticated by special testimony showing that they are *faithful reproductions of the object or person depicted*. However, the amount and type of authentication required will vary with the type of evidence involved.

(a) **Photographs:** [§1147] When dealing with photographs, most courts simply require testimony by a witness familiar with the person or object depicted that the photograph *accurately represents* the person or object. [United States v. McNair, 439 F. Supp. 103 (E.D. Pa. 1977); People v. Bowley, 59 Cal. 2d 855 (1963)]

    1) **Compare:** A few courts, however, still require more—*e.g.,* testimony by the person who actually took the picture, describing the camera angle, speed and lighting (to show absence of distortion), development process, and the care and custody of the negative (to show absence of retouching or tampering). [9 A.L.R.2d 899]

    (b) **X-rays:** [§1148] Unlike a photograph, an X-ray picture *cannot* be authenticated by testimony of a witness that it is a correct representation of the facts. Therefore, authentication of X-ray pictures, electrocardiograms, etc., must show that the process used is *accurate* (the court will usually take judicial notice of this); that the machine itself was in *working order*; that it was *operated* by a qualified operator; and that the evidence has come through a proper *custodial chain*.

d. **View of the scene:** [§1149] Where relevant evidence cannot be brought into court, the trial court may authorize a "view" during which the jury *goes to the scene* to observe the premises or object for themselves.

    (1) **Examples:** The jury's examination of the scene of the collision, its inspection of damage to P's land caused by overflow of water through D's negligence, or the judge's view of property to determine its value in condemnation proceedings may be allowed. [Yeary v. Holbrook, 198 S.E. 441 (Va. 1961)]

    (2) **View as evidence:** [§1150] Some courts have held that the view itself is not evidence, but merely a device to aid the trier of fact in understanding the testimonial evidence. However, the better and majority view is contra: The view constitutes *independent* evidence—and thus can sustain a finding or verdict apart from any testimonial evidence. [Otey v. Carmel Sanitary District, 219 Cal. 310 (1933)]

    (3) **Judge's discretion to allow view:** [§1151] A decision whether or not to allow the jury to view the scene is committed to the trial judge's discretion and will very rarely be reversed. Often trial judges refuse to permit a view, not only because it is difficult to transport the jury, but because the view may bring inadmissible evidence before the jury.

    (4) **Guide required:** [§1152] For the jury to view the scene, the trial judge ordinarily must designate a guide or "shower" to accompany the jurors. [47 A.L.R. 1227]

e. **Paternity cases:** [§1153] In a paternity case, a comparison of the physical characteristics of the baby and alleged father constitutes real evidence.

    (1) **Exhibition of child:** [§1154] Almost all courts permit an exhibition of the child for the purpose of showing whether or not it is of the same race as the putative father. [32 A.L.R.3d 1303]

    (2) **Admissibility:** [§1155] However, the courts are *split* on the admissibility of such exhibition solely to prove physical resemblance of the child to its alleged father. [40 A.L.R. 97]

(a) **Note:** Most courts will permit the exhibition under *certain conditions* (*e.g.,* where the child is sufficiently old to possess settled features). [Berry v. Chaplin, 74 Cal. App. 2d 652 (1946)]

f. **Demonstrations:** [§1156]   The court, in its discretion, may permit experiments or demonstrations to be performed in the courtroom.

(1) **Bodily injuries:** [§1157]   Demonstrations to show the effect of bodily injury (*e.g.,* demonstration of a limp to show disability) are usually *allowed*.

(a) **But note:** The trial judge has the discretion to *exclude* or *limit* such demonstrations—to avoid cries of pain, which might unduly arouse the jury's sympathy, or to protect against false demonstrations of pain or disability. [66 A.L.R.2d 1382]

(2) **Experiments:** [§1158]   Scientific experiments may be performed in the courtroom if the judge finds that: (i) the conditions in the courtroom are *substantially similar* to those that attended the original event; and (ii) the experiment will not result in undue *delay* or *confusion*. (*See also* the discussion of scientific evidence, *infra*, §§1224 *et seq.*)

5. **Documentary Evidence:** [§1159]   As indicated *supra,* §1142, three special rules affect the admissibility of documentary real evidence: (i) authentication; (ii) the best evidence rule; and (iii) the completeness doctrine.

a. **Authentication—general rule:** [§1160]   As with other real evidence, before any writing (or secondary evidence of its content) may be received in evidence, it must be "*authenticated*"; *i.e.,* the proponent must offer a foundation of evidence sufficient to support a finding that the document is genuine and is what it purports to be. [Fed. R. Evid. 901]

(1) **Exceptions:** [§1161]   Of course, authentication is not required where the genuineness of the document is *admitted* in the pleadings or by other evidence, or if the adverse party *fails to raise* timely objection to lack of foundation.

(2) **Preliminary fact determinations:** [§1162]   Again, as with all real evidence, the preliminary facts as to the authenticity of a document are decided by the jury, not the judge. The judge merely determines whether there is sufficient evidence for the jury to find that the document is what it purports to be. If the genuineness of the document is then disputed, it is up to the jury to decide the question.

(3) **Documents requiring independent proof of authenticity:** [§1163]   In most cases, the proponent of the writing (letter, contract, deed, etc.) must produce evidence apart from the document itself to show that it is genuine and is what it purports to be. There is no limit on the kinds of evidence that may be used for this purpose, but the following are the most commonly encountered [Fed. R. Evid. 901(b); Cal. Evid. Code §§1410 *et seq.*]:

(a) **Direct evidence of authenticity**

1) **Testimony of subscribing witnesses**

   a) **At common law:** [§1164]   The *only* method by which a deed, mortgage, or other private document could be authenticated was by testimony of the subscribing witnesses; *i.e.,* a document would not be accepted as genuine *unless* it had been subscribed by attesting witnesses who appeared in court to identify the document (unless such witnesses were unavailable).

   b) **Under modern law:** [§1165]   Testimony of subscribing witnesses is no longer required. [Fed. R. Evid. 903] However, if subscribing witnesses *are* available, their testimony is certainly one method that may be used to authenticate the document. [Fed. R. Evid. 901(b)(1); Cal. Evid. Code §1411]

      1/ **Compare—wills:** [§1166]   Testimony of subscribing witnesses is still required to authenticate wills. However, this is a requirement of probate law, rather than a rule of evidence. (*See* Wills Summary.)

      2/ **Forgetful witness:** [§1167]   If a subscribing witness denies or forgets the document in question, other evidence may be used to prove its authenticity—and to rebut the witness's denial thereof. [Cal. Evid. Code §1412; Matheson v. Caribo, 109 S.E. 102 (S.C. 1921)]

2) **Testimony of other witnesses:** [§1168]   The testimony of any witness who saw the execution of the document, or heard the parties acknowledge the document, may be used to authenticate the document—whether the witness subscribed the document or not. [Fed. R. Evid. 901(b)(1); Cal. Evid. Code §1413]

3) **Opinion testimony as to handwriting identification:** [§1169] A writing may also be authenticated by evidence of the genuineness of the handwriting of the maker.

   a) *Such evidence may be given by any person familiar with the handwriting* of the supposed writer [United States v. Gallagher, 576 F.2d 1028 (3d Cir. 1978)], except when a nonexpert's familiarity with the handwriting was acquired in preparation for litigation. [United States v. Pitts, 569 F.2d 343 (5th Cir. 1978); *but see* United States v. Standing Soldier, 538 F.2d 196 (8th Cir. 1976)—*allowing* nonexpert opinion of handwriting based on familiarity plainly acquired for trial purposes];

   b) *By expert testimony* [Fed. R. Evid. 901(b)(3); Cal. Evid. Code §1418]; or

   c) *By having the trier of fact compare it with some admittedly genuine document* [Fed. R. Evid. 901(b)(3); Cal. Evid. Code §1417].

(b) **Circumstantial evidence of authenticity**

1) **Admissions:** [§1170]   It may be shown that the party against whom the writing is offered has in the past either admitted its authenticity or acted upon it as if it were authentic.

2) **Authentication by content:** [§1171]   A writing may also be authenticated by a showing that it contains information that is unlikely to have been known to anyone other than the person who is claimed to have written it, or that it is written in a manner unique to that person. [Fed. R. Evid. 901(b)(4); Cal. Evid. Code §1421; *and see* United States v. Sinclair, 433 F. Supp. 1180 (D. Del. 1977)]

   a) **Reply letter doctrine:** [§1172]   Thus, a writing may be authenticated by evidence that it was received in response to a communication sent to the claimed author. For example, where A mails a letter to B, and a reply is received in which reference is made to A's letter, this is sufficient evidence to authenticate the reply letter as having actually come from B. [Cal. Evid. Code §1420; 62 A.L.R. 583]

   b) **Connecting link:** [§1173]   Likewise, where a series of correspondence between two persons is established, and a letter is shown to fit in as a connecting link between other letters in that series, this is sufficient evidence to authenticate the letter as being part of the series.

   c) **Style or manner of expression:** [§1174]   A writing may also be authenticated by identification of the writer's style or manner of expression—*e.g.,* the use of certain words, phrases, abbreviations, or idioms shown to have been unique to the person claimed to have written it. [Fed. R. Evid. 901(b)(4)—"appearance, contents, substance, internal patterns, or other distinctive characteristics" may be admitted to authenticate; *and see* United States v. Wilson, 532 F.2d 641 (8th Cir. 1976)]

3) **Authentication by proving document produced by reliable process:** [§1175]   Where documents or other data compilations have been produced by some automatic process or system—*e.g.,* X-rays or computer printouts—testimony describing the process and indicating its reliability is sufficient to authenticate. [Fed. R. Evid. 901(b)(9)]

4) **Authentication by age ("ancient documents doctrine"):** [§1176]   Most states retain the common law rule that a document affecting property (*e.g.,* deed, will, mortgage, etc.) is presumed authentic if shown to be at least **30 years old** and "fair on its face"—*i.e.,* its condition creates no suspicion as to its authenticity, and it was kept or found in a place where, if authentic, it would likely be kept or found. [Cal. Evid. Code §643]

a) **Federal Rules:** [§1177] The Federal Rules are even more liberal: Any document in any form (including data stored electronically) is presumed authentic if shown to be at least *20 years old*, and "fair on its face" (above). [Fed. R. Evid. 901(b)(8)]

(4) **Documents that are "self-authenticating":** [§1178] Certain kinds of documents or records require no independent proof of authenticity. Their nature is such that merely producing the document establishes *prima facie* its own authentication. The burden then shifts to the adverse party to prove that the document is not what it purports to be or otherwise is not authentic.

(a) **Official documents under seal:** [§1179] Documents bearing the seal of any recognized government agency or department and the signature of an authorized signatory may be received into evidence without independent proof of authenticity. [Fed. R. Evid. 902(1); United States v. Trotter, 538 F.2d 217 (8th Cir. 1976)]

(b) **Notarized documents:** [§1180] Documents notarized as required by law (*e.g.,* bearing certificate "subscribed and sworn to before me . . ." and accompanied by notary's seal and signature) need no independent proof of authenticity [Fed. R. Evid. 902(8)], or testimony of the notary will be sufficient to authenticate [*In re* Clifford, 566 F.2d 1023 (5th Cir. 1978)].

1) **Note:** Some states are more stringent and require that the certificate also show that the parties appeared before the notary and acknowledged the genuineness of their signatures thereon. [Cal. Evid. Code §1451]

(c) **Certified copies of public records:** [§1181] A copy of any public record (including data compilations) may be received without further authentication if accompanied by a certificate showing that: (i) the original is a document *authorized by law to be recorded or filed* in a public office, and is so recorded or filed; (ii) the attached copy is a *correct copy* of the original; and (iii) the certificate is *signed by the custodian* of the public record and bears the seal of that office. [Fed. R. Evid. 902(4)]

1) **Recorded private documents:** [§1182] Deeds, mortgages, or other private documents that are authorized by law to be recorded can thus be authenticated without independent proof as to the circumstances surrounding execution and notarization, or testimony of the recording officer, etc.

(d) **Commercial paper:** [§1183] Uniform Commercial Code section 3-307, incorporated also in Federal Rule 902(9), provides that production of a promissory note is prima facie evidence of its validity. [*See* United States v. Carriger, 592 F.2d 312 (6th Cir. 1979); *and see* United States v. Little, 567 F.2d 346 (8th Cir. 1977)—checks admissible as commercial paper]

(e) **Miscellaneous:** [§1184]   The Federal Rules list various other records that may be accepted as *"self-authenticating"*: official publications (*e.g.,* pamphlets published by public agencies), newspapers and periodicals, trade inscriptions and the like affixed in the course of business and indicating ownership or origin, etc. [Fed. R. Evid. 902(5)-(7)]

(5) **Compare—authentication of oral statements:** [§1185]   Oral statements often require authentication as to the *identity* of the speaker, even though they are not documents or even real evidence.

(a) **When authentication necessary:** [§1186]   Authentication of an oral statement is generally required where the statement is admissible only if said by a *particular* person—*e.g.,* admissions by a party or prior inconsistent statements of a witness. In such cases, the proponent of the statement must produce sufficient evidence that the person claimed to have made the statement actually did so.

1) **Authentication not necessary in all cases:** [§1187]   Not *all* oral statements need to be authenticated. In some cases, the identity of the speaker may not matter. Thus, if the only issue is whether the defendant had notice of a defect, the fact that *someone* told the defendant of the defect would be relevant without any showing as to who that person was.

(b) **Methods of authentication:** [§1188]   An oral statement can be authenticated by the testimony of a witness who saw and heard the speaker make it.

1) **Telephone conversations:** [§1189]   Where, however, the statement was made by telephone, the proponent may find it more difficult to prove that the statement was made by a *particular* person. In such a case, the statement must be authenticated in much the same way as a document. [Fed. R. Evid. 901(b)(6)] *Examples:*

a) If A receives a telephone call and A *recognizes* B's voice, this recognition is sufficient to authenticate the call as having actually come from B. [United States v. Cuesta, 597 F.2d 903 (5th Cir. 1979)]

b) The same is true where the speaker has knowledge of *certain facts* that *only* B could have.

c) Similarly, if A calls *B's telephone number* and a voice answers, "This is Mr. B" or "This is the B residence," this acknowledgment is sufficient in itself to authenticate the conversation as being with Mr. B or his agent—the accuracy of the telephone transmission system being *assumed*. [First State Bank of Denton v. Maryland Casualty Co., 918 F.2d 38 (5th Cir. 1990)]

d) Furthermore, most courts hold that when A telephones B's *business establishment*, and engages in a conversation *relevant* to the business with the person answering the phone, this is a sufficient showing that the person answering *in fact* held a position in B's business. [Union Construction Co. v. Western Union Telegraph Co., 163 Cal. 298 (1912)]

b. **Best evidence rule:** [§1190]   The best evidence rule has a misleading name. Contrary to what its title implies, the rule does *not* require a party to present the best or most probative evidence on an issue where more than one means of proof is available. Rather, the best evidence rule is a specific evidentiary requirement applicable to documentary evidence. It might therefore better be referred to as the *"original writing rule."*

(1) **Statement of rule:** [§1191]   To prove the contents of a writing, the *original* writing itself must be produced, unless it is shown to be *unavailable*. [Fed. R. Evid. 1002; United States v. Winkle, 587 F.2d 705 (5th Cir. 1979)]

(a) **Rationale:** Slight differences in written words or symbols may make a vast difference in meaning. Also, production of the original prevents *fraud* and *mistakes* that might occur if oral testimony or copies were used in lieu thereof.

(b) **Waiver by failure to object:** [§1192]   As with most other rules of evidence, the best evidence rule is waived (and secondary evidence of a writing's contents is thus admissible) by the opponent's failure to make a timely and specific objection.

(c) **Limitations on rule**

1) **Not applicable to official records:** [§1193]   Note that the rule applies only to *private* writings: *i.e.,* properly authenticated copies of any *official document* or *recorded writing* (*e.g.,* a recorded deed) *may* be used in lieu of the originals. [Fed. R. Evid. 902(4), 1005]

2) **Not applicable where contents of writing only "collateral":** [§1194]   Note also that the rule applies only where the *secondary* evidence is offered to prove the contents of an *original* writing. It does not apply where the "writing" itself is "not closely related to the controlling issues." [Fed. R. Evid. 1004(4)]

a) **Example:** Where D denies the making of a written contract with P, P may introduce secondary evidence as to its contents without producing the contract itself. Here the issue is not the contract's *contents*, but whether a contract had in fact been *made* at all. [Wigmore §1242]

3) **Not applicable where party admits contents:** [§1195]   The contents of a writing (photograph, recording, etc.) may be proved

by the testimony or deposition of the party against whom it is offered or by that party's written admission, ***without*** accounting for the nonproduction of the original writing. Note that this rule does ***not*** extend to out-of-court oral admissions. [Fed R. Evid. 1007]

4) **Not applicable when proof is of oral conversation rather than a record thereof:** [§1196]   A witness can testify to an ***oral*** conversation heard even though a written or otherwise recorded record (*e.g.,* a tape) of it exists. [*See* United States v. Rose, 590 F.2d 232 (7th Cir. 1978)]

5) **Applies only to affirmative contents of writing, not to absence of contents:** [§1197]   The rule is ***inapplicable*** to testimony that books or records have been examined "and found ***not*** to contain designated matter." [United States v. Madera, 574 F.2d 1370 (5th Cir. 1978)]

(2) **What constitutes "original writing":** [§1198]   The best evidence rule applies to all printed and written documents of any type whatsoever.

(a) **Modern trend expands "writing":** [§1199]   Under the Federal Rules and modern trend, "writing" is expanded to include ***photographs*** (including X-rays and motion pictures), ***recordings in any form*** (*e.g.,* tape recordings), and any other form of data compilation. [Fed. R. Evid. 1001]

(b) **Duplicate originals:** [§1200]   A duplicate includes a carbon copy, photostatic copy, microfilm reproduction, etc. [Fed. R. Evid. 1001(4)]

1) **Federal Rules:** [§1201]   Under the Federal Rules, a duplicate is as admissible as the original unless (i) the authenticity of the original is genuinely disputed, or (ii) it would be unfair under the circumstances to admit the duplicate in lieu of the original (as where only part of the original was reproduced and the rest is necessary for cross-examination). [Fed. R. Evid. 1003; CTS Corp. v. Piher International Corp., 527 F.2d 95 (7th Cir. 1975)— carbon copy admitted as original; United States v. Rodriguez, 524 F.2d 485 (5th Cir. 1975)—photocopy admitted as original]

(3) **Justifications for nonproduction of "original writing":** [§1202]   The best evidence rule does not apply where it is impossible or impractical to produce the original writing in court because it is: (i) lost or destroyed; (ii) unobtainable; (iii) too voluminous; or (iv) in the opponent's possession, and the opponent fails to produce it.

(a) **Lost or destroyed:** [§1203]   Where the original writing has been lost or destroyed without fault of the party offering the secondary evidence, the rule is not applicable. [Fed. R. Evid. 1004(1)]

1) **Limitation—wills:** [§1204]   Note, however, that when dealing with lost wills, most states limit the type of secondary evidence that may be used to prove their contents. [*See, e.g.,* Cal. Prob. Code §350—contents of a lost will may be proved only by the testimony of two credible witnesses who actually saw the will, although they need not be attesting witnesses]

(b) **Unobtainable:** [§1205]   The best evidence rule is usually inapplicable where the original writing is in the possession of a third person who is outside the state (and hence outside the court's subpoena power).

1) **But note:** There is substantial authority that the above situation does not establish the unobtainability of an original—on grounds that secondary evidence as to the contents of the document should be admissible only when the original document (or a properly authenticated copy) cannot be obtained by the use of "letters rogatory" to the foreign jurisdiction. [*See, e.g.,* McDonald v. Erbes, 83 N.E. 162 (Ill. 1907)] This view is apparently taken by Federal Rule 1004(2): A writing is unobtainable only when it cannot be obtained "by any available judicial process or procedure."

(c) **Too voluminous:** [§1206]   Where the original writings are so voluminous that it would be impractical to produce them in court, the court may disregard the rule and allow secondary evidence (*e.g.,* a summary), if the originals are available for inspection by the adverse party. [Fed. R. Evid. 1006; United States v. Clements, 588 F.2d 1030 (5th Cir. 1979)]

(d) **In possession of opponent:** [§1207]   The rule is also inapplicable where the original writing is in the control or possession of the adverse party and that party fails to produce it upon reasonable advance notice. (Such notice is usually in the form of a separate pleading—"notice to produce"—filed before trial.) [Fed. R. Evid. 1004(3)]

1) **Effect of claim of privilege:** [§1208]   There is a split of authority as to whether the above notice may be dispensed with where the original document is in the possession of a party who is claiming a privilege (*e.g.,* a defendant in a criminal case has possession of a document as to which she asserts her privilege against self-incrimination).

a) *Some states* hold that in such cases, *no* prior "notice to produce" need be given, and the adverse party can introduce secondary evidence as to the contents of the documents. [*See, e.g.,* People v. Lowell, 71 Cal. App. 500 (1925)]

1/ Indeed, a demand for the writing made on the defendant in the presence of the jury would be *improper* on the rationale that either surrender or refusal by the defendant would be *self-incriminating*. [Cal. Evid. Code §1503(a)]

                 b)   ***Other courts*** hold that at least ***some*** prior notice ought to be given, since the defendant may prefer to waive her privilege in order to prevent the use of secondary evidence. [*See, e.g.,* McKnight v. United States, 115 F. 972 (6th Cir. 1902)]

    (e) **Preliminary fact question for court:** [§1209] Each of the foregoing justifications for nonproduction of the original is a preliminary fact question going to the fulfillment of a technical rule of evidence—and hence is decided by the ***trial judge*** alone. [Fed. R. Evid. 1008; *and see supra,* §63]

        1) **Compare—relevancy of evidence:** [§1210] Where the question raised is whether the copy offered is a true and correct copy of the original, or whether an original ever existed, these are treated as issues going to the credibility and relevancy of the evidence, and hence are decided by the jury. [Fed. R. Evid. 1008]

  (4) **Rules of preference where secondary evidence allowed:** [§1211] In the situations where the best evidence rule is not applicable (above), and hence secondary evidence as to the contents of the writing may be received, the question arises—what ***kind*** of secondary evidence is admissible?

    (a) **Majority view:** [§1212] Most courts have adopted a rule of preference for a ***copy*** of the original writing, if available. Thus, if the proponent has a copy (or access thereto), that copy must be produced rather than ***oral*** testimony as to the contents. [*See, e.g.,* Cal. Evid. Code §1505]

    (b) **Minority view:** [§1213] The minority view (adopted by the Federal Rules) is that there are ***no*** rules of preference. The proponent may use ***any*** kind of secondary evidence—*i.e.,* copies of the writing, or mere oral testimony of persons who have read it. The ***kind*** of secondary evidence offered goes only to the ***weight***, not the ***admissibility***, of the evidence. [Baroda State Bank v. Peck, 209 N.W. 827 (Mich. 1926)]

  c. **Doctrine of completeness**

  (1) **Traditional approach:** [§1214] The traditional approach to the introduction of documents is that each party is free to present evidence as he chooses. A party may, therefore, elect to introduce only ***part*** of a document or writing. Under this view, it is up to the adverse party, by cross-examination or rebuttal, to bring out whatever additional portions of the document are necessary to correct any misleading impression created by the parts introduced. [*See* Cal. Evid. Code §356]

  (2) **Federal Rules approach:** [§1215] However, the modern approach (Federal Rules) is that if a party seeks to introduce only part of a document or recorded statement (*e.g.,* deposition), the other party may require the introduction at the same time of any other part "which ought in fairness to be considered contemporaneously with it." [Fed. R. Evid. 106]

(a) **Comment:** It is believed that the Federal Rule adopts the better approach because it prevents a party from misleading the jury by presenting matters out of context; otherwise the jury's first impression might be difficult to dislodge.

B. DEMONSTRATIVE EVIDENCE

1. **Distinguished from Real Evidence:** [§1216] Demonstrative evidence must be distinguished from so-called real evidence, discussed *supra*. Real evidence is tangible evidence which itself is alleged to have some direct or circumstantial connection with the transaction at issue. On the other hand, demonstrative evidence is *not* "the real thing"; *i.e.,* it is not *the* alleged murder weapon, or the *actual* engine part involved in the litigation. Instead, it is tangible material used only for *explanatory* or *exemplifying* purposes. It is a *visual aid—e.g.,* an anatomical model, a chart, a diagram, a map, a film, etc.

   a. **Distinction not always clear:** [§1217] As a practical matter, the distinction between real and demonstrative evidence is not always clear. A particular piece of evidence (*e.g.,* a photograph of the murder scene) may be real evidence or demonstrative evidence depending on the use to be made of it.

      (1) **Example:** If the jury is to use the photograph to make any *factual decisions* (*e.g.,* to determine placement of objects), the photograph would be real evidence. On the other hand, if the jury were simply to use the photograph to better *understand* and *picture* the testimony given, the photograph would be demonstrative evidence.

   b. **Distinction sometimes eliminated:** [§1218] Some courts and treatises do not distinguish between real and demonstrative evidence, calling them both demonstrative evidence.

2. **Types of Demonstrative Evidence:** [§1219] There are two basic types of demonstrative evidence:

   a. **Selected demonstrative evidence:** [§1220] Selected demonstrative evidence is existing evidence (*e.g.,* existing, genuine handwriting specimens or exemplars used as standards of comparison by a handwriting expert).

   b. **Prepared or reproduced demonstrative evidence:** [§1221] Evidence made specifically for trial (*e.g.,* scale models, drawings, photographs) is known as prepared or reproduced demonstrative evidence.

      (1) **Testimonial foundation required:** [§1222] Because there is some danger of fabrication, abuse, or distortion with demonstrative evidence prepared specially for trial, the law seeks to minimize these dangers by requiring testimonial assurances of accuracy.

3. **Admissibility of Demonstrative Evidence:** [§1223] Because it does not usually qualify as *substantive* evidence in the case, demonstrative evidence is not ordinarily offered into evidence and thus does not go to the jury's deliberation room.

C. SCIENTIFIC EVIDENCE

1. **In General:** [§1224]   As indicated earlier, where the trial court permits scientific experiments to be conducted in the courtroom, such are admissible as real evidence. More often, however, experiments are conducted out of court and the results offered to the jury through testimonial evidence—in which case the evidence must meet the admissibility requirements for scientific evidence.

2. **Foundation Requirements for Admissibility of Scientific Evidence**

   a. **Substantially similar conditions:** [§1225]   Where experimental evidence is offered, it must always be shown that the experiment was conducted under conditions *"substantially similar"* to those existing at the time of the actual event being litigated. Thus, in a skid test, there must be a showing of same size car, same type pavement, same weather conditions, etc. Conditions must have been *substantially*, but not *absolutely*, identical. [Culpepper v. Volkswagen of America, 33 Cal. App. 3d 510 (1973)]

   b. **Expert testimony:** [§1226]   If the experiment or test was of a *complicated nature* (*e.g.,* chemical analysis, shot-test patterns, etc.), it must have been conducted by qualified experts in the field; those experts must then testify in court as to (i) the *conduct* of the test; and (ii) the *reliability* of the testing procedures. [State v. Allison, 51 S.W.2d 51 (Mo. 1932)]

      (1) *Frye* **"general acceptance" test:** [§1227]   Prior to adoption of the Federal Rules, expert testimony was permitted only where the court found that the scientific principle or discovery underlying the testimony was "sufficiently established to have gained general acceptance in the particular field in which it belongs." [Frye v. United States, 293 F. 1013 (D.C. Cir. 1923)—refusing to admit, as unreliable, testimony based upon an early lie detector test]

      (2) *Daubert* **scientific validity test:** [§1228]   In *Daubert v. Merrell Dow Pharmaceuticals*, 509 U.S. 579 (1993), the Supreme Court rejected the *Frye* "general acceptance" test in favor of a scientific validity test.

         (a) **Rationale:** The Court indicated that the ultimate question in deciding whether to admit evidence over a "junk science" challenge was whether the reasoning or methodology underlying the testimony was *scientifically valid* and applicable to the case at hand. The Court further commented that the *Frye* "general acceptance" test was not mentioned in Federal Rule 702 or the legislative history and that *Frye* was contrary to the general liberal approach of the Federal Rules toward relaxing barriers to opinion testimony. (Despite the *Daubert* decision, many states, including states that have modeled their evidence codes on the Federal Rules, continue to follow some version of the *Frye* test.)

         (b) *Daubert* **factors:** [§1229]   The *Daubert* Court listed several factors for a judge to consider when deciding whether to admit evidence under the scientific validity test:

1) **Testing and testability:** [§1230]   A judge should consider whether the theory or technique in question is testable and, if so, whether it has been tested. A theory can be untestable if it makes indeterminate predictions or has too many escape hatches.

   a) **Example:** A theory that strict toilet training produces adults who are excessively neat, except that sometimes it produces adults who in reaction to the training become extremely messy or obsessively normal is basically untestable.

   b) **Example:** A theory that lying can be detected by blood analysis would be testable, but testimony based on the theory would be inadmissible if its adherents failed to test it using the scientific method.

2) **Peer review and publication:** [§1231]   Another factor a judge should consider is whether the theory or technique has been subjected to scrutiny and criticism by scientific peers. Publication in a peer reviewed journal (*i.e.,* one that asks established experts to evaluate articles before accepting them for publication) counts in favor of admissibility. Publication and peer review are not, however, essential; some theories and techniques are valid but are either too new or of such limited interest that it would be unreasonable to expect them to have been published or subjected to peer review.

3) **Error rate:** [§1232]   The *Daubert* Court noted that a judge should consider the "error rate" of a technique in making judgments about admissibility. This consideration is applicable to a number of forensic tests. For example, experts have sought to study the error rate of the polygraph test—*i.e.,* how many "false positives" (erroneous determinations of deception) and "false negatives" (erroneous determinations of truth-telling) are likely to occur.

4) **Standards:** [§1233]   An additional factor for a judge to consider is the "existence and maintenance of standards controlling the technique's operation." For example, the FBI sets standard protocols for the operation of DNA labs, designed to help prevent lab error. The existence of such standards is a factor that works in favor of admissibility.

5) **General acceptance:** [§1234]   Although *Daubert* does not require that a theory have achieved "general acceptance" in its field as the *sine qua non* of admissibility, it recognizes that general acceptance is one factor that counts in favor of the reception of scientific evidence.

(c) ***Daubert* factors not exclusive:** [§1235]   The Court in *Daubert* also stated that the factors listed were not intended as a "definitive checklist." In a particular case other factors might be relevant in deciding whether scientific evidence was based on acceptable science.

For example, an issue such as whether in testing an hypothesis the researcher used a properly controlled experiment is obviously relevant to a *Daubert* analysis.

(d) ***Daubert* vs. *Frye*—the basic difference:** [§1236]   The basic difference between the *Daubert* and *Frye* tests is that *Frye* instructs judges to defer to scientists, making the question of admissibility turn upon the issue of whether the scientific theory or technique has achieved "general acceptance" in the relevant scientific community. On the other hand, *Daubert* encourages judges to learn enough about the scientific method to decide for themselves whether an expert's testimony is based upon "good" science.

(e) ***Daubert* vs. *Frye*—exclusion of evidence:** [§1237]   Both the *Daubert* and *Frye* tests exclude particular types of scientific evidence. *Frye* tends to exclude ***new techniques*** that have yet to achieve "general acceptance"; whereas *Daubert* would be more likely to exclude techniques that have long been accepted by practitioners (*e.g.*, forensic experts) but are ***scientifically questionable***.

(f) ***Daubert* vs. *Frye*—policy arguments:** [§1238]   Opponents of the *Daubert* approach argue that *Frye* was correct in instructing judges to defer to the scientific community instead of attempting to become amateur scientists. Judges do not know enough science to make the required judgments of validity, and acquiring knowledge of scientific methodology is not the best use of their time. Supporters of *Daubert* say that *Frye* discriminates against science that is valid but that has not had the time (or research funds) to achieve "general acceptance." The supporters of *Daubert* further argue that *Frye's* concept of "general acceptance" in a "field" is vague and subject to manipulation, and that *Daubert* sends a good message to forensic scientists by telling them to test their conclusions using the scientific method.

(g) ***Daubert* guidelines inapplicable to nonscientific experts:** [§1239] *Daubert's* scientific validity requirement applies only to ***scientific experts***. There are, however, many other types of experts (*e.g.*, a police investigator may be an expert on the business methods of drug dealers; an auto mechanic may be an expert on the repair of cars). These nonscientific experts need not meet the scientific validity requirement of *Daubert*.

   1)   **Rationale:** Nonscientific experts do not pretend to be scientists or rely upon hard to understand scientific expertise, so there is less danger that a jury will be fooled by "junk science" testimony.

   2)   **Application:** Although the distinction between scientific experts and nonscientific experts was recognized in *Daubert* and has been applied by subsequent courts, its boundaries are unclear. For example, forensic document examiners have long been allowed to testify whether documents were forged, even

though their field was not developed through rigorous scientific inquiry, and proficiency tests show a high error rate. Based on these facts, are document examiners scientific experts subject to *Daubert*? One federal court has held that examiners are not scientific experts and may testify without meeting the requirements of *Daubert* as long as they do not wrap themselves in the mystique of science. [*See* United States v. Starzecpyzel, 880 F. Supp. 1027 (S.D.N.Y. 1995)]

(3) **Judicial notice in lieu of expert testimony:** [§1240] As scientific knowledge becomes firmly accepted, some courts have shown a willingness to take *judicial notice* of the *reliability* of certain scientific tests—*e.g.,* radar tests, firearms identification tests, fingerprints, blood-alcohol tests, etc. (Judicial notice is discussed *infra,* §§1267 *et seq.*)

(a) **Jury instruction given:** [§1241] In judicial notice cases, the judge simply instructs the jury as to the reliability of the scientific tests, and the need for independent expert testimony on this point is eliminated.

(b) **Proof of proper test administration:** [§1242] Of course, judicial notice as to the reliability of a certain test is no substitute for proof that the test was *properly administered* in the present case (*e.g.,* that the radar device was operating properly at the time in question).

(c) **Jury not bound by results:** [§1243] And even if the test's reliability is judicially noted, this does not invariably mean that the jury is *bound* by the test results (*e.g.,* the jury can find that the defendant was not speeding regardless of the radar test).

c. **Probative value outweighs risk of unfair prejudice, etc.:** [§1244] Finally, it must appear that the test has sufficient *probative* value as to the issues involved and that this probative value *outweighs* any risk of confusing or misleading the jury. In other words, the evidence must aid, rather than confuse, the trier of fact. [*See* Fed. R. Evid. 403]

3. **Types of Scientific Evidence:** [§1245] As human knowledge expands, new scientific and experimental techniques for obtaining or verifying data achieve acceptance and are then generally held to be *receivable* in evidence. Thus, there was a time when firearms identification evidence, so-called ballistics evidence, was considered irrelevant, even (in the words of one court) "preposterous." Such evidence is now considered "highly relevant," and judicial notice is often taken of its general reliability. Today, there are more than a dozen areas of possible scientific proof:

a. **Psychiatry and psychology:** [§1246] Psychiatric or psychological evidence may be allowed as scientific evidence (*e.g.,* psychiatric testing to support or refute an insanity defense to a charge of criminal conduct).

b. **Toxicology and other chemical sciences:** [§1247] Toxicology (*i.e.,* the identification of poisonous substances) and other chemical sciences are accepted areas of scientific evidence. *Examples:*

(1) **Blood tests:** [§1248] Tests on blood found at the scene of a crime may be used to link a suspect to the crime; similarly, a blood test showing the blood type of the victim is admissible, even though the blood type proves to be a common one such as type "O." (The objection of remoteness goes to the weight of the evidence rather than to its admissibility.) [Shanks v. State, 45 A.2d 85 (Md. 1945); *and see* Cal. Evid. Code §§890-897—Uniform Act on Blood Tests to Determine Paternity]

(2) **Breathalyzer:** [§1249] The Breathalyzer machine analyzes a sample of breath to determine the alcoholic content of the blood. Before the result of a Breathalyzer test can be received in evidence, the prosecution must lay a four-phase foundation showing:

    (a) *That the equipment was properly checked* and in proper working order at the time of the test;

    (b) *That the chemicals employed were of the correct type* and were compounded in the right proportions;

    (c) *That the test subject had nothing in his mouth at the time* of the test and had taken no food or drink within 15 minutes of taking the test; and

    (d) *That the test was given in a proper manner by a qualified examiner.* [State v. Baker, 355 P.2d 806 (Wash. 1960)]

(3) **Hair analysis:** [§1250] Radioimmunoassay hair analysis has been held admissible to show drug use, subject to a showing that: (i) the sample was properly obtained (*e.g.,* the hair was taken from the correct parts of the body); (ii) the laboratory's general technique was sound; and (iii) the laboratory was careful in following the technique in the particular case. [*See* United States v. Medina, 749 F. Supp. 59 (E.D.N.Y. 1990) (Weinstein, J.)]

c. **Forensic pathology:** [§1251] Forensic pathology evidence is acceptable (*e.g.,* scientific evidence offered in connection with proof of cause or time of death).

d. **DNA profiling:** [§1252] The basic scientific principles and techniques underlying DNA profiling by RFLP analysis (a technique that examines DNA fragments so that a pattern from a crime-scene sample of DNA may be compared with a known sample of DNA) are widely recognized as valid and acceptable. Courts may admit the evidence after taking judicial notice that it satisfies the *Daubert* scientific validity requirement. [United States v. Beasley, 102 F.3d 1440 (8th Cir. 1996)] However, DNA profiling by PCR analysis (a technique that produces multiple copies from a single test sample of DNA) is more controversial. Many courts still require a *Daubert* hearing, with expert testimony about scientific basis, before admitting PCR profiling. Decisions of trial judges upholding the admissibility of PCR profiling after such a hearing are likely to be upheld. [*See* United States v. Hicks, 103 F.3d 837 (9th Cir. 1996)] Even if the underlying principles of DNA profiling are valid, DNA expert testimony may still be challenged on other grounds (*e.g.,* that it is confusing and prejudicial because the proper laboratory procedures were not followed, or that the expert's statistical testimony is misleading).

e. **Microanalysis:** [§1253]   The analysis of very small samples of substances (*e.g.,* to identify the source of bits of glass, wood, soil, fibers, etc.) is also acceptable scientific evidence.

f. **Neutron activation analysis (NAA); inductively coupled plasma-atomic emission spectrometry (ICP):** [§1254]   These methods of identifying and measuring the various elements of a substance have been considered sufficiently scientific to be received in evidence. [*See, e.g.,* United States v. Stifel, 433 F.2d 431 (6th Cir. 1971)—NAA amissible; United States v. Davis, 103 F.3d 660 (8th Cir. 1996)—ICP admissible] They can be used, for example, to show similarities between the composition of cartridges found at a crime scene and those found in defendant's possession.

g. **Fingerprinting (including soleprints and palmprints):** [§1255]   Today, most courts take judicial notice of the reliability of fingerprint comparison evidence. [*See, e.g.,* Grice v. State, 151 S.W.2d 211 (Tex. 1941); Moenssens, Fingerprints and the Law (1969)]

h. **Firearms identification evidence (so-called ballistics evidence):** [§1256]   Abundant case law upholds the admissibility of firearms identification evidence when presented by an expert. [*See, e.g.,* Cummings v. State, 172 S.E.2d 395 (Ga. 1970)]

i. **Questioned document evidence:** [§1257]   Expert testimony regarding the genuineness of a document (*e.g.,* in a case involving a claim of forgery) is generally considered to be admissible, though some commentators believe that the expertise does not meet the *Daubert* standard because of its high error rate and lack of a scientific basis. Even if it lacks a scientific basis, questioned document testimony may still be admitted on the ground that *Daubert* does not apply to nonscientific experts (*see supra,* §1239). If the testimony is reasonably reliable and the expert does not pretend to be a scientist, it is admissible on the same basis as the testimony of an expert auto mechanic—the expert has nonscientific knowledge that is useful to the jury. [United States v. Jones, 107 F.3d 1147 (6th Cir. 1997)]

j. **Polygraph testing (so-called lie detector):** [§1258]   Most courts continue to *exclude* polygraph results unless *all* parties stipulate *in writing* that the test results are admissible. The stipulation may occur before the test is taken, and hence before the parties know what the final results will be.

    (1) **Minority view:** [§1259]   A few courts now allow polygraph results to be admitted even in the absence of stipulation. For example, the Eleventh Circuit allows polygraph results to be received to impeach or corroborate a witness's testimony, provided that notice is given and procedural safeguards are observed. [United States v. Piccinonna, 885 F.2d 1529 (11th Cir. 1989) (en banc)]

    (2) **Criminal cases:** [§1260]   In criminal cases, the prosecutor, accused, and accused's counsel must all sign the stipulation. Thus, test results clearly may not be admitted in a criminal case without the accused's consent. And the court may not compel an accused to submit to a polygraph examination because of the privilege against self-incrimination. [State v. Nemoir, 214 N.W.2d 297 (Wis. 1974)]

(3) **Judicial discretion:** [§1261]   Notwithstanding a written stipulation, some courts hold that the admissibility of the test results is still subject to the trial court's discretion.

(4) **Right of cross-examination:** [§1262]   If the polygraph results are offered in evidence, the opposing party has the right to cross-examine the examiner as to his *qualifications* and *training*, the *limitations* and *possibilities for error* in polygraph testing, and, in the trial court's discretion, any other matters that appear to be pertinent.

(5) **Limited use by jury:** [§1263]   If the polygraph evidence is received, the trial court will instruct the jury that the examiner's testimony does not tend directly to prove or disprove any element of the crime but, at most, tends to indicate that at the time of the examination the accused was or was not telling the truth. [State v. Valdez, 371 P.2d 894 (Ariz. 1962); State v. McDavitt, 297 A.2d 849 (N.J. 1972); *but see* People v. Potts, 220 N.E.2d 251 (Ill. 1966)—contra]

k. **Vehicular speed detection:** [§1264]   The speed at which a vehicle was traveling may be determined by scientific methods (*e.g.,* by means of radar or VASCAR equipment).

l. **Spectrographic voice identification (so-called voiceprint):** [§1265]   Spectrographic voice identification may also be used as evidence in some courts, but has come under increasing criticism as being unreliable.

m. **Narcoanalysis and hypnosis:** [§1266]   Narcoanalysis and hypnosis are *not* favored as truth-developing devices. [*See* Waltz, *Introduction to Criminal Evidence,* ch. 18 (3d ed. 1991)—detailed discussion of all areas of scientific evidence; *and see supra,* §966] However, the Supreme Court has held that a per se rule excluding all post-hypnosis testimony infringes impermissibly on a criminal defendant's right to testify on his own behalf. [Rock v. Arkansas, 483 U.S. 44 (1987)]

XI. JUDICIAL NOTICE

__chapter approach__

The important thing to remember about judicial notice is that it acts as a *substitute for full, formal proof*. In other words, matters of "common knowledge" may be accepted by the trier of fact as true without any formal proof thereof. To analyze a judicial notice question, determine whether:

1. Judicial notice of this fact is mandatory; *i.e.*, judicial notice *must* be taken (*e.g.*, federal or state laws or rules of procedure, etc.).

2. Judicial notice is permissive; *i.e.*, judicial notice *may* be taken by the court, or *must* be taken if requested by one of the parties (*e.g.*, laws of other states, administrative orders, matters of common knowledge or verifiable facts).

3. The litigants have been informed so that they know what will be judicially noticed and therefore taken as true.

A. NATURE OF JUDICIAL NOTICE

1. **Definition:** [§1267] Judicial notice is the process whereby the trier of fact accepts certain facts as true without the necessity of formal proof. Judicial notice is thus a *substitute for evidence*.

2. **Legislative vs. Adjudicative Facts:** [§1268] The most basic distinction in the area of judicial notice is that between *legislative facts* and *adjudicative facts*.

    a. **Legislative facts:** [§1269] Those facts that are relevant to *legal reasoning* and the *law-making process* are legislative facts.

        (1) **Examples of legislative facts:** That racially separate schools are inherently unequal; that women have at times been the object of invidious legislative and judicial discrimination; that electronic methods exist which, without physical entry, can intrude upon the privacy of citizens; that Congress enacted the National Labor Relations Act to redress what it felt was the imbalance in the bargaining power of the employer as against the worker are all legislative facts.

        (2) **Additional examples:** Legislative facts also include the applicable law, statutes, judicial decisions, etc., without which legal issues cannot be decided.

        (3) **Scarcity of case law:** [§1270] Although a court must take judicial notice of legislative facts in virtually every case in which it makes a decision based upon policy or draws a legal conclusion, there are very few rules governing this type of judicial notice. Most courts simply take judicial notice of legislative facts without any reference to the fact that they are doing so.

b. **Adjudicative facts:** [§1271]   Adjudicative facts are matters of consequence to the *resolution of the factual issues* in the particular case. These facts would be the subject of proof except that, for one reason or another, judicial notice may be taken of them—usually because no reasonable person could dispute them.

(1) **Use of term:** [§1272]   The great majority of cases involving judicial notice concern adjudicative, not legislative, facts. Consequently, when courts or commentators speak of judicial notice, they usually mean judicial notice of *adjudicative facts*.

(2) **Examples of judicially noticed adjudicative facts:** The following are examples of judicially noticed adjudicative facts: That the boiling point of water at sea level is 212°F.; that pork that has been properly cooked cannot cause trichinosis; that the human body cannot survive immersion in molten lead; and, in an action for breach of contract to locate a purchaser of crude oil, that at the time of the alleged breach there was an Arab oil embargo and an increase in the price of oil. [Mainline Investment Corp. v. Gaines, 407 F. Supp. 423 (N.D. Tex. 1976)]

B.   SCOPE OF MATTERS NOTICED   [§1273]

Judicial notice is a formal part of the trial proceedings. It does not permit the trial judge, nor any member of the jury, to substitute his personal knowledge for the evidence in the record. [United States v. Lewis, 833 F.2d 1380 (9th Cir. 1987)]

1. **Common Law:** [§1274]   The common law rule is that judicial notice may be taken only of facts of "*common, everyday knowledge*" that are accepted as "*indisputable*" by persons of average intelligence and experience in the community. [Varcoe v. Lee, 180 Cal. 338 (1919)]

a. **Discretionary:** [§1275]   Traditionally, judicial notice has been largely discretionary with the trial court. Except for noting all applicable laws, the trial court is not *required* to take notice of any particular fact or matters. Hence, most of the case law in this area deals with the circumstances under which a trial court is *permitted* to take notice of facts (thus dispensing with the need for formal proof thereof).

2. **Modern Rules:** [§1276]   In many jurisdictions today, judicial notice is made mandatory as to certain kinds of facts, while remaining discretionary as to others.

a. **Mandatory judicial notice**

(1) **General view:** [§1277]   In most courts, judicial notice *must* be taken of the following matters—whether or not requested by any party:

(a) **Federal and state (local) law:** [§1278]   This includes constitutions, statutes, ordinances, decisions, and rules of procedure (legislative facts).

(b) **Federal and state (local) rules of procedure:** [§1279]   (These are legislative facts.)

(c) **English language:** [§1280]   The true meaning and significance of all English words and phrases and of all legal expressions (legislative facts).

(d) **Indisputable matters:** [§1281]   Facts and propositions of generalized knowledge "that are so universally known that they cannot reasonably be disputed" (adjudicative facts). [Cal. Evid. Code §451]

(2) **Compare—Federal Rules:** [§1282]   The Federal Rules regard legislative facts, such as §§1278-1280 above, as *not* the subject of judicial notice at all but simply part of the court's reasoning process. [Fed. R. Evid. 201(a), note] Items covered by §1281 above are treated as *"adjudicative"* facts, meaning facts relating to the case at hand (*see infra,* §1289).

b. **Permissive judicial notice:** [§1283]   In addition to the foregoing, a court may on its own motion take judicial notice of certain other matters. [Fed. R. Evid. 201(c)] And if an appropriate request is made by a party (below), the court is *required* to take notice thereof; *i.e.,* notice is mandatory upon request. [Fed. R. Evid. 201(d)]

(1) **Matters that may be noted**

(a) **Laws of other states or nations:** [§1284]   (These are legislative facts.)

(b) **Administrative regulations and orders:** [§1285]   The regulations and orders of any agency of state or federal government (legislative facts).

(c) **Court records:** [§1286]   Records of any state or federal court (legislative *or* adjudicative facts). [*See* Schweitzer v. Scott, 469 F. Supp. 1017 (C.D. Cal. 1979)]

(d) **Matters of common knowledge locally:** [§1287]   Facts and propositions that are of such common knowledge *locally* that they cannot be reasonably disputed (*e.g.,* the locality of a certain street; whether a certain area is residential) (adjudicative facts). [United States v. Lavender, 602 F.2d 639 (3d Cir. 1979)]

(e) **Verifiable facts:** [§1288]   Matters that are not reasonably subject to dispute and are capable of immediate and accurate determination by resort to sources of reasonably *indisputable* accuracy (*e.g.,* almanacs, encyclopedias, etc.) (adjudicative facts). [United States v. Gould, 536 F.2d 216 (8th Cir. 1976)]

1) **Note:** What facts are verifiable is a rapidly expanding area of the law. As scientific knowledge becomes more and more precise, courts have shown a willingness to take judicial notice of more and more facts.

2) **Example:** Courts today commonly take judicial notice of the reliability of various scientific evidence—*e.g.,* fingerprints, ballistics, radar, blood-alcohol ratio, etc. The significance is that

the court will instruct the jury as to the reliability of such tests without requiring independent expert testimony in every case. [People v. MacLaird, 264 Cal. App. 2d 972 (1968)—reversal for failure to take notice as to reliability of radar evidence; *but see* State v. Hanson, 270 N.W.2d 212 (Wis. 1978)—trial court erred in taking judicial notice of moving radar device]

(2) **Compare—Federal Rules:** [§1289]   The Federal Rules recognize judicial notice only as to "adjudicative" facts—facts relating to the case at hand. Under this approach, Federal Rule 201 recognizes only §§1286-1288 above as proper subjects of judicial notice. [Fed. R. Evid. 201(b)] Matters covered in §§1284-1285 would be treated as "legislative facts" (although the procedure for bringing such matters to the attention of the court is substantially the same). [*See* Fed. R. Crim. P. 44(1)]

c. **Limitation—criminal cases:** [§1290]   Matters that are beyond reasonable dispute can be judicially noted in criminal as well as civil cases, but the court **cannot** instruct the jury in a criminal case that it is **required to accept** judicially noticed facts as conclusive. Instead, the judge will instruct the jury that it **may accept** the judicially noticed facts as true (*see infra,* §1300). [Fed. R. Evid. 201(g)]

(1) **Example:** In a grand theft auto prosecution in which the value of the stolen car is an essential element, the court could not instruct the jury that it must find, for example, that a new car is worth more than $50. [State v. Lawrence, 234 P.2d 600 (Utah 1951)]

C. PROCEDURE

1. **Stage of Proceeding When Proper:** [§1291]   Judicial notice may be taken at any stage of the proceeding—either by a trial or an appellate court. [Fed. R. Evid. 201(f)]

a. **Notice in appellate court:** [§1292]   In fact, a reviewing court is required to take notice of any matter the trial court improperly failed to notice. For example, *see Meredith v. Fair,* 298 F.2d 696 (5th Cir. 1962), where the appellate court took notice of Mississippi segregation policies, despite a specific finding to the contrary by the trial court.

(1) **Note:** One court suggests in dictum that judicial notice of adjudicative facts on appeal of criminal cases violates the defendant's Sixth Amendment right to trial by jury. [*See* United States v. Dior, 671 F.2d 351 (9th Cir. 1982)—a jury may, in its prerogative, "ignore even uncontroverted facts in reaching a verdict. . . ."]

2. **When Judicial Notice Appropriate:** [§1293]   Where judicial notice is permissive (*see supra,* §§1283-1289), the court may take notice on its own motion without any request by a party. But far more frequently, such notice is taken only after a request therefor has been made by a party to the action—in which event, the court is required to take notice of the matters requested if appropriate (*see supra,* §1283).

a. **Request by party:** [§1294]   The party's request that the court judicially notice some matter may be made through the pleadings or otherwise (oral motion will suffice in most courts), according to the following requirements:

(1) **Opportunity to be heard:** [§1295]   The party's request must be made in a manner that allows the opponent an opportunity to be heard; and

(2) **Sufficient information:** [§1296]   The party making the request must furnish the court with sufficient information to enable it to rule on the request. [Fed. R. Evid. 201(d)]

b.   **Opportunity to be heard:** [§1297]   Even where the trial court is proceeding on its own motion (*i.e.,* no party request), it is required to afford each party an opportunity to be heard as to the propriety of taking judicial notice of the matter in question. And if such opportunity was not afforded previously, the party is entitled to be heard even after judicial notice was taken. [Fed. R. Evid. 201(e)]

c.   **Court's determination:** [§1298]   In ruling on a party's request, the judge may generally consider and rely upon any reliable source of information, whether or not furnished by a party. However, if the judge resorts to outside sources or consultants, this must be made part of the record. [Cal. Evid. Code §455]

D.   EFFECT OF JUDICIAL NOTICE

1.   **Civil Cases—Fact Conclusively Established:** [§1299]   When judicial notice of a fact is taken, it is binding on the jury—at least in civil cases. In other words, the judge should instruct the jury in a civil case to accept as *conclusive* any fact judicially noted; and if such a fact is fatal to one side's case, the judge must direct a verdict against that side.

2.   **Compare—Criminal Cases:** [§1300]   In criminal cases, however, holding the jury bound as to any fact contrary to the accused's position may violate the accused's Sixth Amendment right to a jury trial. Hence, the jury is instructed that it *may*, but is *not required* to, accept as conclusive any fact judicially noted. [Fed. R. Evid. 201(g)—applying same rule to judicially noticed facts contrary to position of prosecution]

XII. BURDENS AND EFFECT OF EVIDENCE

chapter approach

Not all evidence questions are concerned with the admissibility of evidence. The major area of questioning where admissibility is **not** the issue concerns burdens of proof and presumptions. Typically, this kind of question will involve whether the judge should direct the verdict or, if she sends the case to the jury, which party she should indicate has the burden of proof. In this area you should ask:

1. Who has the **burden of proof** and by what **weight** must it be proven (preponderance of the evidence, clear and convincing evidence, or reasonable doubt)?

2. Does the litigant with this burden have available **sufficient evidence** to allow the jury to find in her favor?

3. Does the litigant have a **presumption** in her favor that would entitle her to a directed verdict? If so, then the concern switches to the other litigant to ask the same questions now that he has the burden of going forward with the evidence.

A. INTRODUCTION [§1301]

Except in the limited areas in which the trial judge takes "notice" of a fact in issue (_supra,_ §§1267-1300), one party or the other has the burden of presenting evidence on the issues in the suit. This burden raises the considerations of **which** party is obligated to present the evidence, how **much** evidence the party must present, and the **consequences** of that party's doing or failing to do so.

B. PROOF DEFINED [§1302]

"Proof" is the establishment of a requisite degree of belief in the mind of the trier of fact as to the facts in issue. It is the cumulation of evidence that persuades the trier of fact. [Cal. Evid. Code §190]

C. BURDEN OF PROOF

1. **Definition:** [§1303] "Burden of proof" is a term used loosely to refer to two separate concepts: (i) It primarily refers to a party's obligation to produce the degree of evidence required to **prove the facts** upon which she relies—_i.e.,_ the burden of persuading the trier of fact that the burdened party is entitled to prevail. (ii) The term is also sometimes used to refer to a party's obligation of **introducing** or "**going forward**" with the evidence. To avoid confusion, the first burden is referred to herein as the **burden of persuasion**; the second burden is the burden of **going forward** with the evidence or the burden of **introducing** evidence.

2. **Burden of Persuasion**

    a. **In general:** [§1304] When a case is submitted to the jury, the trial judge will instruct the jury about the burden of persuasion. A party bears the burden of persuasion on a factual issue if the judge's instructions tell the jury that the factual issue should be resolved against that party if the party fails to persuade the jury. In cases tried without a jury, the trial judge as trier of fact will apply the burden of persuasion rules, deciding against the party bearing the burden when the proof is evenly balanced and the judge finds herself in equipoise.

b. **Allocation of the burden:** [§1305]   In civil cases, the plaintiff, as the party disturbing the status quo, bears the burden of persuasion on most issues. In criminal cases, the prosecution normally bears the burden of persuasion. In civil or even criminal cases, however, the burden of persuasion is sometimes allocated to the defendant.

   (1) **Rationale:** The reason for allocating the burden of persuasion to the defendant may be that: (i) *the defense is disfavored* (*e.g.*, a defendant should not be able to escape liability by using a technical defense such as the statute of limitations unless he persuades the trier of fact that the factual basis for the defense exists); (ii) *the defendant has better access to evidence* (*e.g.*, the defendant is in a better position to know what happened to the goods entrusted to him by the plaintiff); or (iii) *the defense is rare* so that it would be a waste of time to make the plaintiff disprove it in every case (*e.g.*, contracts are rarely invalid because of duress, so that plaintiffs should not have to allege and prove a lack of duress in every case where a contract is involved).

   (2) **Relation to burden of pleading:** [§1306]   The burden of pleading and the burden of persuasion are often allocated to the same party; thus, if the defendant is required to plead a defense in his answer or lose it, usually the defendant will also be required to persuade the jury as to that defense. This allocation makes sense because it is convenient and the policy reasons for allocating the burden of pleading often overlap with the policy reasons for allocating the burden of persuasion.

c. **Quantum of evidence required**

   (1) **Preponderance of evidence:** [§1307]   The preponderance of evidence standard is the most generally applicable burden of persuasion used in the law. It applies to almost all issues in civil cases, to preliminary fact determinations committed to the judge and, according to many courts, to some issues in criminal cases (*e.g.,* the statute of limitations, venue).

      (a) **Definition:** [§1308]   "Preponderance of evidence" is sometimes defined as "such evidence as, when weighed against that opposed to it, has more convincing force; and thus the greater probability of truth." [93 A.L.R. 155]

         1) **Example:** Sometimes the preponderance of evidence standard is pictured as a balance scale; hence whichever side produces the greater weight of evidence (that which causes its pan of the scale to sink lower) has presented the preponderance of evidence.

      (b) **Effect of burden:** [§1309]   The party with the burden of persuasion on an issue must end up with the preponderance of evidence on that issue in order to prevail with the trier of fact. Thus, if the preponderance of evidence is against that party, or the balance is in equipoise, the party with the burden of persuasion must lose on the issue.

(2) **Clear and convincing evidence:** [§1310]   In some cases, for reasons of policy, a *higher* burden of persuasion is required.

  (a) **Example—severe sanctions:** For instance, in cases involving severe sanctions—but short of criminal penalties—clear and convincing evidence is often necessary (*e.g.*, disbarment of an attorney, denaturalization of a citizen).

  (b) **Example—fraud:** Many jurisdictions require that a party alleging fraud must prove it by clear and convincing evidence. The reason is that if this contention prevails, the other party will not only lose the lawsuit but be stamped as fraudulent.

  (c) **Example—settled transactions:** Likewise, in cases that seek to upset settled transactions, such as those that attempt to show that what appears to be a mortgage is really a deed or vice versa, clear and convincing evidence is usually necessary.

(3) **Reasonable doubt:** [§1311]   In *criminal cases*, the *guilt* of the accused must be established "beyond reasonable doubt"—*i.e.*, a mere preponderance of the evidence is insufficient.

  (a) **Rationale:** The reasonable doubt standard is an attempt to make sure that the scales of evidence are heavily balanced against a defendant before he may be convicted of a criminal offense.

  (b) **Compare—other issues:** However, other issues in a criminal case (*e.g.*, lawfulness of search, voluntariness of confession) need only be proved by a *preponderance* of evidence. (*See* detailed discussion in Criminal Procedure Summary.)

d. **Effect of burden of persuasion:** [§1312]   The main effect of allocating the burden of persuasion is that the court will instruct the jury as to which party bears this burden.

(1) **Note:** As a practical matter, there is no way to enforce the rules on burden of persuasion once the case goes to the jury; *i.e.,* if, after hearing the instructions on burden of persuasion, the jury decides to ignore them, there is no effective way to prevent this.

(2) **Comment:** Many commentators have pointed out that, at least in preponderance of the evidence cases, the only time the allocation of the burden of persuasion actually makes a difference is when the jury views the evidence as precisely in equipoise—which, they argue, as a practical matter almost never happens.

3. **Burden of Going Forward with the Evidence:** [§1313]   The party who bears the burden of going forward with the evidence (also known as the burden of production)

must satisfy it by introducing legally sufficient evidence on the issue (evidence from which a reasonable jury could infer the fact alleged from the circumstances proved). Satisfaction of this burden allows the jury to decide the issue (in that party's favor, if the jury feels she has met her burden of persuasion). If a party fails to meet her burden of going forward with the evidence on an issue, the trial court will direct a verdict against her on that issue. And if the issue is essential to that party's recovery, she will simply suffer a directed verdict or nonsuit and be thrown out of court.

a. **Example:** In a typical negligence case, P (having the burden of going forward) must first offer competent evidence sufficient to support a verdict as to each element of the prima facie case (*i.e.,* duty, breach, causation, damages). If P fails to meet this burden of going forward with the evidence, P will suffer a directed verdict. If P meets this burden of introducing evidence, P will get to the jury on those issues.

   (1) *At this point, D may offer no evidence* and hope that the jury either disbelieves P's evidence or otherwise finds it so weak on some issue that it does not meet P's burden of persuasion, even by a preponderance of evidence.

   (2) *Alternatively, D may introduce evidence to counter P's* evidence and hence increase the likelihood that the jury will decide that P has not met her burden of persuasion.

   (3) *If the pleadings permit, D may introduce evidence of P's contributory negligence*—an issue on which D has the burden of going forward with the evidence.

   (4) *If D introduces sufficient evidence of contributory negligence* to meet his own burden of going forward with the evidence on that issue, P then has the choice of: (i) allowing the issue to go to the jury with no contrary evidence (hoping that D has not met his burden of persuasion); (ii) introducing contrary evidence to rebut D's evidence of contributory negligence (hence making it more likely the jury will decide D has not met his burden of persuasion on the issue); or (iii) introducing evidence on a new issue such as "last clear chance" (if the substantive law and pleadings permit) on which P may have the burden of introducing evidence.

b. **Effect of failure to meet burden:** [§1314]   Note that the penalty for failing to meet the burden of going forward with the evidence may be significantly different from the penalty for failing to meet the burden of persuasion. In the latter case, it is up to the jury to decide whether a party has met this burden. In the former case, the judge can direct a verdict if the burden is not met.

c. **Inferences:** [§1315]   Another way of stating that a party has met her burden of going forward with the evidence is that the party has raised an *"inference"* in her favor. An inference is a *deduction of fact* made by the jury from the evidence presented. [*See* Cal. Evid. Code §600]

   (1) **Example:** If the issue involved is whether D was negligent in driving his car when it struck P, the trier of fact can conclude that D was negligent by

inference from the facts introduced by P (*e.g.,* D's excess rate of speed, his glancing away from the road just before the impact, his admissions of fault following the accident, etc.).

(2) **Discretion of trier of fact:** [§1316]   The actual drawing of inferences is largely a matter for the discretion of the trier of fact once the party with the burden of introducing evidence has met this burden and hence has raised an inference in her favor.

d. **Shifting of burden:** [§1317]   Sometimes a party with the burden of introducing evidence on an issue introduces so much evidence that she not only meets the burden of going forward with the evidence but *exceeds* it—thereby placing on the opposing party the burden of introducing evidence.

(1) **Rare case:** [§1318]   The shifting of the burden of introducing evidence can occur in the very rare case where such a "great mass of credible competent evidence is introduced that a reasonable trier of fact could not find contrary to it." [Blank v. Coffin, 20 Cal. 2d 457 (1942)] (This kind of case is extremely rare because of the right of the jury to disbelieve all eyewitnesses.)

(2) **More common instance:** [§1319]   Much more commonly, the burden of going forward with the evidence is switched where a party has a "*presumption*" in her favor (*see* below).

4. **Presumptions:** [§1320]   A presumption is a deduction that the law *requires* the trier of fact to draw from particular facts in evidence in the absence of a sufficient contrary showing. In other words, a presumption *shifts* the burden of going forward with the evidence. [*See* Fed. R. Evid. 301—"a presumption imposes on the party against whom it is directed the burden of going forward with evidence to rebut or meet the presumption"]

a. **Rationale:** A presumption is a "procedural tool" based on considerations of probability, practical convenience, or public policy.

(1) **Application:** In certain recurring fact situations, proof of fact A renders the inference of fact B so highly probable, since B so commonly goes hand in hand with A, that it is deemed sensible and fair to assume the truth of fact B—until there is some contrary showing.

(2) **Example:** Proof that a properly stamped and addressed letter was put into the mail renders the inference that it was duly received so probable that courts will "presume" it was received, in the absence of some contrary showing. [Cal. Evid. Code §641]

b. **Source of presumptions:** [§1321]   Most courts recognize that a presumption may arise from consistent judicial practice (case law), as well as by legislative enactment.

(1) **Minority—only statutory presumptions recognized:** [§1322]   A few states (minority view) take the position that due to the greater evidentiary effect of presumptions (*see* below), presumptions can be created only by statute. All other deductions recognized by case law are merely inferences. [20 Minn. L. Rev. 241 (1936)]

(2) **In federal courts—*Erie* doctrine:** [§1323]   In diversity cases involving a claim or defense under state law, the Federal Rules defer to state law; *i.e.*, the burden of proof is deemed a "substantive" matter for *Erie* purposes, so that federal courts will recognize and apply the presumptions that the appropriate state courts would apply. [Fed. R. Evid. 302; *and see* Civil Procedure Summary]

c. **How presumption arises:** [§1324]   Before a presumption comes into operation, the party seeking its benefit must first establish the "basic fact" that is a condition to the "presumed fact." Thus, to invoke the presumption that a person missing for at least seven years is dead, a party must first establish the basic fact that the person has been missing for that period of time, from which the presumed fact (death) arises. [Cal. Evid. Code §667]

   (1) **Basic fact disputed:** [§1325]   If the basic fact is disputed (*e.g.*, by evidence that the person has not been missing that long), the jury must be instructed to make a finding as to the existence or nonexistence of the basic fact—because unless the jury is convinced as to the basic fact, there is obviously no basis for the presumption.

   (2) **Basic fact established:** [§1326]   But if the basic fact is established (either not disputed or established by a jury finding), the presumption arises.

d. **Requirement of rational connection:** [§1327]   Where a presumption is created by statute, it ordinarily must appear that there is some "rational connection" between the basic fact proved and the ultimate fact presumed. [Mobile, Jackson & Kansas City Railroad v. Turnipseed, 219 U.S. 35 (1910)]

   (1) **Civil cases:** [§1328]   Note that Wigmore and various other writers would not recognize any such limitation (in civil cases, at least). They argue that a statutory presumption merely changes the burden of producing evidence, and that the legislature has the power to determine such procedural rules.

   (2) **Criminal cases:** [§1329]   However, in criminal cases, a "rational connection" is a *requirement* of constitutional due process. Unless it can be said with substantial assurance that the presumed fact is *more likely* than not to flow from the proved fact on which it is based, the presumption violates the Fourteenth Amendment Due Process Clause. [Leary v. United States, 395 U.S. 6 (1969)—invalidating statutory presumption that any person in possession of marijuana (proved fact) knew that it was illegally imported (presumed fact); *and see* County Court of Ulster County v. Allen, 442 U.S. 140 (1979)]

e. **Classification of presumptions:** [§1330]   Presumptions are sometimes classified as "*conclusive*" and "*rebuttable*." This discussion refers only to rebuttable presumptions (*i.e.*, "true" presumptions). "Conclusive" presumptions are not really presumptions at all, but rather are simply definitions or rules of law (*see infra*, §1349).

f. **Procedural effect of rebuttable presumptions:** [§1331]   All rebuttable presumptions have the effect of placing upon the *opposing party* the burden of going forward with the evidence (or else having a directed verdict entered against him). If the party against whom the presumption operates meets his burden of going forward with the evidence, the case goes to the trier of fact (usually the jury). The issue then is, "what happens to the burden of persuasion; does it remain as it was before the operation of the presumption, or does it switch?"

(1) **Minority view—presumption is evidence:** [§1332]   A few jurisdictions have taken the position that a presumption is itself evidence, so that even if contradictory evidence is received, the trier of fact (jury) is entitled to "weigh" the presumption against the conflicting evidence. [Mutual Life Insurance Co. v. Maddox, 128 So. 383 (Ala. 1930)]

   (a) **Criticism:** This view requires the jury to perform an intellectually impossible task ("weighing" a legal conclusion). Furthermore, where one party has clearly produced a preponderance of the evidence, including evidence to rebut some presumption invoked against that party, telling the jury it must still "weigh" the presumption gives the presumption far more effect than it should have.

(2) **Majority view—presumption not evidence:** [§1333]   Most modern courts and writers agree that a presumption itself is *not* evidence, but merely a *deduction* the trier of fact is required to draw from the evidence in the absence of a contrary showing. [United States v. Ahrens, 530 F.2d 781 (8th Cir. 1976)] Still, there remains disagreement as to the continuing effect of the presumption when contrary evidence has been introduced.

   (a) **Most courts—presumption dispelled ("bursting bubble" theory):** [§1334]   Some of the writers (*e.g.,* Thayer, Wigmore) assert that a presumption is merely a preliminary assumption of fact, and that it *disappears* from the case upon the introduction of evidence sufficient to sustain a contrary finding (no preponderance required). Thus, the burden of persuading the jury as to the existence of the fact in question remains where it was at the outset. Most courts today follow this approach. [*See* Bongiovi v. Jamison, 718 P.2d 1172 (Idaho 1986)]

      1) **Federal Rules:** [§1335]   The Federal Rules are in accord— except in *diversity* cases, where federal courts look to *state law* to determine the effect of presumptions (*see supra,* §1323). [Fed. R. Evid. 301; Usery v. Turner Elkhorn Mining Co., 428 U.S. 1 (1976); Legille v. Dann, 544 F.2d 1 (D.C. Cir. 1976)]

   (b) **Presumption not dispelled:** [§1336]   Other authorities (*e.g.,* Morgan, Maguire) assert that a presumption does *not* "vanish" on the appearance of counterevidence, but remains in the case until the other party has produced evidence of such caliber as to persuade the trier of fact that the counterevidence, rather than the presumption, is true. In other words, the presumption requires the other party to produce a preponderance of the evidence as to the nonexistence of the presumed fact; *i.e.,* it switches the burden of persuasion.

(c) **Certain presumptions dispelled; others not:** [§1337]   Another approach (California Evidence Code) incorporates both views, making the effect of counterevidence depend on the type of presumption involved.

1)   **Presumptions designed to implement public policy remain:** [§1338]   This approach recognizes that certain types of presumptions are established to implement some independent public policy. Where this is the case, the mere fact that contradictory evidence has been introduced is not sufficient reason to disregard the presumption altogether. Thus, the presumption remains in the case, and it is left to the jury to decide whether the contradictory evidence preponderates. [Cal. Evid. Code §605—"presumptions affecting the burden of proof"]

   a)   **Examples:** The following are examples of commonly recognized presumptions that are established to implement public policy:

      (i)   That persons who have gone through a wedding ceremony are *validly married*;

      (ii)   That a person not heard from in seven years is *dead*;

      (iii)   That a person *intends* the normal consequences of his voluntary act; and

      (iv)   That official duties have been *regularly performed*.

      [Cal. Evid. Code §§660 *et seq.*]

2)   **Presumptions not designed to implement public policy are dispelled:** [§1339]   Presumptions that are established to implement no independent public policy (other than to facilitate determination of the action in which they are applied) are dispelled as soon as evidence sufficient to support a contrary finding is introduced. The jury then decides the case as if the presumption had never arisen (although the jury is still free to draw whatever inference it may choose from the facts). [Cal. Evid. Code §604—"presumptions affecting burden of producing evidence"]

   a)   **Examples:** The following are examples of commonly recognized presumptions that are designed solely for evidentiary purposes (rather than to implement some independent public policy):

      (i)   That a person *owns* that which he possesses;

      (ii)   That money or property delivered by one to another was *due*;

  (iii) That a letter duly mailed has been ***received*** in the ordinary course of mail;

  (iv) That a writing was ***executed*** on the date it bears.

  [Cal. Evid. Code §§630 *et seq.*]

b) **Application:** If P wishes to show that D received a letter P sent to D, proof that P properly posted the letter raises a presumption that it was received by D in the ordinary course of the mail. [Cal. Evid. Code §641] However, that presumption is dispelled if D introduces evidence sufficient to support a contrary finding (*e.g.,* D's testimony that she never received the letter). From that point on, it is up to the jury to decide whether D received the letter (*i.e.,* the presumption no longer compels a finding in P's favor on the issue).

1/ Because of the accepted reliability of the mail, the jury may well choose to disbelieve D and hence find that D did in fact receive the letter. But here the jury relies on an inference; no presumption compels its finding.

3) **Criticism of "mixed rule":** [§1340] The great disadvantage of the approach varying the effect of presumptions is that, as a practical matter, it is often very difficult to tell which category a presumption falls into. It thus introduces a high degree of uncertainty into this area of the law.

g. **Conflicting presumptions:** [§1341] Occasionally, the plaintiff and defendant may each invoke some presumption in their favor on the same issue.

(1) **Example:** Where the validity of a second marriage is attacked by evidence of a prior marriage, the presumption that the first marriage continued (*i.e.,* that bigamy was committed) conflicts with the presumption that a second marriage is valid (no bigamy).

(2) **Rule for resolving conflict:** [§1342] Where conflicting presumptions exist, the judge should apply the presumption that is founded on the weightier considerations of policy and logic (*e.g.,* presumption of validity of second marriage displaces presumption of continuance of first). If one presumption does not predominate, both should be disregarded. [*See* Uniform Rule of Evidence 15]

h. **Rule in criminal cases:** [§1343] Different considerations are encountered in criminal cases. The constitutional requirement that an accused be proved guilty "beyond a reasonable doubt" limits the use of presumptions in criminal cases. Wherever the presumed fact establishes guilt, is an element of the offense, or negatives a defense, the presumption ***cannot*** mandate a conviction in the face of a reasonable doubt about the presumed fact. A jury instruction that suggests that a presumption shifts the burden of production to the defendant on an essential element is likely to be held unconstitutional.

(1) **Example:** The judge instructs the jury in a homicide case that the "acts of a person of sound mind and discretion are presumed to be the product of the person's will, but the presumption may be rebutted." The jury could interpret such an instruction as shifting the burden of persuasion on criminal intent to the defendant, and hence the instruction is unconstitutional. [Francis v. Franklin, 471 U.S. 307 (1985)]

(2) **"Permissive" and "mandatory" presumptions:** [§1344] In criminal cases, the Supreme Court has distinguished between "permissive presumptions" and "mandatory presumptions." [County Court of Ulster County v. Allen, *supra,* §1329] A "permissive presumption" instruction merely tells the jury that a factual deduction is permissible; a "mandatory presumption" instruction shifts the burden of persuasion. Mandatory presumption instructions are subject to constitutional challenge on the ground that they violate the requirement that the prosecution prove its case beyond a reasonable doubt. (*See* Criminal Procedure Summary.)

i. **Res ipsa loquitur:** [§1345] The doctrine of res ipsa loquitur warrants special attention. [*See* Torts Summary; Waltz & Inbau, *Medical Jurisprudence* 88-108 (1971)]

(1) **Minority view—rebuttable presumption:** [§1346] Some authorities characterize res ipsa loquitur as a rebuttable presumption that can be overcome only by preponderating evidence of no negligence by the defendant. [167 A.L.R. 658]

(2) **Majority view—permissible inference:** [§1347] However, the majority and preferable view is that res ipsa loquitur is nothing more than a permissible inference, its weight depending on the circumstances of the case. [*See, e.g.,* Sweeney v. Erving, 228 U.S. 233 (1913); *and see* 20 Minn. L. Rev. 241 (1936)]

(3) **Compromise view:** [§1348] A few states adopt a view in between: California Evidence Code section 646 classifies res ipsa loquitur as a "presumption affecting the burden of producing evidence" meaning that it *is* a presumption (deduction of negligence must be drawn), but that its only real effect is to shift to the defendant the burden of introducing sufficient evidence to support a finding of no negligence on his part. Once the defendant does this—and his evidence need not preponderate—the presumption is dispelled. The jury is then free to accept or reject any inference of negligence arising from the facts upon which the presumption was based. [Cal. Evid. Code §604]

5. **Conclusive Presumptions:** [§1349] Conclusive presumptions are not really presumptions, but rather are rules of substantive law. Where a party has a conclusive presumption in his favor, the law permits no contradictory evidence or finding. Hence, a conclusive presumption cannot be rebutted by disputing its logic or by producing evidence to the contrary.

a. **Example:** In many states, where A purports to "sell" goods to B, but retains possession thereof at all times ("basic fact"), the sale is conclusively presumed to be in fraud of A's creditors ("presumed fact"). No evidence to the contrary will be received.

b. **Statutory presumptions:** [§1350]   Matters that are "conclusively presumed" vary widely from state to state. The following conclusive presumptions are set forth in the California Evidence Code (but the Code recognizes that others may be created by other statutes or case law):

(1) **Legitimacy of issue:** [§1351]   A child born to a *married* woman *cohabiting* with her husband at the time of conception is conclusively presumed legitimate as long as the husband was not impotent or sterile. [Cal. Evid. Code §621]

    (a) **Rationale:** The strong *public policy* favoring legitimacy prevents any proof that a man cohabiting with his wife is not the father of her child. Even a properly conducted blood test showing that it was physically impossible for him to have fathered the child is inadmissible to dispute the presumption!

        1) **Compare:** Of course, if the husband can show that he was not "cohabiting" with his wife at the time of conception, the presumption does *not* apply. [Jackson v. Jackson, 67 Cal. 2d 245 (1967)]

    (b) **Presumption as rule of law:** [§1352]   Note that this conclusive presumption amounts simply to a definition of legitimacy. A "legitimate" child is thus either one whose biological parents were married to each other *or* one born to a mother who was cohabiting with her husband at the time of conception. This latter part of the definition is indifferent to the biological facts.

(2) **Recitals:** [§1353]   The facts recited in a *written instrument* are conclusively presumed to be true as between the parties thereto or their successors in interest. [Cal. Evid. Code §622]

(3) **Estoppel:** [§1354]   Any party who has deliberately led another to believe that a particular thing is true and to act upon such belief is *estopped* to deny the truthfulness thereof in any action arising out of that party's statements or conduct. [Cal. Evid. Code §623]

XIII. THE PAROL EVIDENCE RULE

___chapter approach___

The parol evidence rule is generally seen as more of a rule of contract law than of evidence. The crucial question here is whether there was an integrated, unambiguous contract. If so, the parol evidence may be inadmissible to vary the terms of the agreement.

A. STATEMENT OF RULE [§1355]

Basically, the parol evidence rule stipulates that when the parties have agreed on a writing as the final embodiment of the terms of their agreement (*i.e.,* an integration), then other evidence (be it oral or written) cannot be considered if it would add to, alter, or contradict the terms of that written agreement.

1. **Evidence Excluded:** [§1356] Note that, since this rule makes *both* oral (parol) *and* written evidence inadmissible to vary the terms of an integrated agreement, the name "parol evidence rule" is somewhat incomplete. A more appropriate title would be the "rule protecting complete agreements."

2. **Rationale for Rule:** A written instrument is *more reliable* and accurate than human memory in establishing the terms of an agreement. Also, when there exists a writing that purports to be a memorialization of an agreement, to permit extrinsic evidence of its terms would open the door to possible *fraud* (reasoning similar to the Statute of Frauds and best evidence rule).

B. NATURE OF RULE [§1357]

The parol evidence rule has two aspects—one *procedural* and the other *substantive*:

1. **Rule of Procedure:** [§1358] The rule operates on the one hand as an exclusionary rule of evidence: Subject to certain recognized exceptions (below), where the terms of an agreement have been reduced to writing, extrinsic evidence of the parties' negotiations or promises is inadmissible to vary their written agreement.

2. **Rule of Substantive Law:** [§1359] The rule operates primarily as one of substantive law: "The execution of a contract in writing, whether the law requires it to be in writing or not, supersedes all the negotiations or stipulations concerning the matter which preceded or accompanied the execution of the instrument." [Cal. Civ. Code §1625]

    a. **Effect:** Since all preliminary negotiations are superseded by the integrated contract, thereafter only the writing is material in determining the rights and obligations of the parties; their preliminary negotiations and discussions cannot be considered. [Restatement of Contracts §237]

3. **Effect of Failure to Object in Trial Court:** [§1360] The cases are split as to whether the rule is "waived" by failure to object to the introduction of parol evidence in the trial court.

a. **Majority view—no waiver:** [§1361]   The probable majority view, emphasizing the substantive law aspect of the rule, is that the failure to raise an objection to parol evidence in the trial court is *not* a "waiver" of the rule. Hence, violation of the rule may be used as grounds for appeal, and the appellate court will disregard any improperly admitted parol evidence in review of the case, even though the matter was never raised in the trial court. [92 A.L.R. 810]

b. **Minority view—contra:** [§1362]   However, some courts insist that all issues be raised in the trial court as a prerequisite to appellate review, and therefore hold that the rule *is* waived by failure to make timely objection below; improperly admitted parol evidence can therefore be used to sustain the judgment.

4. **Litigation Involving Third Party:** [§1363]   The rule applies only to litigation between the parties to the instrument (and their successors, assigns, etc.). Therefore, if a *third party* is involved in the action, that party can always introduce parol evidence to vary or contradict the instrument. [Dunn v. Price, 112 Cal. 46 (1896)]

a. **Admissibility in criminal cases:** [§1364]   Thus, parol evidence is usually admissible in criminal cases to contradict the terms of written instruments (*e.g.,* letters, contracts, etc.) because the State was not a party to such instruments.

C. SCOPE AND ANALYSIS OF RULE

1. **Rule Applies Only to Integrated Agreements:** [§1365]   It should be emphasized that the rule prohibits parol evidence only where it is sought to be used to vary or contradict the terms of an *integrated* (finalized) written agreement. Thus, unless the written instrument was intended by both parties as the final and exclusive memorial of their dealings, the rule simply does not apply. Hence, the admissibility of parol evidence turns initially on whether the writing is an "integration."

a. **"Integration" depends on parties' intent**

(1) **Preliminary fact question for judge:** [§1366]   As a question going to the legal competency of evidence, integration is one of the preliminary fact questions that must be decided by the trial judge (*see supra,* §63). [Brawthen v. H. & R. Block, Inc., 52 Cal. App. 3d 139 (1975)]

(a) **Role of jury:** [§1367]   While the jury takes no part in deciding whether the writing was intended as an integration, if the parol evidence is admitted (*i.e.,* the judge finds no integration), the jury *alone* weighs the *effect* of the parol evidence as against the recitals in the written instrument.

(2) **Determining whether writing is an integration**

(a) **"Face of the instrument" test:** [§1368]   The traditional rule and weight of authority is that integration must be determined from the *face of the instrument* itself. The trial judge is limited to an examination of the "four corners" of the instrument in determining whether the parties intended it as a complete expression of their agreement;

the judge cannot consider the circumstances surrounding its execution or any parol evidence at this point. [70 A.L.R 752]

    1) **Criticism:** [§1369] This rule may exclude the most probative evidence of the parties' true intent.

    2) **Effect of merger clause:** [§1370] A provision in the instrument to the effect that "this instrument contains all of the agreements between the parties" or "no other representations have been made," etc., is held by many courts to *establish conclusively* the parties' intent to have an integration.

  (b) **"Any relevant evidence" test:** [§1371] However, the minority and liberal view is that the trial judge, in performing the preliminary fact-finding function, may consider not only the contents of the instrument, but *any extrinsic evidence* that is *relevant* to the parties' intentions regarding integration. [*See, e.g.,* Masterson v. Sine, 68 Cal. 2d 222 (1968)]

b. **"Partial" integration:** [§1372] When a writing is *incomplete* on its face, the parol evidence rule simply does *not* apply because the parties obviously did not intend the writing as an integration. However, even where an instrument appears to be an integration, the proponent of parol evidence may claim that it was intended as a final expression only of the terms covered therein. The agreement would then be only "partially integrated," and the rule would not bar parol evidence on matters not covered in the writing.

c. **"Collateral" oral agreements:** [§1373] Alternatively, the proponent of parol evidence may claim that there were actually *two* agreements between the parties—*i.e.,* one that was embodied in the writing (integrated), and a second "collateral" oral agreement. In such case, the written agreement may be supplemented by evidence of the "collateral" agreement since such evidence does not affect the integrated agreement at all.

  (1) **"Collateral" defined:** [§1374] An agreement is "collateral" if it meets the following requirements:

    (a) *It is collateral in form* (not a part of the integrated written agreement in any way);

    (b) *It is not inconsistent with the written agreement* in any way (including both the express and implied provisions of the written agreement); and

    (c) *It is not so closely connected with the principal transaction as to form "part and parcel thereof."*

      1) *Under the Restatement view*, the parol agreement must be one that is the natural subject of a separate agreement. [Restatement of Contracts §240(1)(b)]

2) ***The Uniform Commercial Code*** (applicable to sales contracts) does not even require this much. The additional terms are admissible unless they "would certainly have been included in the document in the view of the court." [U.C.C. §2-202, comment 3]

(2) **Examples:** [§1375] Cases involving collateral oral agreements occur most frequently where the written agreement is silent on some term or condition, and parol evidence is then offered to show the parties' oral understanding with regard thereto:

(a) **Duration of employment:** Oral agreements may thus be shown to prove the duration of an employment or agency contract where the writing itself omitted the duration. [85 A.L.R.2d 1331]

(b) **Time for performance:** At least some courts have held that oral agreements may be shown to prove the time for performance, where the written contract is silent. [*See* 85 A.L.R.2d 1369]

1) **Compare:** However, other courts are contra on the ground that the law implies performance within a "reasonable time," and that since implied terms are as much a part of the agreement as express terms, parol evidence of an oral agreement fixing time varies the terms of the written agreement. [Waterford Irrigation District v. Modesto Irrigation District, 127 Cal. App. 544 (1932)]

(c) **Limits on option:** Some courts have become increasingly liberal as to what is "collateral." In a leading case, D deeded his ranch to his sister, S, reserving an option to repurchase. Later, D went into bankruptcy, and the bankruptcy trustee attempted to exercise the option. S resisted on the ground that she and D had an "oral understanding" that the option was personal to him and could not be assigned. The court held such parol evidence admissible because the deed itself was silent as to assignability, the limitation on assignment was not inconsistent with the option, and the oral understanding was one which "might naturally be made as a separate agreement." [Masterson v. Sine, *supra*]

(3) **No separate consideration required:** [§1376] Most courts do not require that there be a separate consideration for the "collateral" agreement. Rather, they follow the general concept of contract law that a single promise or performance can support several counterpromises.

(a) **But note:** There is authority contra, requiring ***separate*** consideration for an extrinsic agreement to be upheld as "collateral." [Restatement of Contracts §240]

2. **Admissibility of Parol to "Explain" or "Interpret" Term Used in Integrated Agreement:** [§1377] Even a complete, integrated agreement must be interpreted by the court if it is involved in litigation. The question arises, therefore, to what extent parol evidence is admissible in the ***interpretation process***—*i.e.,* not to vary or contradict the terms of the instrument, but rather to show what the parties meant by the terms used.

a. **Ambiguities:** [§1378]   It has long been recognized that if words in the written instrument are ambiguous, parol evidence *is* admissible to explain the ambiguity.

    (1) **Former law—distinction as to "latent" vs. "patent" ambiguities:** [§1379] According to the older cases, and some statutes, parol was admissible only to explain *latent* ambiguities (*i.e.,* document appears clear on its face, but becomes ambiguous in application—*e.g.,* D sells "my car" and it turns out she owns two cars). But parol was not admissible to explain *patent* ambiguities (*i.e.,* document ambiguous on its face) because this would be tantamount to the court "making" the agreement for the parties. [50 Cal. L. Rev. 294 (1962)]

    (2) **Modern law rejects distinction:** [§1380]   The distinction between latent and patent ambiguities is no longer tenable. Modern courts generally admit parol evidence to clarify ambiguities in a written instrument, whether they be "latent" or "patent," as long as the other parts of the writing are reasonably clear. [104 A.L.R. 287]

        (a) **Compare—no bargaining intent:** [§1381]   Of course, if the ambiguities are *so fundamental* that there is no way the court could determine what the parties intended, parol evidence cannot be admitted because there appears to be no real bargaining intent.

        (b) **Exception as to wills:** [§1382]   Most states still limit the type of evidence that may be admitted to clarify ambiguities in a will by prohibiting use of the testator's own declarations as to what she intended. [*See* Cal. Prob. Code §105; *and see* Wills Summary]

b. **Special meaning established by custom or usage:** [§1383]   Traditionally, parol evidence is admitted to explain any *special meaning* attached to the words used in the instrument, where such special meaning derives from *custom* or *usage* in a particular industry. [89 A.L.R. 1228]

    (1) **Example:** A motion picture distribution contract conferred distribution rights in the "United Kingdom." Parol was admitted to show that by usage in the motion picture industry, "United Kingdom" meant Ireland as well as the British Isles. [Ermolieff v. R.K.O. Radio Pictures, 19 Cal. 2d 543 (1942)]

    (2) **Expansion under U.C.C.:** [§1384]   This custom or usage exception is expanded somewhat by the U.C.C. (applicable to contracts for sale of goods), which provides that the wording of a contract should be interpreted not only in the light of custom or usage in a particular industry, but also by parol evidence as to the parties' course of dealings under previous contracts and by their course of performance under the present contract. [U.C.C. §2-202]

c. **The "plain meaning" rule and the attack thereon:** [§1385]   Where there is no ambiguity (*supra*), nor any special meaning claimed by reason of custom or usage (*supra*), the extent to which parol evidence—*e.g.,* the parties' negotiations, conduct, etc.—is admissible to "interpret" a written instrument depends on which rule the court chooses to follow:

(1) **"Plain meaning" rule:** [§1386]   Most courts still insist that the words used in a written instrument must be interpreted in accordance with their "plain meaning," and that parol evidence is therefore not admissible to show that the parties used them in any different sense. [*See, e.g.,* Rowe v. Chesapeake Mineral Co., 156 F.2d 752 (6th Cir. 1946)]

   (a) **Rationale:** An instrument should be interpreted so as to give effect to the reasonable expectations of the parties, who presumably expect that it will be interpreted according to its "plain meaning." [4 Williston §612]

   (b) **Criticism:** Each party may in fact have his own view as to the "plain meaning" of the terms used, and the judge's view may be altogether different again!

(2) **"Reasonably susceptible" rule:** [§1387]   A minority of courts are much more liberal as to the interpretation of terms used in an instrument. "The test is not whether the instrument appears to the court to be plain and unambiguous on its face, but whether the offered evidence is relevant to prove a meaning to which the language of the instrument is reasonably susceptible." [Pacific Gas & Electric Co. v. Thomas Drayage & Rigging Co., 69 Cal. 2d 33 (1968)]

   (a) **Rationale:** No language is infallible. The fact that the terms of an instrument appear "clear" to the judge does not preclude the possibility that the parties may have used them in some different sense.

   (b) **Example:** D agrees to indemnify P against any "injury to property." Later, P's property is injured. Even though this injury would seem covered by the "plain meaning" of the indemnification agreement, D should be permitted to show that the parties understood and intended that the above phrase covered only injury to property of third persons, and not injury to P's own property. [Pacific Gas & Electric Co. v. Thomas Drayage & Rigging Co., *supra*]

   (c) **Criticism:** The process of "interpretation" is being used to vary and contradict the terms of the instrument. By allowing parol evidence in opposition to the normal or plain meaning of the words used, the parol evidence rule is vitiated. Either party can claim that he "did not mean" what was said, and the stability and integrity of any writing can thus be impaired.

3. **Exceptions to Rule:** [§1388]   There are certain limited situations in which, for policy reasons, parol evidence is admitted to vary or contradict the terms of a written instrument. Some of these are outright "exceptions" to the rule, while others are really specialized rules of substantive law rather than of evidence.

   a. **Recitals of consideration:** [§1389]   As a rule of substantive law in most states, recitals of consideration are not conclusive as to the actual consideration for agreements. [Restatement of Contracts §82] Hence, parol evidence is admissible to show what the real consideration was—or that there was no consideration. [100 A.L.R. 17]

(1) **But note:** This rule does not permit oral evidence of additional or different executory promises under the guise of proving a different consideration. Such would vary or contradict the writing. [29 Cal. L. Rev. 249 (1941)]

b. **Instrument not intended to be effective:** [§1390]   Even a complete agreement may be shown by parol evidence to be ineffective. Here, the parol is not being used to vary or contradict the terms, but simply to show that the agreement was not intended by the parties to be legally effective.

(1) **Sham, forgery, etc.:** [§1391]   Parol evidence is admissible to show that a document, otherwise apparently valid, was really executed in jest, is a forgery, or otherwise was not intended to bind the parties.

(2) **Conditions precedent:** [§1392]   Likewise, it may also be shown by parol evidence that the agreement was executed subject to some external condition precedent—*i.e.,* that it was not intended to take effect until something else happened. [Fontana v. Upp, 128 Cal. App. 2d 205 (1954)] But parol is not admissible where the condition is subsequent in nature.

(a) **Note:** Where a deed is delivered to a grantee, parol is not admissible to show that the delivery was subject to some oral condition. This, however, is a rule of property. (*See* Property Summary.)

c. **Fraud, duress, mistake:** [§1393]   Parol evidence is admissible to show that the written instrument was entered into through fraud, duress, or mistake. Again, the parol is not really being used to alter or vary the terms of the instrument, but to show the external circumstances surrounding its execution. [Simmons v. Ratterree, 217 Cal. 201 (1932)]

(1) **Note:** A provision in the agreement to the effect that "there are no warranties or representations made except as provided herein" does not prevent the use of parol evidence to show fraud or mistake, since such a showing nullifies that provision along with the rest of the agreement. (But such a provision may be considered in establishing the parties' intent to have an integrated agreement; *see* "integration," *supra,* §§1365-1372.)

d. **Miscellaneous**

(1) **Deed intended as mortgage:** [§1394]   Parol evidence is admissible to show that a deed or other instrument that on its face appears absolute was really intended only as a security device—thus contradicting the terms of the instrument. [111 A.L.R. 448]

(2) **Status of title:** [§1395]   Except as against an innocent purchaser for value, a transfer of title that is apparently absolute can be shown by parol evidence to have been in trust for another. (*See* Property Summary.)

(3) **Principal-agent:** [§1396]   Parol evidence is admissible to show that the party who signed the contract was really acting as the agent for an undisclosed principal, at least where the undisclosed principal seeks to enforce the contract, in which event the principal also becomes bound thereby. (*See* Agency and Partnership Summary.)

(a) **Note:** The person who *signs* the instrument may not escape liability to any person who *relied* on the signatory's being bound as a principal by showing that he was only acting as the agent for another.

(b) **And note:** Where a negotiable instrument is involved, one who signs as *maker* may *never* avoid liability by showing he was in reality only *acting as agent* for another. (*See* Commercial Paper Summary.)

(4) **Release, discharge:** [§1397]   Parol evidence is always admissible to show that the obligations under an instrument have subsequently been paid, released, or otherwise discharged. [Wigmore §2441]

APPENDIX
COMPARISON OF SELECTED PROVISIONS OF
COMMON LAW AND FEDERAL RULES

SUBJECT AREA	COMMON LAW	FEDERAL RULES
PRELIMINARY FACT DETERMINATIONS		
Where Facts Decided by Judge	Judge may consider only admissible evidence.	Judge may consider any nonprivileged evidence (including hearsay). [Fed. R. Evid. 104]
RELEVANCY		
Character Evidence		
Where Character in Issue	Reputation and specific act evidence admissible. Opinion evidence inadmissible.	Reputation, opinion, and specific act evidence admissible. [Fed. R. Evid. 405(b)]
Accused's Evidence of Good Character	Only evidence of defendant's reputation in community admissible.	Both reputation and opinion evidence admissible. [Fed. R. Evid. 405(a)]
Cross-Examination of Character Witnesses	Questions must be asked in "Have you heard . . ." form.	Questions may also be asked in "Do you know . . ." form. [Fed. R. Evid. 405(a), note]
HEARSAY		
"Statement"	Nonassertive conduct is hearsay.	Nonassertive conduct *not* hearsay; nonverbal conduct a "statement" only if intended as an assertion. [Fed. R. Evid. 801(a)]
Hearsay Status of Particular Statements		
Prior Inconsistent Statements	Nonhearsay if offered to impeach, but not to prove truth of matter asserted.	Nonhearsay under either of the following conditions: (1) as at common law, if offered only to impeach and not for truth of matter asserted; or (2) as substantive proof of truth of matter asserted if made while testifying under oath at a prior proceeding by a declarant who is present at trial and subject to cross-examination. [Fed. R. Evid. 801(c), (d)(1)(A)]
Prior Consistent Statements	Nonhearsay if offered to rehabilitate, but not to prove truth of matter asserted.	Nonhearsay and admissible as substantive proof of truth of matter asserted if offered to rebut charge of recent fabrication or improper influence and made by a declarant who is present at trial and subject to cross-examination. [Fed. R. Evid. 801(d)(1)(B)]
Prior Statements of Identification	Nonhearsay if offered to corroborate witness's in-court identification, but not to prove truth of matter asserted.	Nonhearsay and admissible as substantive proof of truth of matter asserted if made by a declarant after perceiving the person. [Fed. R. Evid. 801(d)(1)(C)]

Admissions by a Party	Hearsay (but within admissions exception).	All admissions by party-opponent are nonhearsay, including vicarious, co-conspirator, and implied admissions. [Fed. R. Evid. 801(d)(2)]

HEARSAY EXCEPTIONS
Former Testimony

"Identity" of Parties	*Traditional view:* Requires 100% identity of parties. *Modern trend:* Rejects traditional view for an "identity of interest and motive" test.	Party against whom evidence now offered (or predecessor in interest in civil suit) must have been a party to former proceeding and must have had an opportunity and similar motive to develop the witness's testimony. [Fed. R. Evid. 804(b)(1)]

Admissions

Unauthorized Admissions by Employees	Hearsay. Inadmissible in most states, but a few states recognize it as an exception.	Admissible nonhearsay if it concerns a matter within scope of employee's duties and made during employment. [Fed. R. Evid. 801(d)(2)] (Note that all admissions—vicarious, implied, co-conspirator, etc.—are defined in Federal Rules as nonhearsay.)
Co-Conspirator's Statements	Conspiracy must be established by independent evidence (other than co-conspirator's statements).	Co-conspirator's statements must be considered but are not alone sufficient to establish conspiracy. [Fed. R. Evid. 801(d)(2)(E)]

Declarations Against Interest

"Against Interest"	Statement must prejudice declarant's pecuniary or proprietary interest.	May also be (1) statements that would subject declarant to civil liability or would render invalid claim by him against another; and (2) declarations against penal interest (but where offered to show defendant's innocence, must also show corroborating circumstances clearly indicating trustworthiness). [Fed. R. Evid. 804(b)(3)]

Dying Declarations

When Admissible	Only in homicide cases.	In all civil cases and in homicide cases (but not in rape, robbery, larceny, etc., cases). [Fed. R. Evid. 804(b)(2)]
Unavailability of Declarant	Declarant must be dead when evidence offered.	Declarant need only be "unavailable" (although proponent must show why declarant's deposition is unobtainable). [Fed. R. Evid. 804(b)(2)]

Present Sense Impressions

Admissibility	Hearsay. Inadmissible in most states, but some states recognize it as an exception.	Admissible as separate exception to hearsay rule. [Fed. R. Evid. 803(1)]
When Statement Made	Where exception recognized, statement must be made while declarant is engaged in the conduct or perceiving the event that the statement is offered to explain.	Statement must be made while declarant is perceiving event or condition or immediately thereafter. [Fed. R. Evid. 803(1)]

Declarations of Physical Condition ("State of Body" Cases)		
Past Condition	Inadmissible.	Admissible when made for purposes of treatment or diagnosis. Such statements may also describe the cause of an injury if relevant to the diagnosis or treatment. [Fed. R. Evid. 803(4)]
Declarations of Mental Condition ("State of Mind" Cases)	Indirect and direct assertions of intent are hearsay but are admissible as exceptions under limited circumstances.	Indirect assertions are admissible because nonhearsay. Direct assertions are hearsay but admissible under exception. [Fed. R. Evid. 801(c), 803(3)]
Past Recollection Recorded		
Source of Record	Document must have been prepared by witness or "under his direction."	Witness need only have "adopted" document as a record of the event. [Fed. R. Evid. 803(5)]
Business Records		
Content of Record	Only statements of *fact* in business records are admissible.	Any "acts, events, conditions, opinions, or diagnoses" contained in business records are admissible.
Availability of Entrant	Entrant must be unavailable.	Entrant need not be unavailable. [Fed. R. Evid. 803(6)]
As Evidence of Absence of Entry	Business records are admissible only to prove facts contained therein; are inadmissible for negative purposes (*i.e.*, to show no transaction).	Business records are admissible to prove "the occurrence or nonoccurrence of a transaction." [Fed. R. Evid. 803(7)]
Official Records		
Personal Knowledge Requirement	Official who made entry must have had personal knowledge of the facts recorded.	Record of "factual finding" need only be "trustworthy." [Fed. R. Evid. 803(8)]
Judgments		
Of Prior Criminal Conviction	Inadmissible, except to impeach.	Judgments of felony convictions, unless based on plea of nolo contendere, are admissible in both criminal and civil cases to prove any fact essential to judgment. However, in a criminal case, government cannot use conviction of third person for purposes other than impeachment. [Fed. R. Evid. 803(22)]
In Former Civil Case	Inadmissible.	Admissible to prove matter of personal, family, or general history or boundaries of land if such would be provable by reputation evidence. [Fed. R. Evid. 803(23)]
Declarations of Family History ("Pedigree")		
Status of Declarant	Declarant must be related by blood or marriage to family in question.	Includes declarants who are so intimately associated with the family that they are likely to have accurate information. [Fed. R. Evid. 804(b)(4)]
When Statement Made	Admissible only if declaration made before any controversy arose as to matters stated.	Time when statement made does not affect admissibility. [Fed. R. Evid. 803(19), 804(b)(4)]

Ancient Documents	Admits declarations in property-disposing documents if documents are over 30 years old and properly authenticated.	Admits (1) statements in **any** document at least 20 years old, and (2) statements in documents affecting an interest in property regardless of age (unless subsequent dealings with the property have been inconsistent with document). [Fed. R. Evid. 803(15), (16)]
Learned Treatises	Admissible only to impeach expert who relied on it.	May be read into evidence and considered as substantive proof if used by expert as basis for direct, or called to expert's attention on cross. [Fed. R. Evid. 803(18)]
"Catch-All" Exceptions	Hearsay exceptions restricted to specific, rigid categories.	Courts may admit hearsay evidence if it meets the same necessity and trustworthiness standards required of recognized exceptions. However, advance notice must be given to opponent. [Fed. R. Evid. 807]

COMPETENCY OF WITNESSES

Laypersons	*Early common law:* Witness could be disqualified for mental incapacity and immaturity, financial interest, conviction of crime, atheism, or because a spouse of party to the action. *Modern law:* General requirements are capacity to communicate, understanding of duty to tell truth, and personal knowledge.	Only requirements are witness's ability to communicate and to testify from personal knowledge. [Fed. R. Evid. 602-604]
Presiding Judge	*Early view:* Can decline to testify in his discretion. *Modern view:* Incompetent if either party objects.	Incompetent to testify even without objection. [Fed. R. Evid. 605]
Jurors At Trial	Juror can testify even over a party's objection.	May not testify if either party objects. [Fed. R. Evid. 606(a)]
Regarding Jury Deliberations	Juror cannot "impeach his own verdict."	Can testify as to any outside influences improperly brought to bear on any member or any extraneous prejudicial information improperly brought to jury's attention. [Fed. R. Evid. 606(b)]

OPINION TESTIMONY

Basis for Expert Opinion	Opinion must be based on information admissible in evidence.	Material on which expert bases opinion need not be admissible in evidence if reasonably relied on by other experts in the field. [Fed. R. Evid. 703]
	Expert must disclose assumed facts upon which opinion is based.	Prior disclosure of underlying facts not necessary unless judge requires otherwise. [Fed. R. Evid. 705]
On Ultimate Issue	Witness cannot express opinion on ultimate issue.	Opinion testimony not objectionable merely because it embraces an ultimate issue. [Fed. R. Evid. 704(a)] However, ultimate issue testimony on mental state of accused is prohibited. [Fed. R. Evid. 704(b)]

IMPEACHMENT

Who May Be Impeached

Early common law: Party could not impeach own witness. *Modern law:* Same, but exceptions for adversary, hostile, and indispensable witnesses, or where surprise change in testimony of witnesses.

Any party can attack or support credibility of any witness. [Fed. R. Evid. 607]

By Showing Poor Character for Truth and Veracity

Conviction of Crime

What crime

By any felony conviction.

By any felony if court determines probative value outweighs prejudicial effect to defendant, or by any crime involving dishonesty or false statement. [Fed. R. Evid. 609(a)]

Juvenile adjudications

Not admissible to impeach.

Judge has discretion to admit offenses (except those of accused) if necessary to determine guilt or innocence. [Fed. R. Evid. 609(d)]

Effect of pardon

Conviction can still be used to impeach.

Conviction inadmissible if pardon based on innocence or rehabilitation. [Fed. R. Evid. 609(c)]

Remote convictions

Traditional rule: Conviction is admissible to impeach no matter how remote. *Modern rule:* Trial judge has discretion to exclude remote conviction.

Conviction more than 10 years old is inadmissible unless court determines probative value substantially outweighs prejudicial effect and adverse party is given written notice. [Fed. R. Evid. 609(b)]

Character Testimony

Impeaching witness restricted to reputation testimony; cannot state opinion regarding credibility.

Opinion testimony is allowed. [Fed. R. Evid. 608(a)]

By Prior Inconsistent Statements

Laying Foundation

Foundation required (witness must *first* be presented with statement and given opportunity to explain).

Witness need only be given opportunity to explain or deny at some point, and foundation not required at all where interests of justice otherwise require. [Fed. R. Evid. 613]

Evidentiary Effect

Admissible nonhearsay but can be used only to impeach, not as an item of proof.

Admissible nonhearsay for impeachment and, in limited circumstances, for substantive proof (*see* "Hearsay, Hearsay Status of Particular Statements"). [Fed. R. Evid. 801(d)(1)(A)]

REHABILITATION

By Prior Consistent Statements

Evidentiary Effect

Admissible nonhearsay but can be used only to rehabilitate.

Can be used as substantive proof (nonhearsay) in limited circumstances (*see* "Hearsay, Hearsay Status of Particular Statements"). [Fed. R. Evid. 801(d)(1)(B)]

DOCUMENTARY EVIDENCE

Authentication

Private Documents

Testimony by subscribing witness only way to authenticate (unless witness unavailable).

Genuineness of document can be established by alternate means. [Fed. R. Evid. 901]

Ancient Documents Rule	Documents affecting property presumed authentic if shown to be at least 30 years old, free from suspicion on face, and kept or found in place where would likely be if authentic.	Rule modified to apply to any document at least 20 years old if "fair on face." [Fed. R. Evid. 901(b)(8)]
BEST EVIDENCE RULE **Degrees of Secondary Evidence**	Rule of preference for copy of original.	Proponent may use any kind of secondary evidence [Fed. R. Evid. 1004] unless "writing" is a public record, in which case copy is preferred. [Fed. R. Evid. 1005]
DOCTRINE OF COMPLETENESS	Party may introduce only part of document. Adverse party required to introduce other parts on cross-examination.	If party seeks to introduce part of document, adverse party may require introduction at the same time of any other part "which ought in fairness to be considered contemporaneously with it." [Fed. R. Evid. 106]

REVIEW QUESTIONS

In answering the following questions, assume that the Federal Rules of Evidence apply unless instructed otherwise.

PROCEDURE FOR ADMITTING OR EXCLUDING EVIDENCE

1. If evidence is inadmissible, the trial judge has the responsibility to take the initiative in excluding it. True or false?

2. Actress Gloria Glamour sues columnist Rex Read for defamation on grounds that he insulted her in one of his columns. Rex denies her allegations and introduces part of the column in which he stated, "Gloria Glamour has never looked lovelier. . . ."

   a. On rebuttal may Gloria introduce the next line of the article to show that Rex actually said, "Gloria Glamour has never looked lovelier than Godzilla"?

   b. May Gloria compel **Rex** to introduce the entire statement?

3. P calls W to the witness stand and asks him a question. Before W can answer, D jumps up and states, "I object." D later loses the case and appeals on the ground that his objection was erroneously *overruled*. Indicate whether the following are true or false.

   a. The appellate court will not reverse the judgment for P because D's objection was not timely made.

   b. The appellate court will not reverse the judgment because D's objection was not specific enough.

   c. If D had stated, "I object, hearsay," but it turned out that the evidence was not hearsay, D may raise another ground for objection on appeal.

4. P calls W to the witness stand and asks her a question. Before W can answer, D jumps up and states, "I object." P later loses the case and appeals on the ground that D's objection was erroneously *sustained*. Indicate whether the following are true or false.

   a. The appellate court will not reverse the judgment even if P's question called for inadmissible hearsay.

   b. The appellate court will not reverse the judgment if P failed to make an offer of proof as to what W's testimony would have been.

5. Which of the following preliminary facts must be decided by the judge rather than the jury?

   (A) Whether W may refuse to testify against H on the ground that she is married to H. The factual issue is whether W is the same person who went through a wedding ceremony with H.

(B) Whether a document challenged as a forgery is genuine.

(C) Whether an expert is qualified to testify as a witness.

(D) Whether a witness is telling the truth in providing a criminal defendant with an alibi.

(E) Whether a witness is telling the truth about whether a document offered under the business records exception was made in the regular course of business.

6. When a judge decides a preliminary question of fact, must she abide by the same rules of evidence as apply at trial? _____

RELEVANCY AND ITS COUNTERWEIGHTS

7. Is all relevant evidence admissible unless excluded by a specific rule or by the judge in her discretion? _____

8. After an accident on a flight of stairs, Owen installs a railing. Although evidence of this subsequent safety measure is not admissible to show that Owen was negligent prior to the accident, may such evidence be used to prove that Owen owns the stairway? _____

9. Pilar sues Donald for injuries she suffered when she tripped on a crack in Donald's sidewalk, claiming that Donald failed to repair the crack even though he had notice it was there.

   a. May Pilar introduce evidence that others were *previously* injured when they tripped on the same crack? _____

   b. May Donald introduce evidence that he did not receive any reports of the prior accidents? _____

   c. For purposes of proving that Donald knew of the dangerous condition of his sidewalk, may Pilar introduce evidence that others have *subsequently* tripped on the crack and been injured? _____

10. Builder sues Painter for breach of contract on the ground that Painter failed to paint Builder's new apartments the proper shade of green.

    a. May Builder introduce evidence that in his previous contracts with Painter "green" always meant "olive green"? _____

    b. May Painter introduce evidence that under his contracts with most other builders "green" meant "lime green"? _____

CHARACTER EVIDENCE

11. Ace is charged with murdering Vincent.

    a. May the prosecution introduce evidence that Ace once attempted to kill someone else to show that Ace probably committed the murder? _____

b. May the prosecution introduce evidence that Ace tortured Vincent's brother to find out where Vincent was hiding? _____

c. May the prosecution introduce evidence that Ace previously tried to run down Vincent with a steamroller? _____

12. Where Xerxe's character is an ultimate issue in the case, either party may introduce evidence of Xerxe's past conduct to prove his character. True or false? _____

13. Dorothy is on trial for the alleged murder of Brunhilda.

a. May Lionel testify that Dorothy has a reputation for nonviolence even though Dorothy does not plan to take the stand? _____

b. On cross-examination may the prosecution ask Lionel whether he has heard that Dorothy once killed another person? _____

c. If Dorothy claims she killed Brunhilda in self-defense, may Lionel testify that he knew Brunhilda, and that in his opinion she had a violent temperament? _____

14. In a civil case, character evidence is generally admissible to prove that a party was likely to have acted in a particular way. True or false? _____

15. Cuthbert wishes to prove that his car was locked when it was stolen from his driveway.

a. May Cuthbert testify that he is a cautious, security-minded person? _____

b. May Cuthbert testify that every time he gets out of his car he checks to see that the doors are locked? _____

EVIDENCE AFFECTED BY EXTRINSIC POLICIES

16. Pearl sues Dolly for physical injuries, alleging that Dolly sold her a spoiled turkey sandwich. Prior to trial Dolly states, "I wish I had refrigerated that turkey. How about $50 to drop the suit?"

a. May Pearl introduce Dolly's statements at trial? _____

b. Would the answer remain the same if Dolly had said to Pearl, "I'll be happy to pay for your medical expenses"? _____

c. Would the result be the same if Dolly had said to Pearl, "I have some liability insurance"? _____

HEARSAY RULE AND ITS EXCEPTIONS

17. Indicate whether the following are true or false:

a. "Hearsay" includes writings as well as oral statements. _____

b. X nods his head in response to a question put to him out of court; X's conduct is "assertive" and would be hearsay if offered at trial. _____

c. Conduct that is not intended as a substitute for words, but that nevertheless reflects on the actor's state of mind, is inadmissible hearsay. _____

18. Wanda is called as a witness on the issue of whether a transfer of a share of stock from David to Wanda was a gift or a sale. Wanda testifies that David stated at the time of the transfer, "I am giving you this share of stock as a graduation present." Is David's statement hearsay? _____

19. Paula sues Desmond for fraud, alleging that the painting Desmond sold her was not a genuine Van Gogh. To prove that the painting is genuine, Desmond introduces the bill of sale he received from his art dealer describing the painting as a "Van Gogh."

a. Is the bill of sale hearsay? _____

b. Would the answer be different if Desmond introduced the bill of sale to show that his representation to Paula was made in good faith? _____

20. In an action for medical malpractice, Walt testifies that during the operation he heard Nurse tell Doctor that the sponge count was off. Is Walt's testimony hearsay:

a. If offered to show that a sponge was left in Walt's body? _____

b. If offered to show that the doctor had been warned? _____

21. In a slip-and-fall case, Wendell testifies for Plaintiff that immediately after the accident he said to Storekeeper, "That banana skin was black; it must've been on the floor of the aisle all day."

a. Since Wendell was the declarant and is now testifying in court, his statement to Storekeeper cannot be excluded as hearsay. True or false? _____

b. Unless Defendant makes a specific and timely objection, the jury may consider Wendell's statement to prove the truth of the matter asserted. True or false? _____

22. Dennis is on trial for criminal assault. The prosecution introduces evidence that Vic made an obscene gesture at Dennis and called him a liar. If offered to prove Dennis's motive for assaulting Vic, is the evidence admissible? _____

23. Angela is on trial for murdering her husband. She claims his death was accidental. The prosecution offers a letter she wrote to a friend in which she said, "I am planning to kill my husband."

a. Is the letter hearsay? _____

b. A defense witness testifies that Angela recently stated, "My husband is a wonderful person." Is this statement hearsay? _____

24. Which of the following items of evidence constitute nonassertive conduct? _____

(A) Issue: Sanity of Jane. Evidence that Rochester, who has known Jane for 20 years, hired Jane as governess for his children.

(B)   Issue: Whether Plaintiff suffered a concussion. Evidence that Physician treated Plaintiff for a concussion.

(C)   Issue: Did Alicia or Bonnie strike the victim? Evidence that Alicia fled the scene of the crime, whereas Bonnie did not.

25.   If the hearsay declarant is not a witness at trial, his credibility may not be attacked because only the credibility of a trial witness is "at issue." True or false?   _____

26.   Which of the following are admissible within the former testimony exception to the hearsay rule?   _____

(A)   Testimony of passenger, now deceased, in his suit against cable car company, sought to be admitted in another passenger's later action against the company involving the same accident.

(B)   Testimony of victim at D's prior trial, sought to be introduced at D's second trial after D's conviction was reversed. The victim died after the first trial.

(C)   Deposition of eyewitness, sought to be introduced at the trial of the case when the witness refuses to testify because of threats against his life.

(D)   Transcript of a witness's testimony at a coroner's inquest, sought to be admitted in later wrongful death action after the witness cannot be located despite diligent efforts.

27.   Phoebe, a professional waterskier, brings suit for injuries she sustained when Dora's boat ran into her. Dora offers evidence that immediately after the accident Phoebe stated, "I guess it's my fault. I should not have swerved in front of your boat." Indicate whether the following are true or false.

a.   Phoebe's statement is inadmissible since Phoebe is the plaintiff in the case and does not plan to testify.   _____

b.   Phoebe's statement, "I guess it's my fault," is inadmissible because it is just her opinion.   _____

28.   Are superseded or amended pleadings admissions?   _____

29.   Alphonse offers to plead guilty to a charge of income tax evasion.

a.   If his offer is not accepted, may it still be used against him in a later civil suit involving the same conduct?   _____

b.   Would the answer be different if Alphonse's offer had been accepted?   _____

c.   Would the above answers be the same if the offer was to plead "no contest"?   _____

30.   Following a head-on collision, Percy shouts at Drew, "You numbskull, you ran right through the red light!" Drew does not respond. In his subsequent suit against Drew, may Percy introduce Drew's silence as an admission that Drew ran the red light?   _____

31. Dan, a suspect in a murder case, disappears after his release on bail. When the police finally track him down, they find Dan has changed his name to Sylvester. Is Dan's disappearance or change of name admissible against him at trial? _____

32. A bus owned by Bus Co. collides with a car driven by Phyllis. Driver, an employee of Bus Co., tells Phyllis, "I'm so sorry. I was speeding around that corner." If Phyllis sues Bus Co., can she introduce Driver's statement as an admission? _____

33. Indicate whether the following are true or false:

    a.   A conspiracy is considered a "partnership in crime"; thus an admission made by one co-conspirator may be introduced against the other co-conspirators. _____

    b.   A statement by a decedent indicating his fault is admissible as an admission in a wrongful death action brought by his heirs. _____

    c.   Admissions, including those based on nonverbal conduct, are admissible under the Federal Rules as nonhearsay. _____

34. Pam Passenger sues Runaway Railway for injuries she suffered when Runaway's train derailed. Pam seeks to introduce a statement by Elwood, who is available to testify but is hostile to Pam, that he unbolted the rails. Is Elwood's statement admissible as a declaration against interest? _____

35. Livia is on trial for poisoning Tiberius. Livia's defense is that the poisoning was actually done by Caligula. Livia wishes to testify, "Caligula told me that he was the one who poisoned Tiberius." Is Livia's testimony admissible under the declaration against interest exception without laying further foundation? _____

36. Vernon, a professional flagpole sitter, is severely injured in a fall from his flagpole. Immediately after the accident Vernon tells the gathering crowd, "What a lousy way to die. I should have known better. I saw Dexter wax the pole."

    a.   If Vernon dies shortly thereafter, is his statement admissible as a dying declaration in a prosecution of Dexter for malicious mischief? _____

    b.   If Vernon's daughter brings a wrongful death action, is Vernon's statement admissible? _____

    c.   If Vernon had stated, "I'll bet Dexter waxed the pole," would his declaration be admissible in a homicide prosecution against Dexter? _____

    d.   Long after Vernon's accident, Sam makes a deathbed confession that he, not Dexter, waxed the pole. Is Sam's statement within the dying declaration exception to the hearsay rule? _____

37. Vanessa, who was severely beaten, regains consciousness after being in a coma for a year. Vanessa's brother immediately shows her a picture of Dominic, at which time Vanessa screams and shouts, "He did it! He hit me!" May Vanessa's brother testify to her statement at Dominic's trial for battery? _____

38. Ephie is shopping at Theta Zeta Grocery when a customer rushes past her shouting, "Fire! I just saw fire!"

a. To prove there was a fire, may Ephie testify to the unknown customer's statement? _____

b. Assume that Ephie continues shopping when another customer approaches her and says, "It sure is smoky in here. Can you reach that jar of olives?" May Ephie testify to this customer's statement? _____

39. State whether each of the following out-of-court statements is admissible under the exception for declarations of physical condition:

a. After being hit by a truck, Priscilla tells the truck driver, "My leg sure hurts." _____

b. Priscilla tells the paramedic who arrives at the scene, "My leg sure hurt right after the accident." _____

c. Priscilla tells Alex, a friend, "My leg really hurt after the accident." _____

d. Dr. Watson examines Priscilla solely for purposes of testifying as an expert witness at trial. Priscilla tells him, "My leg hurt after the accident." _____

40. Sam's domicile is in issue in a divorce action. Witness testifies that Sam said, "I love living in Las Vegas." Is Sam's statement admissible? _____

41. Harry telephones Martha and says, "Jim and I are going to take Flight No. 102 to San Antonio." Flight No. 102 later crashes and all passengers are killed. May Martha testify as to Harry's statement to prove that Jim is dead? _____

42. Bennie, a nightclub bouncer, is admitted to General Hospital with severe contusions. Bennie tells Doctor treating him, "A bald guy with a red beard did this to me."

a. Assume Doctor writes down this statement on Bennie's medical chart. May the statement be introduced at trial under the business records exception? _____

b. Assume Doctor also writes down his opinion of Bennie's medical condition on the chart. Would the opinion be admissible? _____

c. Assume that Doctor, the entrant, is available to testify as to the medical condition entries on Bennie's chart but is not asked to appear. May the records nevertheless be introduced under the business records exception? _____

d. Assume that Candy, a volunteer nurse's aide, is present during Bennie's examination and takes notes for use in a book she is writing entitled, *Hospital Confessions*. Are Candy's notes admissible as a business record? _____

43. Police Officer prepares a report of an auto accident. She draws a diagram of the positions of the autos, makes measurements of skid marks, etc. She also reports the statement of a witness to the accident that "Driver ran the red light."

a. Is Police Officer's report admissible in a civil case to show the length of the skid marks? _____

b.   Is Police Officer's report admissible in a civil case to show that Driver ran the red light, based on the witness's statement? _____

c.   If Insurance Investigator also made a report of the accident to submit to his employer, Insurance Co., would this report be admissible as a business record? _____

44.   The Bureau of Vital Statistics has no record of Frank's death. If the bureau chief submits a report that he has no death certificate for Frank, is the report admissible under the official records exception to the hearsay rule? _____

45.   a.   Is D's conviction for the murder of X admissible in a later civil action to show that D killed X? _____

b.   If D had been found not guilty on the murder charge, would the judgment of his acquittal be admissible in the subsequent civil case to prove that D did not kill X? _____

46.   Hazel, the live-in maid for the Baxters, tells Martha that Mrs. Baxter has an illegitimate half brother.

a.   If Hazel dies, may Martha testify as to Hazel's statement in a contest over Mrs. Baxter's will? _____

b.   Would community reputation as to Mrs. Baxter's family history be admissible? _____

PRIVILEGES

There are no codified federal rules of privilege. In answering the privilege questions, apply the modern trend of authority as represented by case law and codes such as the California Evidence Code.

47.   Indicate whether the following statements are true or false:

a.   Because of the paramount need to protect particular relationships or interests, privileges tend to be construed broadly. _____

b.   In most states, rules of privilege are subject to judicial expansion. _____

c.   Only a person "interested" in the outcome of litigation may assert a privilege. _____

d.   For a communication to be privileged, it must have been made in confidence. _____

48.   Janitor overhears a confidential conversation between Attorney and Client through the building air conditioning ducts. May Janitor testify as to what he overheard? _____

49.   Holden is called to testify in A's suit against B.

a.   If Holden claims a privilege, but is erroneously compelled to testify, may B, the losing party, base an appeal on that ground? _____

b. Would the result be different if the court had erroneously sustained Holden's claim of privilege? _____

50. Has there been a waiver of privilege in the following situations?

    a. H and W are both holders of a privilege. W makes a privileged disclosure to H, which H reveals to his friend X. _____

    b. Client calls Attorney as a witness and asks Attorney to testify as to a confidential communication Client made to Attorney. _____

    c. Patient signs an insurance application that has a provision waiving his patient-physician privilege in any litigation arising under the insurance contract. _____

51. Claude consults Addie, an attorney, for advice.

    a. If Addie declines the case, may Claude prevent her from testifying as to their conversation? _____

    b. If Claude is not in court, can Addie refuse to testify as to their conversation? _____

    c. If Addie told her friend about Claude's "weird story," can Claude still prevent Addie from testifying? _____

    d. If Claude sues Addie for malpractice, may Addie disclose the fact that Claude wanted her to help him perpetrate a fraud? _____

52. Would the following be considered "confidential communications" within the attorney-client privilege?

    a. Client tells Lawyer's secretary, "Tell Lawyer I hid the gun." _____

    b. Client's conduct in giving Lawyer a gun. _____

    c. Lawyer tells Client, "I'd advise you to turn yourself in." _____

    d. Lawyer tells Client, "I'll charge you $500, but you can take a year to pay me." _____

53. Pat consults Doc, an orthopedic surgeon, to get treatment for a broken arm. Pat tells Doc, "I broke my arm while fighting with Flo."

    a. If Flo sues Pat for personal injuries, may Pat refuse to disclose the statement she made to Doc? _____

    b. In the same suit, may Pat prevent Doc from disclosing the X-rays he took of Pat's arm? _____

    c. If Pat sues Flo for personal injuries, may Pat prevent Doc from testifying as to the information he obtained? _____

d. If Pat is later criminally prosecuted for battery, may Pat keep Doc from testifying as to the information he obtained from her? _____

54. The prosecution seeks to offer Wilma as a witness to testify against her husband, Fred, who is being prosecuted for forgery.

   a. If Fred objects, may Wilma nevertheless testify? _____

   b. Must Wilma testify if Fred's prosecution is for molesting Wilma's child from her previous marriage? _____

55. The privilege to not testify against one's spouse applies only to matters that occurred during the marriage. True or false? _____

56. Desiree, a divorcee, remembers that while she and Horace were married, Horace told her that he had stashed some money in a warehouse. Desiree reads in the newspaper that there is some litigation involving money discovered in a warehouse. If Desiree offers to testify in the case, may Horace appear and prevent her from revealing his statement? _____

57. Indicate whether the following are true or false:

   a. A majority of jurisdictions recognize a psychotherapist-patient privilege. _____

   b. A member of the clergy has a privilege to refuse to disclose the confidential communications of a penitent. _____

   c. The government has an absolute privilege to refuse to disclose confidential "official information." _____

   d. If a police informer is a material witness in a trial against the accused, the police cannot refuse to disclose the informer's identity. _____

   e. A news reporter cannot be compelled to appear in court or to reveal the source of his information because of his First Amendment "free press" privilege. _____

58. Witness, a friend of the accused, is subpoenaed to appear before a grand jury.

   a. May Witness refuse to answer incriminating questions? _____

   b. If Witness is granted immunity from prosecution, may he still refuse to testify? _____

59. a. If the defendant in a criminal case takes the witness stand at his preliminary hearing, has he waived his privilege not to testify at trial? _____

   b. If the defendant takes the stand at trial, has he waived the privilege to refuse to answer incriminating questions on cross-examination? _____

LAY AND EXPERT OPINION

60. Which of the following opinions by a lay witness would be proper? _____

(A) "The man who did it looked about 50."

(B) "I wouldn't have left that dog unchained the way defendant did."

(C) "John looked awfully angry."

(D) "The liquid in the bottle sure tasted like whiskey."

(E) "I've read Ella's handwriting a million times and the writing on that paper is definitely hers."

(F) "Leonardo and Raphael had an agreement about that land."

61. Peg is injured in an auto accident with Dee. Shortly thereafter, the ambulance taking Peg to the hospital collides with a truck. Peg sues Dee and calls Dr. Winston to testify as an expert witness.

a. May Dr. Winston give opinion testimony if he has never examined Peg but has an opinion as to Peg's injuries based on his consultation with other doctors and review of her medical records? _____

b. May Dr. Winston testify if he has never examined Peg but is asked to give an opinion based on a hypothetical question asked by Peg asking him to assume as true certain facts that are in evidence? _____

c. May Dr. Winston testify that in his opinion Peg's injuries were caused by the accident with Dee and not the collision with the truck? _____

d. May Dr. Winston testify that in his opinion Dee was negligent? _____

FORM OF DIRECT AND CROSS-EXAMINATION

62. Are the following questions permissible on direct examination?

a. To an expert witness: "You belong to a number of professional associations, don't you?" _____

b. To a witness whose memory of the event has faded: "Didn't the defendant then push the victim?" _____

c. To a hostile witness: "Even though you knew you were at fault, you didn't stop?" _____

d. To the husband of the adverse party: "Isn't it true that you heard the other pedestrian scream?" _____

63. According to the Federal Rules, a hostile witness may be impeached by either party, although most other witnesses may not. True or false? _____

64. Witness testifies: "I believe I saw the blue sedan drive by." This testimony is an improper opinion by a lay witness. True or false? _____

65. DeWitt is called to testify about a plane crash he witnessed. DeWitt states that he vaguely remembers having once seen a plane crash but that's all.

a. May the examiner show DeWitt a picture of the scene of the crash to re-fresh his memory? _____

b. If, after looking at the picture, DeWitt is then able to testify as to the de-tails of the plane crash, may the adverse party introduce the picture into evidence? _____

66. Polly is called to testify as to the items stolen in the July 1st burglary of her home. Polly testifies that her home has been burglarized 20 times and that she has no memory of which items were taken in the burglary at issue. Polly does state, however, that after each burglary she made a list of missing items and that she has a list captioned "July 1st Burglary."

a. If Polly testifies that she prepared the list and that it is accurate, may its contents be admitted into evidence? _____

b. If Polly had her butler prepare the list, which she later read and initialed, is the list still admissible as a past recollection recorded? _____

c. May the paper on which the list is written be introduced into evidence as an exhibit? _____

67. Witness suffers a stroke after direct examination but before he is cross-examined. Is Witness's direct testimony subject to a motion to strike? _____

68. Judge Solomon warns counsel that the scope of cross-examination must be re-stricted to matters put in issue on direct examination. Is he correct? _____

69. A trial judge has the power to call and interrogate a witness, and neither party may cross-examine that witness. True or false? _____

IMPEACHMENT AND REHABILITATION

70. Wilhelmina testifies that she saw Pedro cross the street against the light. Would the following be proper methods for Pedro to impeach Wilhelmina?

a. Pedro introduces proof that Wilhelmina was convicted of shoplifting (petty larceny with maximum penalty of probation) last year. _____

b. Other witnesses testify that they saw Pedro cross the street with the light. _____

c. Pedro introduces testimony by Tammy that Wilhelmina once cheated on a college history exam. _____

d. Henry testifies that in his opinion Wilhelmina is a liar. _____

71. May extrinsic evidence be used to impeach, for the following purposes, without first asking the witness about the impeaching evidence?

a. To prove a witness's felony conviction. _____

b. To prove prior bad acts (not amounting to convictions) of the witness. _____

c. To prove a prior inconsistent statement (assume the witness is no longer available). _____

72. At Patsy's trial for forgery, Wally testifies, "I saw Patsy sign that check."

    a. May Patsy introduce evidence that prior to trial Wally said, "Patsy never touched that check"? _____

    b. May the jury base its verdict on Wally's prior statement? _____

    c. On redirect, may the prosecution introduce evidence that immediately after Patsy's arrest Wally told the police, "I saw Patsy fooling around with that check"? _____

73. Waldo testifies that on his way home from work he saw the defendant steal a car. May the defendant impeach Waldo by having Imogene testify that Waldo is unemployed and has no permanent residence? _____

74. Ishmael testifies at trial that Duff "looks like the guy who robbed me . . . only the robber was fatter." May the prosecution introduce evidence that, at a police lineup shortly after the robbery, Ishmael identified Duff as the robber? _____

AUTHENTICATION

75. Indicate whether the following statements are true or false:

    a. Real evidence "speaks for itself" and therefore may not be excluded by the trial judge. _____

    b. Photographs need not be authenticated, though X-rays must be. _____

    c. Courts may take judicial notice as to the reliability of a scientific test, but there must be other proof that the test was conducted properly. _____

76. In the following situations, has a document signed by X been properly authenticated?

    a. Witness testifies that he saw X execute the document. _____

    b. Witness testifies that she recognizes the handwriting on the document as X's. _____

    c. Witness testifies that X must have written the document since X never used capital letters or punctuation. _____

    d. The document was a public record certified as required by law. _____

77. P claims that A recorded his telephone conversation. P calls A as a witness and asks, "Did you record my telephone conversation?" D objects that A's answer would violate the best evidence rule.

    a. The objection should be overruled because the best evidence rule applies only to documents and not tape recordings. True or false? _____

b. The objection should be overruled because P is not trying to prove the contents of the tape recording. True or false? _____

78. X wishes to introduce oral testimony as to the contents of a letter. May he do so under the following circumstances?

   a. The original letter was lost through no fault of X, but X has a copy of the letter. _____

   b. Y, who lives out of state, has the letter. _____

   c. An adversary party has possession of the original letter and refuses to produce it, although given notice. _____

JUDICIAL NOTICE

79. Judicial notice is a matter for the trial court. It may not be raised for the first time on appeal. True or false? _____

80. Is a trial court ever required to take judicial notice of a factual matter in a lawsuit? _____

81. True or false—a court may properly take judicial notice that:

   a. Radar tests are reliable. _____

   b. The 4th of January fell on a Wednesday in 1964. _____

   c. Defendant, a friend of the judge, could not have been intoxicated at the time in question. _____

   d. A local neighborhood is residential. _____

BURDEN OF PROOF; PRESUMPTIONS

82. In general, a party bears the burden of proving those facts that he is required to plead. True or false? _____

83. If a party meets the burden of going forward with the evidence, has he satisfied his burden of persuasion? _____

84. State X has a conclusive presumption that a child under the age of seven is incapable of committing a crime. May the prosecution introduce evidence that, even though the accused is only six years old, he actually did commit the crime charged? _____

85. State X recognizes a rebuttable presumption that a person owns the things that she possesses. Patrick alleges that Diego does not own an antique clock that Diego possesses.

   a. If Patrick introduces no evidence, the verdict will be for Diego. True or false? _____

   b. If Patrick introduces testimony that Diego stole the clock, the jury may weigh Patrick's evidence against the presumption of Diego's ownership. True or false? _____

PAROL EVIDENCE RULE

86. The parol evidence rule operates to exclude evidence that contradicts any writing. True or false? _____

87. Emma has a written employment contract with Highram.

   a. Assume Emma's contract fails to mention the duration of her employment. May Emma offer testimony that she and Highram orally agreed that her employment would last as long as Highram remained in business? _____

   b. Assume that the contract calls for Emma to sell greeting cards during the "holiday season." Would Highram's testimony that in the greeting card industry "holiday season" means November 15th to January 1st violate the parol evidence rule? _____

   c. May Emma testify that she was defrauded into signing the agreement? _____

   d. May Highram testify that the agreement was not to be effective until Emma got her driver's license? _____

ANSWERS TO REVIEW QUESTIONS

1. **FALSE**   Ordinarily, the trial judge is not obligated to raise grounds of objection on her own. Unless an objection is made by opposing counsel, almost any kind of evidence can be received. [§§27, 33]

2.a. **YES**   Where a party introduces part of a writing, the other party may introduce rebuttal evidence as to any other part of the writing that is necessary to make the first part understood. [§§35-36] The statement also would be admissible as an admission by a party-opponent. [§294]

b. **YES**   The adverse party can compel the party who first offered one part of a writing to introduce any other part that, in fairness, should be considered contemporaneously with it. [§§35-36]

3.a. **FALSE**   D's objection was timely since it was made before W answered the question. [§44]

b. **TRUE**   Where reversal is sought on the ground that evidence was erroneously *admitted* at trial, the objection must state the specific legal ground upon which the evidence is inadmissible. [§§40-42] Sometimes, however, a general objection will be deemed sufficient on the grounds that the basis for the objection was obvious from its context or the question was objectionable from every standpoint. [§43]

c. **FALSE**   The evidence must have been inadmissible for the reason stated. Other grounds for objection cannot be raised on appeal for the first time. [§48]

4.a. **TRUE**   Where evidence was *excluded* at trial, the judgment will not be reversed if the evidence was inadmissible on *any* ground (in this case hearsay). Thus, even a general objection will preserve the issue on appeal. [§§52-55]

b. **TRUE**   Unless the substance and purpose of W's testimony were apparent from the question asked, P must have made an offer of proof (*i.e.,* a record for appellate review). [§56]

5. **(A),(C),(E)**   Each of these preliminary fact questions concerns the legal admissibility of the evidence and so is decided by the trial judge alone. [§§61, 63] (C) and (E) are fact questions involving the relevancy or credibility of the evidence. Such questions are decided by the jury after an initial determination by the judge that there is sufficient evidence from which the jury can find the preliminary fact. [§§63, 66]

6. **NO**   Under the Federal Rules, any nonprivileged, relevant evidence can be considered. [§74]

7. **YES**   If evidence is relevant it is admissible—unless subject to a specific exclusionary rule, or unless excluded by the judge because its evidentiary dangers outweigh its probative value. [§§86, 91]

8. **YES**   Evidence that is inadmissible for one purpose is not thereby rendered inadmissible for all purposes. [§§87-89] Evidence of subsequent repairs is inadmissible

to prove negligence but is admissible to prove ownership or control of the item required. [§§198-199]

9.a. **YES**   Evidence of prior similar accidents is admissible to show that the condition of the sidewalk was dangerous or that Donald had knowledge of that condition. [§§103-105]

b. **YES**   Such evidence is relevant as showing that Donald lacked notice of the dangerous condition. [§111]

c. **NO**   Evidence of subsequent accidents is admissible only to show that the dangerous crack existed at the time Pilar was injured. It is not admissible to prove causation or notice. [§§106-107]

10.a. **YES**   Past contracts between the parties are admissible to help interpret the terms of their present contract. [§112]

b. **NO**   Evidence of contracts with third persons is generally not relevant for purposes of interpreting a contract between the litigating parties. [§113]

11.a. **NO**   Evidence of other crimes or misconduct is inadmissible when offered to show that the accused had a propensity to commit the crime for which he is now on trial. [§123]

b. **YES**   Evidence of prior crimes is admissible to prove that the crime charged is part of a common scheme or plan. [§131]

c. **YES**   The evidence of Ace's attack on the same person is relevant to show that the later killing was probably not an accident. [§136] It also shows Ace's animosity toward Vincent and explains Ace's motive for killing Vincent. [§§127, 129]

12. **TRUE**   Where character is itself an issue, as in an involuntary commitment proceeding where the question is whether a person is dangerous to himself or others, all courts admit evidence of specific instances of past conduct and reputation. Under the Federal Rules, opinion evidence is also admissible. [§§141-143]

13.a. **YES**   The accused in a criminal case may always offer evidence of her good character to show that she was unlikely to have committed the crime charged. [§145]

b. **YES**   The prosecution may question a defense character witness as to specific misconduct by the accused so long as the conduct is *relevant* to the character trait in issue. [§§153-154]

c. **YES**   A defendant may introduce either reputation or opinion evidence of a homicide victim's violent nature to show that the victim was probably the aggressor. [§§164-165]

14. **FALSE**   As a general rule, character evidence is inadmissible in a civil case to prove either party's probable conduct. [§161]

15.a. **NO**   This is "character" evidence and generally cannot be admitted to prove that a person acted in conformity with such character trait at the time in question. [§§161, 186]

b.	**YES**	Evidence of a person's routine acts in a particular situation (*i.e.,* "habit" evidence) is admissible to prove that the person acted in conformity with that habit on a given occasion. [§§186-188]
16.a.	**NO**	An offer to settle a claim is not admissible as an admission of liability because of the extrinsic policy of the law encouraging compromise and settlement of disputes. Moreover, evidence of any statements made during the course of settlement negotiations is inadmissible. [§§201-205]
b.	**YES**	Evidence of an offer to pay medical expenses is generally held not relevant to prove liability for the injuries. But note that, unlike settlement negotiations, an admission of liability (such as "I wish I had refrigerated that turkey") would be admissible if made in conjunction with an offer to pay medical expenses. [§206]
c.	**YES**	Evidence that a party carries liability insurance is not admissible to establish fault. [§212]
17.a.	**TRUE**	A hearsay "statement" may be either oral or written. [§224]
b.	**TRUE**	X's act is intended as a substitute for words and so is hearsay if offered to prove the truth of the matter to which X nodded. [§§224, 247]
c.	**FALSE**	The Federal Rules specifically require that nonverbal conduct be intended by the actor as an assertion if it is to be excluded as hearsay. (States following the Morgan definition of hearsay are contra.) [§§224-225, 248-254]
18.	**NO**	The words are offered only to show what was said; *i.e.,* they are offered as "legally operative facts" from which the court can determine whether or not the transaction was a gift. [§§230-231, 233]
19.a.	**YES**	The bill of sale is being offered to prove the truth of what it asserts and, as such, is hearsay. [§§223-224, 226]
b.	**YES**	Here the bill of sale is being offered only to show its effect on Desmond (that he thought the painting was a Van Gogh), and not to prove its truth. Therefore, it is not hearsay. [§§236, 239]
20.a.	**YES**	If offered to prove that a sponge was left in the patient, the statement is hearsay and hence is inadmissible. [§§223, 226]
b.	**NO**	If offered to show the *effect* on Doctor (*i.e.,* that he had *notice* that a sponge might still be in the patient), the statement is nonhearsay and therefore admissible. [§§236-237]
21.a.	**FALSE**	Wendell's in-court testimony does not remedy Defendant's lack of opportunity to cross-examine him at the time he made the statement; *i.e.,* the fact that the out-of court declarant is now on the stand does not insure the trustworthiness of his out-of court statement. [§228]
b.	**TRUE**	Failure to object to the introduction of hearsay constitutes a waiver of that ground for objection. [§33]
22.	**YES**	Inflammatory words (or conduct) are not hearsay if offered to reflect on the hearer's subsequent conduct. [§§236, 238]

23.a.	**YES**	A direct assertion by an out-of-court declarant as to her state of mind is hearsay. [§§226, 245] However, the statement in the letter would be admissible under the state of mind exception to the hearsay rule. [§§423-426]
b.	**NO**	If the statement is offered only as circumstantial evidence of Angela's state of mind (that she loved her husband and so would not have murdered him) the statement is not hearsay. [§240]
24.	**(A),(B),(C)**	Nonassertive conduct is conduct the declarant did not intend as an assertion, but is being offered as such. [§§248-251] In none of the cases described was the conduct intended as a substitute for words; thus they are all examples of non-assertive conduct.
25.	**FALSE**	Where the hearsay is admitted under an exception to the hearsay rule, the adverse party may attack the declarant's credibility whether or not the declarant is present at trial. [§266]
26.	**(A),(B),(C)**	In each of these situations, the witness was under oath at the former proceeding and there was opportunity for cross-examination. In each, the party against whom the testimony is now offered had an opportunity and similar motive to cross-examine the witness. And in each, the witness is sufficiently unavailable to testify at the later trial. [§§272-293] (D) is inadmissible under the former testimony exception because, although the witness is unavailable, coroner's inquests generally do not afford the requisite opportunity for cross-examination. [§274]
27.a.	**FALSE**	An admission by a party is admissible not only to impeach a party who testifies, but also as substantive proof of the matters admitted. [§§296-298]
b.	**FALSE**	An admission may be based on the opinion or conclusion of the admitter. It need not depend on the party's personal knowledge. [§§299-300]
28.	**YES**	However, such admissions are not conclusive and so may be explained. [§307]
29.a.	**NO**	Under the Federal Rules, an unaccepted offer to plead guilty is not admissible against an accused in any subsequent proceeding. [§313]
b.	**YES**	A plea of guilty to a criminal charge may be used as an admission against the pleader in any later proceeding involving the same act. [§311]
c.	**NO**	A plea of nolo contendere is not an admission of guilt. Thus, neither an offer to plead nolo contendere, nor the plea itself, is admissible in any subsequent proceeding. [§310]
30.	**DEPENDS**	If Drew heard, understood, and was capable of denying the accusation, his silence might be considered an implied admission. However, if Drew was unable to hear or respond to Percy's charge (*e.g.,* if he was unconscious, in shock, etc.), or if he was afraid to say anything because of Percy's intimidating manner, his silence would not constitute an admission. [§§320-324]
31.	**YES**	Both of Dan's acts reflect his awareness of guilt and so are admissions by conduct. [§330]

| 32. | **YES** | According to the Federal Rules, an employee's statement is admissible against his employer as an admission if made as to a matter within the scope of his authority (here, driving the bus). However, the traditional view is that only authorized statements are admissible against the employer. [§§335-343] |

| 33.a. | **TRUE** | As long as the admission was made during and in furtherance of the conspiracy, and the conspiracy itself is established, one co-conspirator's admission may be received in evidence against the others. [§§344-349] |

| b. | **FALSE** | The Federal Rules do not provide for the reception of admissions by predecessors in interest. [§353] |

| c. | **TRUE** | The Federal Rules admit such statements as nonhearsay. Some jurisdictions view such statements as hearsay but admissible under an exception to the hearsay rule. [§§296-297, 318-319] |

| 34. | **NO** | Although the declaration would be considered contrary to Elwood's interest in avoiding liability in that it constitutes the basis for an action against him for damages, the exception does not apply because Elwood is available. [§§374-375] |

| 35. | **NO** | The Federal Rules admit declarations against penal interest as well as against pecuniary or proprietary interest. However, where the statement offered tends to exculpate the accused and incriminate the declarant, the Rules require corroborating circumstances to indicate the statement's trustworthiness. [§382] Furthermore, Livia must show that Caligula is unavailable to testify and that his testimony cannot be obtained by deposition or similar means. [§§374-375] |

| 36.a. | **NO** | The Federal Rules do not admit dying declarations in *criminal cases* other than homicide. [§391] |

| b. | **YES** | The Federal Rules permit the use of dying declarations in civil actions. [§391] |

| c. | **NO** | All courts require that the statement concern the *facts* of the declarant's impending death based on personal knowledge. Vernon's opinion would thus be inadmissible as a dying declaration. [§§397-398] |

| d. | **NO** | Only declarations made by the victim are admissible as dying declarations. [§393] |

| 37. | **YES** | Vanessa's statement would be admissible as an excited utterance. The display of Dominic's picture upon Vanessa's awakening was a startling event that produced shock and excitement in Vanessa; her statement was made under the stress of that excitement and was related to the event. [§§403-406] |

| 38.a. | **YES** | The declarant of a spontaneous exclamation need not be identified nor shown to be unavailable. [§§410-412] |

| b. | **YES** | Although the customer's statement about the smoke would probably not qualify as an excited utterance under the Federal Rules, it would be admissible as a present sense impression. Again, there are no requirements as to identity or availability of the declarant. [§§415-417] |

39.a.	**YES**	Declarations of present bodily condition made to anyone are admissible. [§§418-419]
b.	**YES**	Statements of past physical condition are admissible when made for the purpose of medical diagnosis or treatment. [§421]
c.	**NO**	Declarations of past physical condition made for purposes other than diagnosis or treatment are inadmissible under the exception. [§421]
d.	**YES**	Statements made solely for *diagnosis* are admissible under the Federal Rules. [§421]
40.	**YES**	Sam's declaration as to his present state of mind is admissible to establish his domicile. [§§424-425]
41.	**NO**	A statement of intent to do an act is admissible to show the probable conduct of the *declarant* (Harry), but not that of a third person (Jim). [§427]
42.a.	**PROBABLY NOT**	To be admissible under the business records exception, a record must be of a type customarily maintained by a business as part of its primary activities. Although a hospital would be considered a "business," the hospital's primary activity is diagnosis and treatment of patients' conditions. Bennie's description of his assailant is not sufficiently related to those activities. [§§448-449]
b.	**YES**	The Federal Rules admit entries of opinions or diagnoses if made in the regular course of business. [§456]
c.	**YES**	Unavailability of the entrant is not required before the record itself may be used. [§460]
d.	**NO**	The entrant of a business record must be under a duty to make the entry in question. Records kept as a hobby do not qualify. [§447]
43.a.	**YES**	The officer's observations about the skid marks, based on her personal knowledge, would be admissible either as business records or as public records. Since this is a civil case, there is no prohibition against using police records. [§§453, 456-457]
b.	**NO**	The hearsay on hearsay would not be admissible as a business record because the person making the statement was under no business duty to contribute to the record. [§457] Nor would it be admissible as a public record, since the officer had no firsthand knowledge of the fact reported by the witness. [§471]
c.	**PROBABLY NOT**	The rule in *Palmer v. Hoffman* excludes accident reports prepared solely in anticipation of litigation (because lacking in trustworthiness). However, some courts would admit the report if offered *against* the insurance company that prepared it. [§§450-452]
44.	**YES**	The fact that there is no record with the agency is admissible to prove that Frank's death was not reported or recorded. Furthermore, if deaths are regularly recorded by the agency, the absence of the record could be used to prove that Frank is not dead. [§481]

| 45.a. | **YES** | The Federal Rules allow the admission of the criminal conviction in a civil case to prove any fact essential to the criminal judgment. [§§485-486] |

45.a. **YES** — The Federal Rules allow the admission of the criminal conviction in a civil case to prove any fact essential to the criminal judgment. [§§485-486]

b. **NO** — The fact that D was acquitted in the criminal case establishes only that he was not found guilty beyond a reasonable doubt. The acquittal does not preclude civil liability based on the same conduct. [§489]

46.a. **YES** — According to the Federal Rules, declarations of pedigree may be made by an "intimate associate" of the person whose family history is in question. [§§497, 505]

b. **YES** — The Federal Rules permit evidence of community reputation to prove any matter of pedigree. [§520]

47.a. **FALSE** — Privileges are usually construed narrowly since they operate to exclude otherwise competent evidence. [§556]

b. **TRUE** — However, in some states only those privileges set forth by statute are recognized. [§§558-559]

c. **FALSE** — Since a privilege is personal in nature, it can be claimed only by the "holder" or a person authorized to claim it on his behalf. [§§563-566]

d. **TRUE** — A claim of privilege always requires a showing that the communication was made in confidence. However, many states recognize a presumption of confidentiality as to communications made in the course of certain relationships. [§567]

48. **NO** — According to the modern trend, as long as the holder of the privilege was not negligent in allowing his conversations to be overheard, the eavesdropper may not testify. [§580]

49.a. **NO** — An appeal cannot be based on the violation of a ***third person's*** privilege. [§581]

b. **YES** — If the court erroneously recognizes an asserted privilege and excludes proffered testimony on this ground, a party may always complain on appeal. [§582]

50.a. **YES and NO** — H has waived the privilege by disclosing the communication to X. However, W may still assert the privilege and prevent either H or X from testifying as to her communication. [§§574, 700-701]

b. **YES** — Since Client is the holder of the privilege, his calling of Attorney constitutes a voluntary waiver of the privilege. (Attorney is not a holder of the privilege and so cannot claim the privilege for himself.) [§§587-588]

c. **YES** — A holder may consent to a contractual provision that waives in advance his right to claim a privilege. [§§574, 649]

51.a. **YES** — Assuming Claude consulted Addie for ***legal*** advice, then he may prevent her or anyone else from testifying as to their confidential conversation. It does not matter that Addie declined the case. [§§599-600]

b. **YES** — Although the privilege belongs to the client, the attorney may assert it on his behalf. [§587]

c.	**YES**	Improper disclosures by the attorney do not "waive" the privilege. Claude could still prevent either Addie or the friend from testifying. [§590]
d.	**YES (on two grounds)**	No privilege exists for communications made to enable the client to perpetrate a crime or fraud. Furthermore, an attorney may testify as to relevant communications between herself and her client where there is a claim that the attorney breached a duty owed the client. [§§620, 624]
52.a.	**YES**	Communications made to third persons are confidential where made for the purpose of transmitting information between the lawyer and client. [§618]
b.	**NO**	The gun itself is not a communication and hence is not privileged. [§609]
c.	**YES**	The privilege covers disclosures by the attorney to the client, including the attorney's advice to the client. [§601]
d.	**NO**	Ordinarily the amount of fees and the method or time of payment of fees are not considered communications within the privilege. [§613]
53.a.	**YES**	A patient may refuse to testify as to any information disclosed to a physician in the course of obtaining treatment. [§§630, 641]
b.	**YES**	The privilege applies to *any* information obtained by the doctor in the course of examination or treatment. [§§637-638]
c.	**NO**	The privilege may not be claimed where the patient places her condition in issue. [§643]
d.	**NO**	In most jurisdictions, the privilege applies in *civil* actions only. [§631]
54.a.	**DEPENDS**	Under federal case law, there is a privilege against adverse spousal testimony in criminal cases. The privilege belongs to the *witness-spouse*. Thus, Wilma will decide if she will testify against her husband. The prosecution cannot compel her to testify, nor can Fred prevent her from testifying if she so chooses. [§§673, 676] (Note that under the traditional view, Fred would be able to prevent Wilma from testifying because the spousal privilege belongs to the party-spouse. [§676])
b.	**YES**	The spousal privilege can never be invoked in a criminal case where one spouse is charged with crimes against the other spouse or a child of either. [§§681-682]
55.	**FALSE**	The privilege may be *asserted* only during the marriage, but is not limited to matters that occurred during marriage. [§§677-678]
56.	**YES**	A confidential communication made during marriage is privileged even after the marriage has ended. *Either* spouse may assert the privilege to bar the other from testifying in either a civil or criminal action. Moreover, the privilege is not limited to actions in which the other spouse is a party. [§§686-696]
57.a.	**TRUE**	Most jurisdictions recognize this privilege. [§654]
b.	**TRUE**	Most states have made both the penitent and the member of the clergy holders of this privilege. [§707]

c.	**DEPENDS**	If disclosure is forbidden by state or federal law, the privilege is absolute. Otherwise, the government must show that disclosure of the information would be contrary to public interest. [§709]
d.	**TRUE**	The identity of such an informer must be disclosed or the court must dismiss the charges against the accused. [§722]
e.	**FALSE**	A news reporter must always *appear* when subpoenaed by a court or grand jury. However, the scope of his privilege to refuse to *disclose* his sources has not yet been fully resolved. [§§729-741]
58.a.	**YES**	The privilege of every witness not to answer incriminating questions applies in any proceeding in which the witness is compelled to appear and take the witness stand. [§§756-759]
b.	**NO**	If the witness is immune from prosecution based on his compelled testimony, the privilege cannot be asserted. [§§780-784]
59.a.	**NO**	An accused does not waive this privilege by testifying at a preliminary hearing. [§§804-805, 808]
b.	**YES**	If the accused takes the stand at trial, he has waived his "witness privilege" and can thus be compelled to answer all questions about the present charges against him. [§803]
60.	**(A),(C), (D),(E)**	Each of these opinions is based on the lay witness's personal observation, and concerns a matter about which laypersons generally form opinions (*i.e.*, age, mood, taste, and handwriting). (B) is improper lay opinion in that it is the witness's opinion as to how he would have acted in a particular situation (and is not based on his perception of the facts in issue). (F) is an opinion on a question of law and so is an improper subject for lay opinion. [§§878-890]
61.a.	**YES**	An expert may base his opinion on the opinion of others where this practice is common in such witness's field of expertise. The expert's opinion is no less admissible because *based on* inadmissible evidence. [§§903-905]
b.	**YES**	The Federal Rules do not require hypothetical questions but such questions are permitted. [§§902, 909-914]
c.	**PROBABLY**	If expert opinion as to which accident caused Peg's injuries would be helpful to the jury, Dr. Winston's opinion would be admissible. [§923] The fact that the opinion may embrace an ultimate issue in the case does not make it objectionable, according to the Federal Rules. [§921]
d.	**NO**	Opinion testimony is admissible as to an ultimate issue of *fact*, but not as to a question of law or where the opinion is unhelpful, prejudicial, or a waste of time. Whether or not a party's conduct failed to meet a relevant legal standard is a conclusion the jury must draw from the facts in evidence. [§§922, 924]
62.a.	**YES**	A leading question is permitted on direct examination to ask about preliminary or background matters [§951]
b.	**YES**	An examiner may use anything, including a leading question, to jog a witness's memory. [§951]

c.	**NO**	*Misleading* questions, which force the witness to admit things he does not want to admit, are *never* allowed. [§§948, 979]
d.	**YES**	Leading questions are permissible on direct examination of a witness identified with the adverse party. [§951]
63.	**FALSE**	The Federal Rules permit impeachment of any witness by any party. [§960]
64.	**FALSE**	The witness's lack of certainty in the phrasing of his testimony goes only to the weight of the testimony and not its admissibility. [§962]
65.a.	**YES**	Anything may be used to refresh a witness's incomplete memory. [§§963-965]
b.	**YES**	The adverse party has the right to inspect the item shown to the witness, and to introduce those parts of the item that relate to the witness's testimony. [§969]
66.a.	**YES**	Since Polly has no independent present memory of the contents of the writing, the list itself may be admitted as a record of what she once knew. [§§433-441, 974]
b.	**YES**	Under the Federal Rules, if Polly read the list while the event was fresh in her memory, and *knew* the list was correct, she would have "adopted" the list as her own recollection of the event. [§435]
c.	**NO**	The witness may only read the document to the jury. [§441]
67.	**YES**	The testimony must be stricken because of the denial of opportunity for cross-examination. [§976]
68.	**YES**	The Federal Rules restrict the scope of cross-examination to matters related to those topics testified to on direct. [§982]
69.	**FALSE**	Either party may cross-examine a witness called by the judge. [§997]
70.a.	**DEPENDS**	Because the conviction is not a felony, it may only be admitted for impeachment if it is a crime of "dishonesty." However, there is no consensus within the federal courts that stealing constitutes a "dishonest" crime within the meaning of Federal Rule 609(a)(2). [§§1022-1023] Therefore, the admissibility of the conviction will depend on the court's interpretation of whether shoplifting is a dishonest crime.
b.	**YES**	A witness's testimony may be discredited by contradictory relevant evidence. [§§1007-1008]
c.	**NO**	Although most courts, and the Federal Rules, leave the admissibility of a witness's past misconduct (not amounting to a criminal conviction) to the discretion of the trial judge, such evidence is limited to the cross-examination of the witness. Extrinsic evidence of past misconduct is not permitted. [§§1044-1046]
d.	**YES**	The Federal Rules allow other witnesses to testify as to their opinions of the witness's credibility. [§§1048, 1054]
71.a.	**YES**	A crime that constitutes grounds for impeachment may be proved by a certified copy of the conviction. The witness need not be questioned about the conviction at all. [§1036]

b.	**NO**	The witness must be asked about prior incidents of misconduct. Furthermore, whether the witness admits or denies the past misconduct, the examiner may *not* introduce extrinsic evidence of the bad acts. [§§1044-1045]
c.	**NO (or usually not)**	Extrinsic evidence may be used, but only after the witness has been given a chance to "explain or deny." The requirement may, however, be excused in special circumstances where the interests of justice so require. [§§1066-1074]
72.a.	**YES**	A witness may be impeached by showing that he has made a prior inconsistent statement regarding the matter to which he testifies at trial. [§1064]
b.	**NO**	Under the Federal Rules, a prior inconsistent statement may be introduced only for impeachment purposes, unless the statement was made under oath at a prior hearing. [§1087] Wally's prior statement was not made under oath; thus, the statement may be introduced only for impeachment purposes.
c.	**DEPENDS**	If the impeachment evidence suggested that Wally had recently fabricated his testimony at trial, federal courts would admit the prior consistent statement to rebut the charge of recent fabrication. [§§1104, 1115]
73.	**PROBABLY NOT**	Whether Waldo was or was not on his way home from work when he witnessed the crime would probably be considered a collateral matter and so not a proper subject for impeachment. [§§1088-1089]
74.	**YES**	Under the Federal Rules, a prior identification of a person is admissible as substantive proof of identity (and not merely as impeachment or corroboration evidence). The prior identification is considered more reliable than the courtroom identification since the accused's appearance may have changed (*e.g.,* he may have lost weight). [§§1122-1126]
75.a.	**FALSE**	As with all types of evidence, the trial judge has discretion to exclude real evidence if its potential for prejudice outweighs its probative value. [§1140]
b.	**FALSE**	Both photographs and X-rays are reproductions and must be authenticated. However, more is required for authentication of an X-ray. [§§1145-1148]
c.	**TRUE**	Where there is sufficient scientific recognition of a certain test, courts have been willing to forgo the requirement of independent expert testimony regarding the test's reliability. [§§1240-1243]
76.a.	**YES**	The testimony of a witness who saw the execution of the document is one method of authentication. [§1168]
b.	**YES**	Any person familiar with the handwriting of the alleged writer of the document may authenticate the document by identifying the handwriting thereon. [§1169]
c.	**YES**	Testimony as to the writer's unique style can serve as circumstantial evidence that he wrote the document in question, and is a proper method of authentication. [§1174]
d.	**YES**	Certified copies of public records are self-authenticating. [§1181]
77.a.	**FALSE**	According to the Federal Rules, the best evidence rule applies to tape recordings, photographs, etc., as well as to documents. [§1199]

| b. | **TRUE** | P is not seeking to prove the contents of the recording, but only that a recording was made. A's testimony is admissible as to whether he recorded P's conversation. [§1194] |

78.a. **YES**   Under the Federal Rules, *any* secondary evidence is admissible to prove the contents of a writing where the best evidence rule is inapplicable (*e.g.,* where the original writing was lost without fault of the proponent). [§§1203, 1211-1213]

   b. **NO**   X would first have to show that the letter could not be obtained by any available judicial process. [§1205]

   c. **YES**   Secondary evidence of the contents of a writing is admissible when the adverse party fails to turn over the original after being given "notice to produce." [§1207]

79. **FALSE**   Judicial notice may be taken at any stage of a proceeding. [§1291]

80. **YES**   Under the Federal Rules, a trial court is required to take judicial notice of adjudicative facts when a party makes a proper request. [§§1282, 1289]

81.a. **TRUE**   [§1288]

   b. **TRUE**   [§1288]

   c. **FALSE**   A judge may not take notice of matters within his personal knowledge which are outside the record. [§1273]

   d. **TRUE**   [§1287]

82. **TRUE**   The burden of persuasion generally, but not always, follows the burden of pleading. [§§1303, 1306]

83. **NOT NECESSARILY**   A party has met his burden of going forward if he has produced enough legally sufficient evidence that the jury *could* decide the issue in his favor. However, the party has met his burden of persuasion only if the jury *does* find for him on an issue as to which he must persuade them. [§§1313-1314]

84. **NO**   A conclusive presumption is in effect a rule of substantive law. As such, it may not be rebutted by contrary evidence. [§§1330, 1349]

85.a. **TRUE**   In the absence of contrary evidence, the jury must find in accordance with the presumption. [§1331]

   b. **FALSE**   Most jurisdictions, and the Federal Rules, follow the view that upon the introduction of counterevidence a rebuttable presumption disappears. Thus, the jury may not weigh the dispelled presumption against the conflicting evidence. [§§1334-1335]

86. **FALSE**   The rule applies only to *integrated* writings. Where the parties have intended the writing to serve as a final embodiment of their agreement, evidence that would alter or contradict the writing is inadmissible. [§§1355-1356, 1365]

87.a. **YES**   Where a written agreement is silent on some term or condition, parol evidence is admissible to prove that the parties had a separate oral agreement regarding that matter. [§§1373-1375]

b. **NO**   Words that have a special meaning because of their custom or usage in a particular industry may be explained by parol evidence. [§1383]

c. **YES**   Parol evidence is admissible to show the circumstances surrounding the execution of the agreement, including fraud by one of the parties. [§1393]

d. **YES**   Extrinsic evidence may be introduced to show that an agreement was not intended to take effect until a condition precedent occurred. [§1392]

SAMPLE EXAM QUESTION I

Dan and Ellen, husband and wife, were tried jointly for shoplifting but were represented by different attorneys. The prosecution contended that the defendants entered Store, that while Ellen distracted the clerk, Dan put a pocket calculator valued at $100 in his pocket, and that the defendants then left with the calculator. At the trial, the following events occurred:

(a) The prosecution called as a witness the manager of Store and asked him whether the missing calculator could possibly have been sold at any time prior to the time Dan and Ellen entered Store. The manager said, "No, I have carefully checked the sales records that we keep in the ordinary course of our business; in those records our clerks enter a description of every item valued at more than $25 immediately after it is sold. The records show no earlier sales of that type of calculator."

(b) The prosecution called as a witness Store's clerk, who testified that as the defendants left Store, he noticed that the calculator was missing from a display stand; that he ran to the door and shouted loudly, "Hey, come back!"; and that the defendants ran to an intersection where they boarded a public bus.

(c) The prosecution called as a witness Wat, who testified that one week before the event charged in the information, Dan and Ellen entered his store and that, while Ellen was asking Wat questions about some merchandise, he saw Dan place a tape recorder in his overcoat pocket.

(d) At the close of the prosecution's case-in-chief, over Dan's objection, Ellen's attorney called Ellen as a witness.

Assume all appropriate objections were timely made. How should the court have ruled on the admissibility of the evidence offered in items (a), (b), (c), and how should the court have ruled on Dan's objection in item (d)? Discuss.

SAMPLE EXAM QUESTION II

Paula, the beneficiary of a $50,000 insurance policy issued on the life of Lola by Insco, an insurance company, sued Insco for the proceeds. The policy excluded coverage for death by suicide, and Insco alleged that Lola had taken her own life.

At the trial before a jury, Ron, a park ranger, testified that he found Lola's body at the foot of a high cliff and described the scene in minute detail. During cross-examination, Ron admitted that he had on the previous day refreshed his recollection from his diary. The court denied a motion by Insco that Ron be ordered to produce the diary, which was at his home.

After evidence of the autopsy findings was introduced, the following evidence was admitted over objection by Insco:

(i) The testimony of Hal, a hiker who was nearby when Lola fell, that in his opinion "the temperature at the top of the cliff was over 110° and the humidity very high."

(ii) The testimony of Med, a qualified medical witness who, after having heard all the evidence referred to above, was asked the following question: "Based on the evidence which you have heard, what is your opinion as to the cause of Lola's fall?" Her answer was that Lola's fall was caused by heat prostration.

Over objection by Paula, the following evidence was admitted:

(iii) Testimony of Fred, a friend of Lola's, that a month before her death Lola said, "I'm so depressed I could end it all!"

(iv) A properly authenticated, officially kept record of a U.S. Weather Bureau Station 45 miles from the cliff showing the maximum temperature at the Weather Bureau Station on the day of Lola's death was 68°.

Among the court's instructions to the jury was the following: "The law presumes that a person will not commit suicide. You will therefore find that Lola did not commit suicide unless you are persuaded to the contrary by a preponderance of the evidence."

(a) Assume that all objections were appropriately and timely made. Was the court correct in its rulings:

    (1) Denying the motion to produce the diary? Discuss.

    (2) Admitting the evidence to which Insco objected and the evidence to which Paula objected? Discuss.

(b) Was the court's instruction to the jury proper? Discuss.

SAMPLE EXAM QUESTION III

Patti sued Dave for personal injuries allegedly sustained when she was struck by an automobile driven by Dave, who was insured by Mutual Insurance Company (Mutual).

(1) In the course of selection of the jury Patti's attorney was allowed, over Dave's objection, to ask prospective jurors whether they or any members of their families owned stock in or were employed by Mutual.

(2) After the jury was impaneled, Patti testified that she was struck in a crosswalk by a yellow sports car driven by a man wearing a purple jacket with a fur collar, that the man immediately drove away, and that she has had disabling headaches ever since. Al testified over Dave's objection that he had investigated the ownership of numerous sports cars fitting the description given by Patti, that he had interviewed and advised Dave's mother of the details of the accident, and that when he asked if Dave had a purple jacket with a fur collar, the mother fainted.

(3) The court received in evidence, over objection by Patti, a certified copy of a judgment of acquittal in a criminal prosecution in which Dave had been charged with hit-and-run driving in connection with Patti's injury.

(4) Dr. Bene was called by Dave and testified over Patti's objection that when he examined Patti a few days following her alleged injury she told him that she had suffered from severe headaches since childhood.

Assume that all objections were timely and appropriately made. Was the court correct in its rulings on:

(a) The question asked the prospective jurors;

(b) The testimony of Al;

(c) The admission of the judgment of acquittal;

(d) The testimony of Dr. Bene concerning his examination of Patti?

Discuss.

SAMPLE EXAM QUESTION IV

X Corporation, wholly owned by Mr. X, operated a drugstore. It was required to keep a record of all narcotic prescriptions filled and all narcotics received. The corporation has been indicted for unlawfully dispensing narcotics. At trial the following events occurred:

(1) The prosecution obtained a subpoena directing X Corporation to produce the narcotic prescription records for the year in question. X Corporation moved to quash the subpoena on two grounds: (i) the records were in the possession of X Corporation's attorney; and (ii) the production of the records would violate the privilege against self-incrimination. The motion to quash was denied.

(2) The prosecution called X Corporation's attorney as a witness. After stating that she had destroyed the records, the attorney was asked to testify as to their contents. An objection to this testimony was overruled.

(3) Mr. X offered to prove that he terminated the corporation's relationship with its attorney when he learned that the records had been destroyed. An objection to this offer was overruled.

(4) In rebuttal, the prosecution offered to prove that during a recess immediately after the attorney's testimony regarding the destruction of the records, Mr. X was overheard saying to the attorney in the hall: "Why did you admit we destroyed those records?" An objection to this offer was sustained.

(5) In final argument, the prosecution, over objection, was allowed to argue that the failure to produce the records might be considered by the jury as an implied admission that the records were incriminating.

Assume that all motions and objections were timely and appropriately made. Was the court's ruling correct on:

(a) The motion to quash the subpoena? Discuss.

(b) The objections to testimony or offers of proof as described in (2), (3), and (4)? Discuss.

(c) The propriety of the prosecution's argument? Discuss.

SAMPLE EXAM QUESTION V

Peter sued Dan for damages for breach of a written contract. Peter's attorney is Row. Dan's answer in the case denied that he had ever signed or entered into any such contract.

At the trial, before a jury, Peter testified that after extensive negotiations, he and Dan executed a written contract. Peter identified a document, purportedly signed and acknowledged by Dan before a notary public, as the original of the contract he and Dan had signed and acknowledged. That document was then offered in evidence by Row and was admitted.

Thereafter, the following took place:

(1)   Abel was called as a witness by Dan. Abel testified without objection that he was a teller in the bank where Dan had his commercial account and that he had seen Dan's signature hundreds of times. Abel was then asked whether, in his opinion, the signature on the contract was Dan's and, over objection, was permitted to answer that it was not.

(2)   On cross-examination, Abel was asked: "Is it not a fact that Peter is suing the bank that employs you?" Defendant's objection was sustained.

(3)   Dan testified in his own behalf that the signature on the contract was not his. On cross-examination Dan admitted attending a meeting in Row's office at which Peter showed him the original of the contract. On further cross-examination Dan was asked: "Didn't Peter then say to you, 'You know that's your signature' and didn't you then smile and shrug your shoulders?" After objection by Dan's attorney, Dan was required to answer the question and his answer was: "No, that never took place."

(4)   In rebuttal, Row was sworn as a witness and, over objection, testified that Peter did say to Dan, "You know that's your signature" and that Dan then smiled and shrugged his shoulders.

At the close of the trial, at Row's request and over Dan's objection the jury was instructed: "The signatures on a document bearing a certificate of acknowledgment are presumed to be genuine. You will therefore assume that the signature on the contract is that of Dan unless you are persuaded to the contrary by a preponderance of the evidence." The Evidence Code of the jurisdiction provides in part: "Presumptions affecting the burden of producing evidence: The signatures on a document bearing a certificate of acknowledgment are presumed to be genuine."

(a)   In each instance in which an objection was made, what might properly have been the grounds of the objection, and how should the court have ruled? Discuss.

(b)   Should the court have given the requested instruction? Discuss.

SAMPLE EXAM QUESTION VI

State X enacted a "Dangerous Drug Control Act." The Act listed several chemicals, including meprobamate (M), as specified dangerous drugs, made possession of any such dangerous drug for the purpose of illegal sale a felony, and provided that possession by an unlicensed person of 20 or more grains of any such dangerous drug without a prescription therefor "shall be presumptive evidence that such drug is being held for sale in violation of this Act."

David was convicted of violation of the Act. At his trial, it was established by legally obtained evidence that he had 40 grains of M in his possession and that he was not then licensed within the meaning of the Act.

The trial court received the following evidence, offered by the prosecution, over objection by the defendant:

(1)   The testimony of Dr. Ash that he had been David's family physician for the 10 years immediately prior to David's arrest and that he had never prescribed M for him.

(2)   The testimony of Watson that he was a former narcotic agent, that he had been present about a year earlier when a person by the name of Bertha died of an overdose of heroin, and that Bertha, after receiving last rites at her request, had said: "David sold me the junk."

On cross-examination of Watson, the trial court sustained an objection by the prosecution to the following question: "Isn't it a fact that last year you were indicted by the grand jury for bribery and that David was the principal witness against you?"

David did not testify in his own behalf. The trial court, over objection by the defendant, instructed the jury that if it found that when David was arrested he was in possession of 20 or more grains of M without a prescription, the jury should presume that he held it for sale in violation of the Act, unless convinced to the contrary by a preponderance of the evidence.

(a)   Assuming that in each case all appropriate objections were made, was the trial court correct in its rulings on:

   (1)   The testimony of Dr. Ash?

   (2)   The testimony of Watson?

   (3)   The cross-examination of Watson? Discuss.

(b)   Was the court correct in giving the instruction on the presumption? Discuss.

SAMPLE EXAM QUESTION VII

Chemicals, Inc., a chemical manufacturer, is being sued by Percy, who claims to have suffered disabling lung damage as a proximate result of breathing air pollutants discharged by Chemicals's plant into the air over Percy's residence. The case is set for trial in a week.

The following sources of possible evidence are available to present at trial:

(a)   An official verbatim transcript of the testimony of Dr. Mobed, a recognized expert, who testified and was cross-examined under oath at a prior hearing on a workers' compensation claim brought against Chemicals by one of its employees who claimed lung damage identical to that claimed by Percy. The transcript contains Dr. Mobed's statement that nothing emitted by Chemicals's plant can injure the human respiratory system. However, Dr. Mobed is on an extended trip to Europe and will not be available to testify.

(b) Baker, a recognized expert, will testify concerning measurements she made of the density of the smoke emitted from Chemicals's plant. Baker will also testify that she made no written record of the readings and does not remember them, but that, as she made the measurements, she called out the three single-digit Ringleman readings to her assistant, Carl. Carl does remember the readings. The Ringleman Chart is a universally accepted standard for measuring smoke emission. Both Baker and Carl will be available to testify at the trial.

(c) A duly certified copy of Circular No. 6888, published by the U.S. Bureau of Mines, which explains Ringleman Chart readings. No one from the Bureau of Mines will be available to testify.

(d) Motion pictures taken by Ed in which Percy is clearly identifiable and is shown engaging in strenuous physical activity at a city park that was not opened until after the filing of the lawsuit. Ed is now deceased.

(e) Darcy's earlier signed sworn statement given to an investigator for Chemicals's attorney that Percy frequently coughed up blood even before Percy moved into the community where Chemicals's plant is located. Darcy will be available as a witness but is likely to change her story.

Discuss the admissibility of each of the enumerated items of possible evidence.

SAMPLE EXAM QUESTION VIII

P sued D for personal injuries. P claimed that D had negligently manufactured a wooden ladder that broke while being used by a man named Carpenter, causing Carpenter to fall upon P. Carpenter died as a result of the injuries received.

(a) Prudent, a police officer, was called as P's witness. She testified without objection that when she arrived at the scene, Carpenter was conscious but lost consciousness before the ambulance arrived, and that when the ambulance came, it backed over the ladder and broke it in several places. Over D's objection, Prudent was allowed to testify that at the scene of the accident she asked Carpenter what happened, and Carpenter said, "The ladder broke and I fell."

(b) P offered in evidence a certified copy of Carpenter's death certificate which stated, among other matters: "IF CAUSED BY INJURY, DESCRIBE HOW INJURY OCCURRED: Rung of ladder broke and victim fell on head." The court sustained an objection thereto.

(c) P called Dr. Dixit. It was stipulated that he was an expert in the fields of strength of materials and accident reconstruction. Over D's objection, Dr. Dixit was permitted to testify that based upon information obtained from the police report, wood fiber analysis reports from an independent laboratory, records of the company from which Carpenter rented the ladder, and his own inspection of the scene, it was his opinion that at least one of the breaks in the ladder preexisted the ladder's being smashed by the ambulance.

(d) D called Hood as a witness. Hood refused to answer any questions about the falling of the ladder, on the ground that his answers might tend to incriminate him. D then called Barber who testified, over P's objection, that Hood told him that he, Hood, had kicked the ladder out from under Carpenter.

(e) On cross-examination, Barber had difficulty remembering anything else that happened the day Hood made the statement to him, but the court sustained D's objection to the question, "How can you remember what Hood said so clearly when you can't remember anything else that happened that day?"

Assume that all appropriate objections were timely made. Were the court's rulings correct? Discuss.

SAMPLE EXAM QUESTION IX

Donna is being prosecuted in federal court for a bank robbery that occurred in January 1995. She claims mistaken identity and will offer Buzzy as an alibi witness. Buzzy will testify that Donna was watching the Super Bowl with him at the time of the robbery. The prosecution has a witness, Tim, who will testify that Buzzy told him that Donna had asked Buzzy to make up an alibi for her for the day of the Super Bowl.

Donna, Buzzy, and Tim are all heroin addicts who have occasionally dealt drugs. None of them, however, has ever been convicted of any crime related to heroin addiction or drug dealing. They have not been involved in any drug deals with each other.

(a) The prosecution seeks to offer evidence of Donna's and Buzzy's heroin involvement, and the defense seeks to offer evidence of Tim's heroin involvement. Evaluate the admissibility of evidence of addiction and sale of heroin by the three individuals. Assume that the defendant will not testify. If you think evidence would be admissible for a limited purpose, describe that purpose.

(b) Buzzy testified that he was certain about his alibi testimony because he and Donna had watched the Super Bowl together every year since the start of the championship. The prosecution did not cross-examine Buzzy about anything that related to watching the Super Bowl in the years before 1995. On rebuttal, the prosecution wishes to impeach Buzzy with testimony by Ms. X that Buzzy had told Ms. X that he had not watched the Super Bowl with Donna in 1992 or 1993. What objection(s) can the defense make to exclude Ms. X's testimony of Buzzy's prior inconsistent statement?

(c) The prosecution has a witness, Mr. Bushmat, who saw the license plate of a suspicious car parked near the bank on the day of the robbery. While the car was still parked, he wrote down the license number. He gave the paper with the number on it to his wife that night. She immediately called the police and gave a police officer the number, which he recorded in writing. The license plate number turned out to be the number of a car owned by Donna. Mr. Bushmat remembers giving his wife the license number but does not remember the number. Mrs. Bushmat remembers the number on the paper that her husband gave her but has lost the slip of paper on which it was written. Could the license plate number be admitted (1) through the record made by the police officer who talked to Mrs. Bushmat, or (2) through the testimony of the Bushmats? (3) Do any Confrontation Clause problems exist?

SAMPLE EXAM QUESTION X

A Tusconna law reformer argues that Tusconna Rules 703 and 705 (which are identical to the Federal Rules) are too permissive in cases in which a law enforcement official testifies for the prosecution as a crime expert (*e.g.*, as an expert on the methods of drug dealers). She proposes that Rules 703 and 705 be amended to provide that in such cases the common law restrictions on the basis and form of expert testimony apply. Discuss how this proposal would change Tusconna's law and assess its merits.

ANSWER TO SAMPLE EXAM QUESTION I

(a) **Manager's Testimony**

Relevance: No one would dispute a finding that the testimony is relevant, because it logically tends to prove that the missing calculator was stolen and not sold.

Hearsay: An out-of-court statement offered to prove the truth of the matter asserted is, as a general rule, inadmissible hearsay because it lacks trustworthiness. Here, Manager is testifying as to the *absence* of a specific entry to prove that no entry was made and that therefore the item in question was not sold. Technically, therefore, it would appear that hearsay concerns are not involved because there is no "statement." Even so, most courts have subjected the absence of business entries to the same hearsay rules that govern affirmative business record assertions.

Assuming the evidence is hearsay, it will nevertheless be admissible if it falls within the *business records exception* to the rule. Under modern codes (and the Federal Rules), evidence of the absence of a business record is admissible to prove the nonoccurrence of an event if such events would ordinarily have been recorded in the regular course of business. Manager's testimony clearly satisfies this limitation; sales of the item in question *are* normally recorded in the ordinary course of business. Accordingly, if the other foundational requirements are met—*e.g.*, if the record has been properly authenticated and the clerk making the entries had personal knowledge of the facts—the hearsay problem has been overcome.

Best evidence rule: The major problem is that Manager is testifying as to the *contents* of a document without producing the record itself or accounting for its nonproduction. Thus, his testimony violates the best evidence rule (under which the original must be used to prove the contents of a writing unless shown to be unavailable) and should be ruled inadmissible.

(b) **Clerk's Testimony**

Relevance: The clerk's testimony is relevant because it shows that the calculator was missing at the time in question *and* it tends to prove a tacit admission of guilt.

Of course, the court might use its discretionary power to exclude the evidence if it finds that the probative dangers outweigh the probative value. For instance, if Dan and Ellen did not hear the clerk, the fact that they boarded a bus at the time in question loses its probative impact; indeed, the evidence might be prejudicial. However, the court's discretion is quite broad here and a decision to admit the evidence as relevant would probably not be reversed.

Hearsay: Although made out of court, the clerk's statement, "Hey, come back!" is not hearsay because it is being used only to show the *effect* on Dan and Ellen and not to prove its truth. However, in some jurisdictions (but not under the Federal Rules), the testimony regarding Dan's and Ellen's flight from Store would be hearsay—*i.e.*, nonassertive conduct manifesting the declarants' belief that they were guilty and offered to prove their guilt. Even so, the evidence is within the *admissions exception* to the hearsay rule and is therefore admissible.

(c) Wat's Testimony

Relevance: Here the prosecution is attempting to introduce evidence of similar misconduct by the defendants. The major problem is whether this is a proper use of character evidence; *i.e.*, can such evidence be used as an item of proof?

As a general rule, the prosecution cannot, as part of its case-in-chief, offer evidence designed solely to establish that the defendants have a "bad" character for the particular trait in question and therefore probably committed the crime with which they are charged. Accordingly, if Wat's testimony is being used only to show that Dan and Ellen had the propensity to shoplift and therefore most likely did so on the occasion in question, it should be ruled inadmissible.

Notwithstanding the above, evidence of past misconduct may be admissible if shown to have some *independent relevancy—i.e.,* if it does more than simply prove the defendants had a criminal propensity. Here, the prosecution can argue that the evidence is admissible (1) to prove absence of mistake (the fact that Dan and Ellen took merchandise before tends to prove that the present act was intentionally committed and was not inadvertent or accidental); (2) to prove a distinctive method of operation that earmarks the present crime as having been committed by Dan and Ellen; and (3) to show that the present act was part of a common scheme or plan.

As to all three of the above points, the evidence is somewhat probative. However, it is also prejudicial in that the jury may be unable to separate the question of past misconduct from the question of present misconduct and may convict the defendants simply because they have demonstrated dishonest characters. In addition, the tangled web of issues that Wat's testimony introduces may be too time-consuming—*i.e.,* the court may find itself trying two theft cases instead of one. Thus, the matter is ultimately one of judicial discretion; although the evidence is technically admissible, it may properly be ruled inadmissible on the basis of its probative danger.

(d) Ellen as a Witness

Privilege: Since Ellen has not yet begun to testify, the issue is whether she can be prevented from testifying at all on the basis of a marital privilege. In *traditional* jurisdictions, a party-spouse can prevent the other spouse from testifying against him in a criminal case. From the facts given, it is unclear what Ellen's testimony was going to be. Assuming she was going to testify "against" Dan, the matter would appear to be straightforward—*i.e.,* since Dan and Ellen are presently married, Dan properly asserted the privilege and Ellen should not be allowed to take the stand.

However, the issue is not that easily resolved: Dan's assertion of the privilege directly conflicts with Ellen's *constitutional right* as an accused to take the stand in her own defense. Thus, the court must either permit her to take the stand or declare a mistrial and order a severance of the cases.

Note: Under the California Evidence Code and *Trammel v. United States*, the privilege belongs only to the witness-spouse. Thus in California (and some other states) and in the federal courts, Dan's objection would have to be overruled and Ellen can proceed with her testimony.

ANSWER TO SAMPLE EXAM QUESTION II

(a) (1) **Motion to Produce Diary**

Where a witness is asked to testify concerning a matter as to which he has no present recollection, he may refer to anything else to refresh his memory. Under the Federal Rules, if extrinsic evidence is so used while the witness is testifying, the opposing party has an absolute right to have that evidence produced and to inspect it (unless of course it is privileged). However, where as here, the same is done *before* the witness testifies, there is no absolute right to compel production of the evidence to which the witness referred; the matter is one of judicial discretion. Here, the court exercised its discretion in favor of denying the motion to produce, and no good reason appears to find an abuse of that discretion. Hence, if the court is bound by the Federal Rules, its ruling on the motion should be upheld.

Other jurisdictions, however, have a *mandatory* rule of production; it is immaterial whether reference was made to the extrinsic matter before or while testifying. If the court is bound by such a rule, it has clearly made an erroneous ruling; no good reason appears why the diary could not be produced (the facts state that Ron has the diary at his home and so it is procurable). Therefore, Ron's testimony should be stricken from the record.

(2) **Hal's Testimony**

Relevance: Hal's testimony is relevant because it logically tends to support Paula's apparent contention that Lola's fall was occasioned by heat prostration and that she did not take her own life.

Opinion: Generally, lay witnesses can testify only as to *facts* they have perceived and in so doing must refrain from giving testimony in the form of an opinion or conclusion. The rationale is that the drawing of inferences from facts observed is a function solely for the trier of fact.

However, lay opinion is admissible in the discretion of the court if it is (1) rationally based on the witness's personal observation of the facts, and (2) helpful to a clearer understanding of the witness's testimony (*i.e.*, if opinion is realistically the only clear way the witness can testify as to the facts perceived). Hal's opinion regarding the temperature would appear to qualify under this exception: He was present at the time of Lola's fall, and there is arguably no better way for him to testify as to the climate (any other form of testimony would be very time-consuming and no doubt confusing). Thus, the court was correct in overruling Insco's objection.

Med's Testimony

Opinion: As discussed above, opinion testimony is generally inadmissible. However, *experts* may testify by way of opinion if the matter in question is a proper subject for expert testimony, the witness is qualified as an expert, the testimony is properly elicited, and the witness bases her testimony on proper information.

Here, the facts state that Med is a "qualified medical witness"; moreover, medical testimony regarding causation is generally held a proper subject of expert opinion. And Med was asked to base her opinion on proper information—*i.e.*, evidence in the case. The major issue then, is whether the testimony has been properly elicited. Since Med apparently did not have firsthand knowledge of the facts, many jurisdictions would require that her testimony be elicited by means of a hypothetical question, specifying the evidence she was considering in forming her opinion. However, modern courts permit this to be developed on cross-examination and allow the testimony to be based on evidence already introduced. Since this is what Med was asked to do, the court acted properly in admitting her testimony.

Fred's Testimony

Relevance: The evidence is clearly relevant as tending to support Insco's position. And while the time that Lola made the statement does affect its probative value, a one-month time differential does not make the evidence so far removed from the event in question as to make it irrelevant as a matter of law. Rather, this factor should more properly bear on the weight to be accorded the evidence than its admissibility.

Hearsay: Although Fred is testifying to Lola's out-of-court statement offered for its truth, the court properly admitted the evidence under the state of mind exception to the hearsay rule. Lola's statement is in the nature of an intent to do a future act (kill herself) and is admissible as tending to show that she did that act.

U.S. Weather Bureau Record

Relevance: The Weather Bureau record is relevant both for purposes of impeaching Hal's prior testimony by contradictory evidence and as tending to prove that Lola did not fall because of heat prostration. The fact that the station was 45 miles from the scene of the occurrence should not affect the record's admissibility but only bear on the weight it is to be given by the trier of fact. At the very least, the issue was one of judicial discretion, and here, the court exercised its discretion in favor of admitting the record.

Hearsay; best evidence rule: As an item of proof, the record is clearly hearsay. However, it is admissible under the official records exception, and the properly authenticated copy satisfies the best evidence rule. Therefore, Paula's objection was correctly overruled.

(b) Propriety of Jury Instruction

Whether the jury instruction was proper depends on the effect of the presumption against suicide once rebuttal evidence is introduced. In some jurisdictions, a presumption *disappears* upon introduction of evidence sufficient to sustain a contrary finding; a preponderance of evidence to the contrary is *not* required. If the court is in such a jurisdiction, its instruction was *improper*. Both Fred's testimony and the Weather Bureau record reduced the presumption to a mere inference, which the jury should have been free to draw or disregard in light of the evidence introduced by Insco.

Other jurisdictions, however, hold that a presumption does not vanish upon introduction of rebuttal evidence. Rather, it remains in the case until the opponent produces evidence sufficient to *persuade* the jury that the counterevidence, rather than the presumption, is true. Thus, if a preponderance of the evidence as to the nonexistence of the presumed fact is not produced, the party in whose favor the presumption operates is entitled to a jury instruction in his favor on the issue. Accordingly, if the court is in this type of jurisdiction, its instruction was correct—*i.e.*, the burden of persuasion was properly placed on Insco.

ANSWER TO SAMPLE EXAM QUESTION III

(a) **Question Put to Prospective Jurors**

Most courts would hold the question asked of the prospective jurors a proper one, since an affirmative answer would tend to show bias in favor of Mutual (and hence, Dave). Admittedly, the question alerts the jury to the fact that there is insurance in the case and thus violates the extrinsic policy against admitting evidence that a party is or is not insured. However, the policy is most probably outweighed by the danger of potential juror prejudice. Moreover, it is doubtful that alluding to the fact that insurance is involved will be very prejudicial, since the probability of insurance protection is now commonplace knowledge in automobile accident cases (either because required by law or because any defendant solvent enough to pay damages would also be prudent enough to carry insurance).

(b) **Al's Testimony**

Relevance: The fact that Dave's mother fainted when asked if Dave had a purple jacket with a fur collar operates as an implied acknowledgment on her part that Dave indeed did own such a jacket. Moreover, it tends to infer an acknowledgment of her son's culpability. Thus, while the defense may contend that the mother's response could mean many other things unconnected with the issues in the case, it is clear that her conduct does have probative value and is relevant as tending to prove Dave's connection with the incident.

Hearsay: Although Al is testifying as to someone's out-of-court conduct, under modern formulations of the hearsay rule, the mother's reaction is *not* hearsay because it is not a "statement." It is simply nonassertive conduct from which an inference can be drawn. Therefore, assuming the court is bound by this formulation of the rule, it correctly overruled Dave's objection.

On the other hand, some jurisdictions classify nonassertive conduct as hearsay if it manifests the actor's belief that a certain fact is true and it is offered to prove that fact. Here, as indicated above, the mother's fainting is being used to show that Dave owned a jacket fitting the description given by Patti and that therefore he was culpable. Hence, the evidence is hearsay in these jurisdictions and inadmissible because not within any exception. If the court was subject to this approach to the rule, its ruling on the evidence was incorrect.

(c) **Judgment of Acquittal**

Relevance: Although Dave would contend that the judgment of acquittal is clearly relevant to prove that he was not the driver who injured Patti, most courts would disagree. The theory is that such a judgment is not necessarily proof of innocence but merely establishes that the prosecution did not prove its case beyond a reasonable doubt. This does not preclude a finding of guilt in a civil trial because a lower evidentiary standard governs civil cases.

Hearsay: In addition, the judgment is hearsay (an out-of-court statement offered for its truth) and should have been ruled inadmissible on that ground, there being no applicable exception. In short, the court acted improperly in overruling Patti's objection to this evidence.

(d) **Dr. Bene's Testimony**

Relevance: Dr. Bene's testimony as to Patti's acknowledgment of childhood headaches is relevant on the issues of causation and damages; *i.e.*, it indicates that the headaches she now complains of were not caused by the hit-and-run accident and at the very least bears on the damages recoverable.

Hearsay: Although the out-of-court statement is offered for its truth, the evidence is admissible as an admission by a party-opponent. Moreover, under the Federal Rules, it is nonhearsay because it is an admission. Thus, it is not objectionable on hearsay grounds.

Privilege: A contention by Patti that her statement to Dr. Bene is protected by the physician-patient privilege must fail. Even assuming the statement was made in the strictest confidence, the privilege is waived when the holder puts her physical condition in issue (as Patti did here by suing for personal injuries). Accordingly, Patti's objection was properly overruled.

ANSWER TO SAMPLE EXAM QUESTION IV

(a) **Motion to Quash**

Attorney-client privilege: The fact that a client's preexisting records are in the custody of an attorney does not bring them within the attorney-client privilege; a preexisting record does not become a confidential communication simply because it is turned over to an attorney. And while some courts have held that a preexisting record in the custody of an attorney will be privileged if it was privileged in the hands of the client, the records here were *not* privileged while in X Corporation's possession.

Privilege against self-incrimination: Production of the records would not violate the privilege against self-incrimination. First of all, only *natural persons* may claim the privilege; a corporation cannot claim it in its own right. Nor could Mr. X himself claim the privilege. Recent Supreme Court decisions indicate that a person's private records and documents (assuming the records in question were "private") are no longer protected by the privilege, the theory being that a subpoena to produce does not amount to *testimonial* compulsion. Thus, the court correctly denied the motion to quash the subpoena.

(b) **Attorney's Testimony**

Hearsay: Although the attorney is being asked to testify as to an out-of-court statement (the records) to prove its truth, the evidence is admissible as an admission (having been made by X Corporation and being offered against it) or under the business records exception to the hearsay rule (assuming the record is properly authenticated).

Best evidence rule: Ordinarily, to prove the *contents* of a writing, the original must be produced. However, secondary evidence is admissible where, as in this case, the original has been destroyed. The fact that the attorney destroyed the records herself—even if she did so fraudulently—does not preclude the use of secondary evidence by the *opposing* party (here, the prosecution).

Although there may be some question as to whether the attorney's oral testimony is proper secondary evidence, there is no indication that a copy of the records was available to the prosecution. Moreover, under the Federal Rules, there are no "rules of preference"; the proponent may offer any kind of secondary evidence. The court correctly overruled the objection to the attorney's testimony.

X's Offer of Proof

Relevance: Mr. X's proffered testimony would be relevant to infer his displeasure with the attorney who destroyed the records and thus tend to prove that the records would have been favorable to the defense. At the very least, the testimony might negate the inference the jury might earlier have drawn that X had authorized the attorney to destroy the records and that, therefore, the records were damaging to X Corporation.

Hearsay: Although X's proffered testimony concerns nonassertive conduct, some jurisdictions would regard it as hearsay on the theory that it manifests his belief that the records were favorable and the evidence is being offered to prove just that. Moreover, the testimony is self-serving and thus carries an inherent danger of untrustworthiness; X has a strong interest in introducing evidence of his own innocence and thus might be prone to manufacturing evidence.

However, under modern formulations of the hearsay rule, the proffered testimony is not objectionable hearsay because nonassertive conduct, even though occurring out of court, is not a "statement." Assuming the court is in a jurisdiction following this approach, its ruling was correct.

Prosecution's Offer of Proof

Relevance: The relevance of the proffered evidence is clear: It creates an inference of a consciousness of guilt on X's part and is circumstantial evidence that the records were indeed damaging.

Hearsay: Although hearsay in many jurisdictions—because the statement manifests X's belief that X Corporation is guilty and it is offered to prove just that—the statement is admissible as an admission.

Privilege: The major issue is whether the evidence is protected by the attorney-client privilege. If the court's ruling sustaining the objection was proper, it must have been because it found that: (i) an attorney-client relationship still existed between X and the attorney, and (ii) the communication was confidential. However, these two findings are questionable.

First of all, X had previously offered to prove that he had terminated the Corporation's relationship with the attorney. Hence, if this is true, the communication cannot be protected as one between the corporation and its attorney. And although there is a possibility that the attorney was X's own private counsel, nothing in the facts so indicates.

Secondly, whether the communication was "confidential" is arguable. The fact that it was overheard does not automatically negate a finding of confidentiality. However, the fact that the statement was made in the hall, as opposed to private quarters, weighs against a finding of confidentiality (although the statement was of a type that one would expect should be kept secret).

On balance, given the serious doubt as to the existence of an attorney-client relationship, it appears that the court improperly sustained the objection.

(c) **Prosecution's Final Argument**

The prosecution was most probably correctly allowed to proceed with its final argument. Since the records were not privileged, the failure to produce them after a proper subpoena can be made a matter of comment to the jury. In other words, since the defendant's assertion of the privilege against self-incrimination was improper, the prosecution is not precluded from commenting about the inferences that can be drawn, particularly where the inference is supported by evidence in the case.

ANSWER TO SAMPLE EXAM QUESTION V

(a) (1) **Abel's Testimony**

Opinion: As a general rule, lay testimony in the form of an opinion is forbidden, the theory being that the drawing of inferences from facts observed (by way of opinion and conclusion) is a function of the trier of fact. However, this rule is subject to several exceptions, including handwriting identification: If a lay witness is shown to be sufficiently familiar with a person's handwriting, the witness's opinion is admissible to identify that handwriting. Since Abel testified that he had seen Dan's signature "hundreds of times," a proper foundation has been laid for his opinion testimony and the objection was properly overruled.

(2) **Cross-Examination of Abel**

Relevance: Although the question does not directly bear on issues going to the merits of the case, it is relevant as tending to show bias on Abel's part. Once Abel took the stand he put his credibility in issue, and evidence that Peter was suing Abel's employer may tend to show that Abel had reason to slant his testimony against Peter.

However, given the fact that Peter's suit is not against Abel himself, the inference of bias that can be drawn is weak at best. Moreover, whether an item of evidence is relevant is largely a matter of judicial discretion. Admissibility must be determined by weighing the probative value against the probative dangers (*e.g.,* potential for confusion of issues, undue waste of time, etc.). Given the relatively weak probative value of the evidence and the strong possibility that the jury may be unduly confused by collateral issues, it would not appear that the court has abused its discretion by choosing to exclude the evidence.

(3) **Cross-Examination of Dan**

Relevance: Dan's response to Peter's accusatory statement is relevant if the response qualifies as an admission. In other words, if a court finds that Dan heard and understood Peter's accusation and that a reasonable person under the circumstances would have made a denial, Dan's silence (or evasive reply) is relevant as an implied admission that the signature was his (*see* Hearsay discussion below).

Hearsay: Peter's statement is not hearsay because it is not offered for its truth but only to lend significance to Dan's reaction. On the other hand, Dan's response would be regarded as hearsay by most courts. It may be treated either as assertive conduct (if shrugging his shoulders is equated with acquiescence in Peter's accusation) or as an admission by silence (if it is found that a reasonable person would have denied the accusation). As an admission, however, Dan's response is admissible under the admissions exception to the hearsay rule. Indeed, under the Federal Rules, it is treated as nonhearsay.

Form of the question: Despite the foregoing discussions, which indicate that the court made a proper ruling, there is a serious problem in this case with the form of the question. Clearly, it is not objectionable simply because suggestive of the answer, since Dan is an adverse party. However, it is properly objectionable as a ***compound question***; *i.e.*, Dan is being asked to answer two questions by a single answer. Accordingly, the court should have sustained the objection and asked counsel to rephrase his question.

(4) **Row's Testimony**

Competency to testify: An objection that Row is incompetent to testify because he is representing Peter in the case must fail. Although an attorney who is called as a witness for his client may be violating professional ethics standards if he continues to handle the case, he is nevertheless a competent witness.

Hearsay: The hearsay objection is overcome much the same as it was on cross-examination of Dan. In short, the evidence is admissible because (1) Peter's accusation is not hearsay, and (2) Dan's response is an implied admission. Moreover, the evidence may also be admissible to ***impeach*** Dan by a prior inconsistent statement, as he has just testified in court that the signature on the contract was not his. A proper foundation has already been laid during cross-examination of Dan. Accordingly, Row's testimony was properly received into evidence.

(b) **Propriety of Jury Instruction**

The propriety of the instruction given the jury turns on what is meant by "presumptions affecting the burden of producing evidence." Had this been a presumption affecting the burden of persuasion, the instruction would have been correct; *i.e.*, Peter would be entitled to a ruling in his favor unless the jury was convinced by a preponderance of the evidence that the signature was not Dan's. However, the result is otherwise where, as here, the presumption affects only the burden of producing evidence. Once evidence has been introduced sufficient to sustain a contrary finding (as it was in this case in light of Abel's and Dan's testimony), the presumption is reduced to a mere ***inference***, which the jury is free to draw or disregard. It does not stay in the case as a presumption and does ***not*** shift the burden of persuasion. Therefore, given the jurisdiction's Evidence Code, the court should not have instructed the jury as it did.

ANSWER TO SAMPLE EXAM QUESTION VI

(a) (1) **Dr. Ash's Testimony**

Relevance: A proffered item of evidence is relevant if it logically tends to prove a fact properly in issue. Here, Dr. Ash's testimony is relevant as tending to prove not only that David had no prescription for the M, but also that he therefore had the drug for the purpose of selling it and not for his personal use. In other words, the testimony is relevant to support application of the presumption.

Privilege: An objection based on the physician-patient privilege must be overruled. First of all, in the majority of jurisdictions, the privilege is inapplicable in criminal proceedings. Of greater significance, however, is the fact that the privilege protects only confidential *communications* between doctor and patient; here, Dr. Ash is not testifying as to a communication. Therefore, the court correctly overruled the objection.

(2) **Watson's Testimony**

Relevance: Watson's testimony would appear relevant in that it creates an inference that if David sold dangerous drugs in the past, he more than likely had M for purposes of sale at the time in question. However, there is a serious problem with admissibility on public policy grounds. The testimony is a form of *character evidence* concerning an alleged act of similar misconduct on a prior occasion. Generally, such evidence cannot be introduced by the prosecution as part of its case-in-chief to show that because the accused has perpetrated similar acts he had a propensity to commit the crime in question. The theory is that to hold otherwise would create serious dangers of undue prejudice; for instance, the jury might be inclined to convict the defendant on the basis of his past misconduct alone.

Notwithstanding the general rule, character evidence of the type in question is admissible if it has some *independent relevancy*—*i.e.*, if it is being used to show something other than the fact that the accused had a criminal propensity. Arguably here, the evidence tends to prove absence of inadvertence or mistake; *i.e.*, it shows that David did not come by the drug without knowing what it was, but acted purposefully and intentionally. Moreover, his possession of a dangerous drug a year ago may be indicative of a common scheme or plan. Accordingly, the court could have been properly convinced that the evidence did have independent relevancy, and therefore it acted correctly in overruling the objection on relevancy grounds.

Hearsay: Watson's testimony regarding Bertha's out-of-court statement is hearsay in that it is offered for its truth. Arguably, it is admissible under the dying declarations exception to the hearsay rule as it appears clearly to have been made under a sense of impending death ("after receiving last rites"). However, there is one major problem: Traditionally, the exception is applicable only to criminal homicide cases; and while the Federal Rules admit dying declarations in all civil cases, in criminal cases the Rules follow the homicide-charge limitation. Therefore, unless this court is subject to the few broader evidence codes that admit dying declarations in all cases, it should have excluded the evidence as inadmissible hearsay.

(3) **Cross-Examination of Watson**

Admissibility for purposes of impeachment: Whenever a witness takes the stand, he puts his character for truth and veracity in issue, and he can therefore be impeached by showing that he had a "bad" character regarding those traits. Moreover, a witness can also be impeached by a showing of bias—*i.e.*, that he had reason to distort his testimony for or against a party. The fact that David previously testified against Watson clearly indicates that Watson had an ulterior motive to fabricate evidence against David and thus is quite relevant on the issue of bias. Further, Watson's indictment for bribery bears on the issue of his truth and veracity as a witness (*i.e.*, whether his present testimony should be believed). The problem, however, is that Watson apparently was not *convicted* of the crime. Although a criminal conviction is admissible for impeachment purposes, ordinarily, a mere showing of *indictment* is not. Additionally, not all courts allow impeachment by inquiry into specific acts of misconduct. Thus, while that part of the question going to Watson's bias was not objectionable, the portion bearing on his indictment was.

Form of the question: Notwithstanding the above discussion, the court correctly sustained the objection because the defense asked a *compound question*; it improperly asked Watson to give a single answer to two questions.

(b) Propriety of Jury Instruction

Even assuming that the presumption is constitutional (*i.e.*, that it can be said with substantial assurance that the presumed fact more likely than not flows from the proved facts), the instruction given the jury was not correct. Despite the varying theories as to the effect of presumptions in civil cases, it is clear that in a criminal case a presumption cannot be used to shift the burden of persuasion. Thus, although the jury could properly have been authorized to find in accordance with the presumption, it should not have been instructed to change the burden of persuasion—the presumption is not a substitute for the prosecution's obligation to prove its case beyond a reasonable doubt.

ANSWER TO SAMPLE EXAM QUESTION VII

(a) Transcript of Dr. Mobed's Testimony

Relevance: The testimony in the transcript is relevant as tending to prove that Percy's claim against Chemicals is without merit. It is direct evidence on the issue of whether Percy's condition was in fact caused by fumes from Chemicals's plant.

Hearsay: Since the transcript is an out-of-court statement offered to prove its truth, it is hearsay. However, the evidence appears admissible under the *former testimony exception* to the hearsay rule. Under that exception, testimony given at a former proceeding is admissible if (1) the witness is presently unavailable to testify; (2) the testimony was given under oath and the opposing party was given the opportunity to cross-examine; (3) there is sufficient identity of parties; and (4) there is sufficient identity of issues.

Here, Dr. Mobed is "unavailable" because he is beyond the subpoena power of the court. Moreover, there is no problem with the oath, cross-examination, or identity of issues requirements. There is some question, however, as to whether there is sufficient identity of parties. Traditionally *both* the proponent of the evidence and his adversary in the present case must have been parties to the former proceeding. Under the Federal Rules, former testimony is admissible if the party against whom the testimony is offered was a *party* or *predecessor in interest* to the former proceeding. In this case, Percy was not a party or predecessor in interest to the prior suit. Hence, in jurisdictions strictly following the traditional approach or the literal Federal Rules approach, the transcript would be inadmissible hearsay. However, under some modern codes, it is sufficient if the adverse party in the former action had a similar interest and motive to cross-examine as does the adverse party in the present proceeding. Arguably, a strong case can be made that the employee who brought the earlier suit had motives and interests identical to those of Percy. Accordingly, courts subject to modern codes would probably overrule a hearsay objection.

Opinion: Arguably, Dr. Mobed's former testimony is nothing more than an opinion and inadmissible as such. Generally, testimony in the form of an opinion is forbidden, the theory being that it is within the exclusive province of the trier of fact to form opinions and conclusions from the facts presented in the case. However, this objection can be overcome on two grounds. First of all, most courts hold that counsel in the present case cannot object to former testimony on the ground that it was a statement of opinion. However, even assuming an opinion objection would otherwise be allowed, experts may testify by way of opinion provided the matter is a proper subject of expert opinion and the witness is qualified as an expert. Here, there would appear to be no problem, since Dr. Mobed is a "recognized expert" and the subject matter is not one of common lay knowledge. Of course, Chemicals would also have to prove that Dr. Mobed based his opinion on proper information (*i.e.*, personal knowledge and/or a reliable source); assuming it did so, the opinion would be admissible.

(b) **Baker's Testimony**

Relevance: Relevance is not a problem since the testimony regarding the density of the smoke bears on the issue of whether the plant emissions were hazardous to health.

Hearsay: The major problem with the evidence is that its relevance turns on the testimony of Carl, since Baker does not remember what the readings were. Thus, if Carl must testify as to what Baker said out of court, that testimony will be hearsay and inadmissible because not within any exception. (Since there is apparently no record of the readings, the past recollection recorded and business records exceptions are not on point.)

Notwithstanding the above, arguably the problem can be overcome if Baker can *refresh her memory* and thus testify from *present recollection*. Generally, when a witness has no present recollection she may refer to anything to refresh her memory. If the item referred to does refresh her memory, so that she can testify on the basis of present recollection, there is no hearsay problem. Accordingly, Baker could consult Carl and presumably testify as to what the readings were. Moreover, since Carl is available to testify, there would be no problem with the opposing party's right to "inspect" the source used to refresh the witness's memory. Carl's testimony for this purpose would not be hearsay because it would not be offered to prove the truth of what Baker said to him but only to satisfy the procedural rules governing the use of extrinsic evidence to refresh a witness's memory. Thus, following the "refreshed memory" theory, this item of evidence would be admissible.

(c) **Certified Copy of Circular**

Relevance: Clearly, the circular is relevant because it explains the Ringleman Chart, which is properly in issue, assuming Baker's testimony regarding the Ringleman readings is admitted into evidence.

Hearsay: The circular is subject to the hearsay rule, because it is an out-of-court statement offered for its truth. However, assuming it was compiled by the U.S. Bureau of Mines as well as published by that agency, it is admissible under the ***official records exception*** to the rule. The fact that no one from the Bureau will be available to testify is immaterial, since as a public record, the publication need not be authenticated. Alternatively, modern codes recognize a hearsay exception for published compilations (learned treatises) generally relied upon as accurate by persons in the field. Although it is not known whether the circular is generally relied upon in the field, the facts state that the Ringleman Chart itself is a "universally accepted standard for measuring smoke emission." Arguably, then, the circular itself is similarly accepted as reliable, so that this exception to the rule would also be applicable.

Best evidence rule: Although the original of the circular is not being offered, there is no problem with the best evidence rule; the rule does not apply to public records where a certified copy is available.

(d) Ed's Motion Pictures

Relevance: Ed's film is relevant as bearing both on the merits of Percy's claim and on the issue of damages. If he was in fact engaging in "strenuous physical activity" after initiating the suit, arguably he did not suffer disabling lung damage at all or, at the very least, the injury was only of a temporary nature and the damages to be awarded should be negligible.

Authentication: The major problem is whether the film can be properly authenticated; *i.e.*, it must be shown that the film is genuine and what it purports to be. Since Ed is now deceased, he is clearly unavailable to perform the authentication function. The film can be authenticated only by someone with personal knowledge of the scene depicted who can testify that the film accurately represents what he saw. Admissibility therefore turns on the procurement of such testimony.

(e) Darcy's Sworn Statement

Relevance: Darcy's statement is relevant to show that the injuries Percy allegedly suffered were not caused by Chemicals's fumes at all.

Hearsay: The pivotal issue regarding admissibility is that the out-of-court statement is hearsay. Hence, even assuming Darcy changes her story in court, the statement cannot be admitted as an ***item of proof*** because, traditionally, it is not within any exception to the hearsay rule.

However, if Darcy changes her story on the stand, the evidence will most probably be admissible as a prior inconsistent statement to ***impeach*** her. Although some courts still adhere to the common law rule against impeaching one's own witness, the modern trend adheres to no such limitation. Moreover, if the statement is admissible for impeachment purposes, under modern evidence codes it might also be admissible as an item of proof—*i.e.*, within an exception to the hearsay rule. The Federal Rules follow this approach—indeed, the Rules classify the statement as nonhearsay—but require that it have been given under oath at a prior proceeding or in a deposition. While Darcy did give a "sworn statement," it is questionable whether such a statement given to an investigator would qualify.

ANSWER TO SAMPLE EXAM QUESTION VIII

(a) **Prudent's Testimony**

Relevance: No one would argue that the testimony regarding Carpenter's statement was irrelevant. It undeniably tends to support P's position that the ladder was negligently manufactured.

Hearsay: Since Prudent is testifying as to Carpenter's out-of-court statement, which is being offered to prove the truth of the matter asserted, the evidence is hearsay and therefore inadmissible unless within a recognized exception to the hearsay rule. Arguably, there are three applicable exceptions:

(1) **Excited Utterance:** A statement made under the stress of an exciting event by one who has been involved in or who has observed that event is admissible. The theory is that the shock of the event guarantees the trustworthiness of the statement; there is said to be no opportunity for the reasoned reflection which might otherwise lead to deliberate fabrication.

Here, there was a startling event preceding Carpenter's statement—the fall. However, there is some question as to whether the time lapse between the fall and the statement was such that Carpenter had the opportunity to reflect and fabricate. Because the statement came in response to a question, an argument can be made that it was not the product of excitement but of the question. Of course, an argument can be made that "blurted" responses made under stress should qualify, but here again, the question turns on whether Carpenter was in fact still influenced by the "excitement" when he spoke. Given the ambiguity in the facts as to just what the time interval was, the issue is debatable, and a finding either way would probably be upheld.

(2) **Present sense impression:** An argument might be advanced that the evidence should be received under the present sense impression exception to the rule as a statement describing the declarant's impression of an event he is then witnessing. However, this theory is weak at best. First of all, not all courts recognize the exception; and while it is adopted by the Federal Rules, the requirements are strict. Specifically, the statement must have been made while the declarant was perceiving the event or immediately thereafter. Here, given the apparent interval of time between the fall and Prudent's arrival on the scene when she questioned Carpenter, it is unlikely that this exception would be held applicable.

(3) **Dying declaration:** If it can be shown that Carpenter spoke under a fear of impending death, the evidence can be introduced under the dying declarations exception. Although at common law the exception only applies in criminal homicide cases, modern evidence codes (and the Federal Rules) extend the exception to all civil cases. The major problem here, however, is that it is not enough to show that Carpenter in fact died soon after speaking. It is the *consciousness* of impending death that guarantees trustworthiness, and the facts are not clear as to just what Carpenter was thinking. Again, a finding either way would probably be reasonable. Accordingly, the court's ruling should be upheld.

(b) **Copy of Death Certificate**

Relevance: Clearly, this item is relevant as tending to prove that the ladder was defective, the crucial issue in the case.

Best evidence rule: A best evidence objection is without merit, because even though the proffered death certificate is not the original, certified copies of public records satisfy the rule.

Hearsay: As an out-of-court "statement" offered for its truth, the death certificate is hearsay but arguably admissible under the *official records exception* to the hearsay rule. However, the facts raise a major problem with admissibility. Such records are said to carry an inherent element of trustworthiness only if the person who made the record had *personal knowledge* of the facts recorded; a record stating mere opinions or conclusions, or reports given the entrant by others will not suffice. Alternatively, if the record is not based on the entrant's personal knowledge, it must be shown that he was under a public duty to accurately report the facts. It is doubtful under these facts that the person who made the record had personal knowledge that the rung of the ladder broke (it can be deduced from the fact that the public employee was not at the scene of the accident); indeed, the record was probably based on the hearsay statements of others. Presumably, since the court sustained the objection, it also found that it was not within the scope of the entrant's duties to report the cause of the injury; or, alternatively, it found that the matter was only conjecture and not a report of facts at all. Accordingly, the evidence was properly excluded as inadmissible hearsay.

(c) **Dr. Dixit's Testimony**

Relevance: Dr. Dixit's testimony is relevant, and indeed crucial to P's case, because it bears on whether the ladder was broken before Carpenter's fall. Since the ambulance virtually destroyed the direct evidence on this issue, testimony such as Dr. Dixit's takes on added importance.

Opinion: As a general rule, testimony in the form of an opinion is inadmissible, the theory being that the drawing of inferences from facts presented in the case by way of opinion and conclusion is a function of the trier of fact. Qualified experts may give opinion testimony, however, if the subject is appropriate for expert opinion and if the opinion is properly elicited and based on proper information.

The facts indicate that Dr. Dixit is a qualified expert and that the matter is appropriate for expert opinion (since the subjects of strength of materials and accident reconstruction are not ones of common lay knowledge). However, some jurisdictions adhere to the traditional limitation that the opinion must be elicited by a hypothetical question directing the expert's attention to facts already received into evidence. Such was not the case here. Nevertheless, modern courts allow the witness to base his opinion on outside sources if those materials are of a type reasonably relied on by other experts in the field in forming opinions; moreover, the underlying facts supporting the opinion need not be admissible evidence. Assuming the court is subject to an evidence code that adopts this more liberal approach, and that the information Dr. Dixit relied on (police report, wood fiber analysis report, etc.) was found to be accepted for such purpose in the field, it correctly overruled D's objection.

(d) **Barber's Testimony**

Relevance: Barber's testimony is relevant on the issue of whether the accident was in fact occasioned by a defect in the ladder. In other words, the evidence operates to negate the merits of P's position.

Hearsay: Since Barber is testifying as to what Hood told him out of court and the statement is being offered for its truth, it is hearsay. Consequently, it should have been ruled inadmissible unless within the ***declarations against interest exception*** to the hearsay rule.

The major issues are whether Hood is "unavailable to testify" within the meaning of the exception, and whether the statement is sufficiently "against his interest" (it is this latter element that is said to guarantee the trustworthiness of the statement). The unavailability limitation is easily overcome since, although Hood is physically present in court, he has exempted himself from testifying by assertion of the privilege against self-incrimination. A more serious problem is presented, however, by the fact that traditionally, declarations against interest have been restricted to those against ***pecuniary*** or ***proprietary*** interests. Arguably, Hood's statement was against his pecuniary interest when made because it might well form the basis of a wrongful death action and therefore prejudice him in a monetary sense. Assuming this theory fails, modern codes also recognize declarations against ***penal*** interest; clearly, the statement subjected Hood to a risk of criminal liability when made and is therefore within the modern scope of the exception. Accordingly, relying on either of the above two theories, the court properly admitted Barber's testimony.

(e) **Cross-Examination of Barber**

Form of the question: Although the question put to Barber bears on his credibility as a witness and is therefore relevant for impeachment purposes, the court properly acted within its discretion in sustaining D's objection. It was the form of the question, and not the testimony it called for, that was objectionable. Specifically, the question was ***argumentative***—*i.e.,* it was an attempt to lure Barber into an argument and most probably would not have advanced the course of the trial. Moreover, it improperly reflected the cross-examiner's interpretation of the facts; although Barber had "difficulty" remembering anything else that happened on the day in question, it was only the cross-examiner's opinion that Barber could not remember "***anything else***" that happened that day.

ANSWER TO SAMPLE EXAM QUESTION IX

(a) **Heroin Evidence**

Donna (defendant)

Because Donna is not testifying, the evidence relating to her heroin involvement cannot be used to impeach her under Federal Rule 608. Rule 608 allows a ***witness's*** credibility to be attacked with evidence of untruthful character.

However, evidence of Donna's addiction to heroin may be admissible under Federal Rule 404(b) to show a motive for the robbery. Rule 404(b) will admit evidence of other crimes, wrongs, or acts for a purpose other than proving character, such as proving motive. The value of the evidence for this purpose would depend on the cost of Donna's addiction and the resources available to her to pay for it. Even if some degree of financial need could be shown, a judge might exclude the evidence under Rule 403 because of the danger of prejudice. If the evidence of addiction is admitted, the evidence of ***drug dealing*** should be ***excluded*** on the ground that it carries a high potential for prejudice and is not strongly probative of motive.

Buzzy (defense witness)

Evidence of Buzzy's addiction and sale of heroin is not admissible under Rule 608 to attack his character for truthfulness. Courts do not generally find that a person's selling or using heroin reflects on that person's character for truthfulness. If the only theory of admission is that Buzzy as a heroin addict and dealer is likely to be untruthful, the evidence will be excluded. Even if the evidence were admissible on this theory, the prosecution would be limited to asking Buzzy questions about heroin involvement, and could not offer extrinsic evidence under Rule 608.

If it could be shown that Buzzy was under the influence of heroin while watching the Super Bowl, or at the time of giving testimony, then extrinsic evidence of that heroin use would be admissible to *impeach* his sensory capacity.

Tim (prosecution witness)

As discussed above, evidence of addiction or sale of heroin will not be admissible to attack Tim's character for truthfulness under Rule 608 on the theory that addicts/dealers are unlikely to be truthful.

However, as with Buzzy, evidence of heroin use might be admissible to show impairment of Tim's sensory capacity at the time he had the conversation with Buzzy or at the time of giving testimony.

In addition, evidence of Tim's selling heroin may be admissible to show Tim's *bias* as a witness. If Tim was worried about being prosecuted for drug dealing, he might have decided to curry favor with the prosecution. This argument would be strengthened if Tim had been charged with a drug crime or if the defense can otherwise show that Tim felt vulnerable to the prosecution. If, however, Tim's alleged drug dealing had not been charged and was not under investigation—*i.e.*, if the allegations became known to the prosecution only because they were put forth by the defense in this case—then the value of the evidence in showing bias would be highly speculative and the danger that the jury would use it as character evidence would justify exclusion under Rule 403.

(b) Buzzy's Prior Inconsistent Statement

Although Buzzy's prior inconsistent statement would be admissible as nonhearsay to impeach Buzzy's testimony, there are two objections that the defense can make to exclude the statement. First, the prosecution did not lay a foundation for the admission of extrinsic evidence contradicting Buzzy's testimony. Under Federal Rule 613, extrinsic evidence of a prior statement by a witness is not admissible unless the witness is afforded an opportunity to *explain or deny* the statement, or the "interests of justice" otherwise require. If Buzzy is still available he could be recalled to explain or deny the statement; otherwise, the prosecution would have to argue the "interests of justice" escape clause of Rule 613 to get the inconsistent statement admitted.

The second objection to Ms. X's testimony is *collateral impeachment*. The defense can argue that Buzzy's watching the Super Bowl in prior years is not independently relevant to any issue other than impeachment so Ms. X's testimony should be excluded as collateral impeachment. However, the Federal Rules arguably give the judge discretion to allow collateral impeachment. Here, Buzzy volunteered an assertion about prior Super Bowls on direct examination; the prosecution could argue that it would be unfair to permit the defense to bolster its witness's testimony by advancing the Super Bowl custom as a memory aid without allowing the prosecution to rebut it.

(c) (1) **Police Department Record**

The use of the police department record would present a hearsay on hearsay problem. The evidence would be admissible, however, if each out-of-court statement falls within an exception or exemption to the hearsay rule. The first two levels of hearsay pose no problem. Mr. Bushmat's statement would fall within the ***present sense impression exception*** if he wrote down the license number while looking at it or immediately thereafter, as seems likely. Mrs. Bushmat's report to the police of what was on the paper also falls within the present sense impression exception because she immediately called the police and told the officer what she had just seen on the paper. It is the police report itself that poses a problem to admissibility.

Public records exception: The police record may be admissible under the public records exception. [Fed. R. Evid. 803(8)] However, the public records exception prevents law enforcement records from being used ***against*** criminal defendants unless the records are of routine, nonadversarial matters. The purpose behind Rule 803(8) is to prevent prosecutorial use of police records to convict a defendant without placing the recorder on the stand for cross-examination. Here, if the prosecution can argue that the recording of the information was routine, nonadversarial, and objective, the danger of inaccuracy that exists when the police are recording incriminating evidence against a known suspect does not exist. Nonetheless, the court might refuse to admit the record under the public records exception on the ground that the police were investigating a particular crime at the time of the recording and therefore the record was not of a routine, nonadversarial matter.

Business records exception: Because of concern exemplified in the legislative history of Rule 803(8) about the trustworthiness dangers of admitting police records against a defendant, some courts have held that those records are equally inadmissible under the business records exception. Such a decision could be grounded in the text of the business records exception, which allows hearsay to be excluded if lacking in trustworthiness.

Past recollection recorded: If the police officer who made the record is still available, then the record may be admissible as the past recollection of the officer. This use of the record would not violate the purpose of Rule 803(8) because the officer would be available for cross-examination.

Present sense impression: If the officer wrote down the number while talking to Mrs. Bushmat, the prosecution can argue that it is admissible as a present sense impression. However, the purpose behind Rule 803(8) would pose an obstacle if the prosecution attempted to admit the evidence on this theory without calling the officer to the stand.

Refreshing recollection: If Mr. Bushmat's recollection can be refreshed by the record, it could be used for that purpose without placing it into evidence.

(2) **Testimony by the Bushmats**

Present sense impression: The license number may be admissible without the use of police records if both Bushmats testify. Mr. Bushmat does not remember the number, but he does remember the circumstances under which he wrote it down. He can lay the foundation for his written statement as a present sense impression.

When written, it was his present sense impression. When shown to his wife, it was still his present sense impression. (He was showing her the record of his prior statement, not making a new one.) Statements that he made in conjunction with handing over the record would not fall within the exception.

Mrs. Bushmat does not have the slip of paper, but she could testify from memory about the number on the paper. That would be analogous to testimony by her that Mr. Bushmat talked to her on the telephone and said, "I am now looking at a license plate number 12345." There is no double hearsay problem here, only a single level of hearsay—Mr. Bushmat's out-of-court statement, which is a present sense impression.

(3) **Confrontation Clause**

If the license plate number falls under a hearsay exception, the Confrontation Clause may still pose an obstacle to its admission. A Confrontation Clause analysis is necessary when the prosecution relies on a hearsay exception that is not "firmly rooted," such as the present sense impression exception or the residual catch-all exception. If the court applies *Ohio v. Roberts* broadly, the prosecution might have to show indicia of reliability and either produce the declarants or show them to be unavailable. To show reliability, the prosecution could argue that the declarants had no motive to fabricate and that not much time elapsed between the observations and the statements.

ANSWER TO SAMPLE EXAM QUESTION X

Rule 703 allows experts to use hearsay and other inadmissible evidence in forming a conclusion, so long as it is the type of evidence reasonably relied upon by experts in the particular field. Rule 705 allows experts to testify to a conclusion without prior revelation of the basis for the conclusion.

If applied literally and without restriction to police experts, these Rules would allow a police expert to testify to a conclusion that, for example, the defendant had been acting as a lookout for a drug dealer, without any need for the prosecution to show that the basis facts were admissible in evidence. The expert also would not have to specify the basis facts before giving the conclusion. Any evidence reliable enough to allow a competent investigator to draw conclusions might be a basis for testimony at trial, even if the evidence would otherwise be inadmissible hearsay.

The proposal to follow the common law approach would change Tusconna law (or at least the literal interpretation of it described above) by requiring that the basis facts be admitted in evidence and that they be specified. This can be accomplished by the use of a hypothetical question.

The return to the common law approach would avoid some of the dangers of the Tusconna (Federal Rules) approach. The common law approach would reveal an expert's reliance on the credibility of other witnesses in forming an opinion. It would prevent the police expert from relying on unreliable hearsay evidence or evidence that was otherwise not admissible (*e.g.*, the product of an illegal search). In addition, the common law approach would ameliorate the danger that the jury would believe that the expert was giving it the "inside story" based on evidence not presented at trial, and would allow the jury to disregard the expert's opinion if it found that the factual basis for it had not been satisfactorily established. Furthermore, the common law approach might lessen the danger that juries would give undue deference to police experts because of their official positions and experience in solving crimes.

On the other hand, by making the hypothetical question necessary, one would invite appeals that quibble over the exact wording of the hypothetical, mandate the use of a form of witness examination that could consume an undue amount of time, and encourage prosecutors to use hypotheticals to "sum up" evidence in the middle of a case (the sort of dangers that led to the reform of the Federal Rules).

TABLE OF CITATIONS TO FEDERAL RULES OF EVIDENCE

TABLE OF CASES

Carver v. United States - §266
Casey v. Phillips Pipeline Co. - §535
Cassidy, State v. - §§169, 175
Castenada, United States v. - §43
Castillo, United States v. - §1110
Castro-Ayon, United States v. - §1087
Cestero v. Ferrara - §405
Chambers v. Mississippi - §§175, 374, 381, 383, 961
Charter v. Chleborad - §216
Check, United States v. - §221
Chesapeake & Delaware Canal Co. v. United States - §§467, 481
City v. - see name of defendant
Clayton v. Canida - §599
Clements, United States v. - §1206
Clewis v. Texas - §360
Clifford, In re - §1180
Clifford-Jacobs Forging Co. v. Industrial Commission - §924
Clifton v. Ulis - §1065
Cline, United States v. - §238
Coleman, Commonwealth v. - §415
Collette v. Sarrasin - §606
Collins v. Wayne Corp. - §340
Collins, People v. - §167
Collins, United States v. - §292
Colyer, United States v. - §979
Commerce Union Bank v. Horton - §466
Commission, United States v. - §728
Commonwealth v. - see name of defendant
Contemporary Mission, Inc. v. Famous Music Corp. - §94
Coran, United States v. - §258
Corey, United States v. - §152
Coslow v. State - §1017
Costello, United States v. - §787
Couch v. United States - §799
County Court of Ulster County v. Allen - §§1329, 1344
Cox v. Selover - §279
Creaghe v. Iowa Home Mutual Casualty Co. - §232
Crisafi, United States v. - §1096
Crooks, People v. - §892
Cuesta, United States v. - §1189
Culpepper v. Volkswagen of America - §1225
Cummings v. Illinois Central Railroad - §391
Cummings v. State - §1256
Cunningham, United States v. (1971) - §1087
Cunningham, United States v. (1981) - §1034
Cushing v. Nantasket Beach Railroad - §470

Cylkowski, United States v. - §146

D.I. Chadbourne, Inc. v. Superior Court - §596
Dabney v. Investment Corp. of America - §598
Dankel, Commonwealth v. - §1140
Dartez v. Fibreboard Corp. - §530
Daubert v. Merrell Dow Pharmaceuticals - §§1228, 1229, 1234, 1235, 1236, 1237, 1238, 1239, 1252, 1257
Davidson v. Prince - §205
Davis v. Alaska - §1029
Davis v. California Powder Works - §1010
Davis v. Hearst - §141
Davis, United States v. (1978) - §543
Davis, United States v. (1996) - §1254
Deaver v. Hickox - §918
DeGeorgia, United States v. - §466
Department of Youth Services v. A Juvenile - §904
Dick, State v. - §271
Dietsch v. Mayberry - §981
DiNapoli, United States v. - §§1032, 1069
Dior, United States v. - §1292
Diversified Industries, Inc. v. Meredith - §594
Dobbins v. Crain Bros., Inc. - §215
Doe, United States v. - §§767, 798
Doern v. Crawford - §425
Doerr, United States v. - §349
Doll v. Loesel - §623
Dow Jones v. Superior Court - §735
Dunn v. Price - §1363
Duntley v. Inman, Poulsen & Co. - §875
Dutton v. Evans - §351
Dwyer, United States v. - §94

Ebasco Services, Inc. v. Pennsylvania Power & Light Co. - §425
Edney v. Smith - §618
Edwards, People v. - §382
Edwards, United States v. - §434
Egbert v. Egbert - §378
Eisenlord v. Clum - §510
Elijah, State v. - §§1005, 1061
Ellis v. Ellis - §655
Ellis v. Kneifl - §337
Emich Motors Corp. v. General Motors Corp. - §487
English, State v. - §236
Envirex, Inc. v. Ecological Recovery Associations, Inc. - §188
Erie Railroad v. Tompkins, - §§562, 814, 1323
Ermolieff v. R.K.O. Radio Pictures - §1383

Esch, United States v. - §922
Exum v. General Electric Co. - §104

Fahy v. Connecticut - §50
Farr v. Pitchess - §734
Fatico, United States v. - §721
Federal Underwriters' Exchange v. Cost - §878
Finch v. Monumental Life Insurance Co. - §43
Firlotte v. Jessee - §113
First National Bank v. Osborne - §384
First State Bank of Denton v. Maryland Casualty
   Co. - §1189
Fisher v. United States - §799
Fontana v. Upp - §1392
Ford v. Schmidt - §198
Fosher, United States v. - §892
Francis v. Franklin - §1343
Fraser-Smith Co. v. Chicago Rock Island &
   Pacific Railway - §535
Frederick v. Federal Insurance Co. - §653
Frost v. United States - §1059
Frye v. United States - §§1227, 1228, 1236, 1237,
   1238

G.M. McKelvey Co. v. General Casualty Co. of
   America - §386
Gallagher, United States v. - §1169
Garcia, United States v. - §88
Gibson, People v. - §1144
Gichner v. Antonio Troiano Tile & Marble Co. -
   §376
Gilbert v. Allied Chemical Corp. - §734
Gilbert v. California - §800
Glasser, United States v. - §456
Goff v. State - §375
Golden, United States v. - §904
Goodfader's Appeal, *In re* - §739
Gordon v. United States - §1034
Gould, People v. - §294
Gould, United States v. - §1288
Grady, United States v. - §477
Grand Jury Impaneled January 21, 1975, *In re* -
   §747
Grand Jury Proceedings (Jackier), *In re* - §597
Grand Jury Proceedings (Witnesses Mary Agosto
   et al.), *In re* - §750
Grand Jury Subpoena Duces Tecum, *In re* - §628
Gray v. Grayson - §486
Greenwood, Village of Lawrence v. - §114
Grice v. State - §1255
Griffin v. California - §810
Grissom v. Bunch - §378

Guillette, United States v. - §288

Hackett, Commonwealth v. - §382
Haldeman, United States v. - §74
Hamilton v. State - §1052
Hankins v. United States - §506
Hanson v. Johnson - §233
Hanson, State v. - §1288
Harris v. New York - §§373, 807
Harris, United States v. - §123
Hartford Steam Boiler Inspection & Insurance
   Co. v. Schwartzman Packing Co. - §112
Hatfield v. Continental Imports, Inc. - §201
Hawley, United States v. - §1039
Hawthorne, State v. - §1033
Hayes, United States v. - §288
Hendricks, People v. - §123
Herbert v. Lando - §732
Hickman v. Taylor - §611
Hicks, United States v. - §1252
Hileman v. Northwest Engineering Co. - §379
Hiss, United States v. - §1055
Hitchman Coal & Coke Co. v. Mitchell - §336
Hodge and Zweig, United States v. - §620
Hoffman v. Cedar Rapids & M.C. Railway - §210
Hoffman v. United States - §768
Hogan, United States v. - §960
Honore v. Superior Court - §722
Hopkins v. Grimshaw - §686
Houston Oxygen Co. v. Davis - §415

Iaconetti, United States v. - §543
Idaho v. Wright - §§549, 551
In re - *see* name of party
Inadi, United States v. - §§351, 549, 550
Ingram v. McCruston - §895

Jackson v. Denno - §§67, 68, 362
Jackson v. Jackson - §1351
Jackson, United States v. (1967) - §725
Jackson, United States v. (5th Cir. 1978) - §827
Jackson, United States v. (7th Cir. 1978) - §882
Jaffee v. Redmond - §§654, 665, 666, 667
Jencks v. United States - §973
Jenkins v. United States - §905
Jenness, State v. - §1018
John Hancock Mutual Life Insurance Co. v.
   Dutton - §885
Johnson v. Chrans - §427
Johnson v. Lutz - §457
Johnson v. Minihan - §991
Johnson v. Ohls - §405

Johnson v. United States - §§803, 809
Johnson, State v. - §918
Johnson, United States v. - §918
Jolly, State v. - §1083
Jones v. Commonwealth - §123
Jones, State v. - §416
Jones, United States v. - §1257
Joseph v. Krull Wholesale Drug Co. - §118
Juarez, United States v. - §588

Kale v. Douthitt - §901
Kampiles, United States v. - §340
Kastigar v. United States - §783
Kelly v. Sheehan - §449
Kennedy v. Great Atlantic & Pacific Tea Co. - §837
Khan v. Zemansky - §1051
Kim, United States v. - §458
Kirk v. Marquis - §864
Kirtdoll, People v. - §461
Kline v. Ford Motor Co. - §819
Knapp, State v. - §1030
Knight v. Otis Elevator Co. - §915
Kovel, United States v. - §618
Krause v. Apodaca - §925
Kristiansen, United States v. - §922
Krulewitch v. United States - §350

L.J. Brosius & Co. v. First National Bank - §465
Landof, United States v. - §578
Lange, United States v. - §457
LaPorte v. United States - §467
Larson, State v. - §1088
Latimer, United States v. - §997
Lavender, United States v. - §1287
Lawrence, State v. - §1290
Leary v. United States - §1329
Lee, People v. - §154
Lee, United States v. - §481
Legille v. Dann - §1335
Lego v. Twomey - §§365, 366
Leisure, United States v. - §56
Leon v. Penn Central Co. - §451
Leong, State v. - §382
Lewis v. Insurance Co. of North America - §267
Lewis v. Marshall - §497
Lewis v. Radcliff Materials, Inc. - §561
Lewis, United States v. - §1273
Liddy, United States v. - §605
Lint, People v. - §274
Lira v. Albert Einstein Medical Center - §415
Lissak v. Crocker Estate Co. - §651

Little, United States v. - §1183
Littlewind, United States v. - §951
Lloyd v. American Export Lines, Inc. - §§281, 486
Lohrmann v. Pittsburgh Corning Corp. - §277
Los Angeles, County of, v. Faus - §114
Love v. Common School District No. 28 - §471
Love, United States v. - §541
Lowe v. Inhabitants of Clinton - §192
Lowell, People v. - §1208
Luce v. United States - §1039
Luck v. United States - §1034
Luick v. Arends - §694
Lustig, United States v. - §679
Lutwak v. United States - §669
Lyon, United States v. - §542

MacKnight v. United States - §1036
MacLaird, People v. - §1288
McCray v. Illinois - §§723, 728
McCurdy v. Greyhound Corp. - §405
McDavitt, State v. - §1263
McDonald v. Erbes - §1205
McGinty v. Brotherhood of Railway Trainmen - §641
McInnis & Co. v. Western Tractor & Equipment Co. - §887
McKee v. State - §113
McKelvy, State v. - §1045
McKnight v. United States - §1208
McNair, United States v. - §1147
McNaulty v. State - §154
Madera, United States v. - §1197
Mahlandt v. Wild Canid Survival & Research Center, Inc. - §299
Mahone, United States v. - §1034
Mainline Investment Corp. v. Gaines - §1272
Malloy v. Hogan - §752
Mandell, United States v. - §1054
Mangan, United States v. - §427
Marchand v. Public Service Co. - §965
Markley v. Beagle - §343
Marks v. Columbia County Lumber Co. - §185
Marques, United States v. - §844
Marr v. State - §918
Martineau, State v. - §405
Mason v. United States - §775
Massey, People v. - §140
Mastberg, United States v. - §886
Masterson v. Sine - §§1371, 1375
Maston, People v. - §134
Matheson v. Caribo - §1167

INDEX

effect on hearer, §§236-239
elements, §§226-227
exempt statements, §§257-262. *See also* Nonhearsay
        under Federal Rules
Federal Rules, §§223-224
good faith words, §239
hearsay on hearsay, §265
lack of personal knowledge compared, §§817, 829-832
Morgan definition, §225
nonassertive conduct, §§225, 248-255
nonhuman evidence, §256
prior statements affecting credibility, §§241-244
rationale, §228
silence as nonassertive conduct, §§252, 320
state of mind assertions, §§240, 245-246
statements not offered to prove truth, §§229-244
untrustworthy hearsay, §263
verbal acts, §247

HOLDER OF PRIVILEGE, §563
See also Privilege
HOSPITAL RECORDS, §449
HOSTILITY, §§951, 957, 1056, 1060
HYPNOSIS, §§966, 1266
HYPOTHETICAL QUESTIONS, §§902, 909, 914, 931

I

IDENTITY
attorney-client privilege, §604
nonexpert opinion, §884
past crimes, §134
police informers, §§720-728
rehabilitation, §§1117-1127
ILLEGALLY OBTAINED EVIDENCE, §1141
IMMUNITY
news reporter's, §§729-741. *See also* Privilege
self-incrimination, §§767, 780-784
IMPEACHMENT
See also Character evidence; Cross-examination;
        Rehabilitation; Reputation
bias, §§1056-1063
character, §§1014-1055
collateral matters, §§1088-1089
confessions, §373. *See also* Confessions
contrary evidence, §§1007-1008
convictions
    appeal of, §1031
    constitutional defects in, §1030
    criminal cases, §1039
    foundation, §§1036-1038
    jury instruction, §1040
    juvenile, §1029
    out-of-state, §1028
    pardon, §1032
    proof, §§1036-1038
    remoteness, §§1033-1035
    what crimes, §§1016-1027
credibility, §§1011-1013
hostility, §1060
inconsistent acts or statements, §§1064-1087
juvenile convictions, §1029

lack of knowledge, §1009
memory, §1010
methods, §§1006-1087
noncriminal misconduct, §§1041-1047
opinions about credibility, §§1053-1055
own witness, §§952-961
    adverse party, §§955-956
    constitutional issues, §961
    cross-examination, §§987-988
    hostile on stand, §957
    surprise testimony, §957
pardon, §1032
perceptive capacity, §1009
relevancy, §1008
reputation for truthfulness, §§1048-1052
IMPLIED ADMISSIONS, §§318-331
conduct other than silence, §§330-331
hearsay status, §319
silence, §§252, 320-329
    constitutional limits, §§328-329
    criminal cases, §§326-329
INDIRECT EVIDENCE
See Circumstantial evidence
INFERENCES, §§1315-1316
See also Presumptions
INJURIES
See Accidents and injuries; Exhibition of injuries
injuries, similar, §100
INSTRUCTION TO DISREGARD, §47
INSUFFICIENT MEMORY
See Past recollection recorded
INSURANCE, LIABILITY
admissibility, §§212-217
INTEGRATED AGREEMENTS, §§1365-1376
INTERNAL AFFAIRS INFORMATION, §711
INVESTIGATIVE REPORTS, §§478-480

JK

JUDGE AS WITNESS, §§833-837
JUDGE, ROLE OF
See also Admissibility; Judicial discretion
admissibility of evidence, §§30, 32
as witness, §§833-837
authenticity, §1136
comment on evidence, §§1001-1002
conditional relevance, §75
examination of witnesses, §§996-1000
modern trend, §68
nonproduction of document, §1209
preliminary facts, §§61-64, 73-75
voluntariness of confessions, §§362-368
JUDGMENTS, §§482-496
See also Judicial admissions
acquittal, §489
civil case, §§490-496
criminal convictions, §§483-488, 1015-1040. *See also*
        Character evidence; Impeachment;
        Reputation
JUDICIAL ADMISSIONS, §§303-317
amended pleadings, §§306-308

Notes

Notes

Notes

Notes

Notes

Notes

Notes

Publications Catalog

Publishers of America's Most Popular Legal Study Aids!

All Titles Available At Your Law School Bookstore.

Gilbert Law Summaries are the best selling outlines in the country, and have set the standard for excellence since they were first introduced more than twenty-five years ago. It's Gilbert's unique combination of features that makes it the one study aid you'll turn to for all your study needs!

Accounting and Finance for Lawyers
Professor Thomas L. Evans, University of Texas
Basic Accounting Principles; Definitions of Accounting Terms; Balance Sheet; Income Statement; Statement of Changes in Financial Position; Consolidated Financial Statements; Accumulation of Financial Data; Financial Statement Analysis.
ISBN: 0-15-900382-2   Pages: 136 $19.95

Administrative Law
By Professor Michael R. Asimow, U.C.L.A.
Separation of Powers and Controls Over Agencies; (including Delegation of Power) Constitutional Right to Hearing (including Liberty and Property Interests Protected by Due Process, and Rulemaking- Adjudication Distinction); Adjudication Under Administrative Procedure Act (APA); Formal Adjudication (including Notice, Discovery, Burden of Proof, Finders of Facts and Reasons); Adjudicatory Decision Makers (including Administrative Law Judges (ALJs), Bias, Improper Influences, Ex Parte Communications, Familiarity with Record, Res Judicata); Rulemaking Procedures (including Notice, Public Participation, Publication, Impartiality of Rulemakers, Rulemaking Record); Obtaining Information (including Subpoena Power, Privilege Against Self-incrimination, Freedom of Information Act, Government in Sunshine Act, Attorneys' Fees); Scope of Judicial Review; Reviewability of Agency Decisions (including Mandamus, Injunction, Sovereign Immunity, Federal Tort Claims Act); Standing to Seek Judicial Review and Timing.
ISBN: 0-15-900000-9   Pages: 278 $20.95

Agency and Partnership
By Professor Richard J. Conviser, Chicago Kent
Agency: Rights and Liabilities Between Principal and Agent (including Agent's Fiduciary Duty, Right to Indemnification); Contractual Rights Between Principal (or Agent) and Third Persons (including Creation of Agency Relationship, Authority of Agent, Scope of Authority, Termination of Authority, Ratification, Liability on

Agents, Contracts); Tort Liability (including Respondeat Superior, Master-Servant Relationship, Scope of Employment). Partnership: Property Rights of Partner; Formation of Partnership; Relations Between Partners (including Fiduciary Duty); Authority of Partner to Bind Partnership; Dissolution and Winding up of Partnership; Limited Partnerships.
ISBN: 0-15-900327-X   Pages: 149 $17.95

Antitrust
By Professor Thomas M. Jorde, U.C. Berkeley, Mark A. Lemley, University of Texas, and Professor Robert H. Mnookin, Harvard University
Common Law Restraints of Trade; Federal Antitrust Laws (including Sherman Act, Clayton Act, Federal Trade Commission Act, Interstate Commerce Requirement, Antitrust Remedies); Monopolization (including Relevant Market, Purposeful Act Requirement, Attempts and Conspiracy to Monopolize); Collaboration Among Competitors (including Horizontal Restraints, Rule of Reason vs. Per Se Violations, Price Fixing, Division of Markets, Group Boycotts); Vertical Restraints (including Tying Arrangements); Mergers and Acquisitions (including Horizontal Mergers, Brown Shoe Analysis, Vertical Mergers, Conglomerate Mergers); Price Discrimination—Robinson-Patman Act; Unfair Methods of Competition; Patent Laws and Their Antitrust Implications; Exemptions From Antitrust Laws (including Motor, Rail, and Interstate Water Carriers, Bank Mergers, Labor Unions, Professional Baseball).
ISBN: 0-15-900328-8   Pages: 210 $18.95

Bankruptcy
By Professor Ned W. Waxman, College of William and Mary
Participants in the Bankruptcy Case; Jurisdiction and Procedure; Commencement and Administration of the Case (including Eligibility, Voluntary Case, Involuntary Case, Meeting of Creditors, Debtor's Duties); Officers of the Estate (including

Trustee, Examiner, United States Trustee); Bankruptcy Estate; Creditor's Right of Setoff; Trustee's Avoiding Powers; Claims of Creditors (including Priority Claims and Tax Claims); Debtor's Exemptions; Nondischargeable Debts; Effects of Discharge; Reaffirmation Agreements; Administrative Powers (including Automatic Stay, Use, Sale, or Lease of Property); Chapter 7-Liquidation; Chapter 11-Reorganization; Chapter 13-Individual With Regular Income; Chapter 12-Family Farmer With Regular Annual Income.
ISBN: 0-15-900442-X   Pages: 311 $21.95

Business Law
By Professor Robert D. Upp, Los Angeles City College
Torts and Crimes in Business; Law of Contracts (including Contract Formation, Consideration, Statute of Frauds, Contract Remedies, Third Parties); Sales (including Transfer of Title and Risk of Loss, Performance and Remedies, Products Liability, Personal Property Security Interest); Property (including Personal Property, Bailments, Real Property, Landlord and Tenant); Agency; Business Organizations (including Partnerships, Corporations); Commercial Paper; Government Regulation of Business (including Taxation, Antitrust, Environmental Protection, and Bankruptcy).
ISBN: 0-15-900005-X   Pages: 277 $17.95

California Bar Performance Test Skills
By Professor Peter J. Honigsberg, University of San Francisco
Hints to Improve Writing; How to Approach the Performance Test; Legal Analysis Documents (including Writing a Memorandum of Law, Writing a Client Letter, Writing Briefs); Fact Gathering and Fact Analysis Documents; Tactical and Ethical Considerations; Sample Interrogatories, Performance Tests, and Memoranda.
ISBN: 0-15-900152-8   Pages: 216 $18.95

Civil Procedure
By Professor Thomas D. Rowe, Jr., Duke University, and Professor Richard L. Marcus, U.C. Hastings
Territorial (Personal) Jurisdiction, including Venue and Forum Non Conveniens; Subject Matter Jurisdiction, covering Diversity Jurisdiction, Federal Question Jurisdiction; Erie Doctrine and Federal Common Law; Pleadings including Counterclaims, Cross-Claims, Supplemental Pleadings; Parties, including Joinder and Class Actions; Discovery, including Devices, Scope, Sanctions, and Discovery Conference; Summary Judgment; Pretrial Conference and Settlements; Trial, including Right to Jury Trial, Motions, Jury Instruction and Arguments, and Post-Verdict Motions; Appeals; Claim Preclusion (Res Judicata) and Issue Preclusion (Collateral Estoppel).
ISBN: 0-15-900429-2   Pages: 410 $22.95

Commercial Paper and Payment Law
By Professor Douglas J. Whaley, Ohio State University
Types of Commercial Paper; Negotiability; Negotiation; Holders in Due Course; Claims and Defenses on Negotiable Instruments (including Real Defenses and Personal Defenses); Liability of the Parties (including Merger Rule, Suits on the Instrument, Warranty Suits, Conversion); Bank Deposits and Collections; Forgery or Alteration of Negotiable Instruments; Electronic Banking.
ISBN: 0-15-900367-9   Pages: 166 $19.95

Community Property
By Professor William A. Reppy, Jr., Duke University
Classifying Property as Community or Separate; Management and Control of Property; Liability for Debts; Division of Property at Divorce; Devolution of Property at Death; Relationships Short of Valid Marriage; Conflict of Laws Problems; Constitutional Law Issues (including Equal Protection Standards, Due Process Issues).
ISBN: 0-15-900422-5   Pages: 161 $18.95

Conflict of Laws
By Dean Herma Hill Kay, U.C. Berkeley
Domicile; Jurisdiction (including Notice and Opportunity to be Heard, Minimum Contacts, Types of Jurisdiction); Choice of Law (including Vested Rights Approach, Most Significant Relationship Approach, Governmental Interest Analysis); Choice of Law in Specific Substantive Areas; Traditional Defenses Against Application of Foreign Law; Constitutional Limitations and Overriding Federal Law (including Due Process Clause, Full Faith and Credit Clause, Conflict Between State and Federal Law); Recognition and Enforcement of Foreign Judgments.
ISBN: 0-15-900424-1   Pages: 250 $20.95

Constitutional Law
By Professor Jesse H. Choper, U.C. Berkeley
Powers of Federal Government (including Judicial Power, Powers of Congress, Presidential Power, Foreign Affairs Power); Intergovernmental Immunities, Separation of Powers; Regulation of Foreign Commerce; Regulation of Interstate Commerce; Taxation of Interstate and Foreign Commerce; Due Process, Equal Protection; "State Action" Requirements; Freedoms of Speech, Press, and Association; Freedom of Religion.
ISBN: 0-15-900375-X   Pages: 312 $21.95

Contracts
By Professor Melvin A. Eisenberg, U.C. Berkeley
Consideration (including Promissory Estoppel, Moral or Past Consideration); Mutual Assent; Defenses (including Mistake, Fraud, Duress, Unconscionability, Statute of Frauds, Illegality); Third-Party Beneficiaries; Assignment of Rights and Delegation of Duties; Conditions; Substantial Performance; Material vs. Minor Breach; Anticipatory Breach; Impossibility; Discharge; Remedies (including Damages, Specific Performance, Liquidated Damages).
ISBN: 0-15-900014-9   Pages: 278 $21.95

Corporations
By Professor Jesse H. Choper, U.C. Berkeley, and Professor Melvin A. Eisenberg, U.C. Berkeley
Formalities; "De Jure" vs. "De Facto"; Promoters; Corporate Powers; Ultra Vires Transactions; Powers, Duties, and Liabilities of Officers and Directors; Allocation of Power Between Directors and Shareholders; Conflicts of Interest in Corporate Transactions; Close Corporations; Insider Trading; Rule 10b-5 and Section 16(b); Shareholders' Voting Rights; Shareholders' Right to Inspect Records; Shareholders' Suits; Capitalization (including Classes of Shares, Preemptive Rights, Consideration for Shares); Dividends; Redemption of Shares; Fundamental Changes in Corporate Structure; Applicable Conflict of Laws Principles.
ISBN: 0-15-900342-3   Pages: 282 $21.95

Criminal Law
By Professor George E. Dix, University of Texas
Elements of Crimes (including Actus Reus, Mens Rea, Causation); Vicarious Liability; Complicity in Crime; Criminal Liability of Corporations;

Defenses (including Insanity, Diminished Capacity, Intoxication, Ignorance, Self-Defense); Inchoate Crimes; Homicide; Other Crimes Against the Person; Crimes Against Habitation (including Burglary, Arson); Crimes Against Property; Offenses Against Government; Offenses Against Administration of Justice.
ISBN: 0-15-900217-6   Pages: 271 $20.95

Criminal Procedure
By Professor Paul Marcus, College of William and Mary, and Professor Charles H. Whitebread, U.S.C.
Exclusionary Rule; Arrests and Other Detentions; Search and Seizure; Privilege Against Self-Incrimination; Confessions; Preliminary Hearing; Bail; Indictment; Speedy Trial; Competency to Stand Trial; Government's Obligation to Disclose Information; Right to Jury Trial; Right to Counsel; Right to Confront Witnesses; Burden of Proof; Insanity; Entrapment; Guilty Pleas; Sentencing; Death Penalty; Ex Post Facto Issues; Appeal; Habeas Corpus; Juvenile Offenders; Prisoners' Rights; Double Jeopardy.
ISBN: 0-15-900376-8   Pages: 244 $20.95

Estate and Gift Tax
By Professor John H. McCord, University of Illinois
Gross Estate; Allowable Deductions Under Estate Tax (including Expenses, Indebtedness, and Taxes, Deductions for Losses, Charitable Deduction, Marital Deduction); Taxable Gifts; Deductions; Valuation; Computation of Tax; Returns and Payment of Tax; Tax on Generation-Skipping Transfers.
ISBN: 0-15-900425-X   Pages: 298 $20.95

Evidence
By Professor Jon R. Waltz, Northwestern University, and Roger C. Park, University of Minnesota
Direct Evidence; Circumstantial Evidence; Rulings on Admissibility; Relevancy; Materiality; Character Evidence; Hearsay and the Hearsay Exceptions; Privileges; Competency to Testify; Opinion Evidence and Expert Witnesses; Direct Examination; Cross-Examination; Impeachment; Real, Demonstrative, and Scientific Evidence; Judicial Notice; Burdens of Proof; Parol Evidence Rule.
ISBN: 0-15-900385-7   Pages: 342 $22.95

Federal Courts
By Professor William A. Fletcher, U.C. Berkeley
Article III Courts; "Case or Controversy" Requirement; Justiciability; Advisory Opinions; Political Questions; Ripeness; Mootness; Standing; Congressional Power Over Federal Court Jurisdiction; Supreme Court Jurisdiction; District Court Subject Matter Jurisdiction (including Federal Question Jurisdiction, Diversity Jurisdiction);

Pendent and Ancillary Jurisdiction; Removal Jurisdiction; Venue; Forum Non Conveniens; Law Applied in the Federal Courts (including Erie Doctrine); Federal Law in the State Courts; Abstention; Habeas Corpus for State Prisoners; Federal Injunctions Against State Court Proceedings; Eleventh Amendment.
ISBN: 0-15-900232-X   Pages: 270 $21.95

Future Interests & Perpetuities
By Professor Jesse Dukeminier, U.C.L.A.
Reversions; Possibilities of Reverter; Rights of Entry; Remainders; Executory Interest; Rules Restricting Remainders and Executory Interest; Rights of Owners of Future Interests; Construction of Instruments; Powers of Appointment; Rule Against Perpetuities (including Reforms of the Rule).
ISBN: 0-15-900218-4   Pages: 162 $19.95

Income Tax I - Individual
By Professor Michael R. Asimow, U.C.L.A.
Gross Income; Exclusions; Income Splitting by Gifts, Personal Service Income, Income Earned by Children, Income of Husbands and Wives, Below-Market Interest on Loans, Taxation of Trusts; Business and Investment Deductions; Personal Deductions; Tax Rates; Credits; Computation of Basis, Gain, or Loss; Realization; Nonrecognition of Gain or Loss; Capital Gains and Losses; Alternative Minimum Tax; Tax Accounting Problems.
ISBN: 0-15-900421-7   Pages: 279 $21.95

Income Tax II - Partnerships, Corporations, Trusts
By Professor Michael R. Asimow, U.C.L.A.
Taxation of Partnerships (including Current Partnership Income, Contributions of Property to Partnership, Sale of Partnership Interest, Distributions, Liquidations); Corporate Taxation (including Corporate Distributions, Sales of Stock and Assets, Reorganizations); S Corporations; Federal Income Taxation of Trusts.
ISBN: 0-15-900384-9   Pages: 210 $19.95

Labor Law
By Professor James C. Oldham, Georgetown University, and Robert J. Gelhaus
Statutory Foundations of Present Labor Law (including National Labor Relations Act, Taft-Hartley, Norris-LaGuardia Act, Landrum-Griffin Act); Organizing Campaigns, Selection of the Bargaining Representative; Collective Bargaining (including Negotiating the Agreement, Lockouts, Administering the Agreement, Arbitration); Strikes, Boycotts, and Picketing; Concerted Activity Protected Under the NLRA; Civil Rights Legislation; Grievance; Federal Regulation of Compulsory Union Membership Arrangements; State Regulation of Compulsory Membership Agreements; "Right to Work" Laws; Discipline of Union Members; Election of Union Officers; Corruption.
ISBN: 0-15-900340-7   Pages: 221 $19.95

Legal Ethics
By Professor Thomas D. Morgan, George Washington University
Regulating Admission to Practice Law; Preventing Unauthorized Practice of Law; Contract Between Client and Lawyer (including Lawyer's Duties Regarding Accepting Employment, Spheres of Authority of Lawyer and Client, Obligation of Client to Lawyer, Terminating the Lawyer-Client Relationship); Attorney-Client Privilege; Professional Duty of Confidentiality; Conflicts of Interest; Obligations to Third Persons and the Legal System (including Counseling Illegal or Fraudulent Conduct, Threats of Criminal Prosecution); Special Obligations in Litigation (including Limitations on Advancing Money to Client, Duty to Reject Certain Actions, Lawyer as Witness); Solicitation and Advertising; Specialization; Disciplinary Process; Malpractice; Special Responsibilities of Judges.
ISBN: 0-15-900026-2   Pages: 221 $20.95

Legal Research, Writing and Analysis
By Professor Peter J. Honigsberg, University of San Francisco
Court Systems; Precedent; Case Reporting System (including Regional and State Reporters, Headnotes and the West Key Number System, Citations and Case Finding); Statutes, Constitutions, and Legislative History; Secondary Sources (including Treatises, Law Reviews, Digests, Restatements); Administrative Agencies (including Regulations, Looseleaf Services); Shepard's Citations; Computers in Legal Research; Reading and Understanding a Case (including Briefing a Case); Using Legal Sourcebooks; Basic Guidelines for Legal Writing; Organizing Your Research; Writing a Memorandum of Law; Writing a Brief; Writing an Opinion or Client Letter.
ISBN: 0-15-900436-5   Pages: 162 $17.95

Multistate Bar Examination
By Professor Richard J. Conviser, Chicago Kent
Structure of the Exam; Governing Law; Effective Use of Time; Scoring of the Exam; Jurisdictions Using the Exam; Subject Matter Outlines; Practice Tests, Answers, and Subject Matter Keys; Glossary of Legal Terms and Definitions; State Bar Examination Directory; Listing of Reference Materials for Multistate Subjects.
ISBN: 0-15-900246-X   Pages: 776 $24.95

Personal Property
Gilbert Staff
Acquisitions; Ownership Through Possession (including Wild Animals, Abandoned Chattels); Finders of Lost Property; Bailments; Possessory Liens; Pledges; Trover; Gift; Accession; Confusion (Commingling); Fixtures; Crops (Emblements); Adverse Possession; Prescriptive Rights (Acquiring Ownership of Easements or Profits by Adverse Use).
ISBN: 0-15-900360-1   Pages: 118 $14.95

Professional Responsibility
(see Legal Ethics)

gilbert
LAW SUMMARIES

Property
By Professor Jesse Dukeminier, U.C.L.A.

Possession (including Wild Animals, Bailments, Adverse Possession); Gifts and Sales of Personal Property; Freehold Possessory Estates; Future Interests (including Reversion, Possibility of Reverter, Right of Entry, Executory Interests, Rule Against Perpetuities); Tenancy in Common; Joint Tenancy; Tenancy by the Entirety; Condominiums; Cooperatives; Marital Property; Landlord and Tenant; Easements and Covenants; Nuisance; Rights in Airspace and Water; Right to Support; Zoning; Eminent Domain; Sale of Land (including Mortgage, Deed, Warranties of Title); Methods of Title Assurance (including Recording System, Title Registration, Title Insurance).

ISBN: 0-15-900426-8   Pages: 445 $22.95

Remedies
By Professor John A. Bauman, U.C.L.A., and Professor Kenneth H. York, Pepperdine University

Damages; Equitable Remedies (including Injunctions and Specific Performance); Restitution; Injuries to Tangible Property Interests; Injuries to Business and Commercial Interests (including Business Torts, Inducing Breach of Contract, Patent Infringement, Unfair Competition, Trade Defamation); Injuries to Personal Dignity and Related Interests (including Defamation, Privacy, Religious Status, Civil and Political Rights); Personal Injury and Death; Fraud; Duress, Undue Influence, and Unconscionable Conduct; Mistake; Breach of Contract; Unenforceable Contracts (including Statute of Frauds, Impossibility, Lack of Contractual Capacity, Illegality).

ISBN: 0-15-900325-3   Pages: 349 $22.95

Sale and Lease of Goods
By Professor Douglas J. Whaley, Ohio State University

UCC Article 2; Sales Contract (including Offer and Acceptance, Parol Evidence Rule, Statute of Frauds, Assignment and Delegation, Revision of Contract Terms); Types of Sales (including Cash Sale Transactions, Auctions, "Sale or Return" and "Sale on Approval" Transactions); Warranties (including Express and Implied Warranties, Privity, Disclaimer, Consumer Protection Statutes); Passage of Title; Performance of the Contract; Anticipatory Breach; Demand for Assurance of Performance; Unforeseen Circumstances; Risk of Loss; Remedies; Documents of Title; Lease of Goods; International Sale of Goods.

ISBN: 0-15-900367-9   Pages: 196 $19.95

Secured Transactions
By Professor Douglas J. Whaley, Ohio State University

Coverage of Article 9; Creation of a Security Interest (including Attachment, Security Agreement, Value, Debtor's Rights in the Collateral); Perfection; Filing; Priorities; Bankruptcy Proceedings and Article 9; Default Proceedings; Bulk Transfers.

ISBN: 0-15-900231-1   Pages: 191 $18.95

Securities Regulation
By Professor David H. Barber, and Professor Niels B. Schaumann, William Mitchell College of Law

Jurisdiction and Interstate Commerce; Securities Act of 1933 (including Registration Requirements and Exemptions); Securities Exchange Act of 1934 (including Rule 10b-5, Tender Offers, Proxy Solicitations Regulation, Insider Transactions); Regulation of the Securities Markets; Multinational Transactions; State Regulation of Securities Transactions.

ISBN: 0-15-9000437-3   Pages: 421 $22.95

Torts
By Professor Marc A. Franklin, Stanford University

Intentional Torts; Negligence; Strict Liability; Products Liability; Nuisance; Survival of Tort Actions; Wrongful Death; Immunity; Release and Contribution; Indemnity; Workers' Compensation; No-Fault Auto Insurance; Defamation; Invasion of Privacy; Misrepresentation; Injurious Falsehood; Interference With Economic Relations; Unjustifiable Litigation.

ISBN: 0-15-900220-6   Pages: 400 $22.95

Trusts
By Professor Edward C. Halbach, Jr., U.C. Berkeley

Elements of a Trust; Trust Creation; Transfer of Beneficiary's Interest (including Spendthrift Trusts); Charitable Trusts (including Cy Pres Doctrine); Trustee's Responsibilities, Power, Duties, and Liabilities; Duties and Liabilities of Beneficiaries; Accounting for Income and Principal; Power of Settlor to Modify or Revoke; Powers of Trustee Beneficiaries or Courts to Modify or Terminate; Termination of Trusts by Operation of Law; Resulting Trusts; Purchase Money Resulting Trusts; Constructive Trusts.

ISBN: 0-15-900039-4   Pages: 238 $20.95

Wills
By Professor Stanley M. Johanson, University of Texas

Intestate Succession; Simultaneous Death; Advancements; Disclaimer; Killer of Decedent; Elective Share Statutes; Pretermitted Child Statutes; Homestead; Formal Requisites of a Will; Revocation of Wills; Incorporation by Reference; Pour-Over Gift in Inter Vivos Trust; Joint Wills; Contracts Relating to Wills; Lapsed Gifts; Ademption; Exoneration of Liens; Will Contests; Probate and Estate Administration.

ISBN: 0-15-900040-8   Pages: 262 $21.95

Gilbert's Pocket Size Law Dictionary
Gilbert

A dictionary is useless if you don't have it when you need it. If the only law dictionary you own is a thick, bulky one, you'll probably leave it at home most of the time — and if you need to know a definition while you're at school, you're out of luck!

With Gilbert's Pocket Size Law Dictionary, you'll have any definition you need, when you need it. Just pop Gilbert's dictionary into your pocket or purse, and you'll have over 4,000 legal terms and phrases at your fingertips. Gilbert's dictionary also includes a section on law school shorthand, common abbreviations, Latin and French legal terms, periodical abbreviations, and governmental abbreviations.

With Gilbert's Pocket Size Law Dictionary, you'll never be caught at a loss for words!

Available in your choice of 5 colors

■ **Brown**   ISBN: 0-15-900252-4 $7.95
■ **Blue**   ISBN: 0-15-900362-8 $7.95
■ **Burgundy**   ISBN: 0-15-900366-0 $7.95
■ **Green**   ISBN: 0-15-900365-2 $7.95

Limited Edition: Simulated Alligator Skin Cover

■ **Black**   ISBN: 0-15-900364-4 $7.95

The Eight Secrets Of Top Exam Performance In Law School
Charles Whitebread

Wouldn't it be great to know exactly what your professor's looking for on your exam? To find out everything that's expected of you, so that you don't waste your time doing anything other than maximizing your grades?

In his easy-to-read, refreshing style, nationally recognized exam expert Professor Charles

Whitebread will teach you the eight secrets that will add precious points to every exam answer you write. You'll learn the three keys to handling any essay exam question, and how to add points to your score by making time work for you, not against you. You'll learn flawless issue spotting, and discover how to organize your answer for maximum possible points. You'll find out how the hidden traps in "IRAC" trip up most students… but not you! You'll learn the techniques for digging up the exam questions your professor will ask, before your exam. You'll put your newly-learned skills to the test with sample exam questions, and you can measure your performance against model answers. And there's even a special section that helps you master the skills necessary to crush any exam, not just a typical essay exam — unusual exams like open book, take home, multiple choice, short answer, and policy questions.

"The Eight Secrets of Top Exam Performance in Law School" gives you all the tools you need to maximize your grades — quickly and easily!
ISBN: 0-15-900323-7 $9.95

LAW SCHOOL LEGENDS SERIES

America's Greatest Law Professors on Audio Cassette

We found the truly gifted law professors most law students can only dream about — the professors who draw rave reviews not only for their scholarship, but for their ability to make the law easy to understand. We asked these select few professors to condense their courses into a single lecture. And it's these lectures you'll find in the Law School Legends Series. With Law School Legends, you'll get a brilliant law professor explaining an entire subject to you in one simple, dynamic lecture. The Law School Legends make even the most difficult concepts crystal clear. You'll understand the big picture, and how all the concepts fit together. You'll get hundreds of examples and exam tips, honed over decades in the classroom. But best of all, you'll get insights you can only get from America's greatest law professors!

Administrative Law
Professor Patrick J. Borchers
Albany Law School of Union University

TOPICS COVERED: Classification Of Agencies; Adjudicative And Investigative Action; Rulemaking Power; Delegation Doctrine; Control By Executive; Appointment And Removal; Freedom Of Information Act; Rulemaking Procedure; Adjudicative Procedure; Trial-Type Hearings; Administrative Law Judge; Power To Stay Proceedings; Subpoena Power; Physical Inspection; Self Incrimination; Judicial Review Issues; Declaratory Judgment; Sovereign Immunity; Eleventh Amendment; Statutory Limitations; Standing; Exhaustion Of Administrative Remedies; Scope Of Judicial Review.
4 Audio Cassettes
ISBN: 0-15-900189-7 $45.95

Agency & Partnership
Professor Thomas L. Evans
University of Texas

TOPICS COVERED: Agency: Creation; Rights And Duties Of Principal And Agent; Sub-Agents; Contract Liability — Actual Authority: Express And Implied; Apparent Authority; Ratification; Liabilities Of Parties; Tort Liability — Respondeat Superior; Frolic And Detour; Intentional Torts. Partnership: Nature Of Partnership; Formation; Partnership By Estoppel; In Partnership Property; Relations Between Partners To Third Parties; Authority of Partners; Dissolution And Termination; Limited Partnerships.
4 Audio Cassettes
ISBN: 0-15-900351-2 $45.95

Antitrust
Professor Thomas D. Morgan
George Washington University Law School

TOPICS COVERED: Antitrust Law's First Principle; Consumer Welfare Opposes Market Power; Methods of Analysis; Role of Reason, Per Se, Quick Look; Sherman Act §1: Civil & Criminal Conspiracies In Unreasonable Restraint Of Trade; Sherman Act §2: Illegal Monopolization, Attempts To Monopolize; Robinson Patman Act Price Discrimination, Related Distribution Problems; Clayton Act §7: Mergers, Joint Ventures; Antitrust & Intellectual Property; International Competitive Relationships; Exemptions & Regulated Industries; Enforcement; Price & Non-Price Restraints.
4 Audio Cassettes
ISBN: 0-15-900341-5 $39.95

Bankruptcy
Professor Elizabeth Warren
Harvard Law School

TOPICS COVERED: The Debtor/Creditor Relationship; The Commencement, Conversion, Dismissal, and Reopening Of Bankruptcy Proceedings; Property Included In The Bankruptcy Estate; Secured, Priority And Unsecured Claims; The Automatic Stay; Powers Of Avoidance; The Assumption And Rejection Of Executory Contracts; The Protection Of Exempt Property; The Bankruptcy Discharge; Chapter 13 Proceedings; Chapter 11 Proceedings; Bankruptcy Jurisdiction And Procedure.
4 Audio Cassettes
ISBN: 0-15-900273-7 $45.95

Civil Procedure
By Professor Richard D. Freer
Emory University Law School

TOPICS COVERED: Subject Matter Jurisdiction; Personal Jurisdiction; Long-Arm Statutes; Constitutional Limitations; In Rem And Quasi In Rem Jurisdiction; Service Of Process; Venue; Transfer; Forum Non Conveniens; Removal; Waiver; Governing Law; Pleadings; Joinder Of Claims; Permissive And Compulsory Joinder Of Parties; Counter-Claims And Cross-Claims; Ancillary Jurisdiction; Impleader; Class Actions; Discovery; Pretrial Adjudication; Summary Judgment; Trial; Post Trial Motions; Appeals; Res Judicata; Collateral Estoppel.
5 Audio Cassettes
ISBN: 0-15-900322-9 $59.95

Commercial Paper
By Professor Michael I. Spak
Chicago Kent College Of Law

TOPICS COVERED: Types Of Negotiable Instruments; Elements Of Negotiability; Statute Of Limitations; Payment-In-Full Checks; Negotiations Of The Instrument; Becoming A Holder-In-Due Course; Rights Of A Holder In Due Course; Real And Personal Defenses; Jus Teril; Effect Of Instrument On Underlying Obligations; Contracts Of Maker And Indorser; Suretyship; Liability Of Drawer And Drawee; Check Certification; Warranty Liability; Conversion Of Liability; Banks And Their Customers; Properly Payable Rule; Wrongful Dishonor; Stopping Payment; Death Of Customer; Bank Statement;

Check Collection; Expedited Funds Availability; Forgery Of Drawer's Name; Alterations; Imposter Rule; Wire Transfers; Electronic Fund Transfers Act.
3 Audio Cassettes
ISBN: 0-15-900275-3 $39.95

Conflict Of Laws
Professor Patrick J. Borchers
Albany Law School

TOPICS COVERED: Domicile; Jurisdiction—In Personam, In Rem, Quasi In Rem; Court Competence; Forum Non Conveniens; Choice Of Law; Foreign Causes Of Action; Territorial Approach To Choice/Tort And Contract; "Escape Devices"; Most Significant Relationship; Governmental Interest Analysis; Recognition Of Judgments; Foreign Country Judgments; Domestic Judgments/Full Faith And Credit; Review Of Judgments; Modifiable Judgments; Defenses To Recognition And Enforcement; Federal/State (Erie) Problems; Constitutional Limits On Choice Of Law.
4 Audio Cassettes
ISBN: 0-15-900352-0 $39.95

Constitutional Law
By Professor John C. Jeffries, Jr.
University of Virginia School of Law

TOPICS COVERED: Introduction; Exam Tactics; Legislative Power; Supremacy; Commerce; State Regulation; Privileges And Immunities; Federal Court Jurisdiction; Separation Of Powers; Civil Liberties; Due Process; Equal Protection; Privacy; Race; Alienage; Gender; Speech And Association; Prior Restraints; Religion—Free Exercise; Establishment Clause.
5 Audio Cassettes
ISBN: 0-15-900373-3 $45.95

Contracts
By Professor Michael I. Spak
Chicago Kent College Of Law

TOPICS COVERED: Offer; Revocation; Acceptance; Consideration; Defenses To Formation; Third Party Beneficiaries; Assignment; Delegation; Conditions; Excuses; Anticipatory Repudiation; Discharge Of Duty; Modifications; Rescission; Accord & Satisfaction; Novation; Breach; Damages; Remedies; UCC Remedies; Parol Evidence Rule.
4 Audio Cassettes
ISBN: 0-15-900318-0 $45.95

Copyright Law
Professor Roger E. Schechter
George Washington University Law School

TOPICS COVERED: Constitution; Patents And Property Ownership Distinguished; Subject Matter Copyright; Duration And Renewal; Ownership And Transfer; Formalities; Introduction; Notice, Registration And Deposit; Infringement; Overview; Reproduction And Derivative Works; Public Distribution; Public Performance And Display; Exemptions; Fair Use; Photocopying; Remedies; Preemption Of State Law.
3 Audio Cassettes
ISBN: 0-15-900295-8 $39.95

Corporations
By Professor Therese H. Maynard
Loyola University Law School

TOPICS COVERED: Ultra Vires Act; Corporate Formation; Piercing The Corporate Veil; Corporate Financial Structure; Stocks; Bonds; Subscription Agreements; Watered Stock; Stock Transactions; Insider Trading; 16(b) & 10b-5 Violations; Promoters; Fiduciary Duties; Shareholder Rights; Meetings; Cumulative Voting; Voting Trusts; Close Corporations; Dividends; Preemptive Rights; Shareholder Derivative Suits; Directors; Duty Of Loyalty; Corporate Opportunity Doctrine; Officers; Amendments; Mergers; Dissolution.
4 Audio Cassettes
ISBN: 0-15-900320-2 $45.95

Criminal Law
By Professor Charles H. Whitebread
USC School of Law

TOPICS COVERED: Exam Tactics; Volitional Acts; Mental States; Specific Intent; Malice; General Intent; Strict Liability; Accomplice Liability; Inchoate Crimes; Impossibility; Defenses; Insanity; Voluntary And Involuntary Intoxication; Infancy; Self-Defense; Defense Of A Dwelling; Duress; Necessity; Mistake Of Fact Or Law; Entrapment; Battery; Assault; Homicide; Common Law Murder; Voluntary And Involuntary Manslaughter; First Degree Murder; Felony Murder; Rape; Larceny; Embezzlement; False Pretenses; Robbery; Extortion; Burglary; Arson.
4 Audio Cassettes
ISBN: 0-15-900279-6 $39.95

Legalines

Legalines gives you authoritative, detailed briefs of every major case in your casebook. You get a clear explanation of the facts, the issues, the court's holding and reasoning, and any significant concurrences or dissents. Even more importantly, you get an authoritative explanation of the significance of each case, and how it relates to other cases in your casebook. And with Legalines' detailed table of contents and table of cases, you can quickly find any case or concept you're looking for. But your professor expects you to know more than just the cases. That's why Legalines gives you more than just case briefs. You get summaries of the black letter law, as well. That's crucial, because some of the most important information in your casebooks isn't in the cases at all … it's the black letter principles you're expected to glean from those cases. Legalines is the only series that gives you both case briefs and black letter review. With Legalines, you get everything you need to know—whether it's in a case or not!

Administrative Law
Keyed to the Breyer Casebook
ISBN: 0-15-900169-2   176 pages $19.95
Keyed to the Gellhorn Casebook
ISBN: 0-15-900170-6   186 pages $21.95
Keyed to the Schwartz Casebook
ISBN: 0-15-900171-4   145 pages $18.95

Antitrust
Keyed to the Areeda Casebook
ISBN: 0-15-900405-5   165 pages $19.95
Keyed to the Handler Casebook
ISBN: 0-15-900390-3   158 pages $18.95

Civil Procedure
Keyed to the Cound Casebook
ISBN: 0-15-900314-8   241 pages $21.95
Keyed to the Field Casebook
ISBN: 0-15-900415-2   310 pages $23.95
Keyed to the Hazard Casebook
ISBN: 0-15-900324-5   206 pages $21.95
Keyed to the Rosenberg Casebook
ISBN: 0-15-900052-1   284 pages $21.95
Keyed to the Yeazell Casebook
ISBN: 0-15-900241-9   206 pages $20.95

Commercial Law
Keyed to the Farnsworth Casebook
ISBN: 0-15-900176-5   126 pages $18.95

Conflict of Laws
Keyed to the Cramton Casebook
ISBN: 0-15-900331-8   113 pages $16.95
Keyed to the Reese (Rosenberg) Casebook
ISBN: 0-15-900057-2   247 pages $21.95

Constitutional Law
Keyed to the Brest Casebook
ISBN: 0-15-900338-5   172 pages $19.95
Keyed to the Cohen Casebook
ISBN: 0-15-900378-4   301 pages $22.95
Keyed to the Gunther Casebook
ISBN: 0-15-900060-2   367 pages $23.95
Keyed to the Lockhart Casebook
ISBN: 0-15-900242-7   322 pages $22.95

Constitutional Law (cont'd)
Keyed to the Rotunda Casebook
ISBN: 0-15-900363-6   258 pages $21.95
Keyed to the Stone Casebook
ISBN: 0-15-900236-2   281 pages $22.95

Contracts
Keyed to the Calamari Casebook
ISBN: 0-15-900065-3   234 pages $21.95
Keyed to the Dawson Casebook
ISBN: 0-15-900268-0   188 pages $21.95
Keyed to the Farnsworth Casebook
ISBN: 0-15-900332-6   219 pages $19.95
Keyed to the Fuller Casebook
ISBN: 0-15-900237-0   184 pages $19.95
Keyed to the Kessler Casebook
ISBN: 0-15-900070-X   312 pages $22.95
Keyed to the Murphy Casebook
ISBN: 0-15-900387-3   207 pages $21.95

Corporations
Keyed to the Cary Casebook
ISBN: 0-15-900172-2   383 pages $23.95
Keyed to the Choper Casebook
ISBN: 0-15-900173-0   219 pages $21.95
Keyed to the Hamilton Casebook
ISBN: 0-15-900313-X   214 pages $21.95
Keyed to the Vagts Casebook
ISBN: 0-15-900078-5   185 pages $18.95

Criminal Law
Keyed to the Boyce Casebook
ISBN: 0-15-900080-7   290 pages $21.95
Keyed to the Dix Casebook
ISBN: 0-15-900081-5   103 pages $15.95
Keyed to the Johnson Casebook
ISBN: 0-15-900175-7   149 pages $18.95
Keyed to the Kadish Casebook
ISBN: 0-15-900333-4   167 pages $18.95
Keyed to the La Fave Casebook
ISBN: 0-15-900084-X   202 pages $20.95

Criminal Procedure
Keyed to the Kamisar Casebook
ISBN: 0-15-900336-9   256 pages $21.95

Decedents' Estates & Trusts
Keyed to the Ritchie Casebook
ISBN: 0-15-900339-3   204 pages $21.95

Domestic Relations
Keyed to the Clark Casebook
ISBN: 0-15-900168-4   119 pages $16.95
Keyed to the Wadlington Casebook
ISBN: 0-15-900377-6   169 pages $18.95

Estate & Gift Taxation
Keyed to the Surrey Casebook
ISBN: 0-15-900093-9   100 pages $15.95

Evidence
Keyed to the Sutton Casebook
ISBN: 0-15-900096-3   271 pages $19.95
Keyed to the Waltz Casebook
ISBN: 0-15-900334-2   179 pages $19.95
Keyed to the Weinstein Casebook
ISBN: 0-15-900097-1   223 pages $20.95

Family Law
Keyed to the Areen Casebook
ISBN: 0-15-900263-X   262 pages $21.95

Federal Courts
Keyed to the McCormick Casebook
ISBN: 0-15-900101-3   195 pages $18.95

Income Tax
Keyed to the Freeland Casebook
ISBN: 0-15-900361-X   134 pages $18.95
Keyed to the Klein Casebook
ISBN: 0-15-900383-0   150 pages $18.95

Labor Law
Keyed to the Cox Casebook
ISBN: 0-15-900238-9   221 pages $18.95
Keyed to the Merrifield Casebook
ISBN: 0-15-900177-3   195 pages $20.95

Property
Keyed to the Browder Casebook
ISBN: 0-15-900110-2   277 pages $21.95
Keyed to the Casner Casebook
ISBN: 0-15-900111-0   261 pages $21.95
Keyed to the Cribbet Casebook
ISBN: 0-15-900239-7   328 pages $22.95
Keyed to the Dukeminier Casebook
ISBN: 0-15-900432-2   168 pages $18.95
Keyed to the Nelson Casebook
ISBN: 0-15-900228-1   288 pages $19.95

Real Property
Keyed to the Rabin Casebook
ISBN: 0-15-900262-1   180 pages $18.95

Remedies
Keyed to the Re Casebook
ISBN: 0-15-900116-1   245 pages $22.95
Keyed to the York Casebook
ISBN: 0-15-900118-8   265 pages $21.95

Sales & Secured Transactions
Keyed to the Speidel Casebook
ISBN: 0-15-900166-8   202 pages $21.95

Securities Regulation
Keyed to the Jennings Casebook
ISBN: 0-15-900253-2   324 pages $22.95

Torts
Keyed to the Epstein Casebook
ISBN: 0-15-900335-0   193 pages $20.95
Keyed to the Franklin Casebook
ISBN: 0-15-900240-0   146 pages $18.95
Keyed to the Henderson Casebook
ISBN: 0-15-900174-9   162 pages $18.95
Keyed to the Keeton Casebook
ISBN: 0-15-900406-3   252 pages $21.95
Keyed to the Prosser Casebook
ISBN: 0-15-900301-6   334 pages $22.95

Wills, Trusts & Estates
Keyed to the Dukeminier Casebook
ISBN: 0-15-900337-7   145 pages $19.95

Call To Order: 1-800-787-8717 or Order On-Line at http://www.gilbertlaw.com

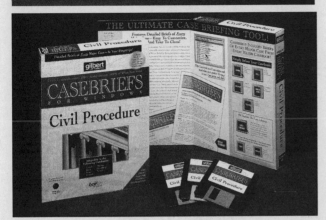
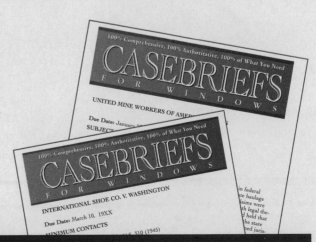

on the Internet!

Employment Guides

A collection of best selling titles that help you identify and reach your career goals.

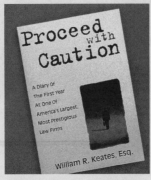

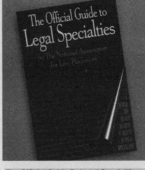

Guerrilla Tactics for Getting the Legal Job of Your Dreams
Kimm Alayne Walton, J.D.

Whether you're looking for a summer clerkship or your first permanent job after school, this revolutionary book is the key to getting the job of your dreams!

Guerrilla Tactics for Getting the Legal Job of Your Dreams leads you step-by-step through everything you need to do to nail down that perfect job! You'll learn hundreds of simple-to-use strategies that will get you exactly where you want to go. You'll Learn:

- The seven magic opening words in cover letters that ensure you'll get a response.
- The secret to successful interviews every time.
- Killer answers to the toughest interview questions they'll ever ask you.
- Plus Much More!

Guerrilla Tactics features the best strategies from the country's most innovative law school career advisors. The strategies in *Guerrilla Tactics* are so powerful that it even comes with a guarantee: Follow the advice in the book, and within one year of graduation you'll have the job of your dreams ... or your money back!

Pick up a copy of *Guerrilla Tactics* today ... you'll be on your way to the job of your dreams!

ISBN: 0-15-900317-2   **$24.95**

Proceed With Caution: A Diary Of The First Year At One Of America's Largest, Most Prestigious Law Firms
William R. Keates

Prestige. Famous clients. High-profile cases. Not to mention a starting salary approaching six figures.

In *Proceed With Caution*, the author takes you behind the scenes, to show you what it's really like to be a junior associate at a huge law firm. After graduating from an Ivy League law school, he took a job as an associate with one of New York's blue-chip law firms.

He also did something not many people do. He kept a diary, where he spelled out his day-to-day life at the firm in graphic detail.

Proceed With Caution excerpts the diary, from his first day at the firm to the day he quit. From the splashy benefits, to the nitty-gritty on the work junior associates do, to the grind of long and unpredictable hours, to the stress that eventually made him leave the firm — he tells story after story that will make you feel as though you're living the life of a new associate.

Whether you're considering a career with a large firm, or you're just curious about what life at the top firms is all about — *Proceed With Caution* is a must read!

ISBN: 0-15-900181-1   **$17.95**

The Official Guide To Legal Specialties
Lisa Shanholtzer

With *The Official Guide To Legal Specialties* you'll get a behind the scenes glimpse at dozens of legal specialties. Not just lists of what to expect, real life stories from top practitioners in each field. You'll learn exactly what it's like to be in some of America's most desirable professions. You'll get expert advice on what it takes to get a job in each field. How much you'll earn and what the day-to-day life is really like, the challenges you'll face, and the benefits you'll enjoy. With *The Official Guide To Legal Specialties* you'll have a wealth of information at your fingertips!

Includes the following specialties:

Banking	Intellectual Property
Communications	International
Corporate	Labor/Employment
Criminal	Litigation
Entertainment	Public Interest
Environmental	Securities
Government Practice	Sports
Health Care	Tax
Immigration	Trusts & Estates

ISBN: 0-15-900391-1   **$17.95**

Beyond L.A. Law: Inspiring Stories of People Who've Done Fascinating Things With A Law Degree
National Association for Law Placement

Anyone who watches television knows that being a lawyer means working your way up through a law firm — right?

Wrong!

Beyond L.A. Law gives you a fascinating glimpse into the lives of people who've broken the "lawyer" mold. They come from a variety of backgrounds — some had prior careers, others went straight through college and law school, and yet others have overcome poverty and physical handicaps. They got their degrees from all different kinds of law schools, all over the country. But they have one thing in common: they've all pursued their own, unique vision.

As you read their stories, you'll see how they beat the odds to succeed. You'll learn career tips and strategies that work, from people who've put them to the test. And you'll find fascinating insights that you can apply to your own dream, whether it's a career in law or anything else!

From Representing Baseball In Australia. To International Finance. To Children's Advocacy. To Directing a Nonprofit Organization. To Entrepreneur.

If You Think Getting A Law Degree Means Joining A Traditional Law Firm — Think Again!

ISBN: 0-15-900182-X   **$17.95**

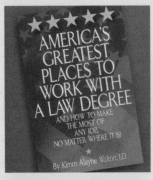

America's Greatest Places To Work With A Law Degree
Kimm Alayne Walton, J.D.

"Where do your happiest graduates work?" That's the question that author Kimm Alayne Walton asked of law school administrators around the country. Their responses revealed the hundreds of wonderful employers profiled in *America's Greatest Places To Work With A Law Degree*.

In this remarkable book, you'll get to know an incredible variety of great places to work, including:

- Glamorous sports and entertainment employers — the jobs that sound as though they would be great, and they are!
- The 250 best law firms to work for between 20 and 600 attorneys.
- Companies where law school graduates love to work and not just as in-house counsel.
- Wonderful public interest employers – the "white knight" jobs that are so incredibly satisfying.
- Court-related positions, where lawyers entertain fascinating issues, tremendous variety, and an enjoyable lifestyle.
- Outstanding government jobs, at the federal, state, and local level.

Beyond learning about incredible employers, you'll discover:

- The ten traits that define a wonderful place to work ... the sometimes surprising qualities that outstanding employers share.
- How to handle law school debt, when your dream job pays less than you think you need to make.
- How to find — and get! — great jobs at firms with fewer than 20 attorneys.

And no matter where you work, you'll learn expert tips for making the most of your job. You'll learn the specific strategies that distinguish people headed for the top ... how to position yourself for the most interesting, high-profile work ... how to handle difficult personalities ... how to negotiate for more money ... and what to do now to help you get your next great job!

ISBN: 0-15-900180-3   **$24.95**

About The Author

Kimm Alayne Walton is the author of numerous books and articles including two national best seller's — *America's Greatest Places To Work With A Law Degree* and *Guerrilla Tactics For Getting The Legal Job Of Your Dreams*. She is a renowned motivational speaker, lecturing at law schools and bar associations nationwide, and in her spare time, she has taken up travel writing, which has taken her swimming with crocodiles in Kakadu, and scuba diving with sharks on the Great Barrier Reef.

E-mail the Job Goddess with your own legal job search questions!

Visit www.gilbertlaw.com for details.

Employment Guides

A collection of best selling titles that help you identify and reach your career goals.

The National Directory Of Legal Employers
National Association for Law Placement

The National Directory of Legal Employers brings you a universe of vital information about 1,000 of the nation's top legal employers— *in one convenient volume!*

It includes:

- Over 22,000 job openings.
- The names, addresses and phone numbers of hiring partners.
- Listings of firms by state, size, kind and practice area.
- What starting salaries are for full time, part time, and summer associates, plus a detailed description of firm benefits.
- The number of employees by gender and race, as well as the number of employees with disabilities.
- A detailed narrative of each firm, plus much more!

The National Directory Of Legal Employers has been the best kept secret of top legal career search professionals for over a decade. Now, for the first time, it is available in a format specifically designed for law students and new graduates. *Pick up your copy of the Directory today!*

ISBN: 0-15-900434-9 $39.95

SAMPLE PAGE

Everything You Need To Know About 1,000 Of the Nation's Top Legal Employers — Fully Indexed For Quick Reference!

Including:

Law Firms and Corporations
Listed Alphabetically

Law Firms and Corporations
Listed by State

Public Interest Organizations and Government Agencies
Listed Alphabetically

Public Interest Organizations and Government Agencies
Listed by State

All Employers
Listed By Practice Area

All Employers
Listed By Office Size

Company Information

1. Name, Address, and Phone Number Of Hiring Partner
2. Demographics
3. Primary Practice Areas
4. Benefits
5. Pro Bono
6. Public Interest Fellowships
7. Minority Recruitment Efforts
8. Non-Discrimination Policy
9. Narrative

Employment Information

10. Office Size
11. Total Firm Size
12. Job Opportunities
13. Summer Associate Information
14. Application Timeline For Summer Associates
15. Hiring Criteria For All Job Openings
16. Salary Information
17. Other Compensation
18. Other Data
19. Partnership Data
20. Other Offices
21. Campus Interviews

The Best Of The Job Goddess
Kimm Alayne Walton, J.D.

In her popular **Dear Job Goddess** column, legal job-search expert Kimm Alayne Walton provides the answers to even the most difficult job search dilemmas facing law students and law school graduates. Relying on career experts from around the country, the Job Goddess provides wise and witty advice for every obstacle that stands between you and your dream job!

ISBN: 0-15-900393-8 $14.95

SAMPLE COLUMN

Business Card Resumes: Good Idea, Or Not?

Dear Job Goddess,

One of my friends showed me something called a "business card resume." What he did was to have these business cards printed up, with his name and phone number on one side, and highlights from his resume on the other side. He said a bunch of people are doing this, so that when they meet potential employers they hand over these cards. Should I bother getting some for myself?

Curious in Chicago

Dear Curious,

Sigh, You know, Curious, that the Job Goddess takes a fairly dim view of resumes as a job-finding tool, even in their full-blown bond-papered, engraved 8-1/2x11" incarnation. And here you ask about a business card resume, two

steps further down the resume food chain. So, no, you *shouldn't* bother with business card resumes. Here's why.

Think for a moment, Curious, about the kind of circumstance in which you'd be tempted to whip out one of these incredible shrinking resumes. You're at a social gathering. You happen to meet Will Winken, of the law firm Winken, Blinken, and Nod, and it becomes clear fairly quickly that Will is a) friendly, and b) a potential employer. The surest way to turn this chance encounter into a job is to use it as the basis for future contact. As Carolyn Bregman, Career Services Director at Emory Law School, points out, "Follow up with a phone call or note, mentioning something Winken said to you." You can say that you'd like to follow up on whatever it is he said, or that you've since read more about him and found that he's an expert on phlegm reclamation law and how that's a topic that's always fascinated you, and invite him for coffee at his convenience so you can learn more about it. What have you done? *You've taken a social encounter and*

turned it into a potential job opportunity. And that makes the Job Goddess very proud.

But what happens if you, instead, whip out your business card resume, and say, "Gee, Mr. Winken, nice meeting you. Here's my business card resume, in case you ever need anybody like me." *Now* what have you done? You have, with one simple gesture, wiped out any excuse to follow up! Instead of having a phone call or a note from you that is personalized to Winken, you've got a piddling little standardized card with your vital statistics on it. Ugh. I know you're much more memorable, Curious, than anything you could possibly fit on the back of a business card.

So there you have it, Curious. Save the money you'll spend on a business card resume, and spend it later, when you have a *real* business card to print, reading, "Curious, Esq. Winken, Blinken, and Nod, Attorneys at Law."

Yours Eternally,

The Job Goddess

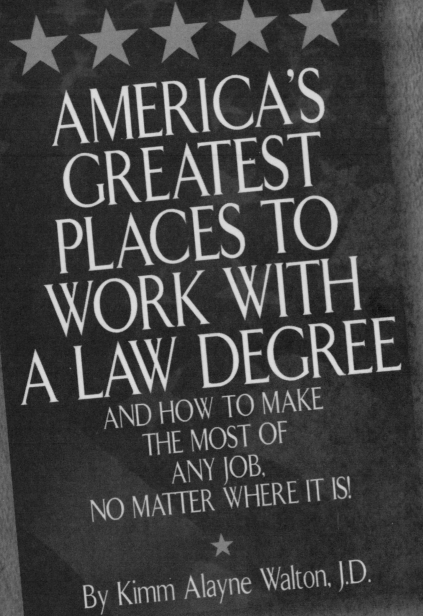